Takeshi Obata

I always get Hotta Sensei to do the bonus pages because I look forward to her storyboards... Every time I see her she says she has no ideas, but she always comes up with something interesting!

—Takeshi Obata

It all began when Yumi Hotta played a pick-up game of go with her father-in-law. As she was learning how to play, Ms. Hotta thought it might be fun to create a story around the traditional board game. More confident in her storytelling abilities than her drawing skills, she submitted the beginnings of **Hikaru no Go** to **Weekly Shonen Jump**'s Story King Award. The Story King Award is an award that picks the best story, manga, character design and youth (under 15) manga submissions every year in Japan. As fate would have it, Ms. Hotta's story (originally named, "*Kokonotsu no Hoshi*"), was a runner-up in the "Story" category of the Story King Award. Many years earlier, Takeshi Obata was a runner-up for the Tezuka Award, another Japanese manga contest sponsored by **Weekly Shonen Jump** and **Monthly Shonen Jump**. An editor assigned to Mr. Obata's artwork came upon Ms. Hotta's story and paired the two for a full-fledged manga about go. The rest is modern go history.

HIKARU NO GO VOL. 18
SHONEN JUMP Manga Edition

STORY BY YUMI HOTTA
ART BY TAKESHI OBATA
Supervised by YUKARI UMEZAWA (5 Dan)

Translation & English Adaptation/Naoko Amemiya
English Script Consultant/Janice Kim (3 Dan)
Touch-up Art & Lettering/Inori Fukuda Trant
Design/Julie Behn
Editor/Gary Leach

VP, Production/Alvin Lu
VP, Sales & Product Marketing/Gonzalo Ferreyra
VP, Creative/Linda Espinosa
Publisher/Hyoe Narita

HIKARU-NO GO © 1998 by Yumi Hotta, Takeshi Obata. All rights reserved.
First published in Japan in 1998 by SHUEISHA Inc., Tokyo. English translation
rights arranged by SHUEISHA Inc.

Printed in Canada

Published by VIZ Media, LLC
P.O. Box 77010
San Francisco, CA 94107

10 9 8 7 6 5 4 3 2 1
First printing, February 2010

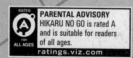

18 SIX CHARACTERS, SIX STORIES

HIKARU no GO

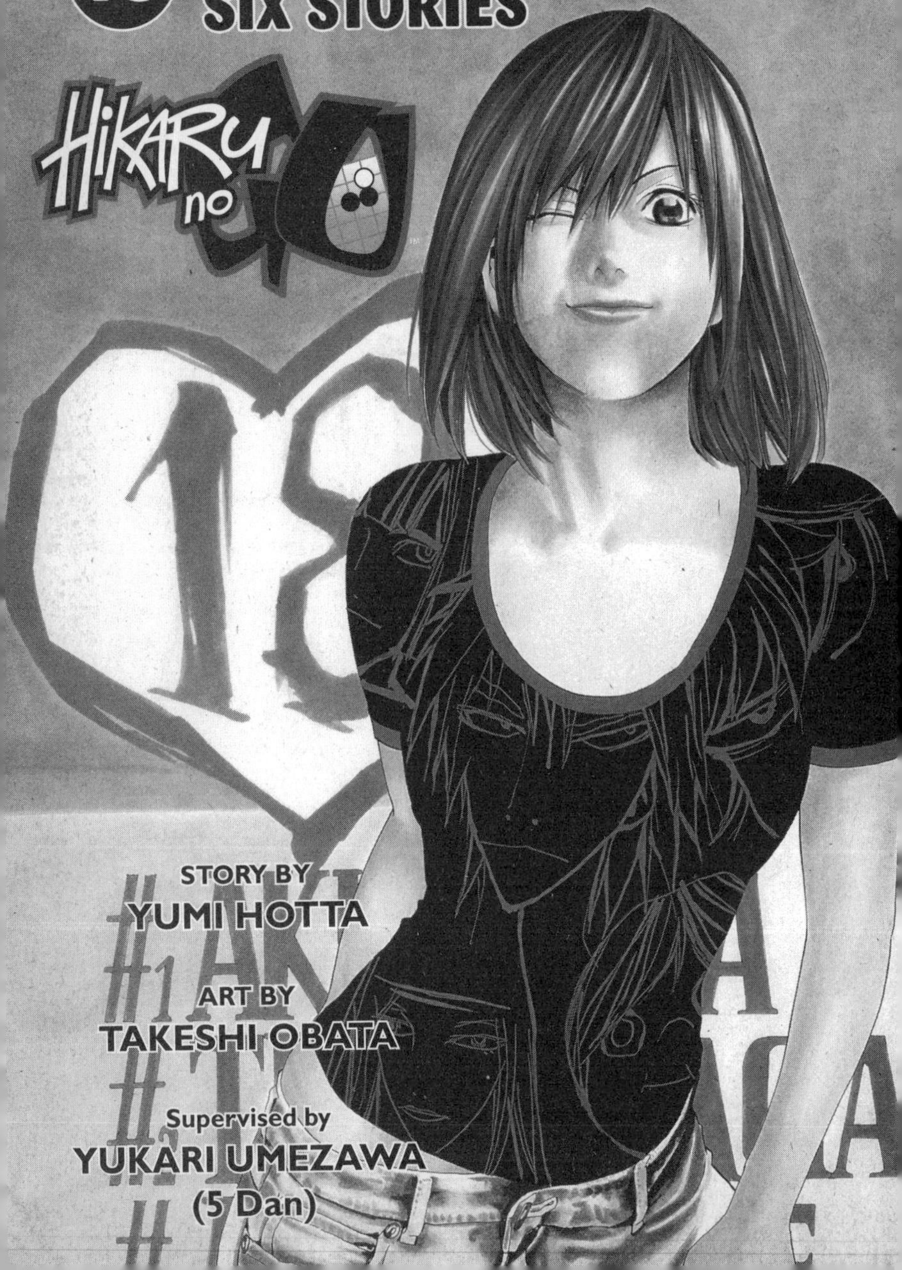

STORY BY
YUMI HOTTA

ART BY
TAKESHI OBATA

Supervised by
YUKARI UMEZAWA
(5 Dan)

Meet the Characters

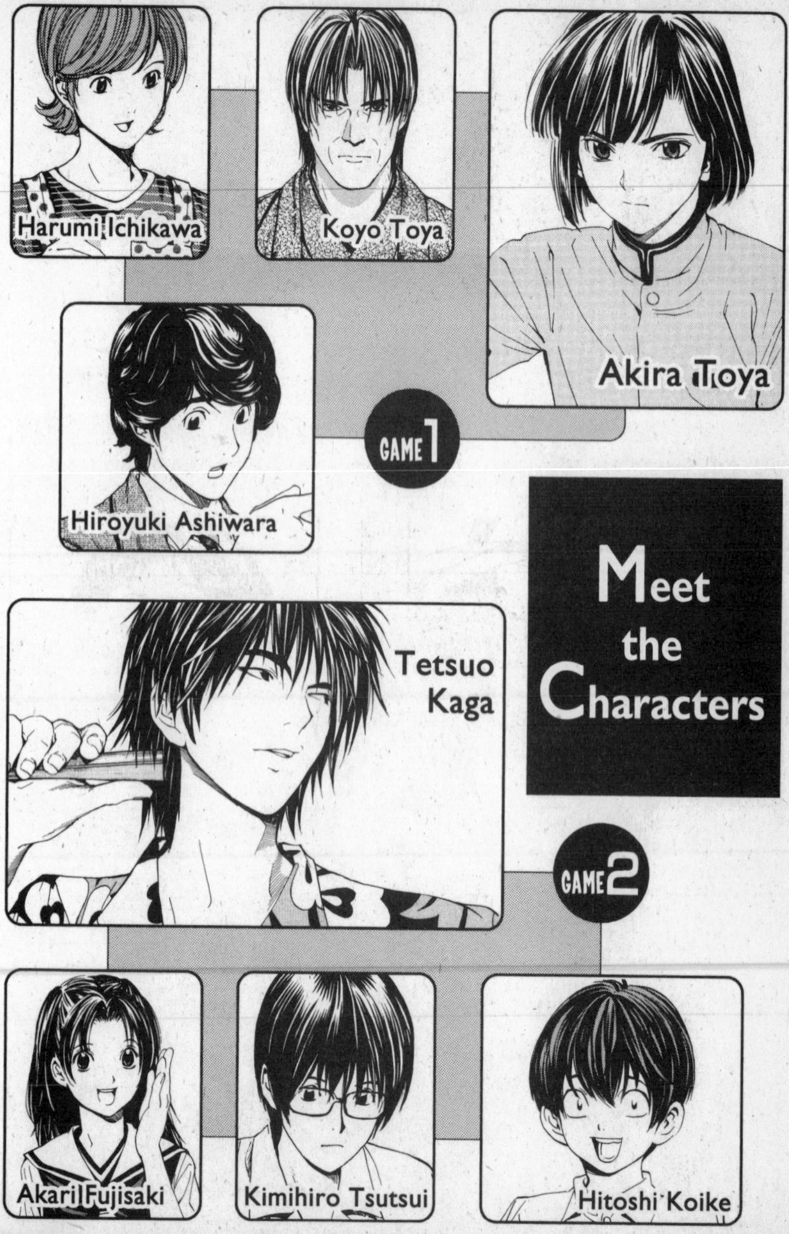
GAME 1
Akira Toya
Koyo Toya
Harumi Ichikawa
Hiroyuki Ashiwara
GAME 2
Tetsuo Kaga
Hitoshi Koike
Kimihiro Tsutsui
Akari Fujisaki

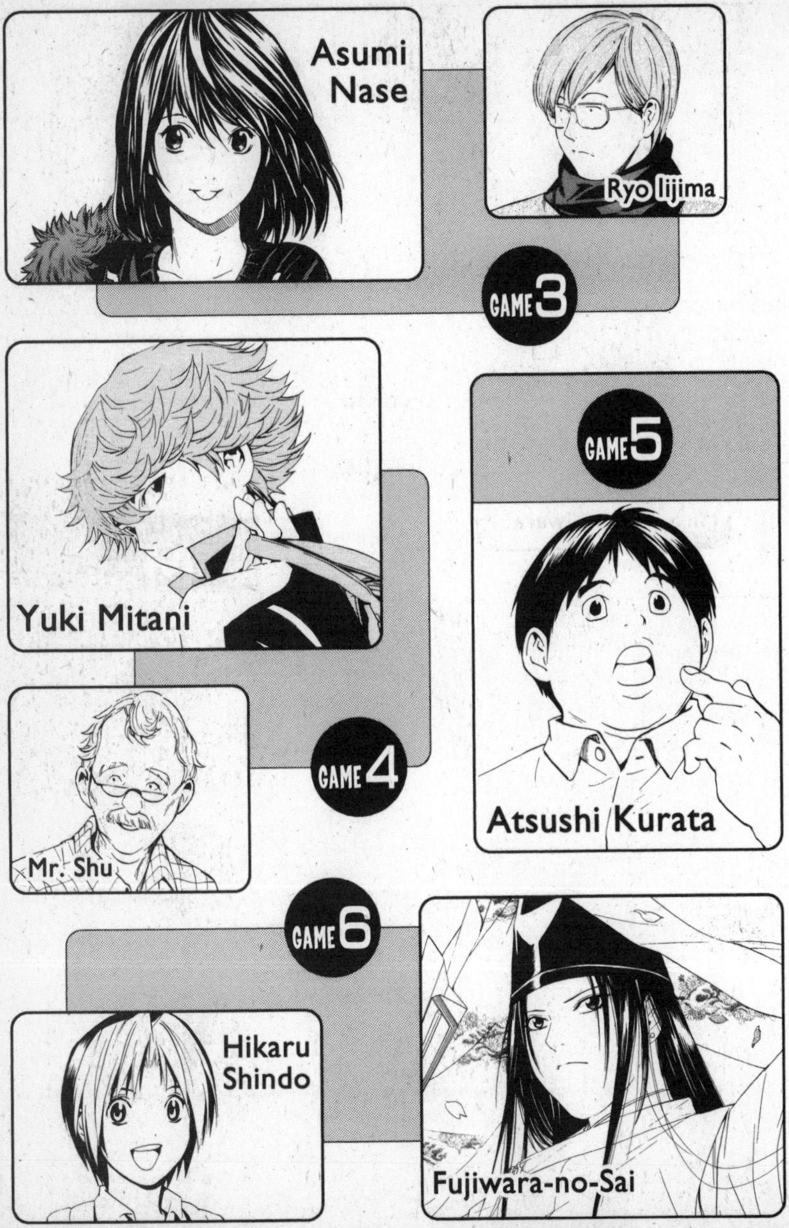
Ryo Iijima
Asumi Nase
GAME 3
GAME 5
Atsushi Kurata
Yuki Mitani
Mr. Shu
GAME 4
Fujiwara-no-Sai
GAME 6
Hikaru Shindo

CONTENTS

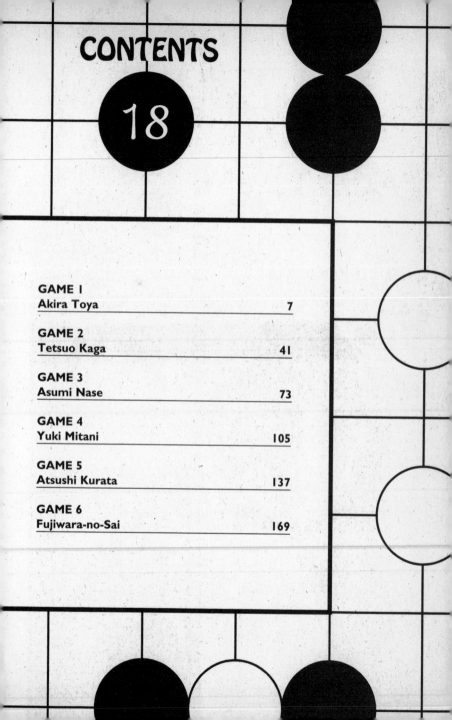

18

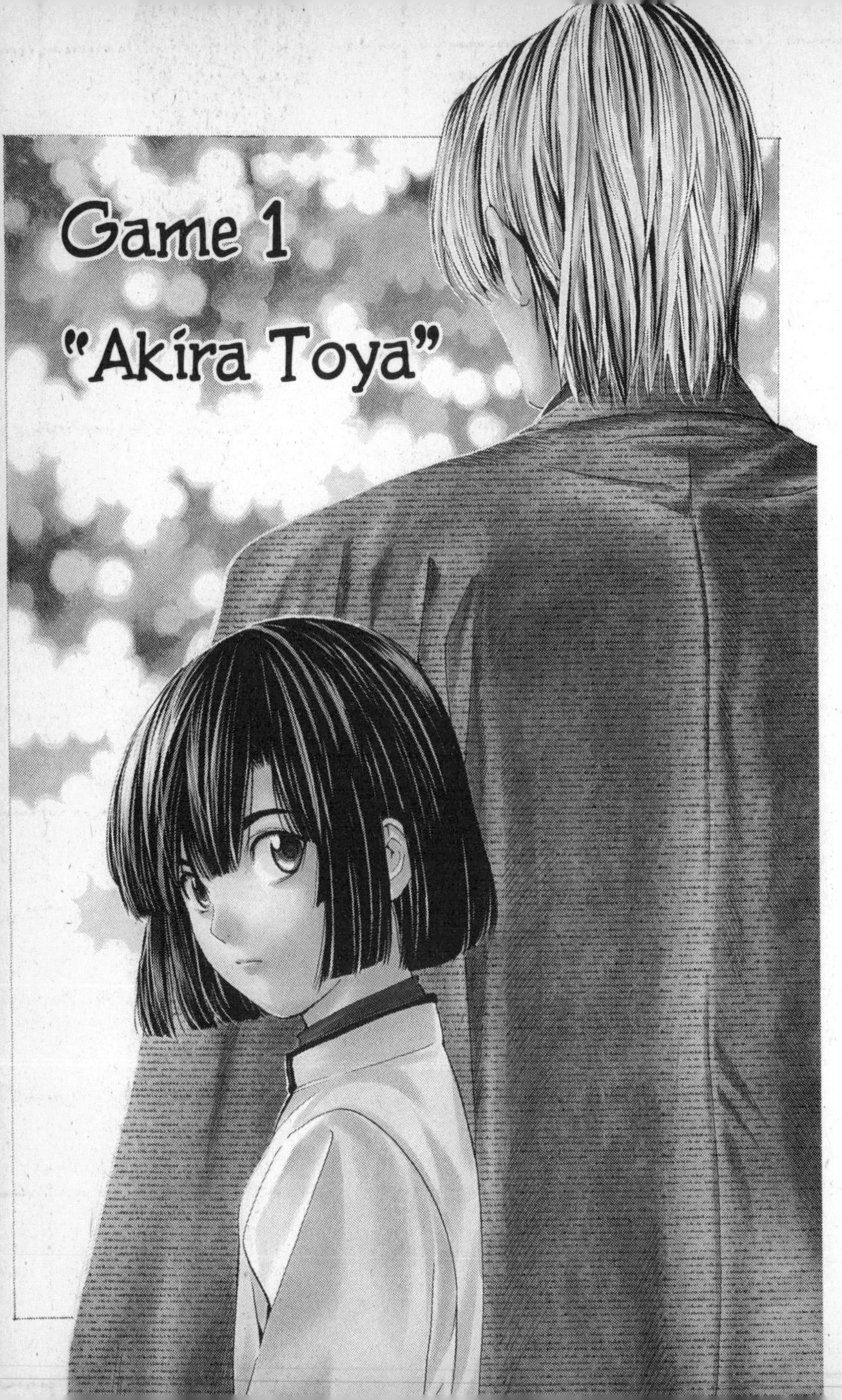
Game 1
"Akira Toya"

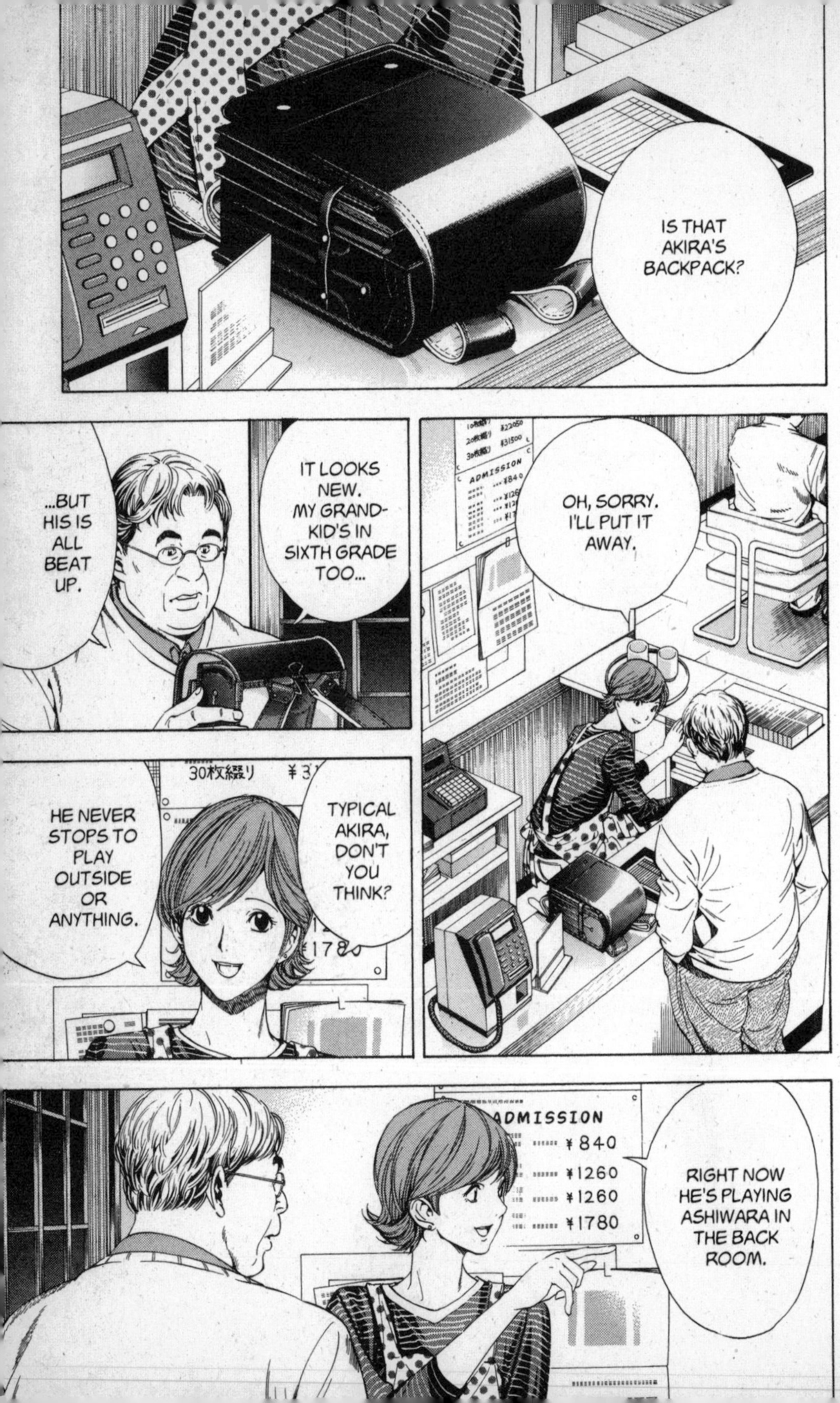
IS THAT AKIRA'S BACKPACK?
OH, SORRY. I'LL PUT IT AWAY.
IT LOOKS NEW. MY GRAND-KID'S IN SIXTH GRADE TOO...
...BUT HIS IS ALL BEAT UP.
TYPICAL AKIRA, DON'T YOU THINK?
HE NEVER STOPS TO PLAY OUTSIDE OR ANYTHING.
ADMISSION
¥840
¥1260
¥1260
¥1780
RIGHT NOW HE'S PLAYING ASHIWARA IN THE BACK ROOM.

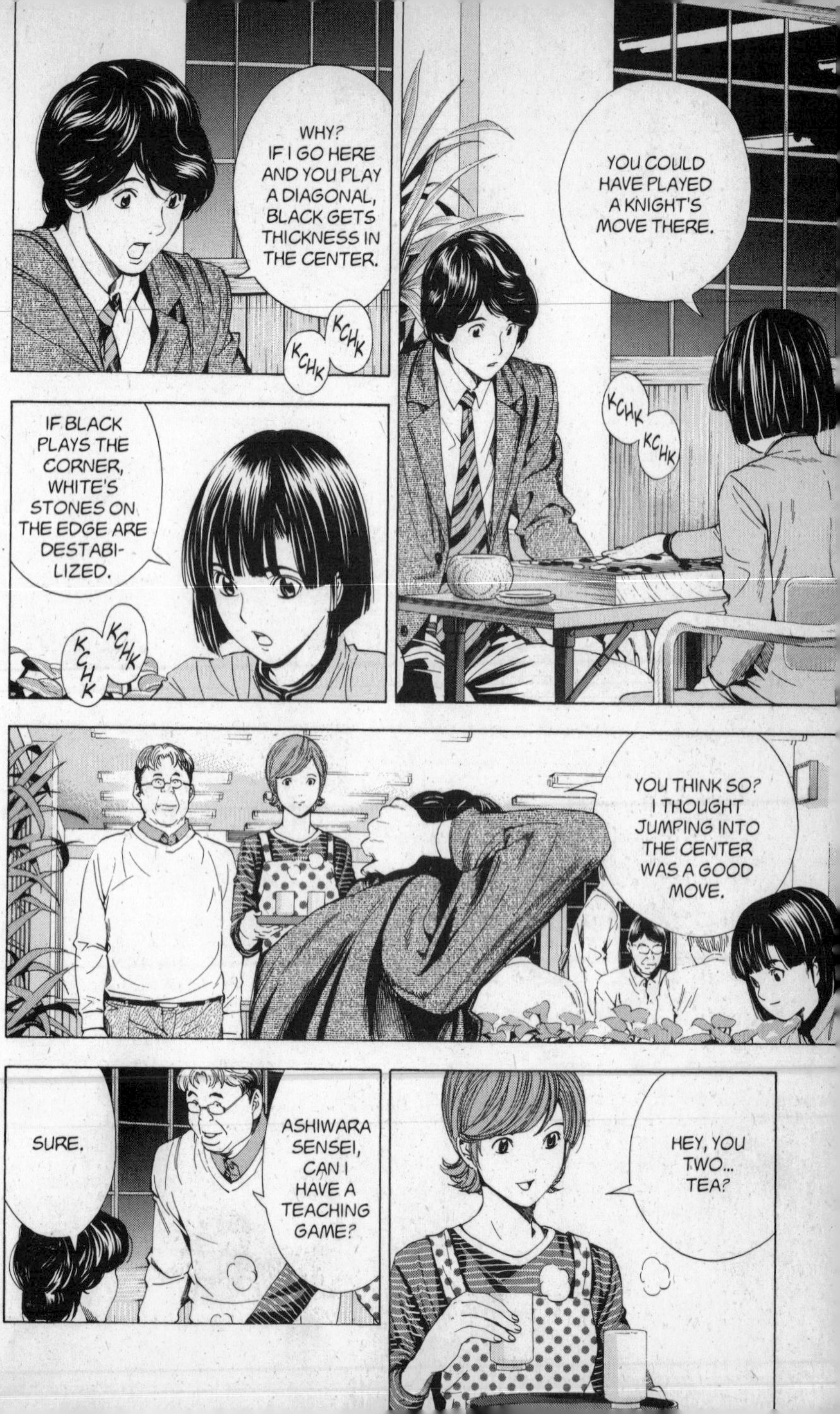

YOU COULD HAVE PLAYED A KNIGHT'S MOVE THERE.
KCHK KCHK
WHY? IF I GO HERE AND YOU PLAY A DIAGONAL, BLACK GETS THICKNESS IN THE CENTER.
KCHK KCHK
IF BLACK PLAYS THE CORNER, WHITE'S STONES ON THE EDGE ARE DESTABI-LIZED.
KCHK KCHK
YOU THINK SO? I THOUGHT JUMPING INTO THE CENTER WAS A GOOD MOVE.
HEY, YOU TWO... TEA?
ASHIWARA SENSEI, CAN I HAVE A TEACHING GAME?
SURE.

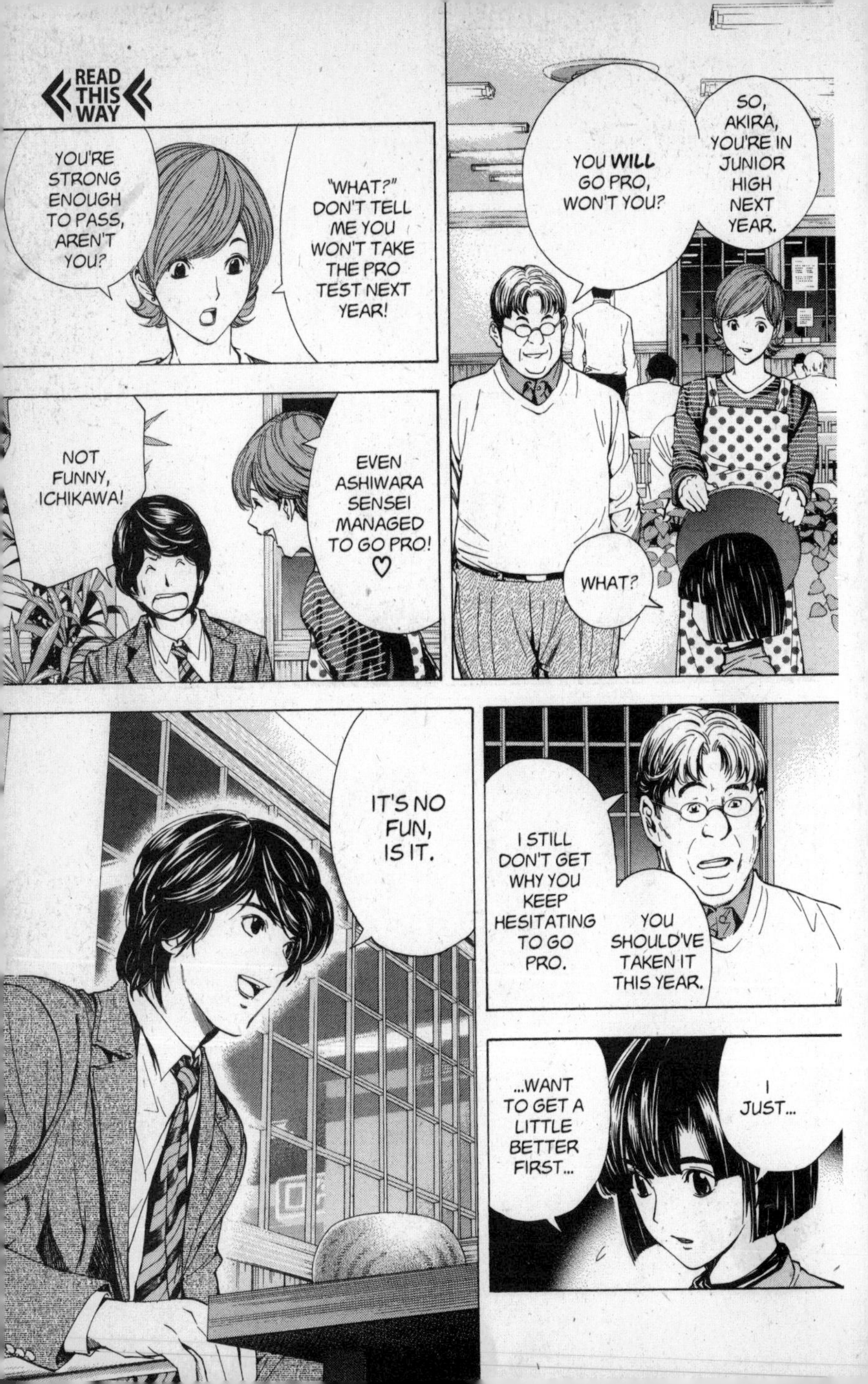
READ THIS WAY
SO, AKIRA, YOU'RE IN JUNIOR HIGH NEXT YEAR.
YOU **WILL** GO PRO, WON'T YOU?
WHAT?
"WHAT?" DON'T TELL ME YOU WON'T TAKE THE PRO TEST NEXT YEAR!
YOU'RE STRONG ENOUGH TO PASS, AREN'T YOU?
EVEN ASHIWARA SENSEI MANAGED TO GO PRO! ♡
NOT FUNNY, ICHIKAWA!
I STILL DON'T GET WHY YOU KEEP HESITATING TO GO PRO.
YOU SHOULD'VE TAKEN IT THIS YEAR.
I JUST...
...WANT TO GET A LITTLE BETTER FIRST...
IT'S NO FUN, IS IT.

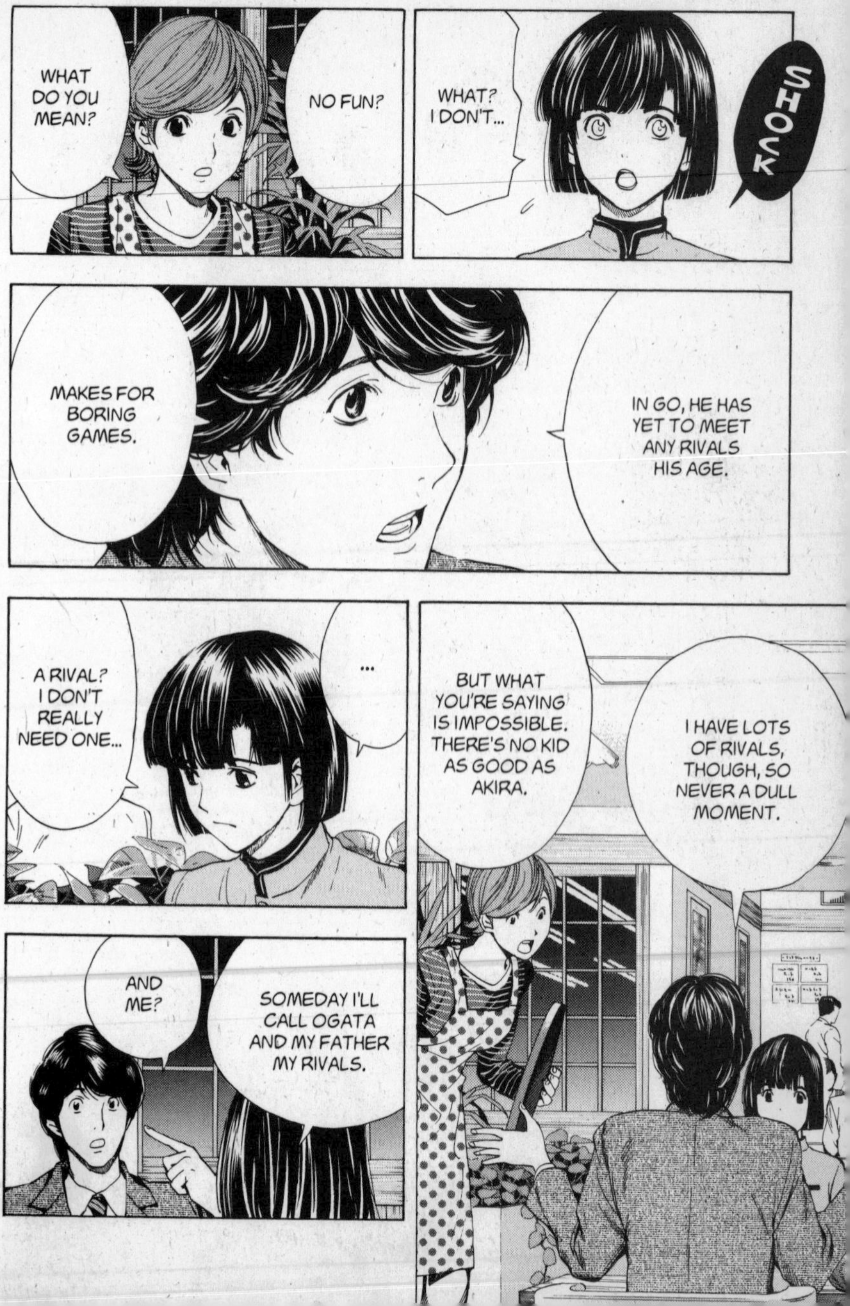
WHAT? I DON'T...
SHOCK
NO FUN?
WHAT DO YOU MEAN?
IN GO, HE HAS YET TO MEET ANY RIVALS HIS AGE.
MAKES FOR BORING GAMES.
I HAVE LOTS OF RIVALS, THOUGH, SO NEVER A DULL MOMENT.
BUT WHAT YOU'RE SAYING IS IMPOSSIBLE. THERE'S NO KID AS GOOD AS AKIRA.
...
A RIVAL? I DON'T REALLY NEED ONE...
SOMEDAY I'LL CALL OGATA AND MY FATHER MY RIVALS.
AND ME?

READ THIS WAY

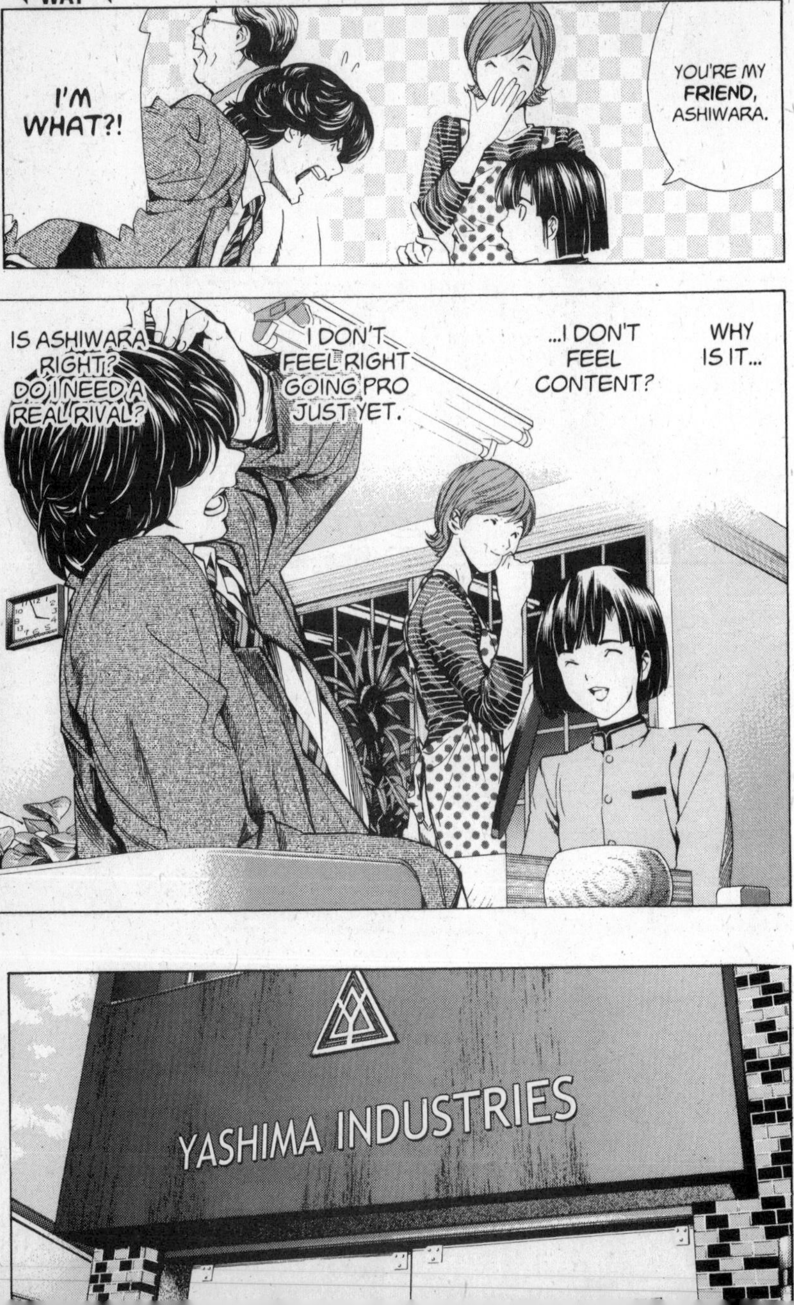

YOU'RE MY FRIEND, ASHIWARA.
I'M WHAT?!
WHY IS IT...
...I DON'T FEEL CONTENT?
I DON'T FEEL RIGHT GOING PRO JUST YET.
IS ASHIWARA RIGHT? DO I NEED A REAL RIVAL?
YASHIMA INDUSTRIES

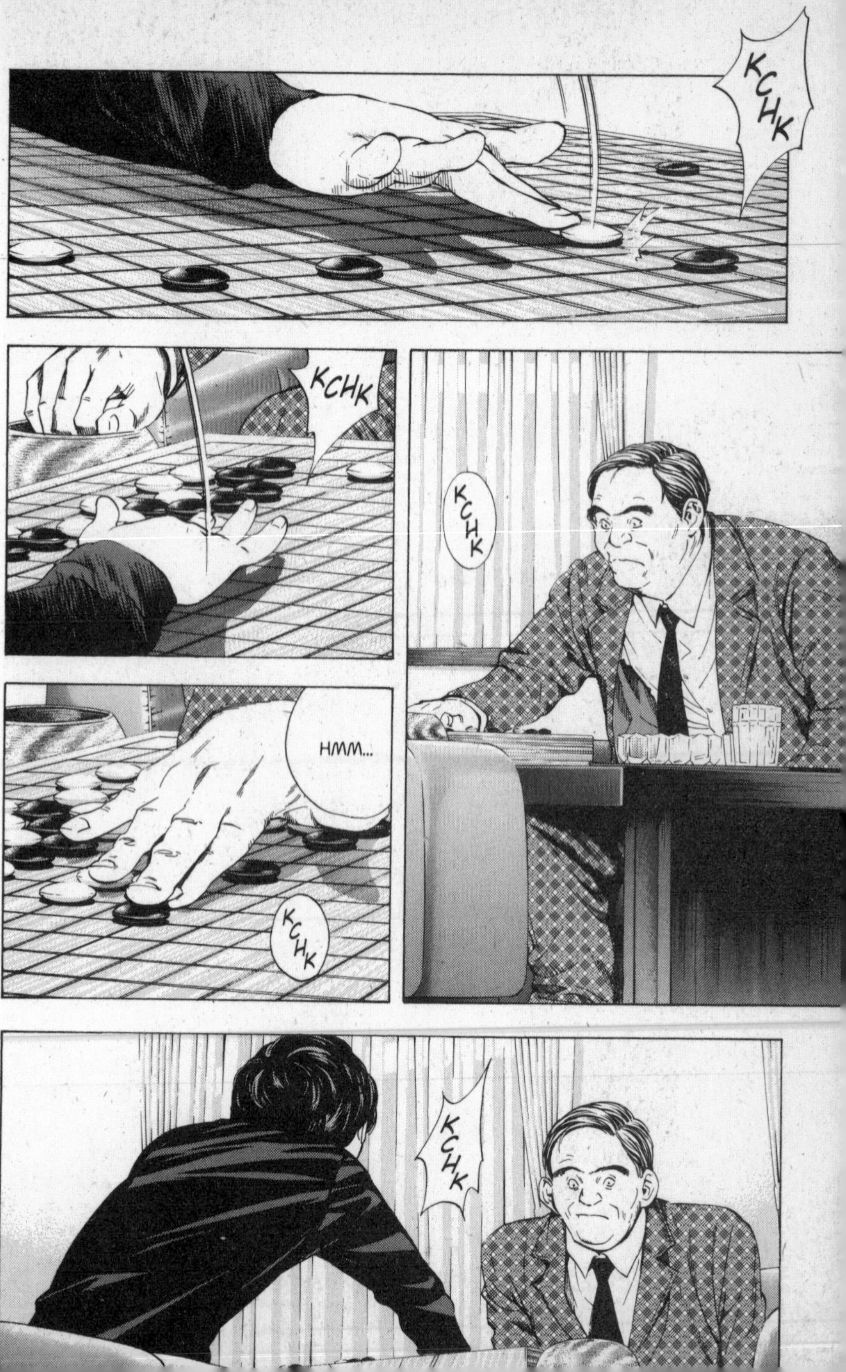
KCHK
KCHK
KCHK
HMM...
KCHK
KCHK

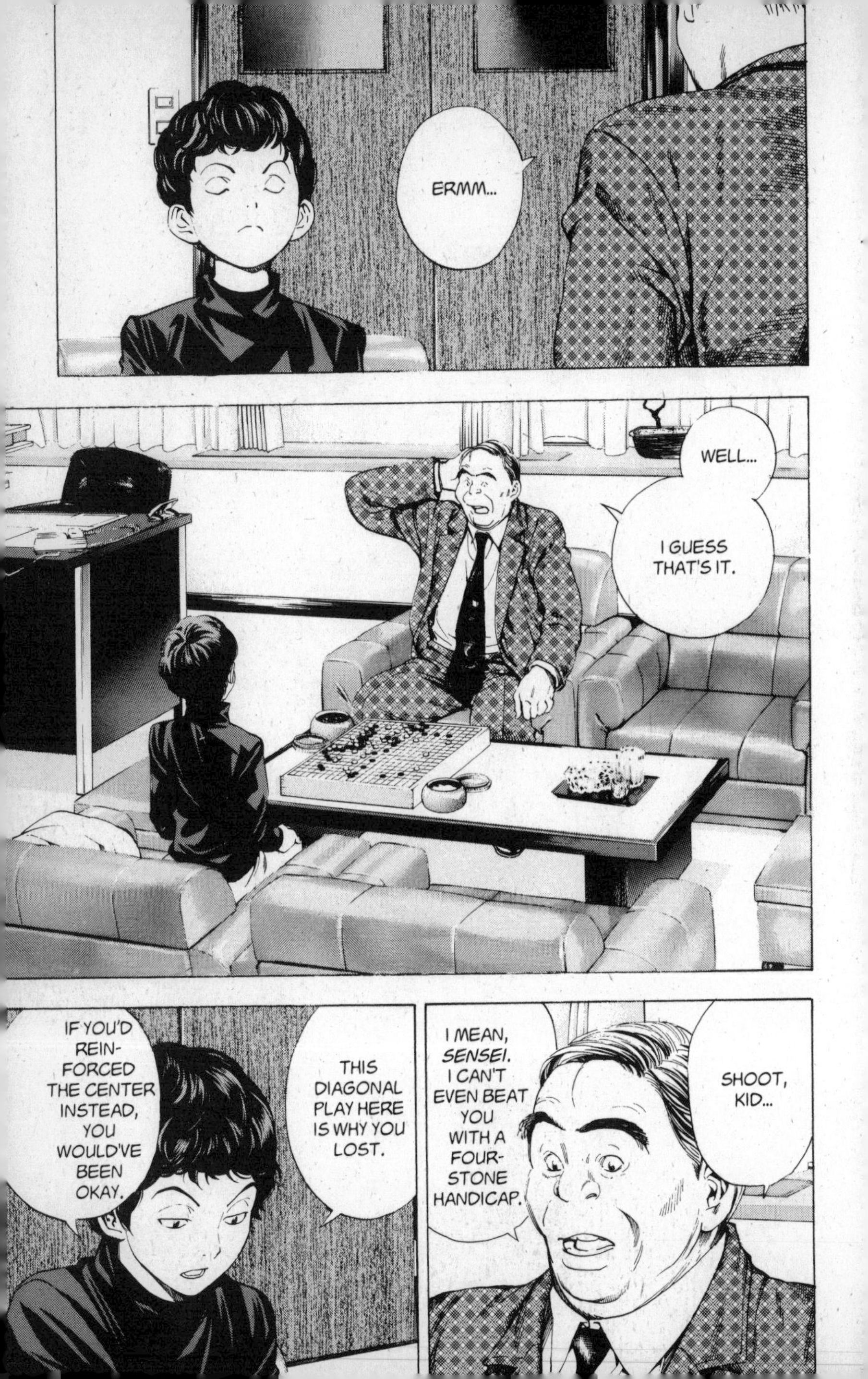
ERMM...
WELL...
I GUESS THAT'S IT.
SHOOT, KID...
I MEAN, *SENSEI*. I CAN'T EVEN BEAT YOU WITH A FOUR-STONE HANDICAP.
THIS DIAGONAL PLAY HERE IS WHY YOU LOST.
IF YOU'D REIN-FORCED THE CENTER INSTEAD, YOU WOULD'VE BEEN OKAY.

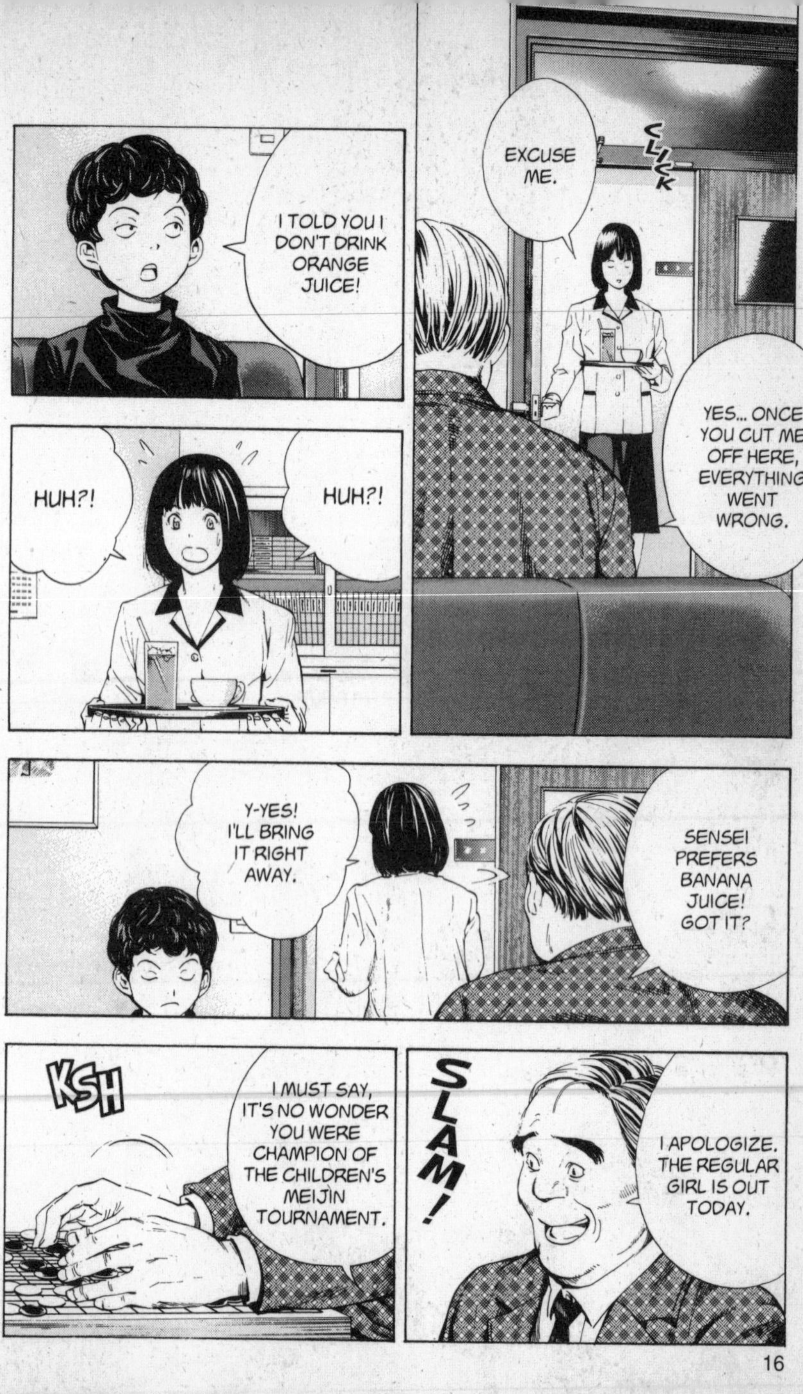
CLICK
EXCUSE ME.
YES... ONCE YOU CUT ME OFF HERE, EVERYTHING WENT WRONG.
I TOLD YOU I DON'T DRINK ORANGE JUICE!
HUH?!
HUH?!
SENSEI PREFERS BANANA JUICE! GOT IT?
Y-YES! I'LL BRING IT RIGHT AWAY.
SLAM!
I APOLOGIZE. THE REGULAR GIRL IS OUT TODAY.
I MUST SAY, IT'S NO WONDER YOU WERE CHAMPION OF THE CHILDREN'S MEIJIN TOURNAMENT.
KSH

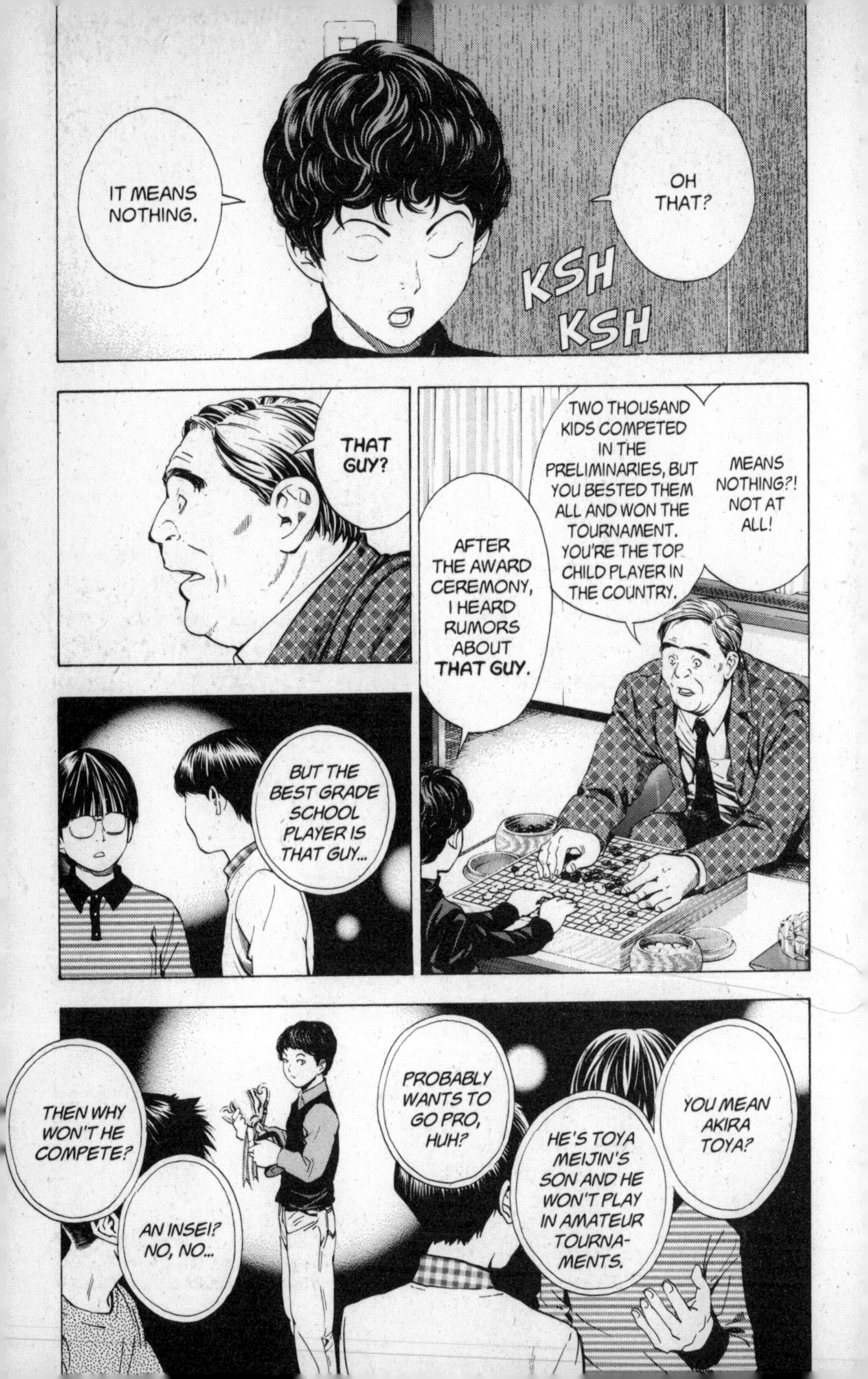
OH THAT?
KSH KSH
IT MEANS NOTHING.
MEANS NOTHING?! NOT AT ALL!
TWO THOUSAND KIDS COMPETED IN THE PRELIMINARIES, BUT YOU BESTED THEM ALL AND WON THE TOURNAMENT. YOU'RE THE TOP CHILD PLAYER IN THE COUNTRY.
AFTER THE AWARD CEREMONY, I HEARD RUMORS ABOUT THAT GUY.
THAT GUY?
BUT THE BEST GRADE SCHOOL PLAYER IS THAT GUY...
YOU MEAN AKIRA TOYA?
HE'S TOYA MEIJIN'S SON AND HE WON'T PLAY IN AMATEUR TOURNA-MENTS.
PROBABLY WANTS TO GO PRO, HUH?
THEN WHY WON'T HE COMPETE?
AN INSEI? NO, NO...

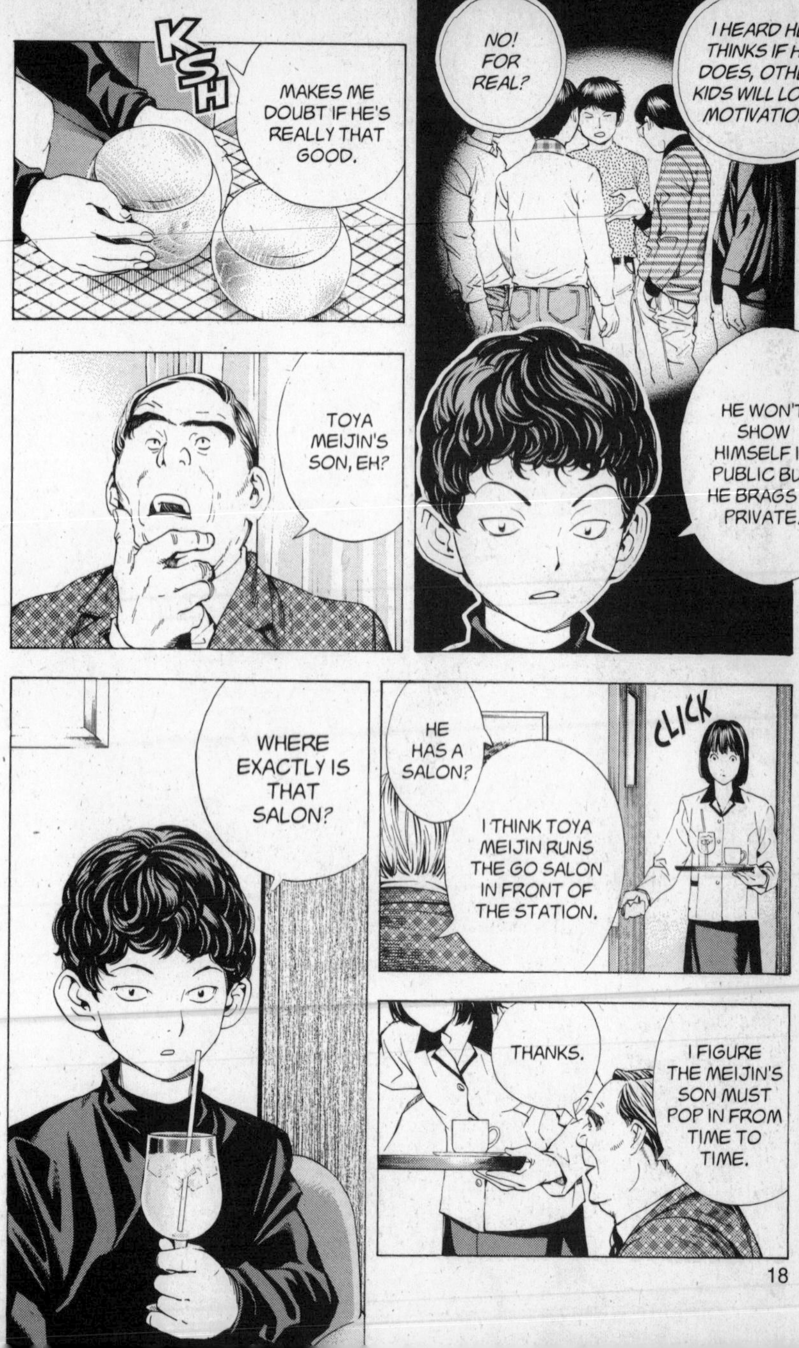
I HEARD HE THINKS IF HE DOES, OTHER KIDS WILL LOSE MOTIVATION.
NO! FOR REAL?
HE WON'T SHOW HIMSELF IN PUBLIC BUT HE BRAGS IN PRIVATE.
KSH
MAKES ME DOUBT IF HE'S REALLY THAT GOOD.
TOYA MEIJIN'S SON, EH?
CLICK
HE HAS A SALON?
I THINK TOYA MEIJIN RUNS THE GO SALON IN FRONT OF THE STATION.
I FIGURE THE MEIJIN'S SON MUST POP IN FROM TIME TO TIME.
THANKS.
WHERE EXACTLY IS THAT SALON?

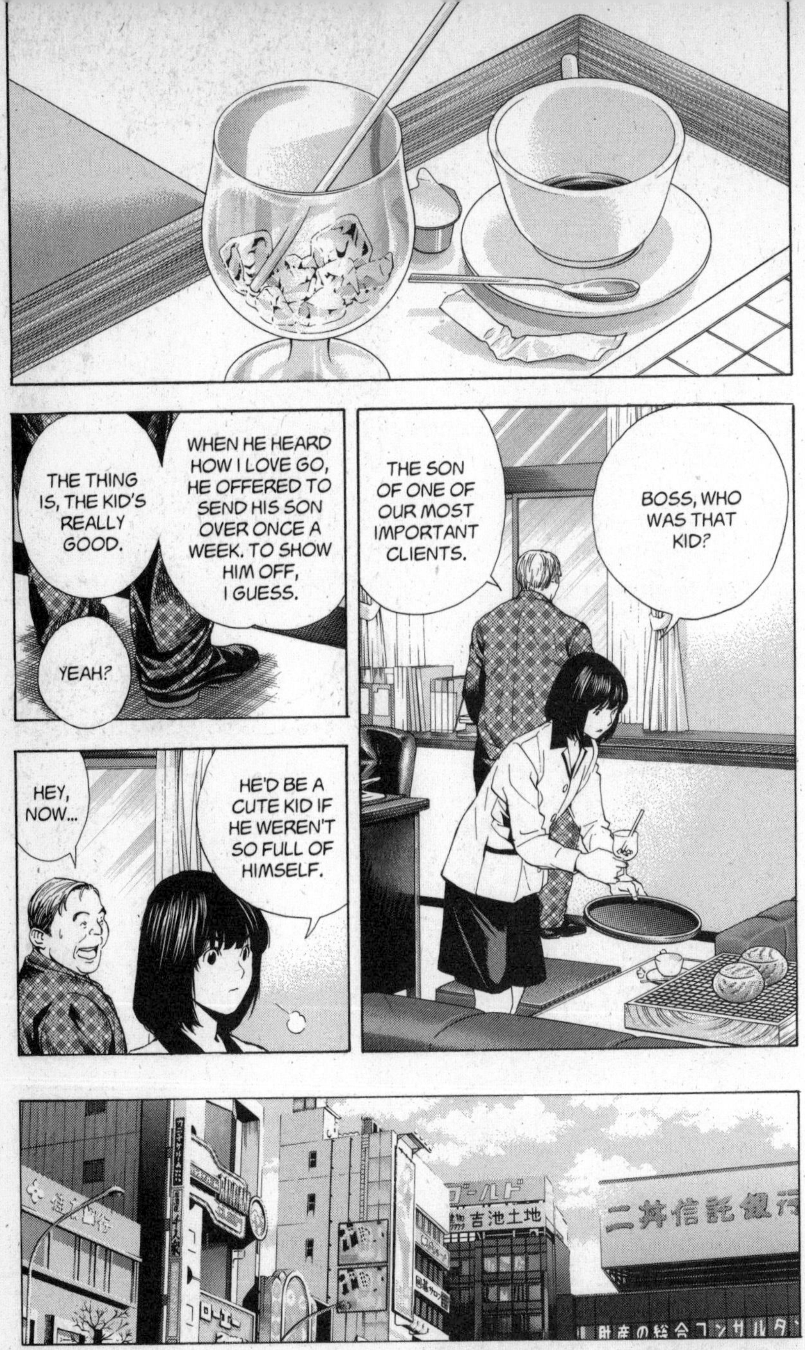
BOSS, WHO WAS THAT KID?
THE SON OF ONE OF OUR MOST IMPORTANT CLIENTS.
WHEN HE HEARD HOW I LOVE GO, HE OFFERED TO SEND HIS SON OVER ONCE A WEEK. TO SHOW HIM OFF, I GUESS.
THE THING IS, THE KID'S REALLY GOOD.
YEAH?
HE'D BE A CUTE KID IF HE WEREN'T SO FULL OF HIMSELF.
HEY, NOW...
吉池土地
二井信託銀行

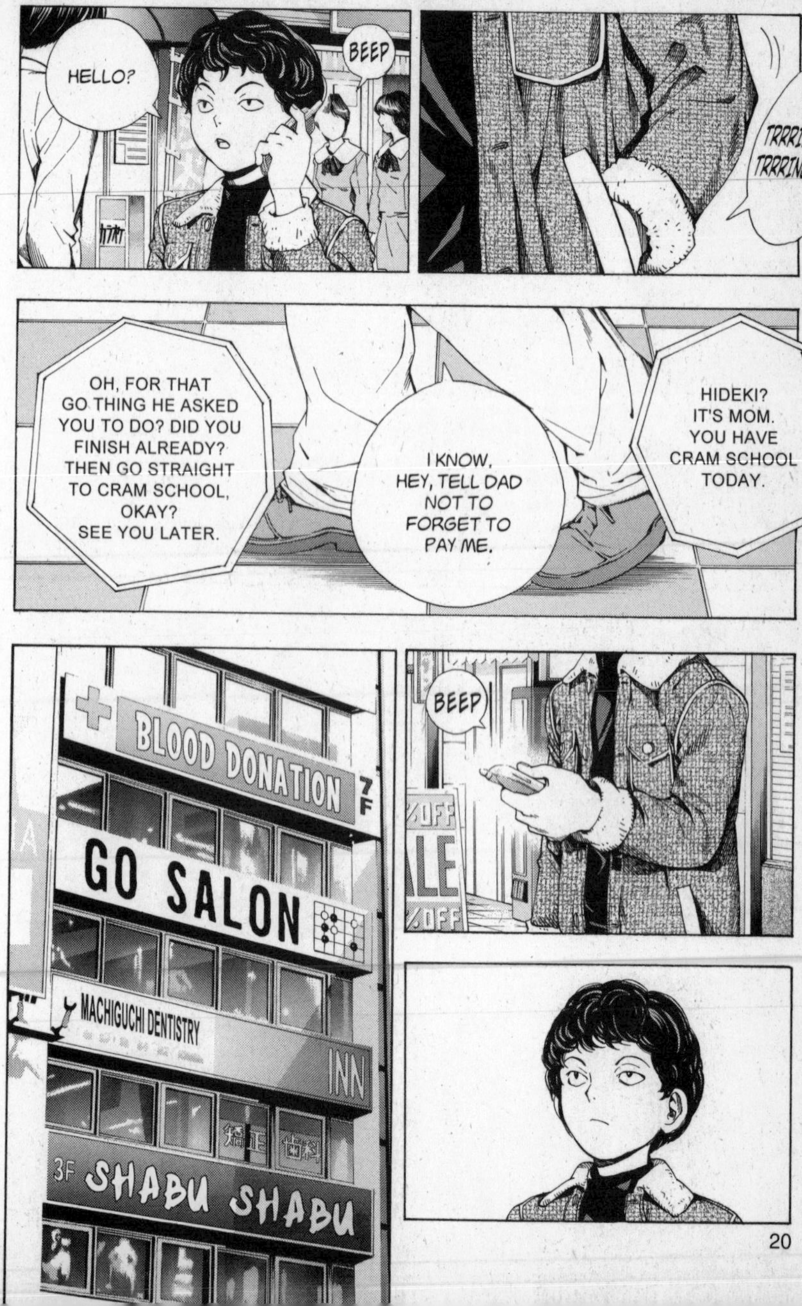
TRRRING TRRRING
BEEP
HELLO?
HIDEKI? IT'S MOM. YOU HAVE CRAM SCHOOL TODAY.
I KNOW, HEY, TELL DAD NOT TO FORGET TO PAY ME.
OH, FOR THAT GO THING HE ASKED YOU TO DO? DID YOU FINISH ALREADY? THEN GO STRAIGHT TO CRAM SCHOOL, OKAY? SEE YOU LATER.
BEEP
BLOOD DONATION
7F
GO SALON
MACHIGUCHI DENTISTRY
INN
3F SHABU SHABU

READ THIS WAY

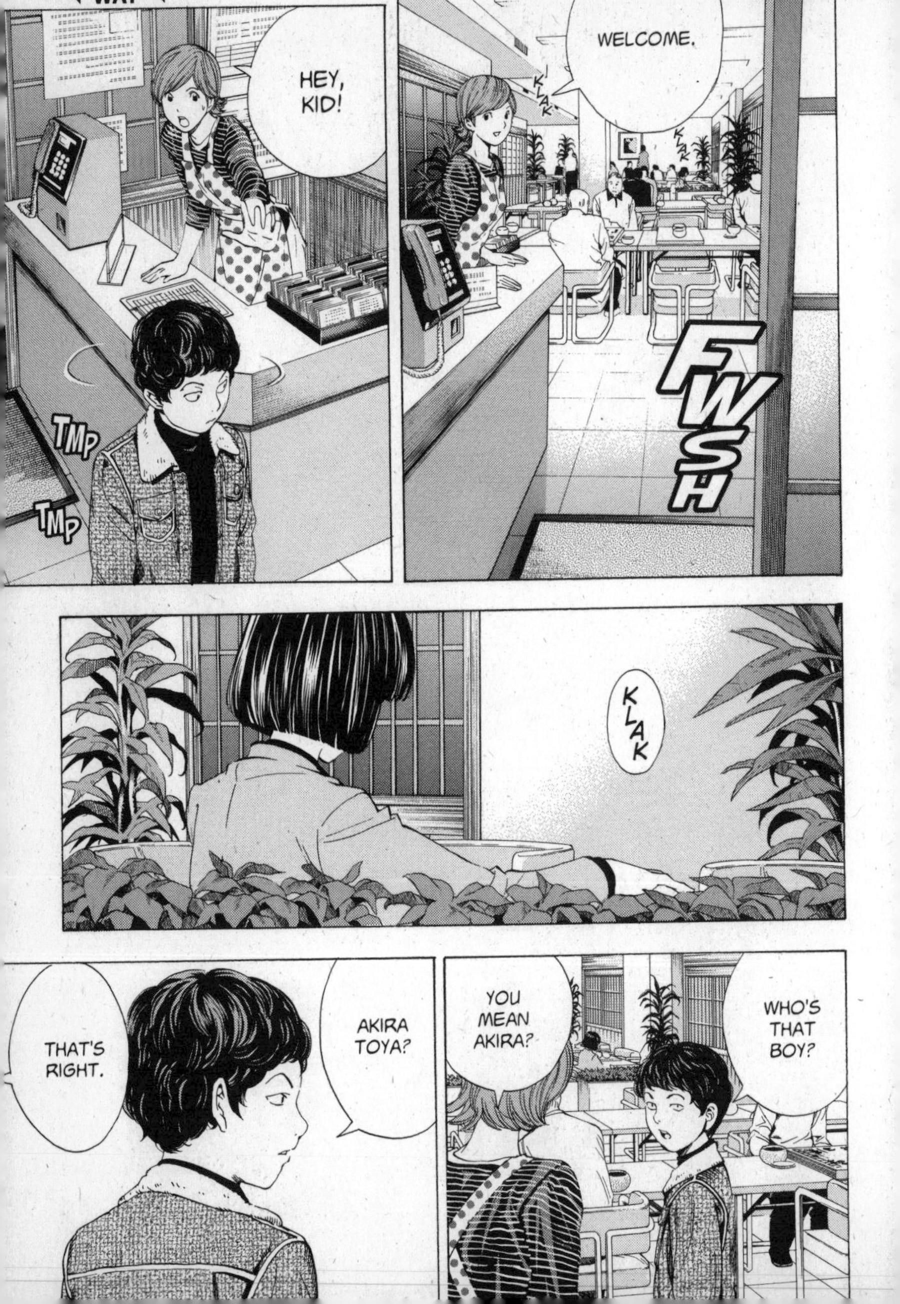

WELCOME.
KLAK
KLAK
FWSH
HEY, KID!
TMP
TMP
KLAK
WHO'S THAT BOY?
YOU MEAN AKIRA?
AKIRA TOYA?
THAT'S RIGHT.

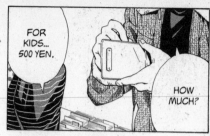

HMPH! SO THAT'S HIM.
HOW MUCH?
FOR KIDS... 500 YEN.
I HEAR AKIRA TOYA'S GOOD. IS IT TRUE?
OF COURSE! YOU DOUBT IT?!
THEN WHY DON'T YOU HAVE HIM PLAY YOU?
THAT'S WHY I'M HERE.
WAIT! LET ME...
AKIRA?

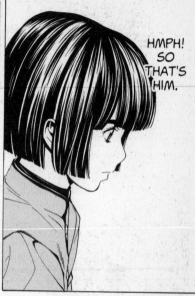

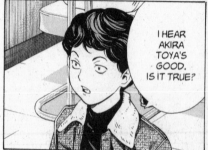

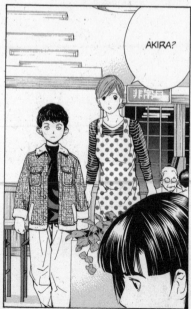

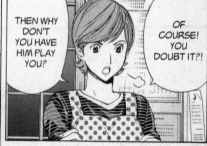

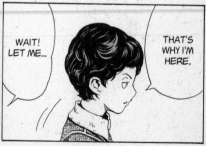

READ THIS WAY

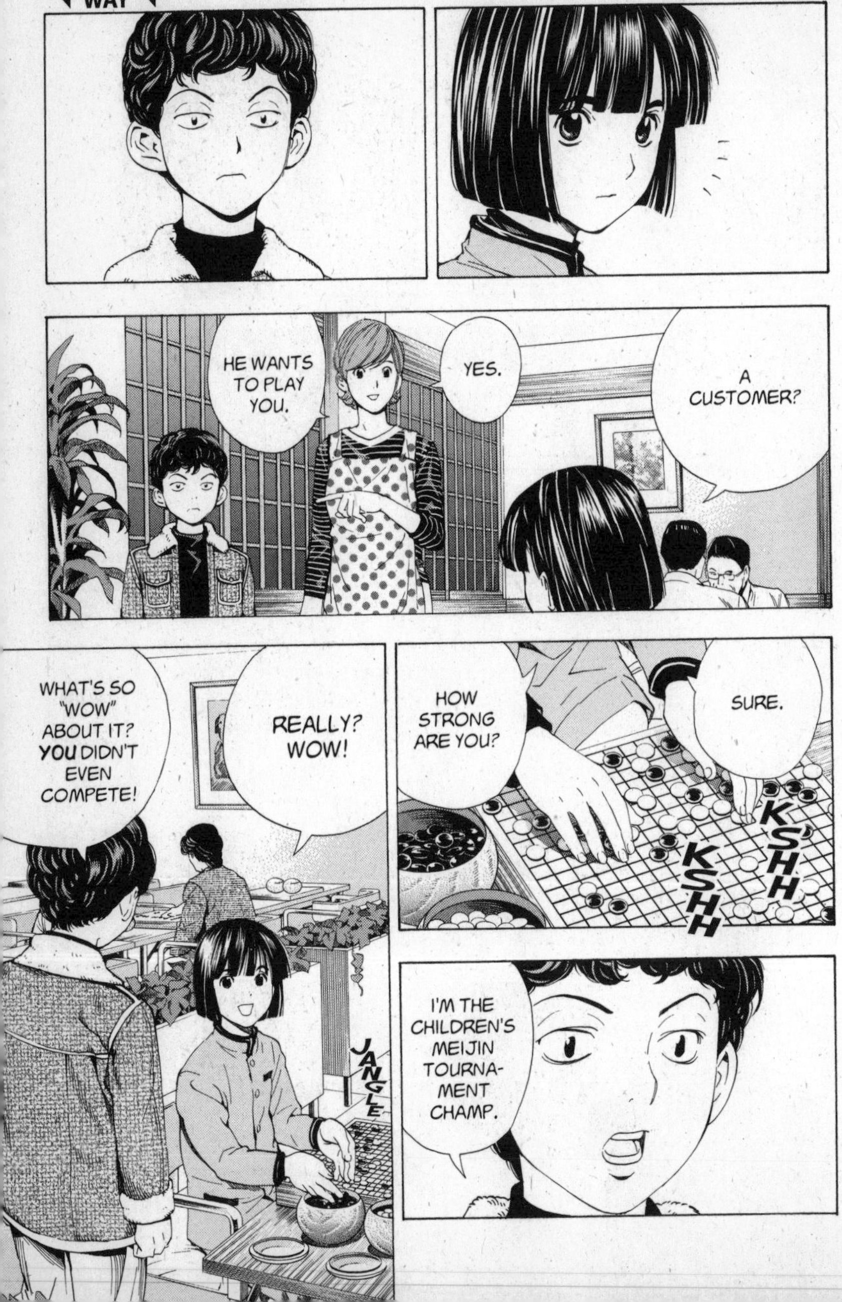
A CUSTOMER?
YES.
HE WANTS TO PLAY YOU.
SURE.
HOW STRONG ARE YOU?
KSHH
KSHH
I'M THE CHILDREN'S MEIJIN TOURNA-MENT CHAMP.
REALLY? WOW!
WHAT'S SO "WOW" ABOUT IT? YOU DIDN'T EVEN COMPETE!
JANGLE

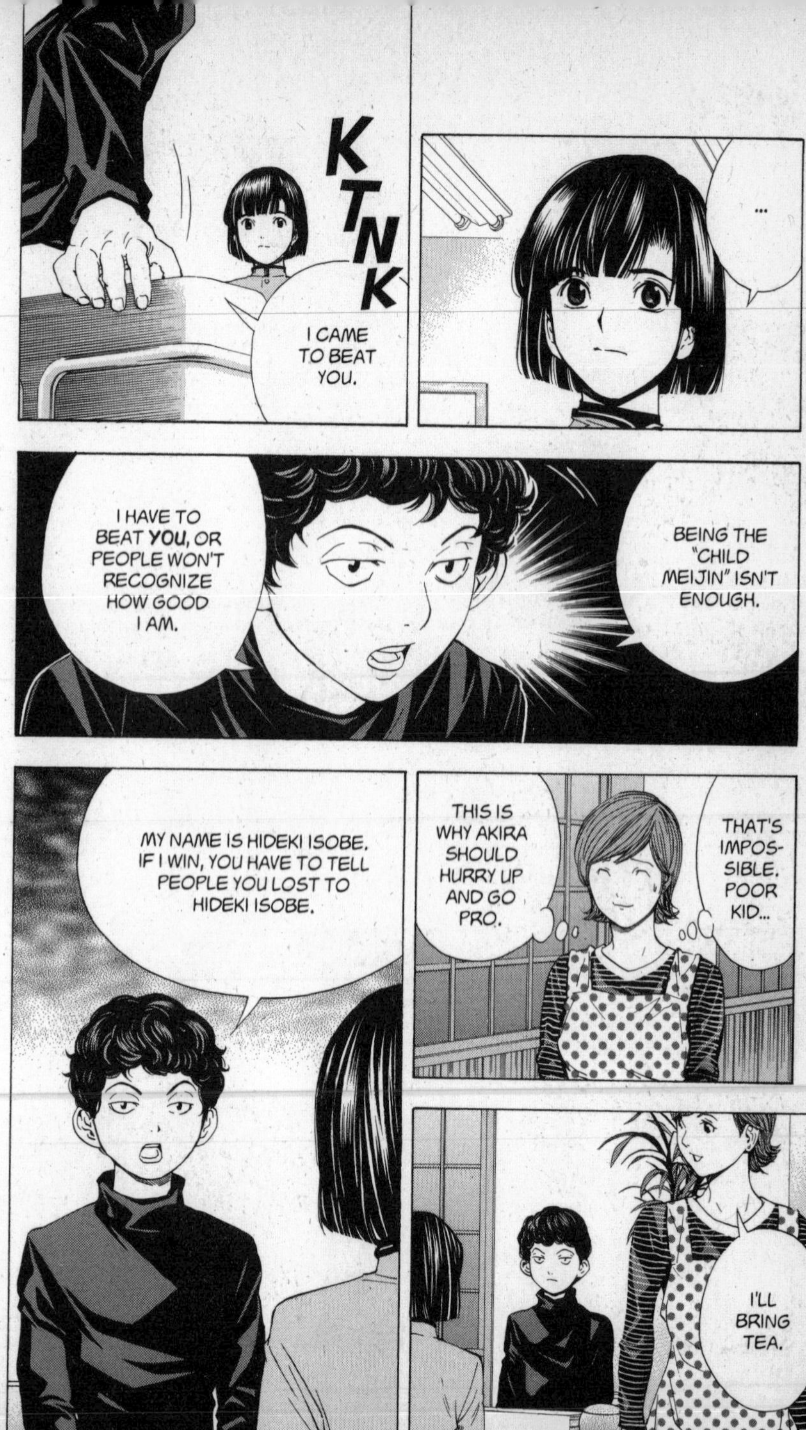
...
KTNK
I CAME TO BEAT YOU.
BEING THE "CHILD MEIJIN" ISN'T ENOUGH.
I HAVE TO BEAT **YOU**, OR PEOPLE WON'T RECOGNIZE HOW GOOD I AM.
THAT'S IMPOSSIBLE. POOR KID...
THIS IS WHY AKIRA SHOULD HURRY UP AND GO PRO.
I'LL BRING TEA.
MY NAME IS HIDEKI ISOBE. IF I WIN, YOU HAVE TO TELL PEOPLE YOU LOST TO HIDEKI ISOBE.

READ THIS WAY

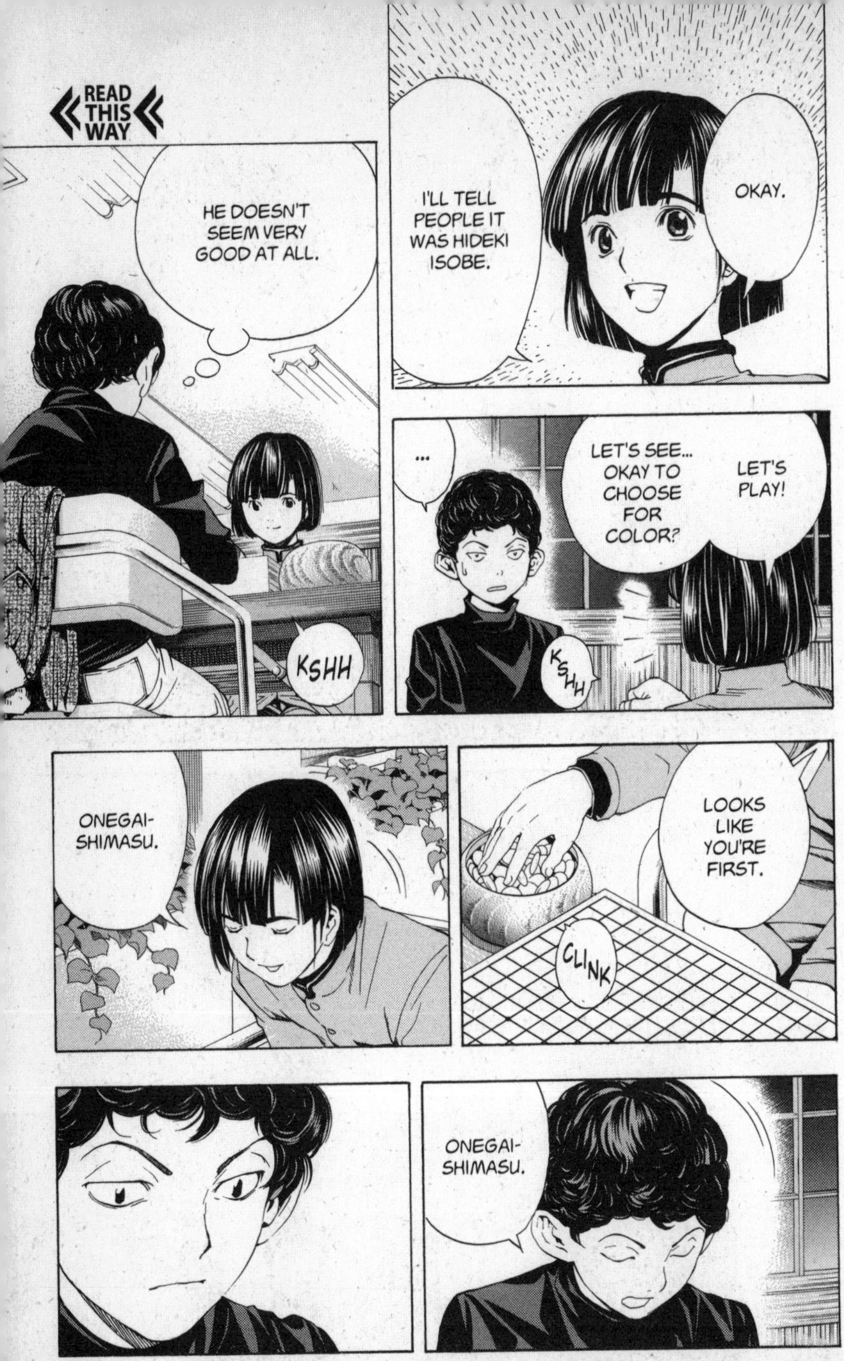
OKAY.
I'LL TELL PEOPLE IT WAS HIDEKI ISOBE.
LET'S PLAY!
LET'S SEE... OKAY TO CHOOSE FOR COLOR?
...
KSHH
HE DOESN'T SEEM VERY GOOD AT ALL.
KSHH
LOOKS LIKE YOU'RE FIRST.
CLINK
ONEGAI-SHIMASU.
ONEGAI-SHIMASU.

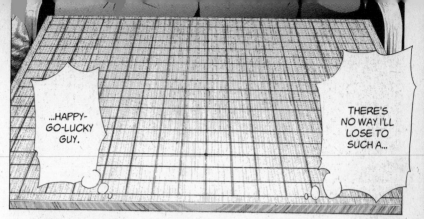

THERE'S NO WAY I'LL LOSE TO SUCH A...
...HAPPY-GO-LUCKY GUY.
KCHK
HIS EXPRESSION JUST CHANGED...
...COM-PLETELY!

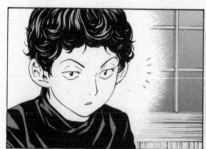

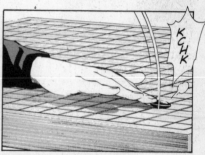

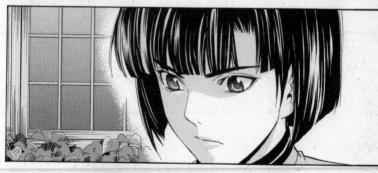

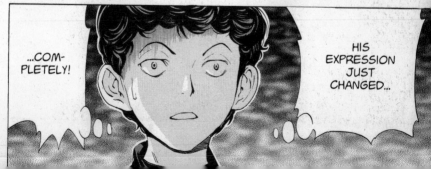

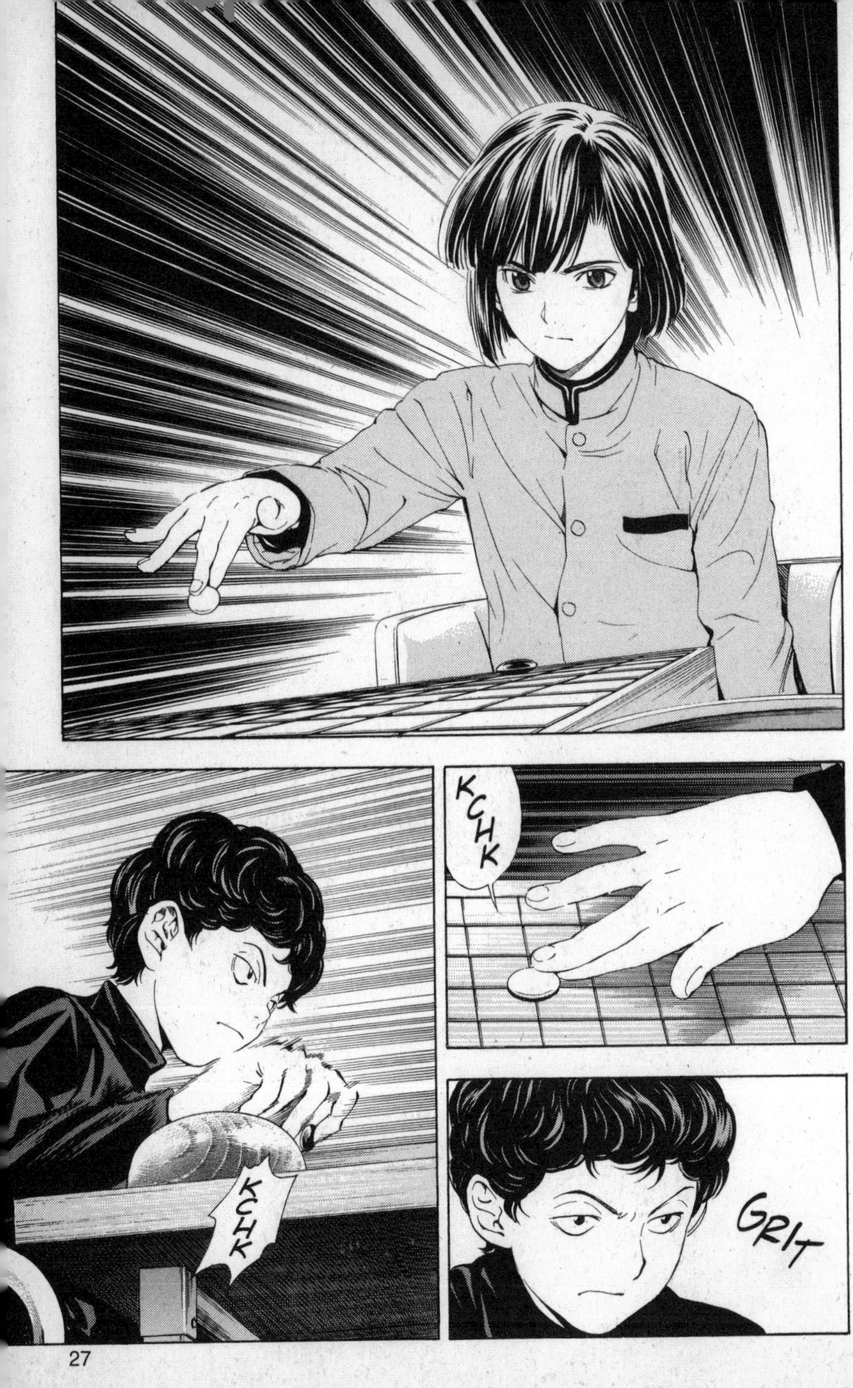
KCHK
GRIT
KCHK

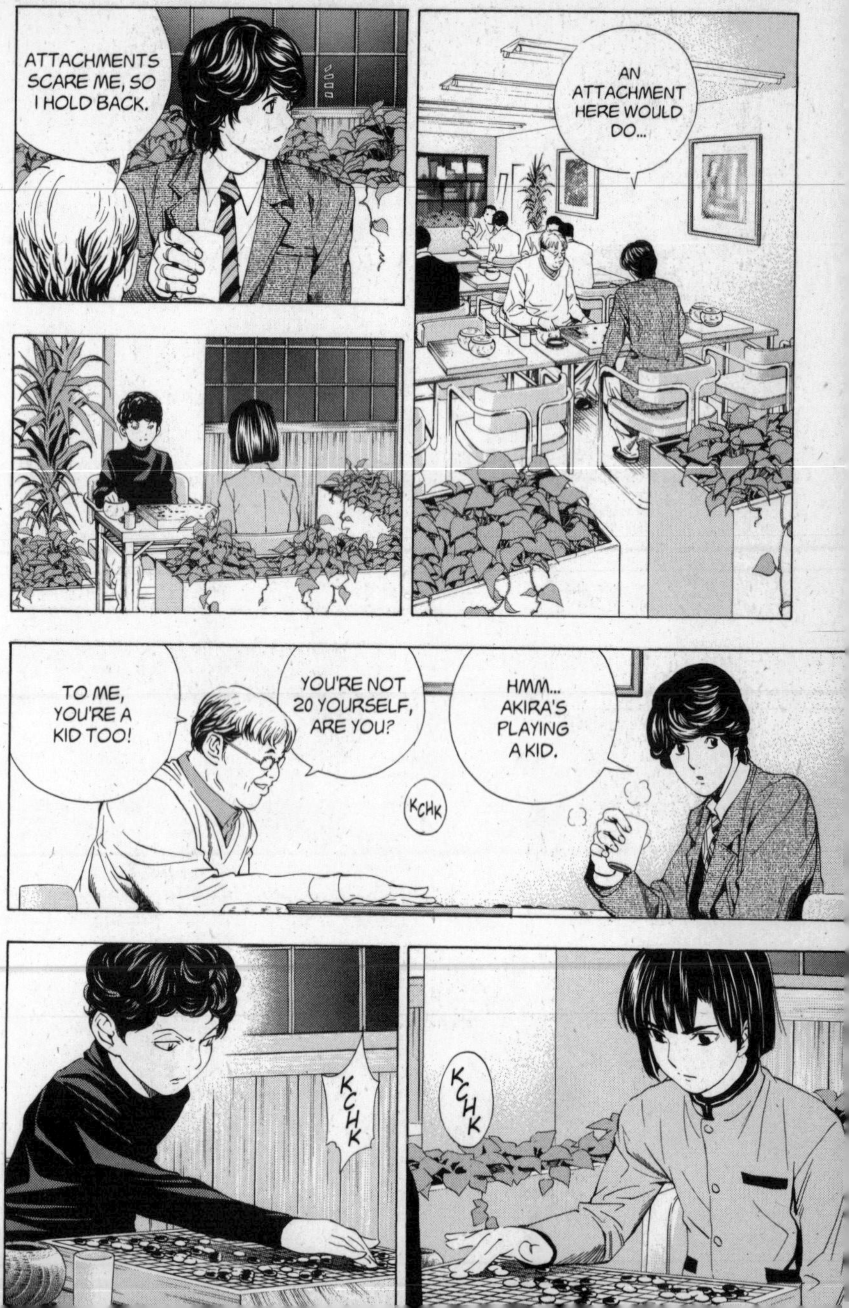
AN ATTACHMENT HERE WOULD DO...
ATTACHMENTS SCARE ME, SO I HOLD BACK.
HMM... AKIRA'S PLAYING A KID.
KCHK
YOU'RE NOT 20 YOURSELF, ARE YOU?
TO ME, YOU'RE A KID TOO!
KCHK
KCHK

READ THIS WAY

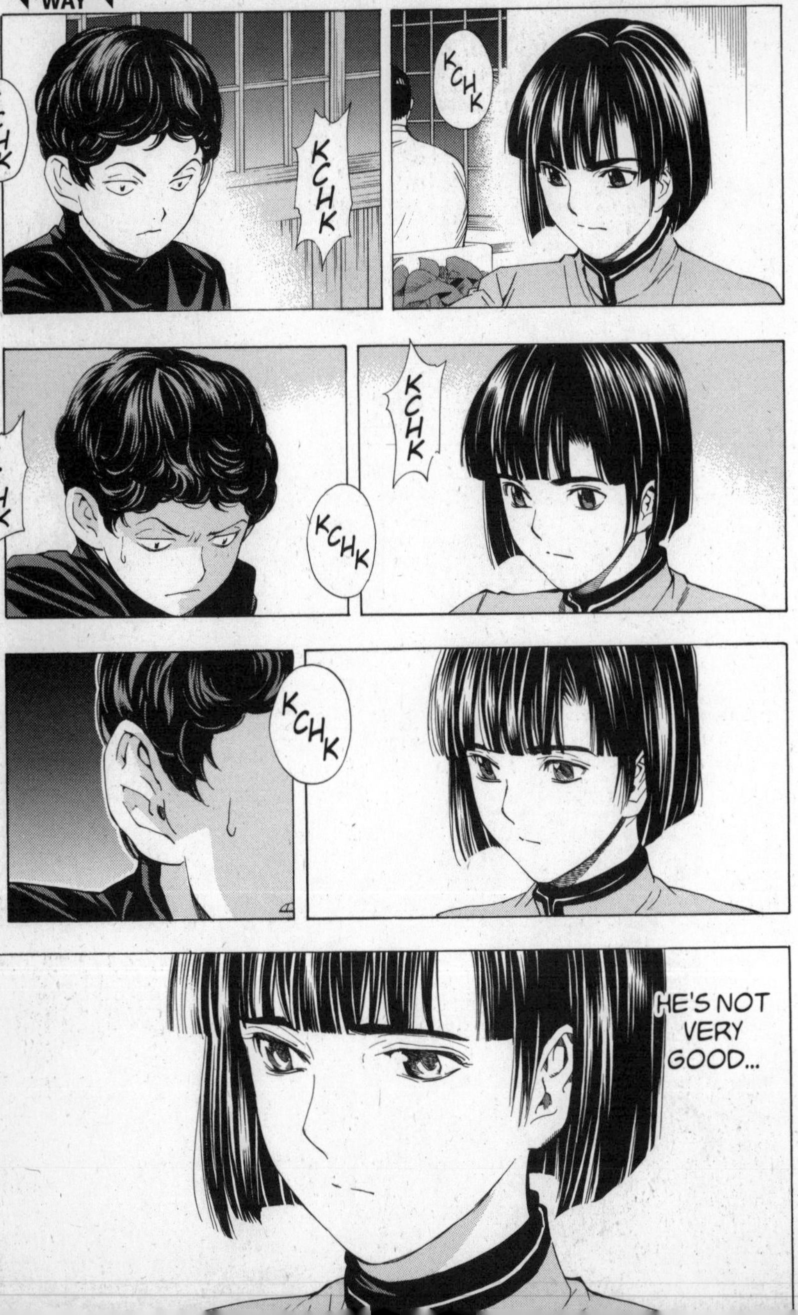

KCHK
KCHK
KCHK
KCHK
KCHK
KCHK
KCHK
HE'S NOT VERY GOOD...

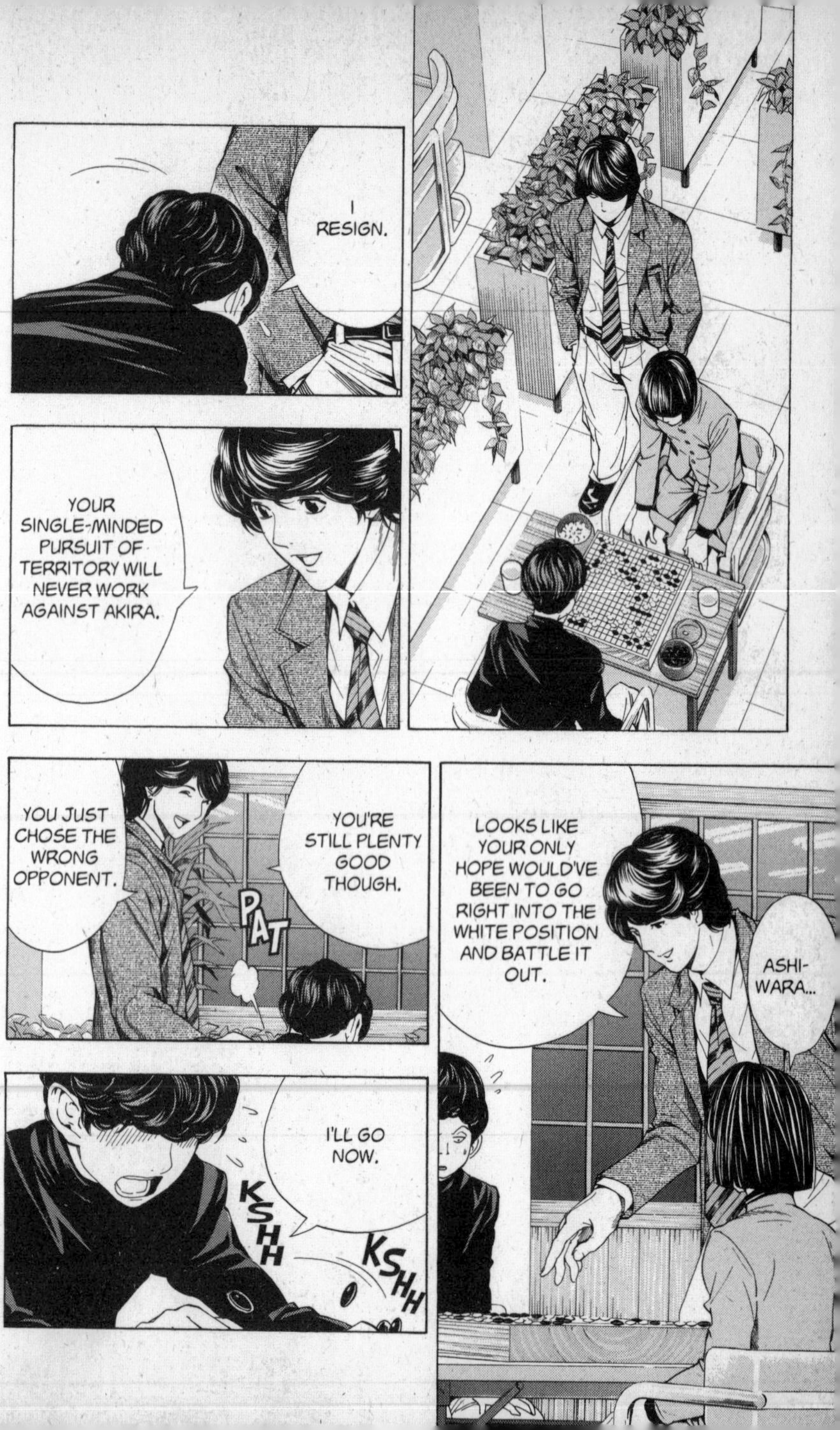
I RESIGN.
YOUR SINGLE-MINDED PURSUIT OF TERRITORY WILL NEVER WORK AGAINST AKIRA.
LOOKS LIKE YOUR ONLY HOPE WOULD'VE BEEN TO GO RIGHT INTO THE WHITE POSITION AND BATTLE IT OUT.
ASHI-WARA...
YOU'RE STILL PLENTY GOOD THOUGH.
YOU JUST CHOSE THE WRONG OPPONENT.
PAT
I'LL GO NOW.
KSHH
KSHH

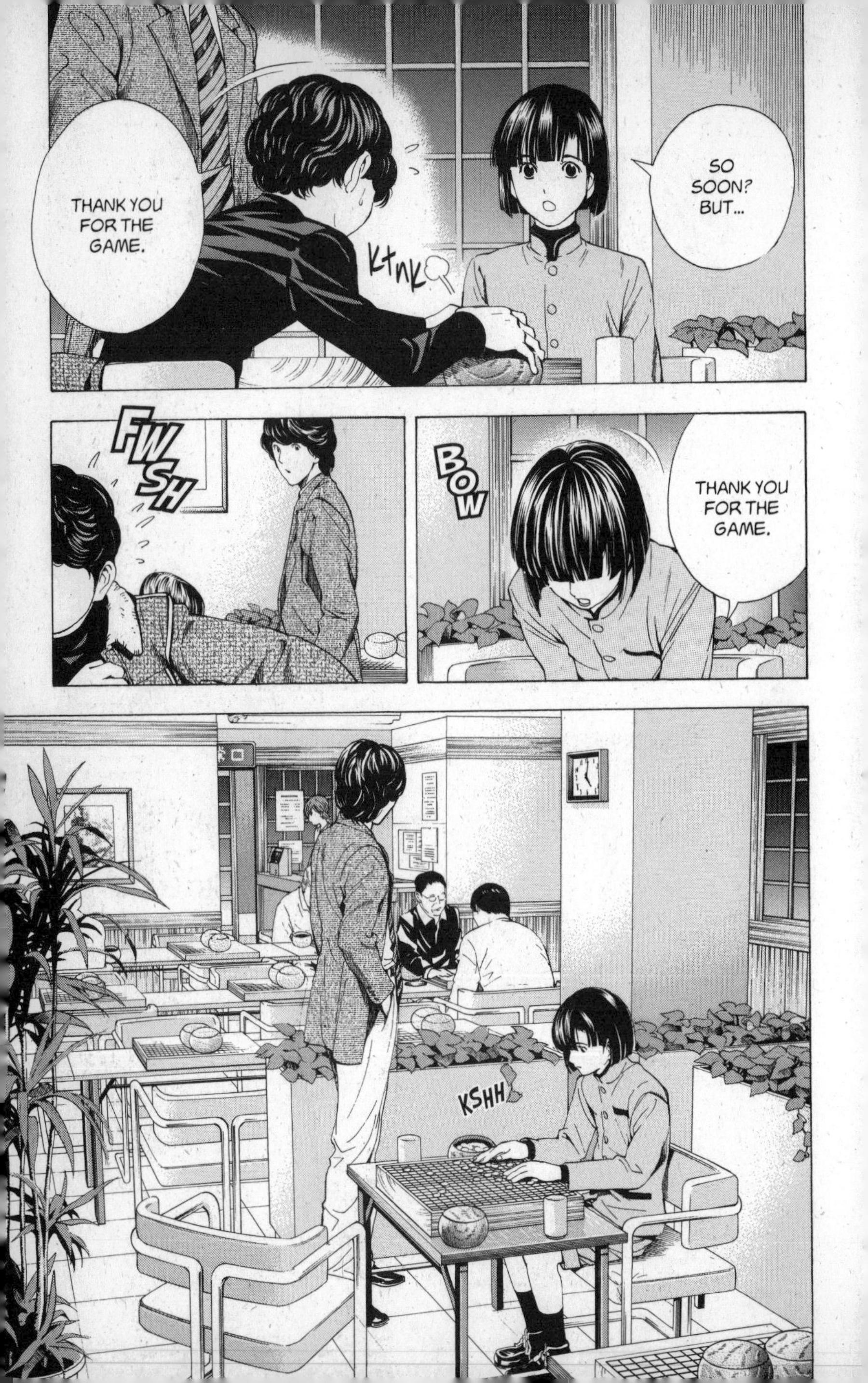
SO SOON? BUT...
KTNK
THANK YOU FOR THE GAME.
THANK YOU FOR THE GAME.
BOW
FWSH
KSHH

EH?

WHO WAS HE?

KSHH

ALREADY?!

I FORGET.

UM... WHAT WAS HIS NAME?

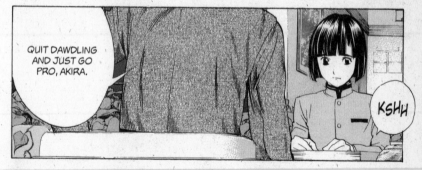

QUIT DAWDLING AND JUST GO PRO, AKIRA.

KSHH

MAYBE I SHOULD...

YEAH...

KSHH

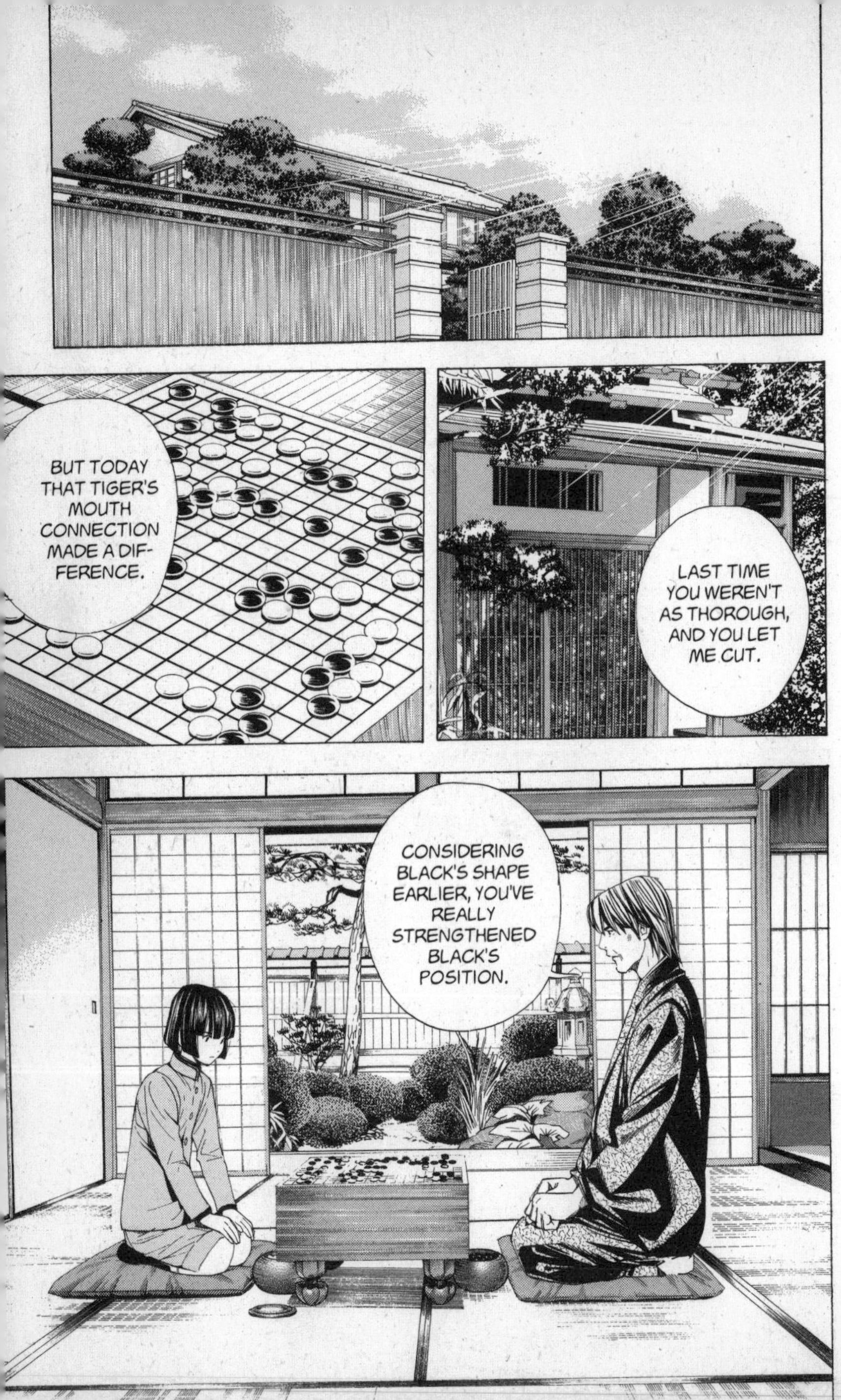
LAST TIME YOU WEREN'T AS THOROUGH, AND YOU LET ME CUT.
BUT TODAY THAT TIGER'S MOUTH CONNECTION MADE A DIF-FERENCE.
CONSIDERING BLACK'S SHAPE EARLIER, YOU'VE REALLY STRENGTHENED BLACK'S POSITION.

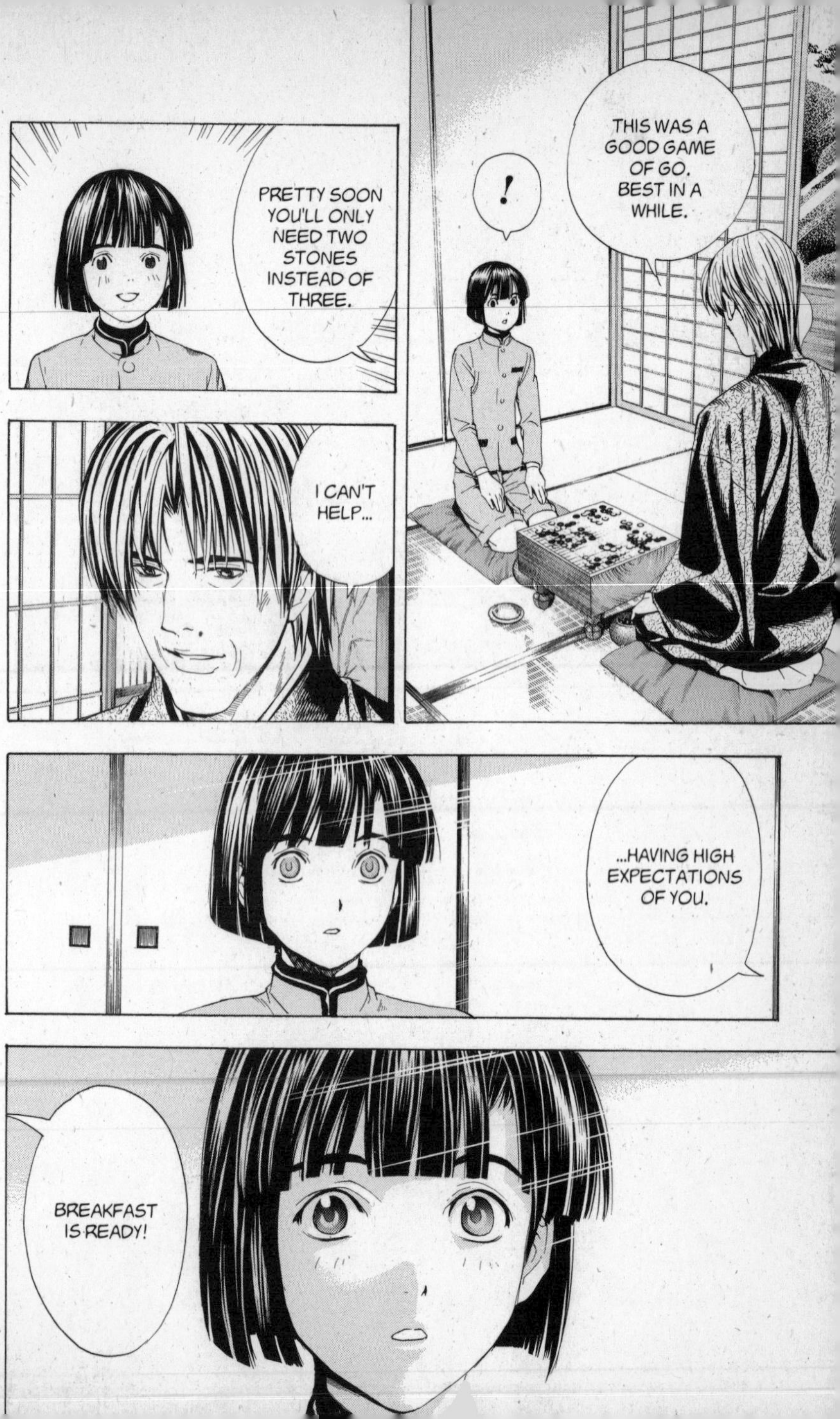
THIS WAS A GOOD GAME OF GO. BEST IN A WHILE.
!
PRETTY SOON YOU'LL ONLY NEED TWO STONES INSTEAD OF THREE.
I CAN'T HELP...
...HAVING HIGH EXPECTATIONS OF YOU.
BREAKFAST IS READY!

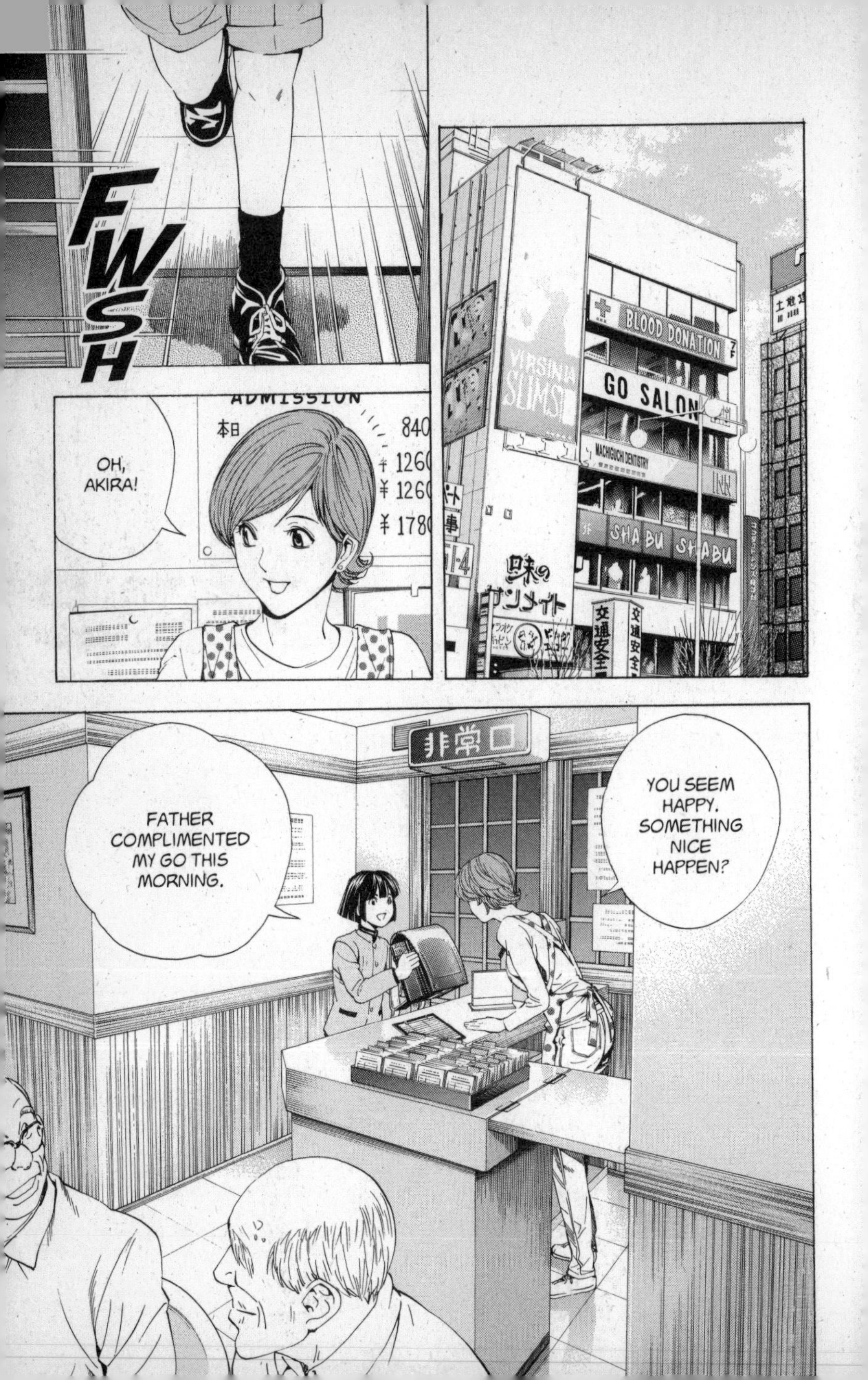
BLOOD DONATION 7F
GO SALON
MACHIGUCHI DENTISTRY
INN
SHABU SHABU
味のサンメイト
FWSH
ADMISSION
本日
OH, AKIRA!
非常口
YOU SEEM HAPPY. SOMETHING NICE HAPPEN?
FATHER COMPLIMENTED MY GO THIS MORNING.

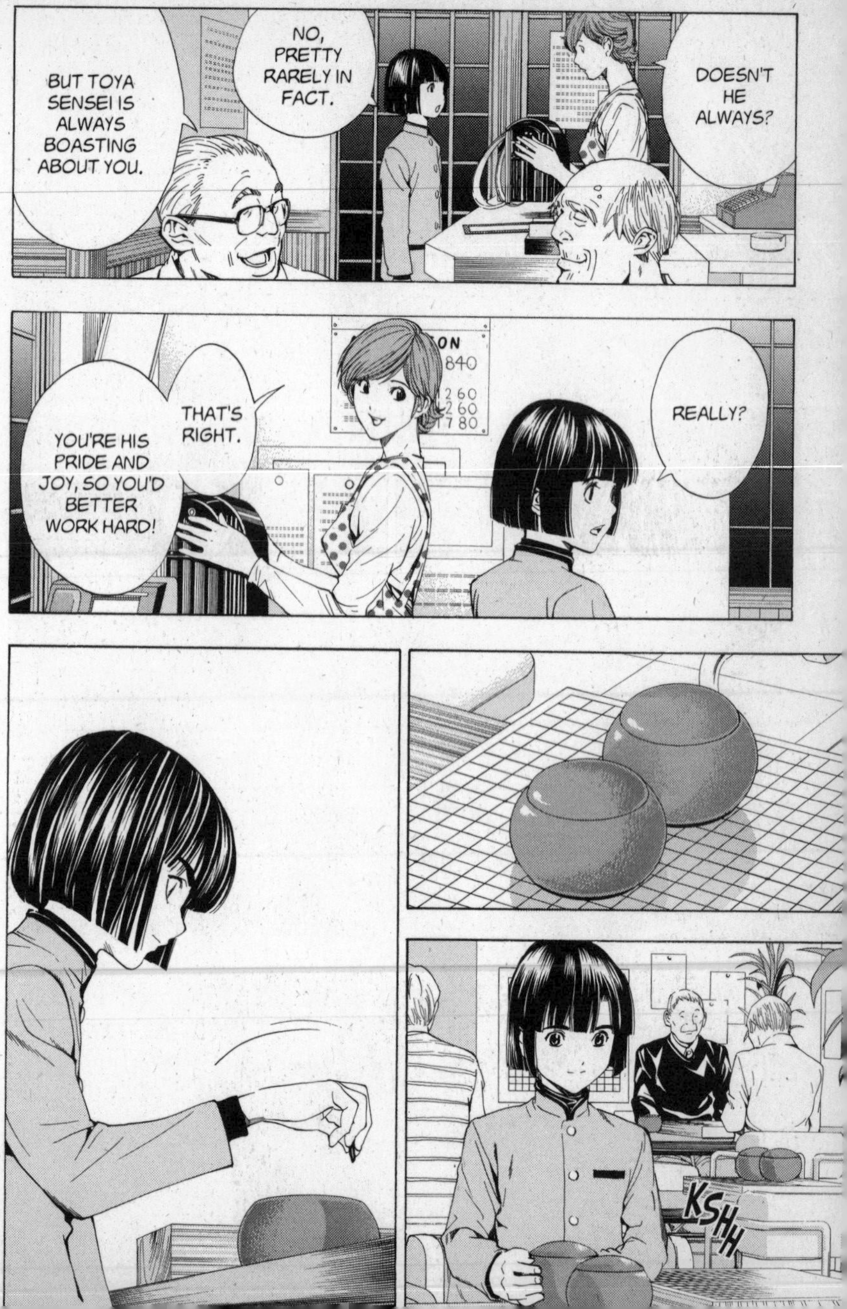
DOESN'T HE ALWAYS?
NO, PRETTY RARELY IN FACT.
BUT TOYA SENSEI IS ALWAYS BOASTING ABOUT YOU.
REALLY?
THAT'S RIGHT.
YOU'RE HIS PRIDE AND JOY, SO YOU'D BETTER WORK HARD!
KSHH

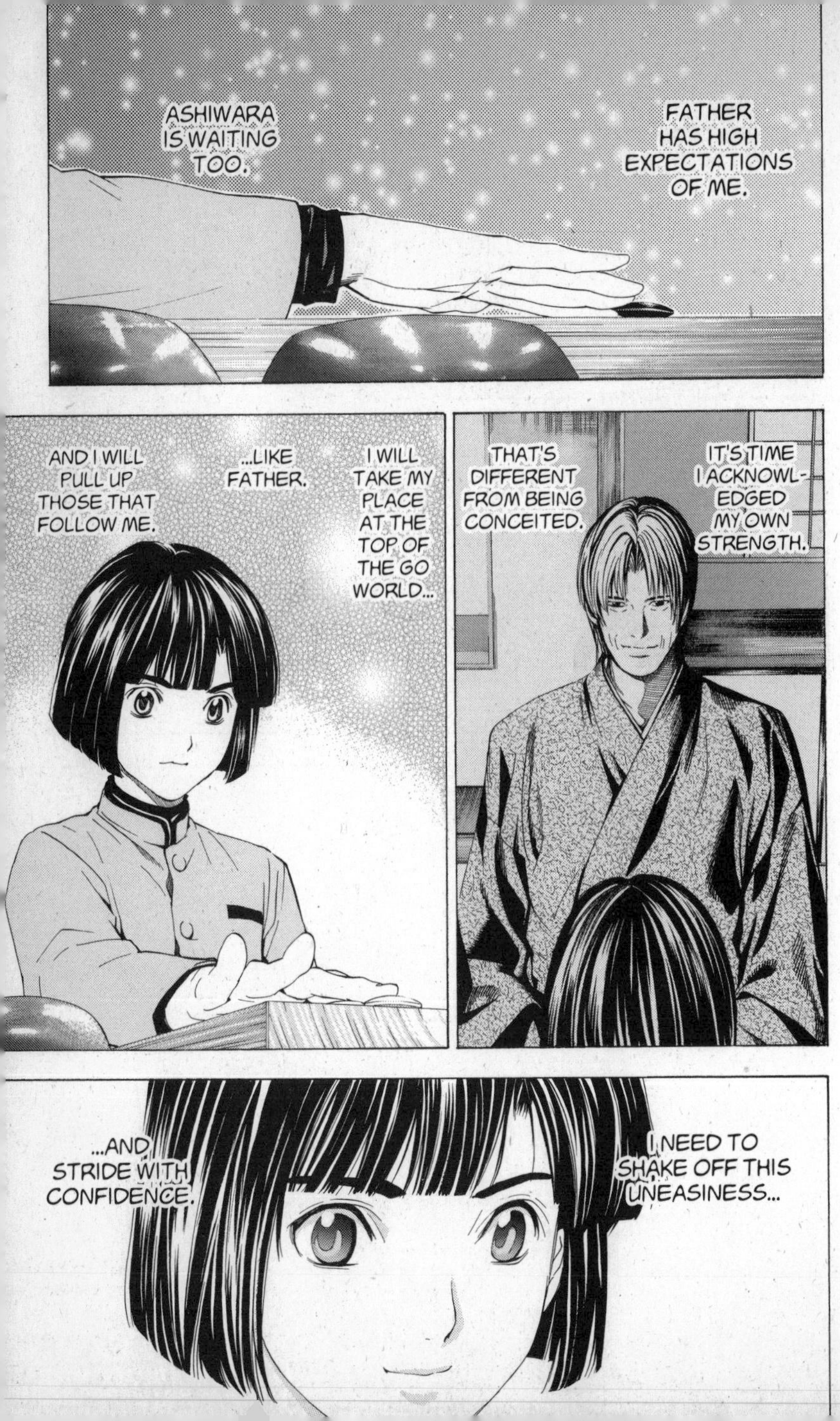
FATHER HAS HIGH EXPECTATIONS OF ME.
ASHIWARA IS WAITING TOO.
IT'S TIME I ACKNOWL-EDGED MY OWN STRENGTH.
THAT'S DIFFERENT FROM BEING CONCEITED.
I WILL TAKE MY PLACE AT THE TOP OF THE GO WORLD...
...LIKE FATHER.
AND I WILL PULL UP THOSE THAT FOLLOW ME.
I NEED TO SHAKE OFF THIS UNEASINESS...
...AND STRIDE WITH CONFIDENCE.

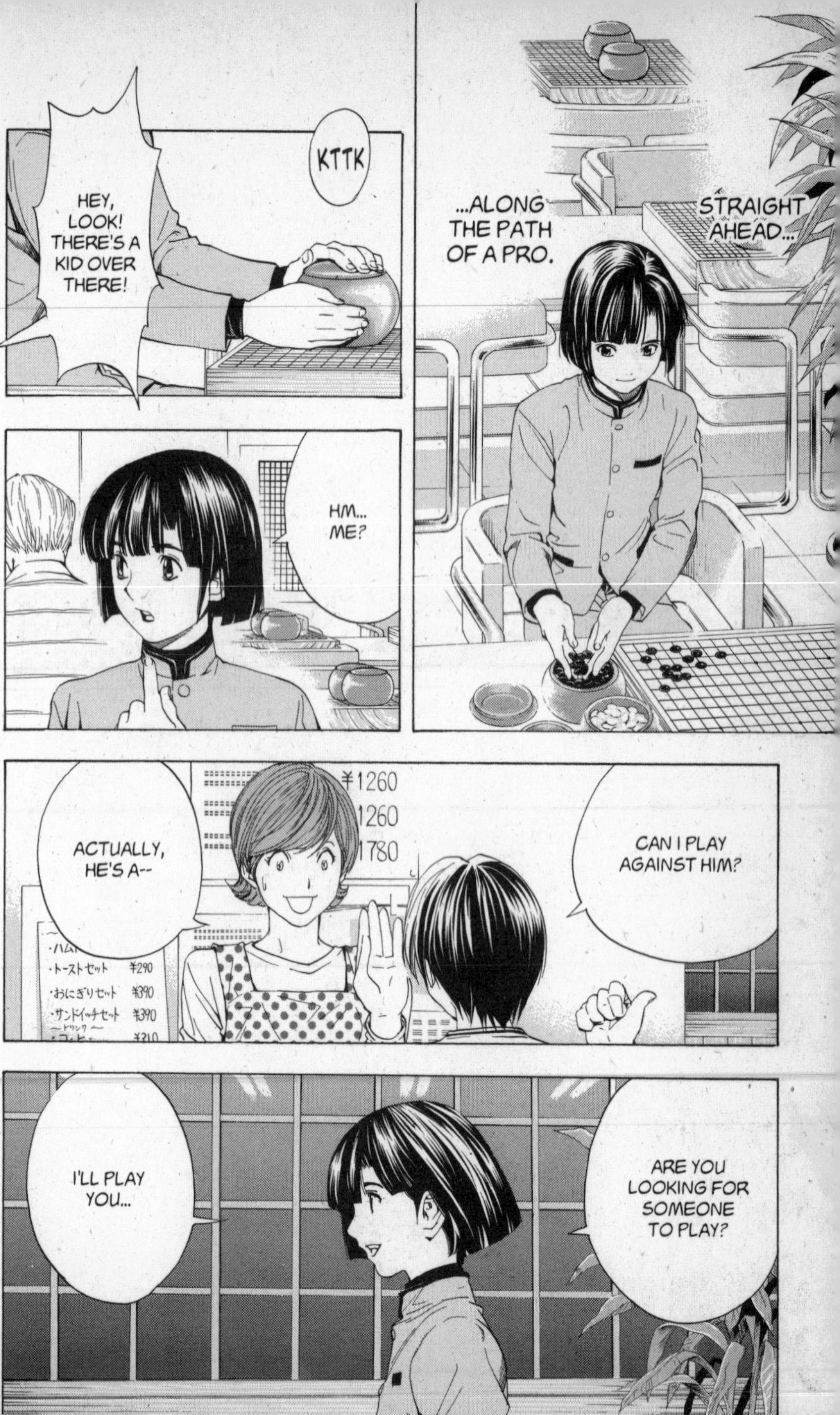
STRAIGHT AHEAD...
...ALONG THE PATH OF A PRO.
KTTK
HEY, LOOK! THERE'S A KID OVER THERE!
HM... ME?
CAN I PLAY AGAINST HIM?
¥1260
1260
1780
ACTUALLY, HE'S A--
トーストセット ¥290
おにぎりセット ¥390
サンドイッチセット ¥390
ドリンク
ARE YOU LOOKING FOR SOMEONE TO PLAY?
I'LL PLAY YOU...

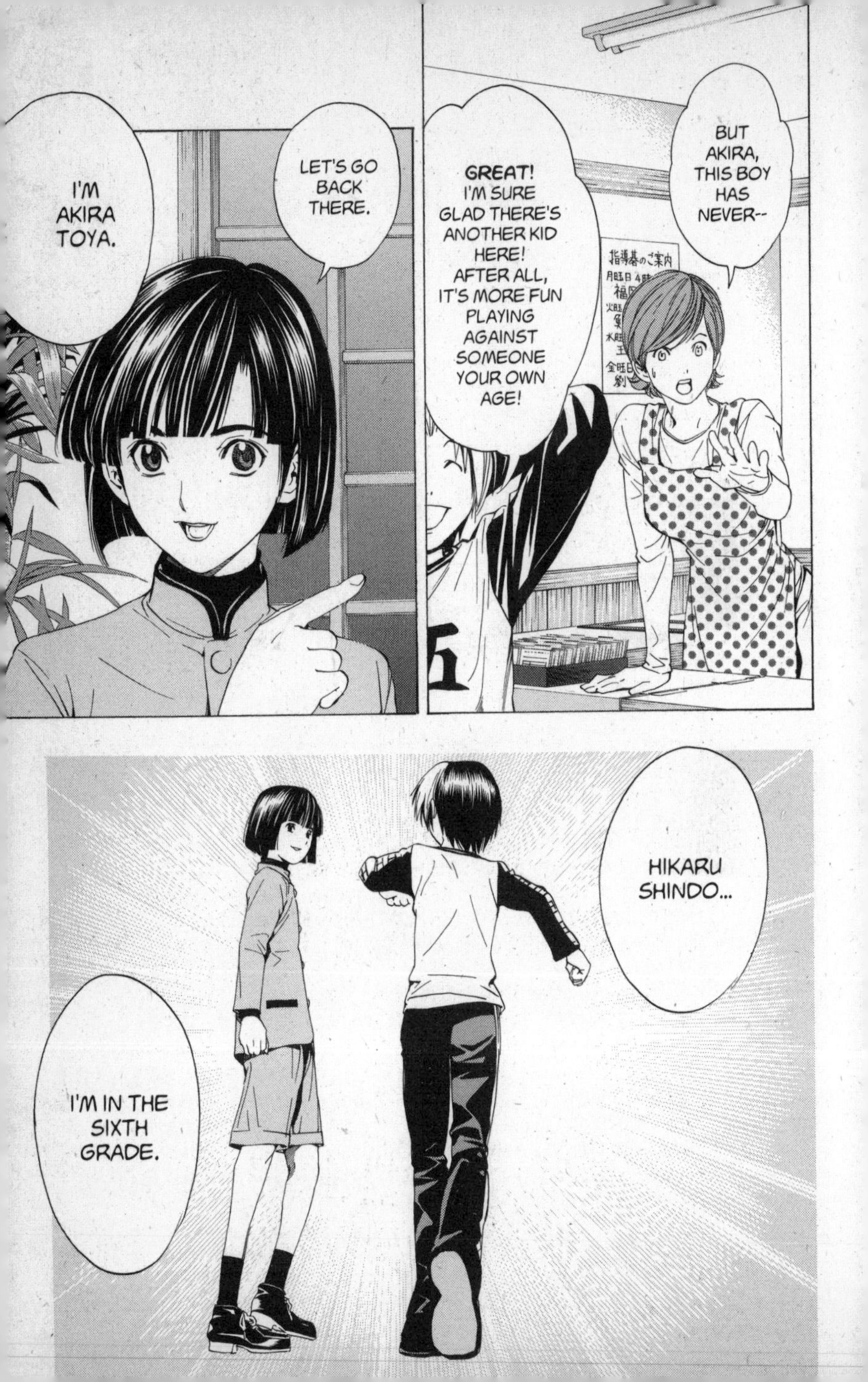
BUT AKIRA, THIS BOY HAS NEVER--
GREAT! I'M SURE GLAD THERE'S ANOTHER KID HERE! AFTER ALL, IT'S MORE FUN PLAYING AGAINST SOMEONE YOUR OWN AGE!
指導碁のご案内
LET'S GO BACK THERE.
I'M AKIRA TOYA.
HIKARU SHINDO...
I'M IN THE SIXTH GRADE.

YUMI HOTTA'S

LONG INTERVIEW WITH TAKESHI OBATA SENSEI: ①

2002.5.28

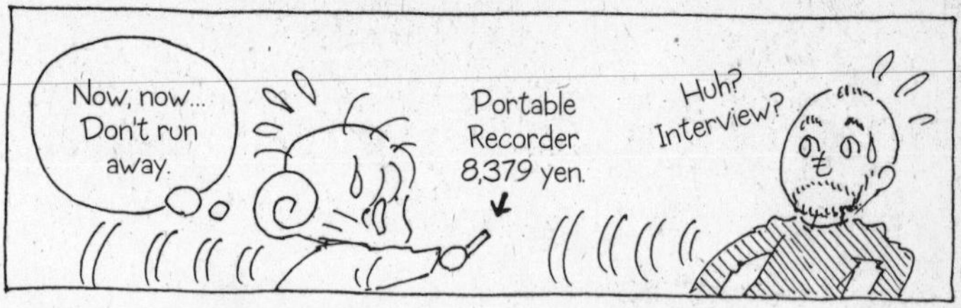

Huh? Interview?
Portable Recorder 8,379 yen.
Now, now... Don't run away.

● ILLUSTRATION COLLECTION: SAI

Ⓗ FIRST OF ALL, THERE ARE MANY ILLUSTRATIONS CREATED JUST FOR THIS COLLECTION.

Ⓞ THIS FOLD-OUT POSTER IS A DRAWING I'D BEEN WANTING TO DO FOR A WHILE. I DIDN'T DO IT IN THE MAGAZINE BECAUSE I THOUGHT I'D BE CONSIDERED A MANIAC. SO THIS IS THE FIRST ONE I DID FOR THIS COLLECTION.

Ⓗ ALL OF THE FOUR SEASONS ARE BEAUTIFUL (PAGE 005, PAGE 033, PAGE 059, PAGE 077).

Ⓞ I WANTED TO CONVEY THE PHYSICALITY OF SAI IN THE SUMMER BY HAVING THE LIGHT REFLECT OFF HIS FACE, IN THE FALL BY HAVING HIS BODY FLOAT OUT IN FRONT OF THE SUNSET, IN THE WINTER BY SEEING HIS BREATH. I WANTED THE READER TO FEEL HIS BODILY PRESENCE. I COULDN'T THINK OF ONE FOR SPRING. I THOUGHT MAYBE I'D HAVE BLOSSOMS (ON HIS HAIR AND BODY) OR SOMETHING.

Ⓗ YOU HAVE A NEW ONE OF HIKARU TOO.

Ⓞ THERE'S HIKARU IN A LEATHER JACKET (ON THE RIGHT SIDE OF THE FOLD-OUT POSTER), BUT I DREW THAT BECAUSE I WANTED TO DRAW A LEATHER JACKET. BUT MAYBE (THAT FASHION) ISN'T REALLY HIKARU'S STYLE. IT'S MORE MITANI'S STYLE. THE ONE OF HIKARU AND THE ELECTRIC SKATEBOARD (PAGE 095) IS MY FAVORITE IN THIS COLLECTION. I LIKE HIS FACIAL EXPRESSION. I PREFER STILL PHOTOS TO THOSE WITH MOVEMENT.

(Continued on page 72)

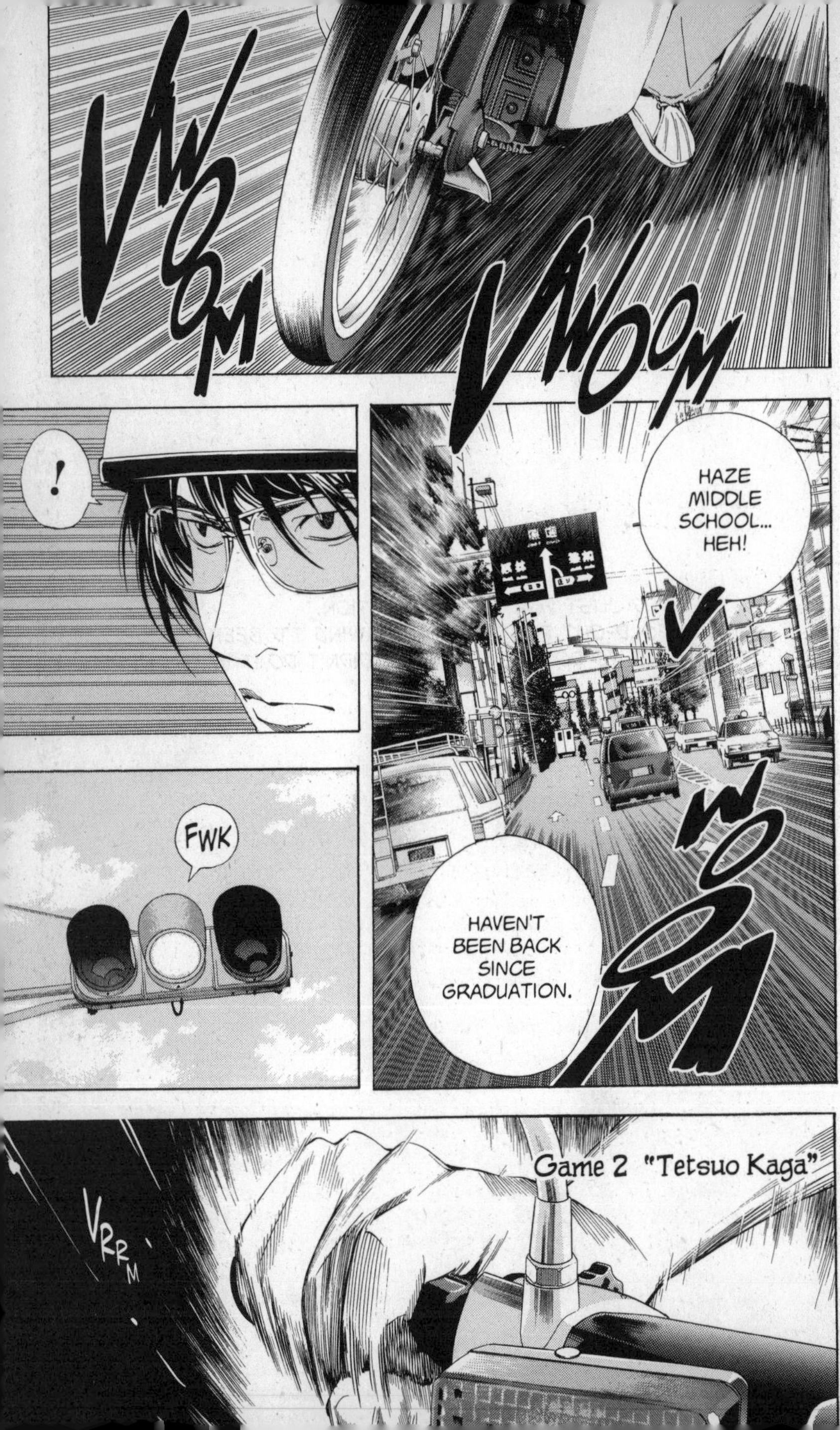
VWOOM
VWOOM
HAZE MIDDLE SCHOOL... HEH!
VWOOM
HAVEN'T BEEN BACK SINCE GRADUATION.
!
FWK
Game 2 "Tetsuo Kaga"
VRRM

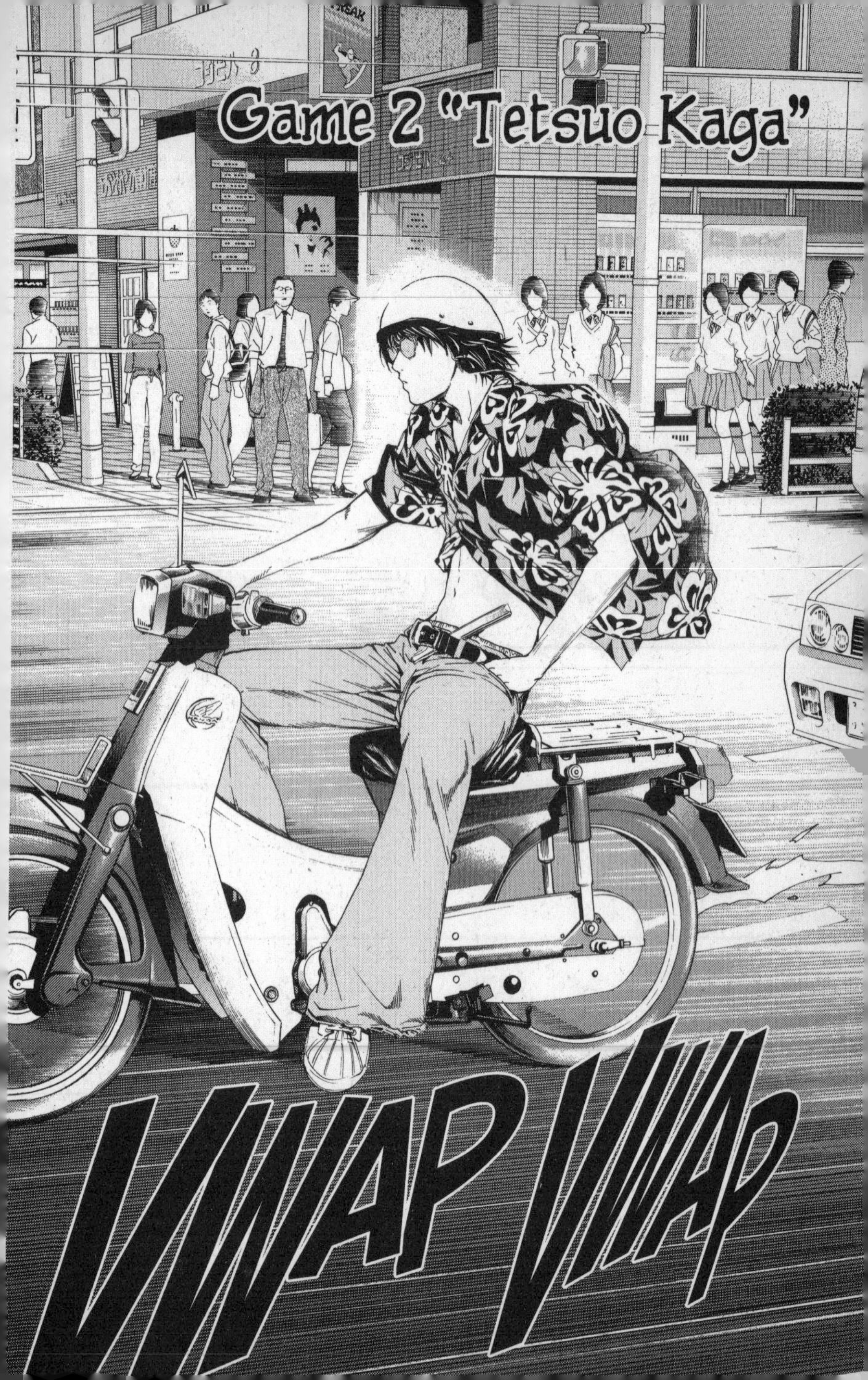
Game 2 "Tetsuo Kaga"
VWAP VWAP

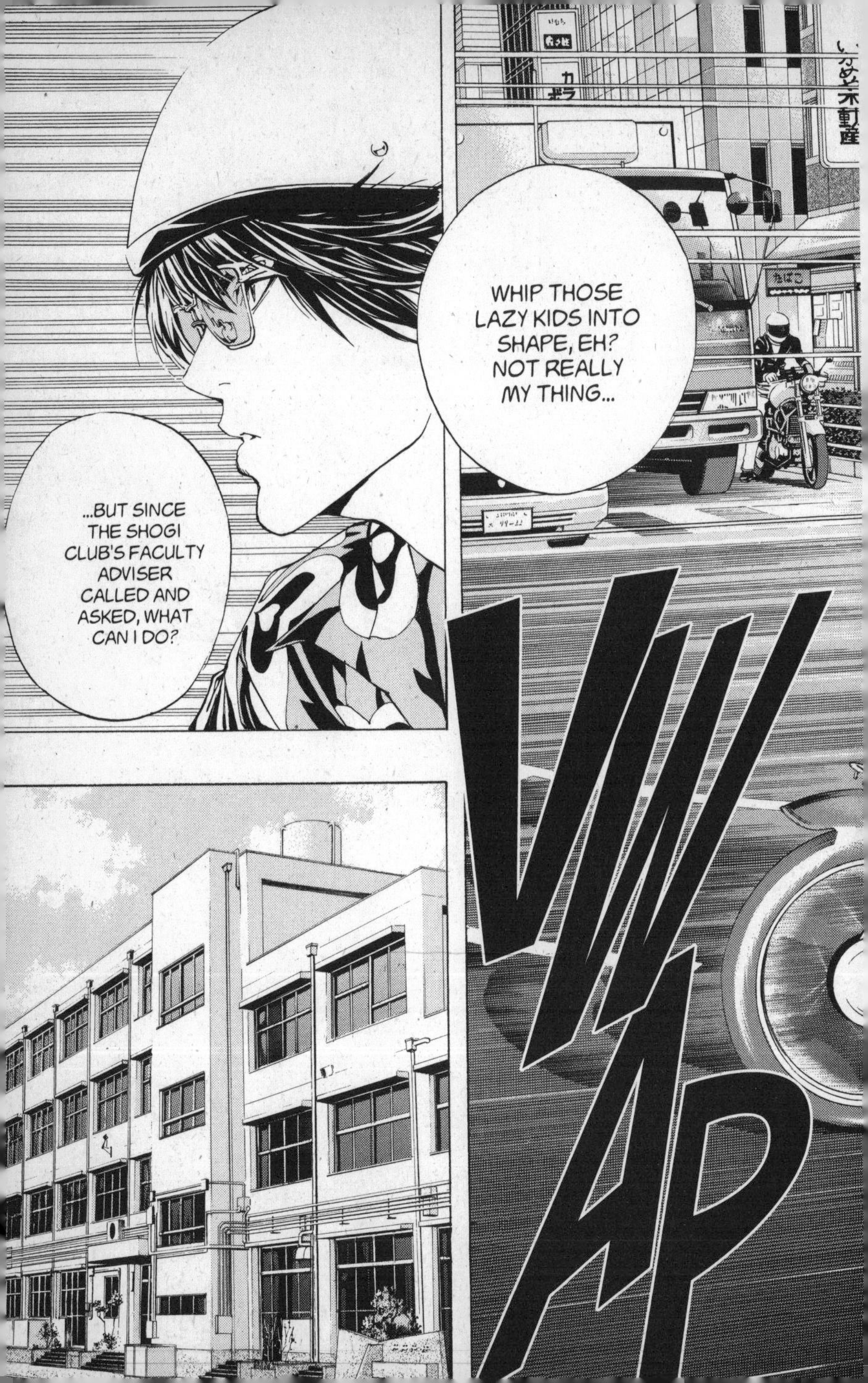
WHIP THOSE LAZY KIDS INTO SHAPE, EH? NOT REALLY MY THING...
...BUT SINCE THE SHOGI CLUB'S FACULTY ADVISER CALLED AND ASKED, WHAT CAN I DO?
VWAP

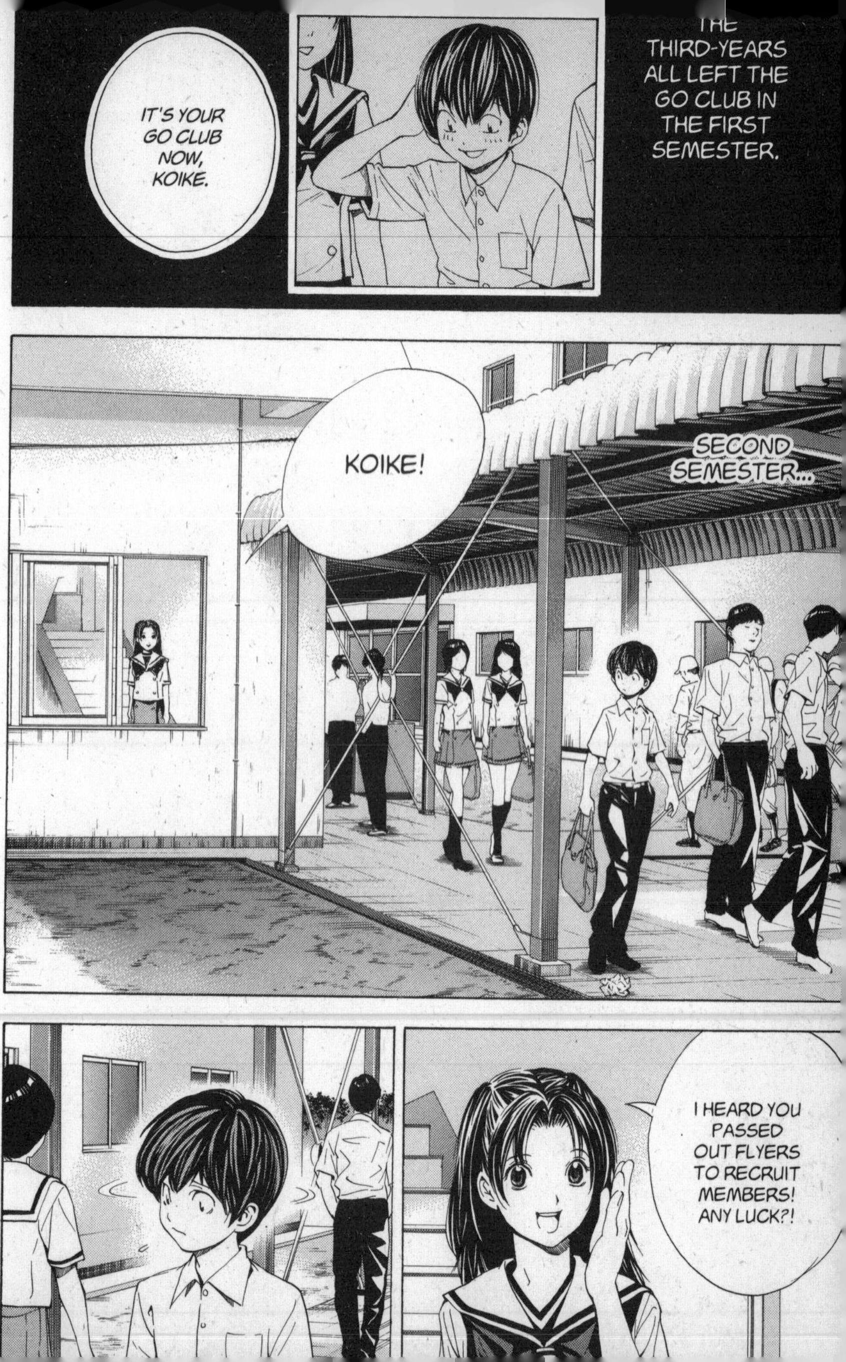
THE THIRD-YEARS ALL LEFT THE GO CLUB IN THE FIRST SEMESTER.
IT'S YOUR GO CLUB NOW, KOIKE.
SECOND SEMESTER...
KOIKE!
I HEARD YOU PASSED OUT FLYERS TO RECRUIT MEMBERS! ANY LUCK?!

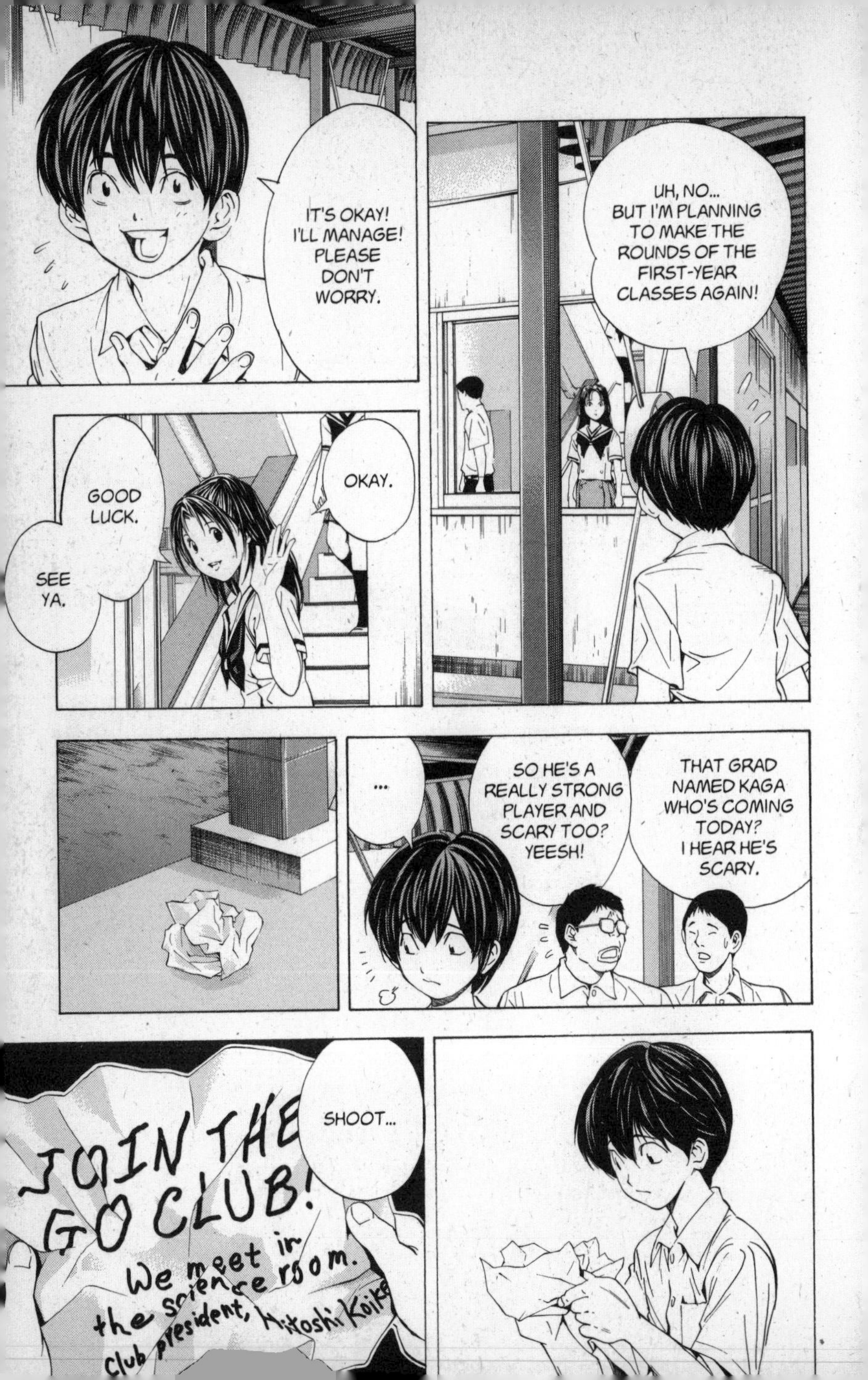
UH, NO... BUT I'M PLANNING TO MAKE THE ROUNDS OF THE FIRST-YEAR CLASSES AGAIN!
IT'S OKAY! I'LL MANAGE! PLEASE DON'T WORRY.
OKAY.
GOOD LUCK.
SEE YA.
THAT GRAD NAMED KAGA WHO'S COMING TODAY? I HEAR HE'S SCARY.
SO HE'S A REALLY STRONG PLAYER AND SCARY TOO? YEESH!
...
SHOOT...
JOIN THE
GO CLUB!
We meet ir
the science room.
Club president, Hitoshi Koike

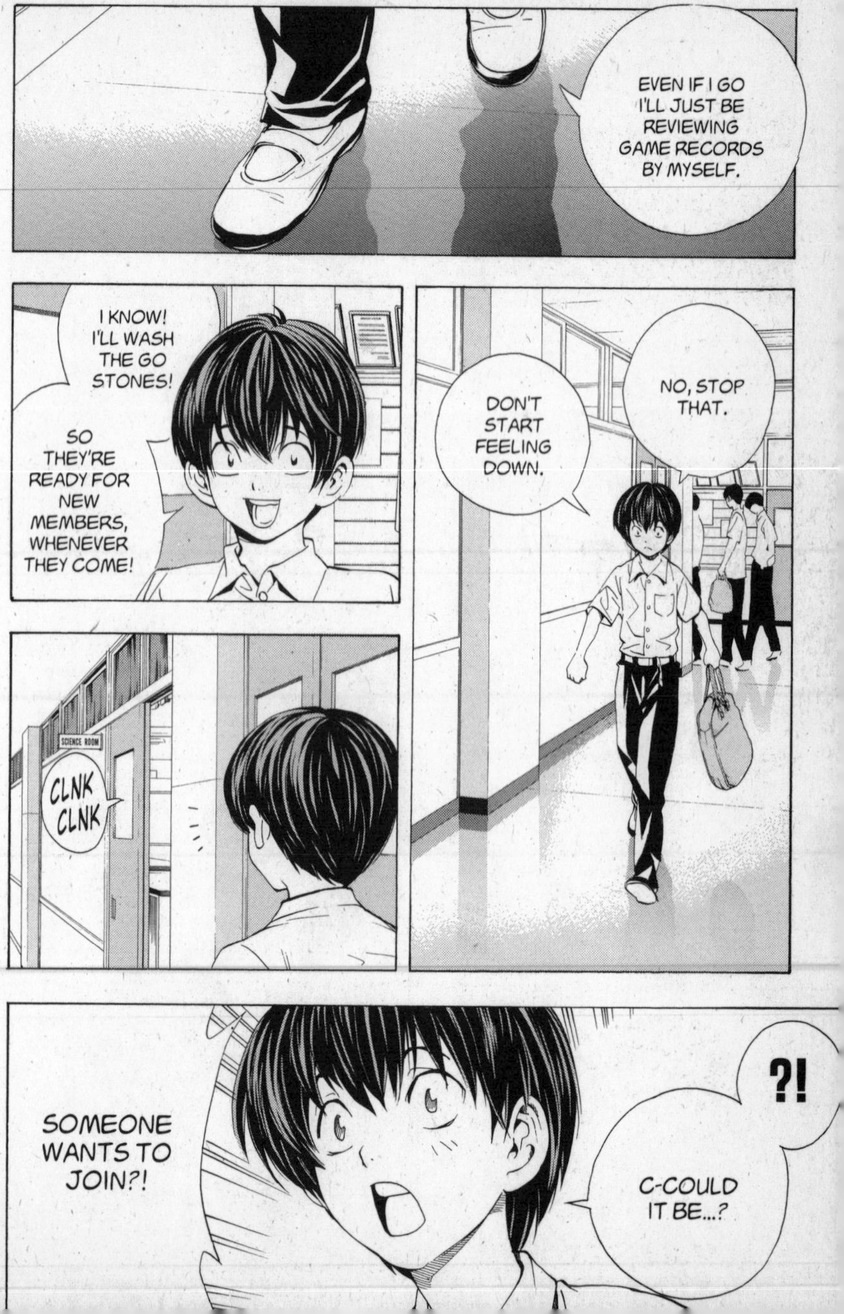
EVEN IF I GO I'LL JUST BE REVIEWING GAME RECORDS BY MYSELF.
NO, STOP THAT.
DON'T START FEELING DOWN.
I KNOW! I'LL WASH THE GO STONES!
SO THEY'RE READY FOR NEW MEMBERS, WHENEVER THEY COME!
SCIENCE ROOM
CLNK CLNK
?!
C-COULD IT BE...?
SOMEONE WANTS TO JOIN?!

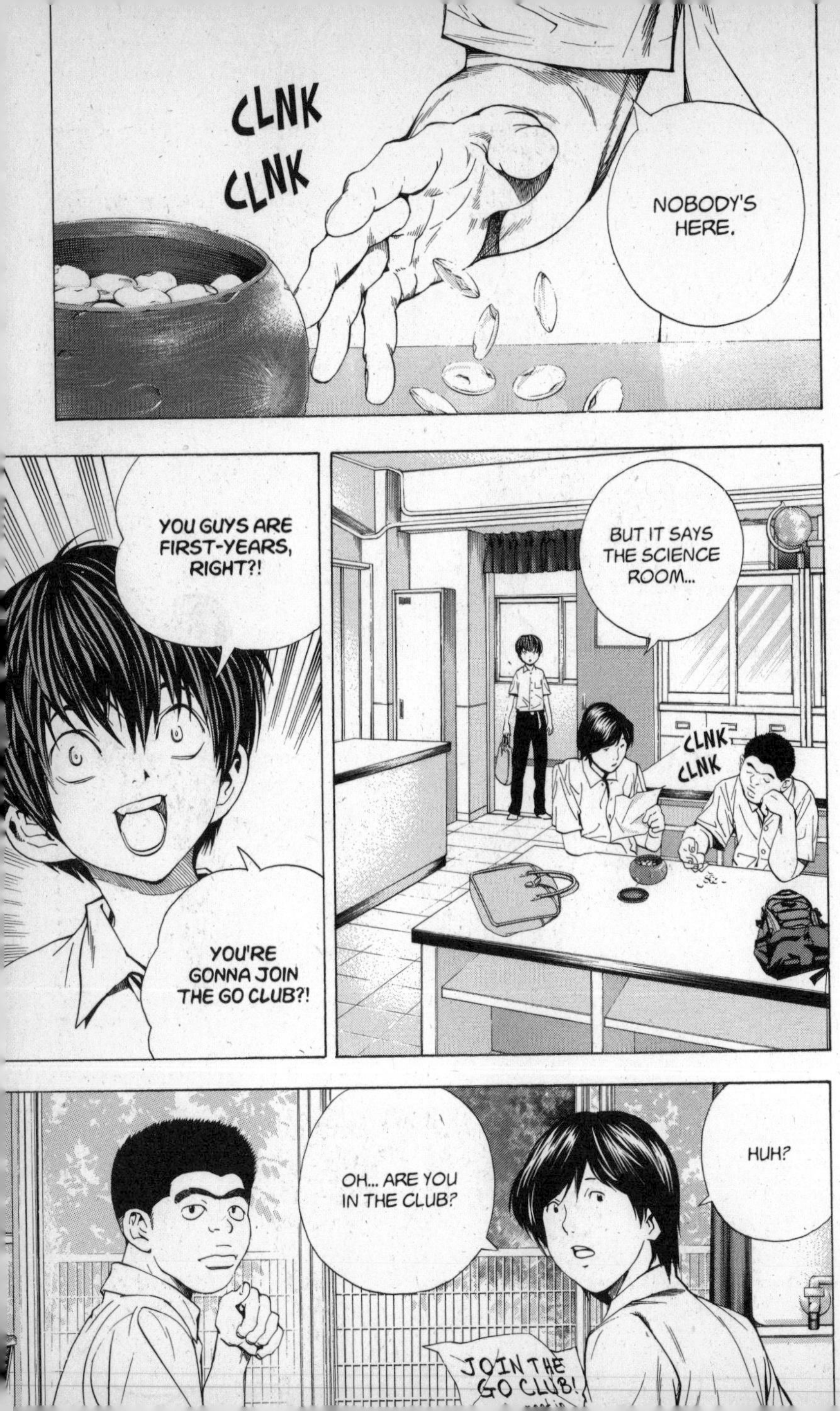
NOBODY'S HERE.
CLNK
CLNK
BUT IT SAYS THE SCIENCE ROOM...
CLNK
CLNK
YOU GUYS ARE FIRST-YEARS, RIGHT?!
YOU'RE GONNA JOIN THE GO CLUB?!
HUH?
OH... ARE YOU IN THE CLUB?
JOIN THE GO CLUB!

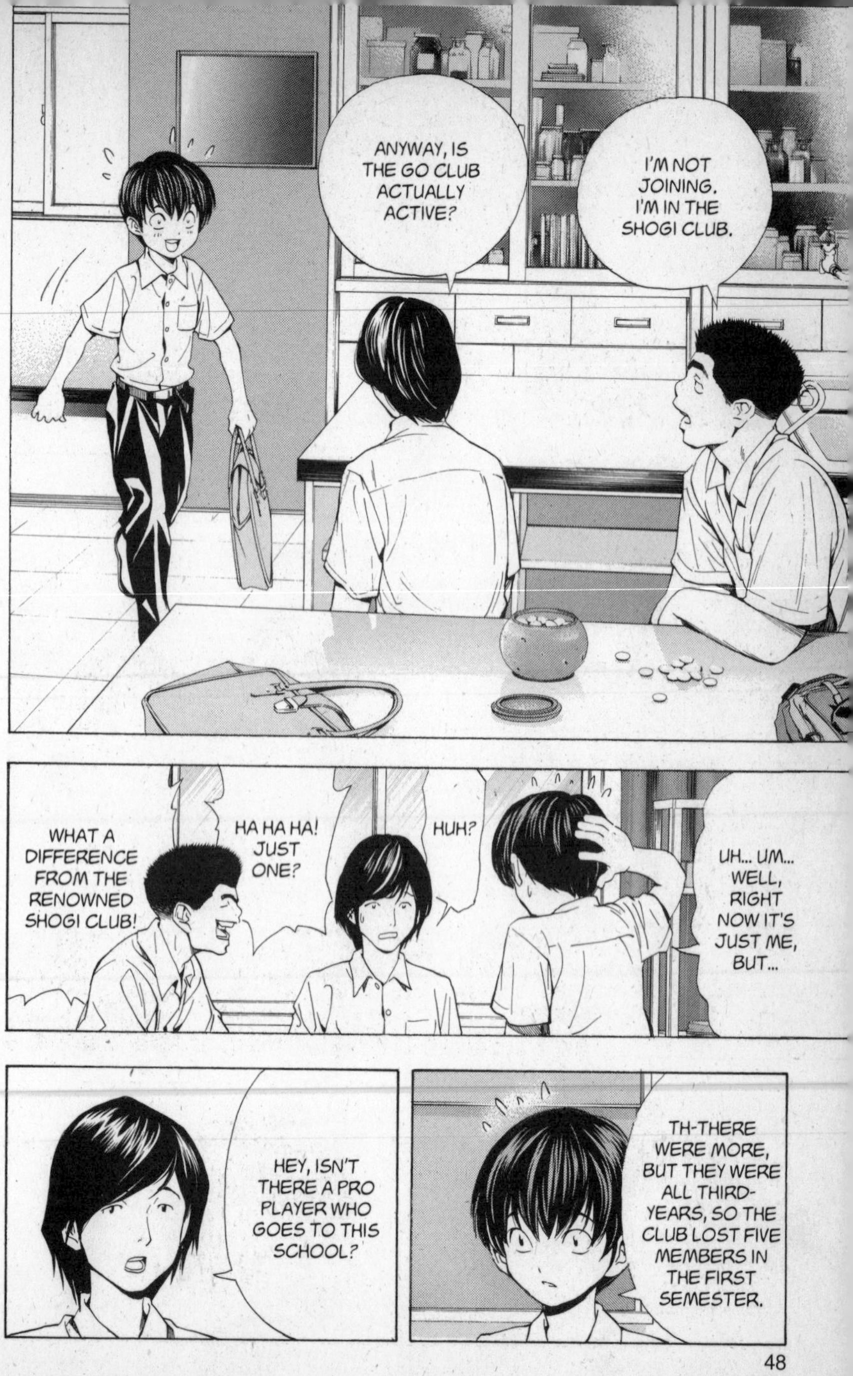
I'M NOT JOINING. I'M IN THE SHOGI CLUB.
ANYWAY, IS THE GO CLUB ACTUALLY ACTIVE?
UH... UM... WELL, RIGHT NOW IT'S JUST ME, BUT...
HUH?
HA HA HA! JUST ONE?
WHAT A DIFFERENCE FROM THE RENOWNED SHOGI CLUB!
TH-THERE WERE MORE, BUT THEY WERE ALL THIRD-YEARS, SO THE CLUB LOST FIVE MEMBERS IN THE FIRST SEMESTER.
HEY, ISN'T THERE A PRO PLAYER WHO GOES TO THIS SCHOOL?

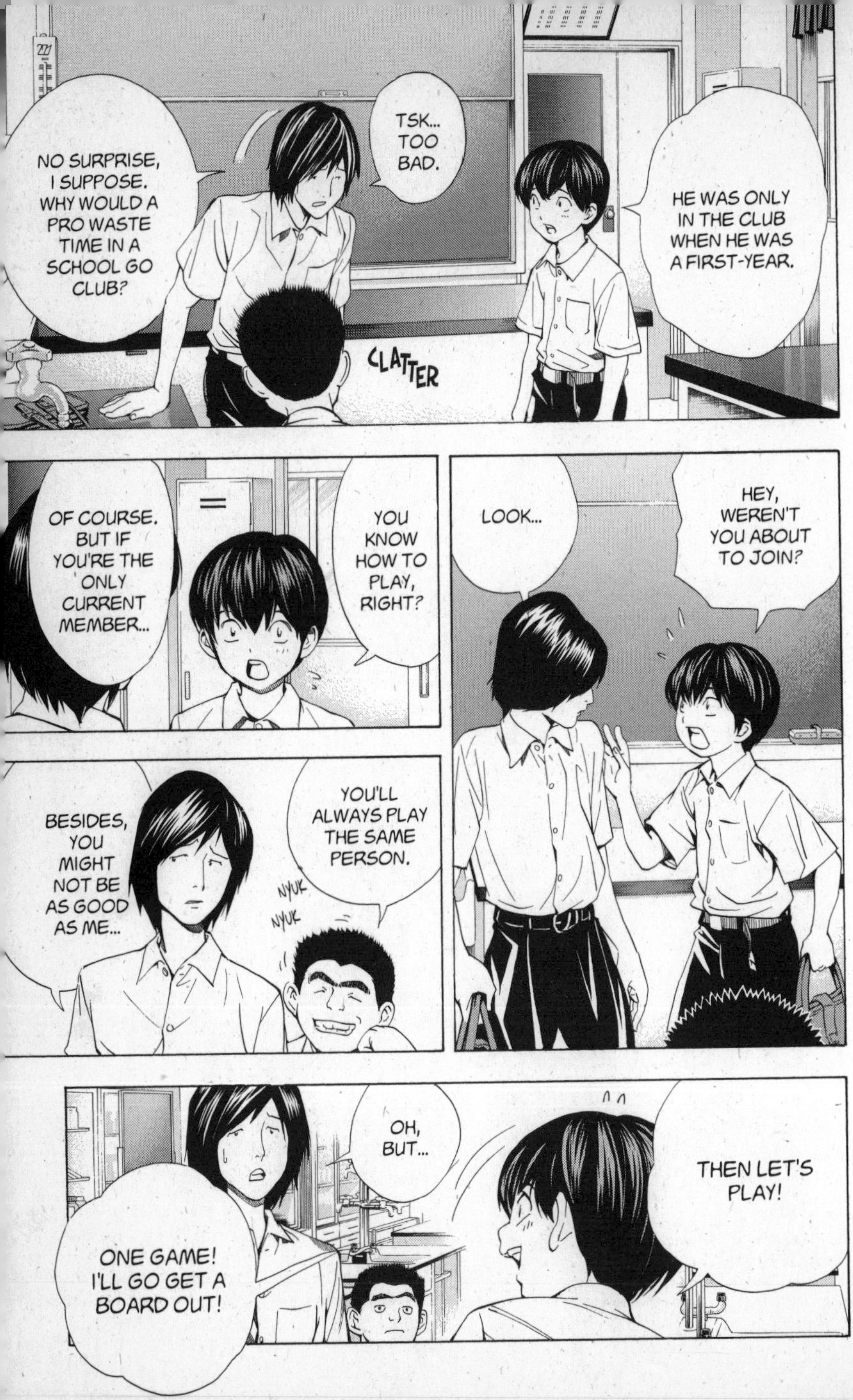
HE WAS ONLY IN THE CLUB WHEN HE WAS A FIRST-YEAR.
TSK... TOO BAD.
NO SURPRISE, I SUPPOSE. WHY WOULD A PRO WASTE TIME IN A SCHOOL GO CLUB?
CLATTER
HEY, WEREN'T YOU ABOUT TO JOIN?
LOOK...
YOU KNOW HOW TO PLAY, RIGHT?
OF COURSE. BUT IF YOU'RE THE ONLY CURRENT MEMBER...
YOU'LL ALWAYS PLAY THE SAME PERSON.
NYUK
NYUK
BESIDES, YOU MIGHT NOT BE AS GOOD AS ME...
THEN LET'S PLAY!
OH, BUT...
ONE GAME! I'LL GO GET A BOARD OUT!

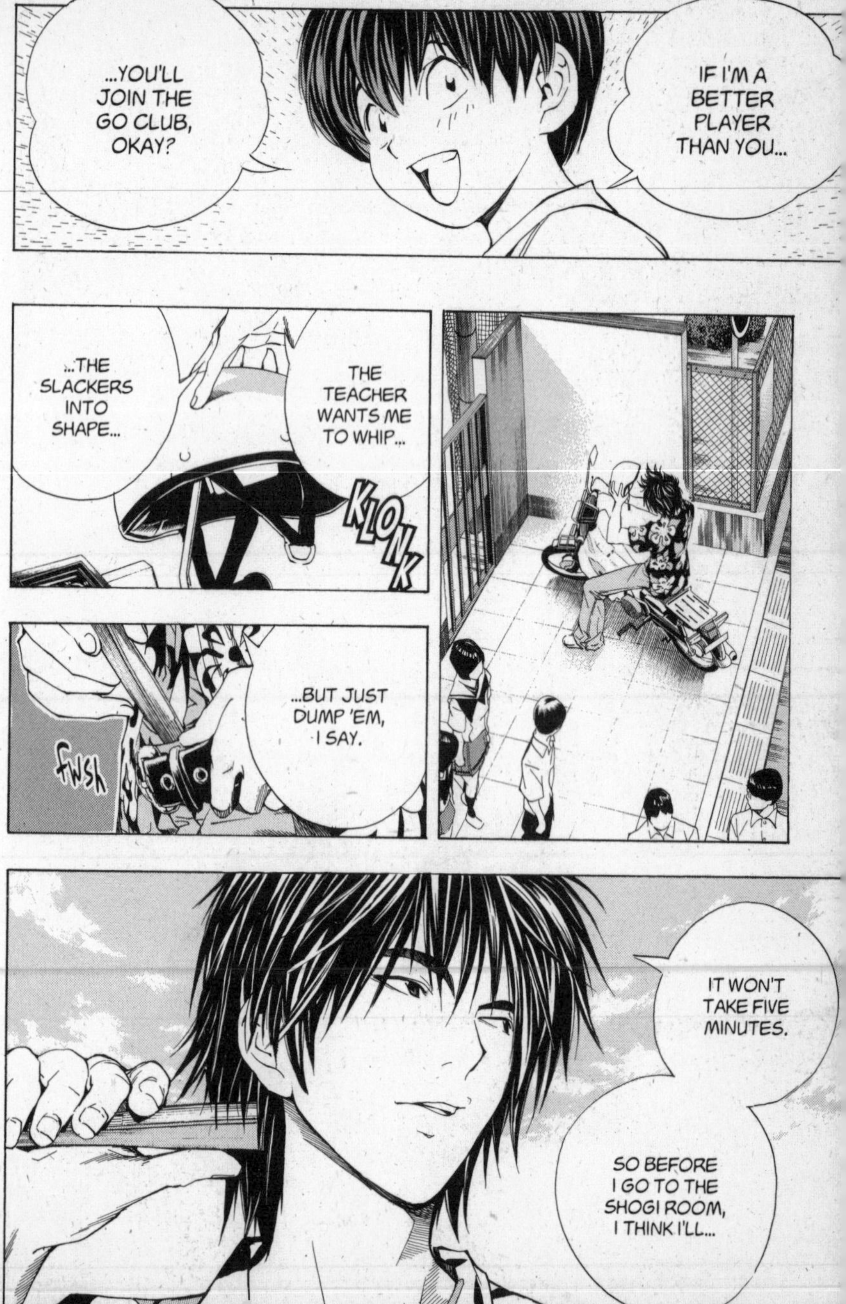
IF I'M A BETTER PLAYER THAN YOU...
...YOU'LL JOIN THE GO CLUB, OKAY?
THE TEACHER WANTS ME TO WHIP...
...THE SLACKERS INTO SHAPE...
KLONK
...BUT JUST DUMP 'EM, I SAY.
fwsh
IT WON'T TAKE FIVE MINUTES.
SO BEFORE I GO TO THE SHOGI ROOM, I THINK I'LL...

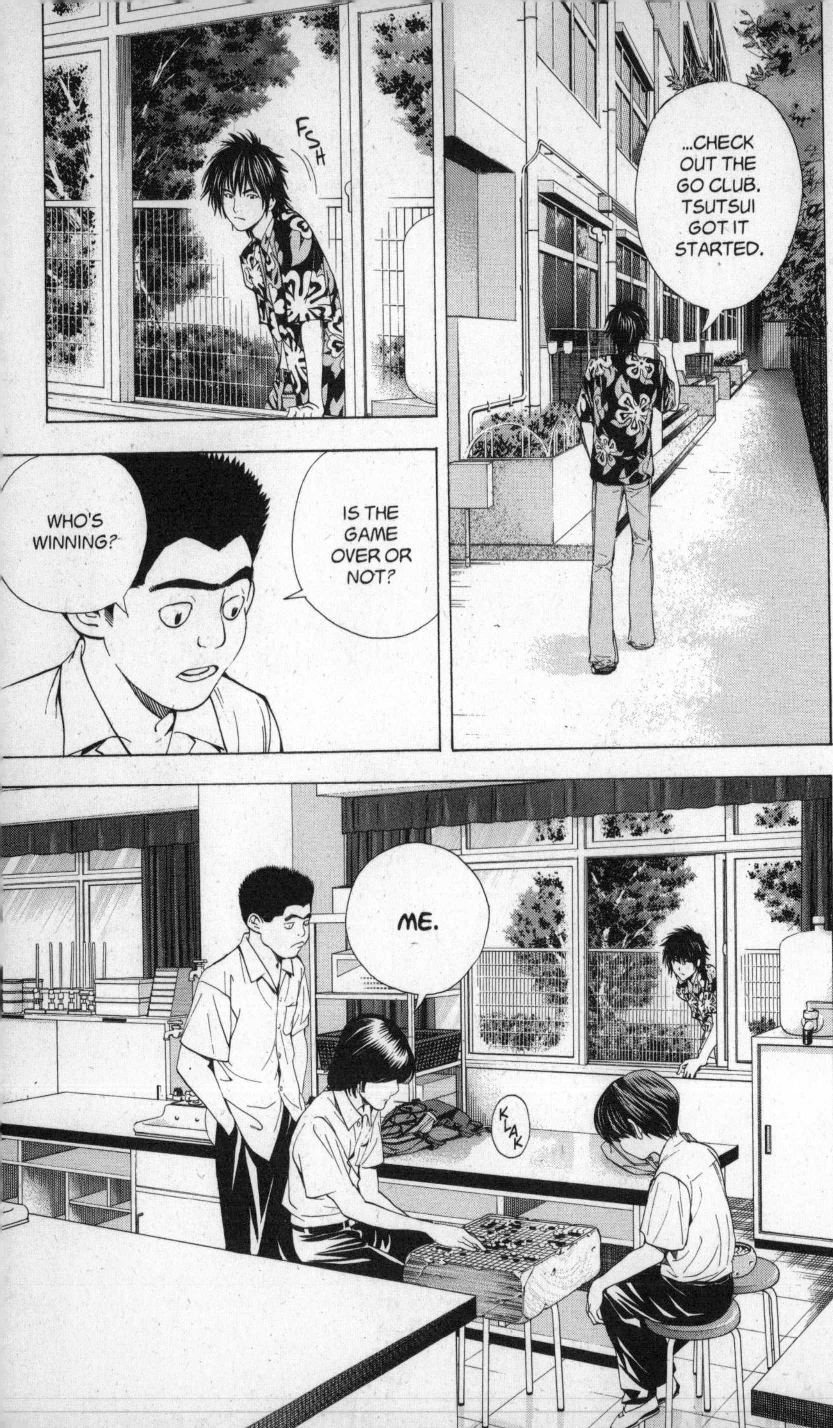
...CHECK OUT THE GO CLUB. TSUTSUI GOT IT STARTED.
FSH
IS THE GAME OVER OR NOT?
WHO'S WINNING?
ME.
KLAK

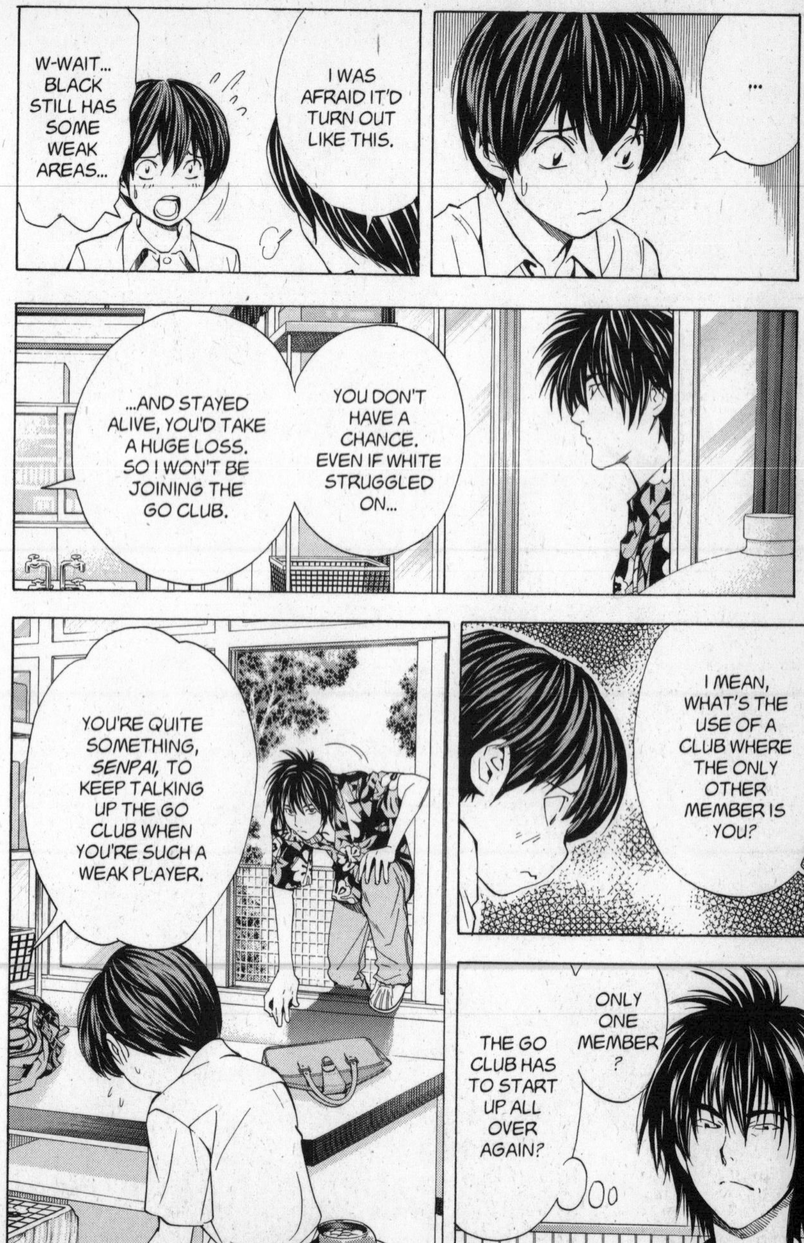
...
I WAS AFRAID IT'D TURN OUT LIKE THIS.
W-WAIT... BLACK STILL HAS SOME WEAK AREAS...
YOU DON'T HAVE A CHANCE. EVEN IF WHITE STRUGGLED ON...
...AND STAYED ALIVE, YOU'D TAKE A HUGE LOSS. SO I WON'T BE JOINING THE GO CLUB.
I MEAN, WHAT'S THE USE OF A CLUB WHERE THE ONLY OTHER MEMBER IS YOU?
ONLY ONE MEMBER?
THE GO CLUB HAS TO START UP ALL OVER AGAIN?
YOU'RE QUITE SOMETHING, *SENPAI*, TO KEEP TALKING UP THE GO CLUB WHEN YOU'RE SUCH A WEAK PLAYER.

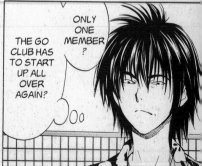

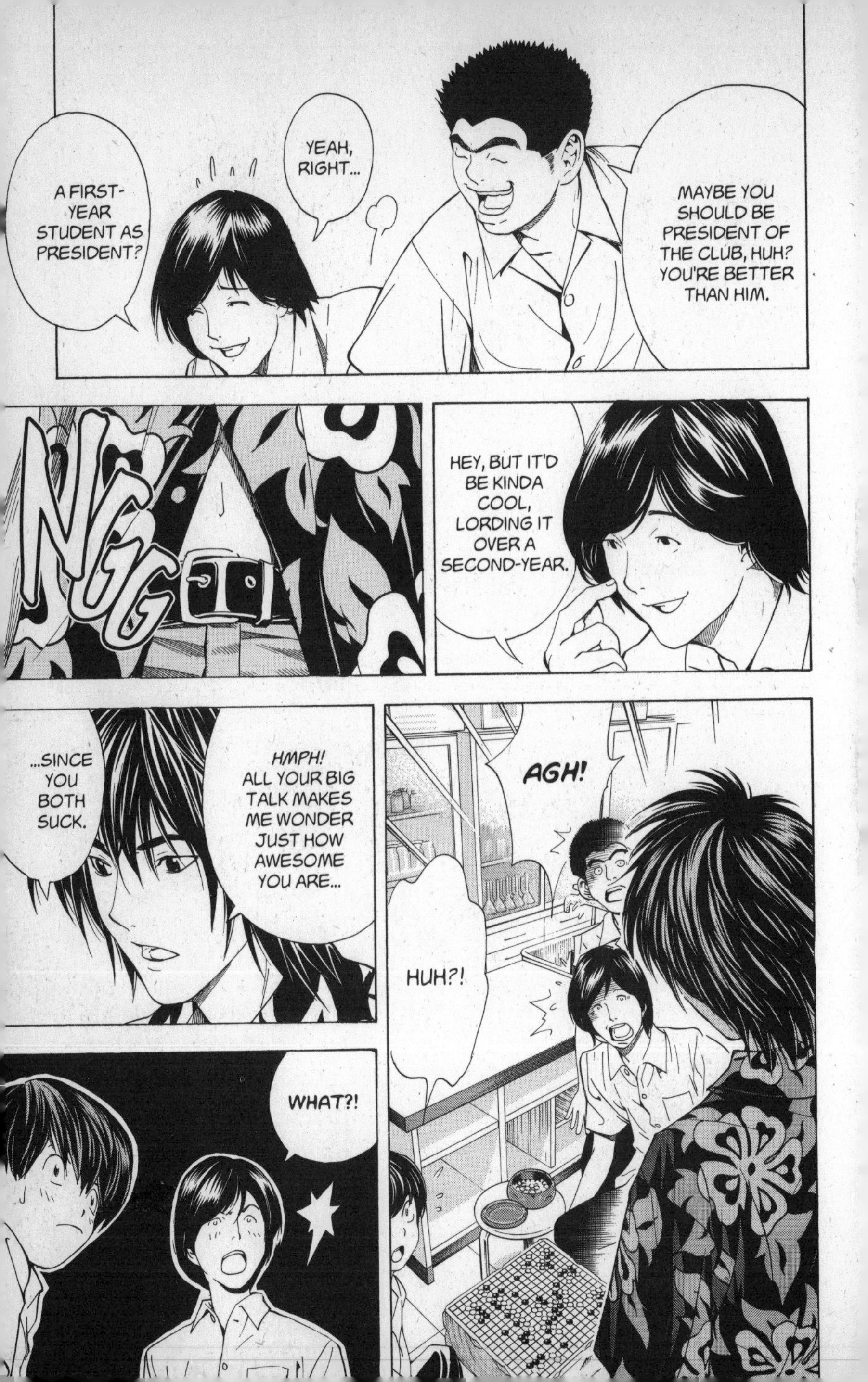
MAYBE YOU SHOULD BE PRESIDENT OF THE CLUB, HUH? YOU'RE BETTER THAN HIM.
YEAH, RIGHT...
A FIRST-YEAR STUDENT AS PRESIDENT?
HEY, BUT IT'D BE KINDA COOL, LORDING IT OVER A SECOND-YEAR.
NGG
AGH!
HUH?!
HMPH! ALL YOUR BIG TALK MAKES ME WONDER JUST HOW AWESOME YOU ARE...
...SINCE YOU BOTH SUCK.
WHAT?!

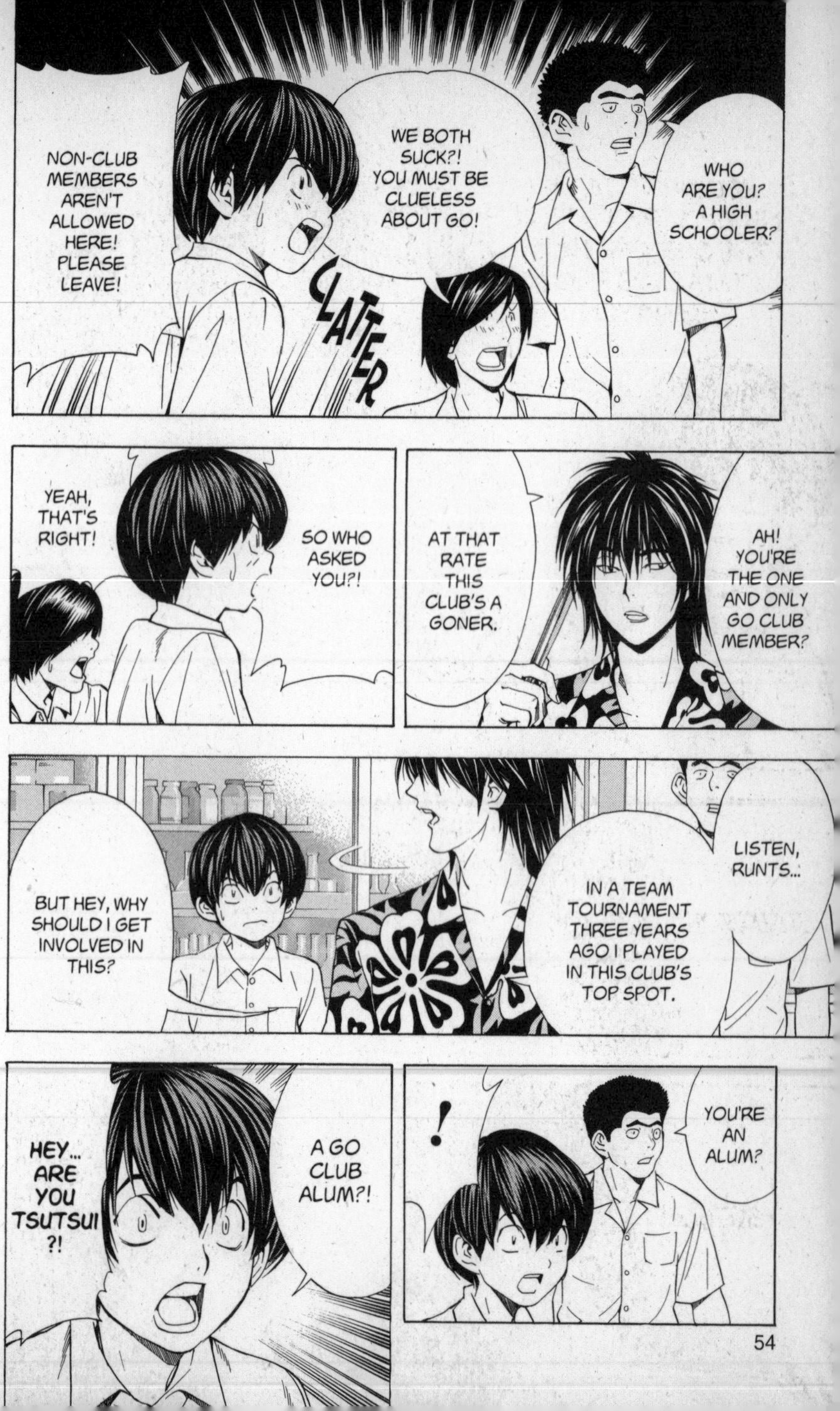
WHO ARE YOU? A HIGH SCHOOLER?
WE BOTH SUCK?! YOU MUST BE CLUELESS ABOUT GO!
NON-CLUB MEMBERS AREN'T ALLOWED HERE! PLEASE LEAVE!
CLATTER
AH! YOU'RE THE ONE AND ONLY GO CLUB MEMBER?
AT THAT RATE THIS CLUB'S A GONER.
SO WHO ASKED YOU?!
YEAH, THAT'S RIGHT!
LISTEN, RUNTS...
IN A TEAM TOURNAMENT THREE YEARS AGO I PLAYED IN THIS CLUB'S TOP SPOT.
BUT HEY, WHY SHOULD I GET INVOLVED IN THIS?
YOU'RE AN ALUM?
!
A GO CLUB ALUM?!
HEY... ARE YOU TSUTSUI ?!

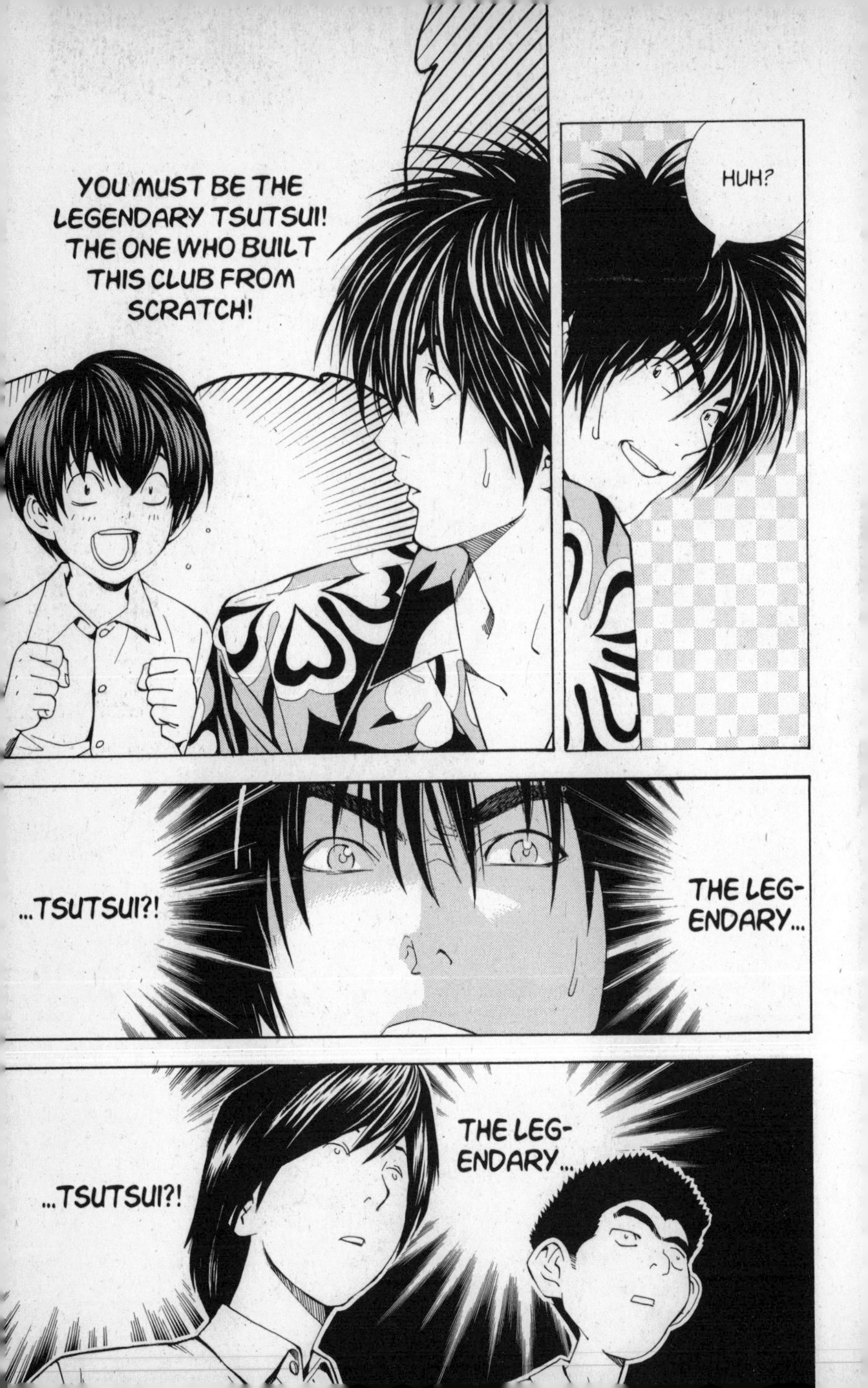
HUH?
YOU MUST BE THE LEGENDARY TSUTSUI! THE ONE WHO BUILT THIS CLUB FROM SCRATCH!
THE LEG-ENDARY...
...TSUTSUI?!
THE LEG-ENDARY...
...TSUTSUI?!

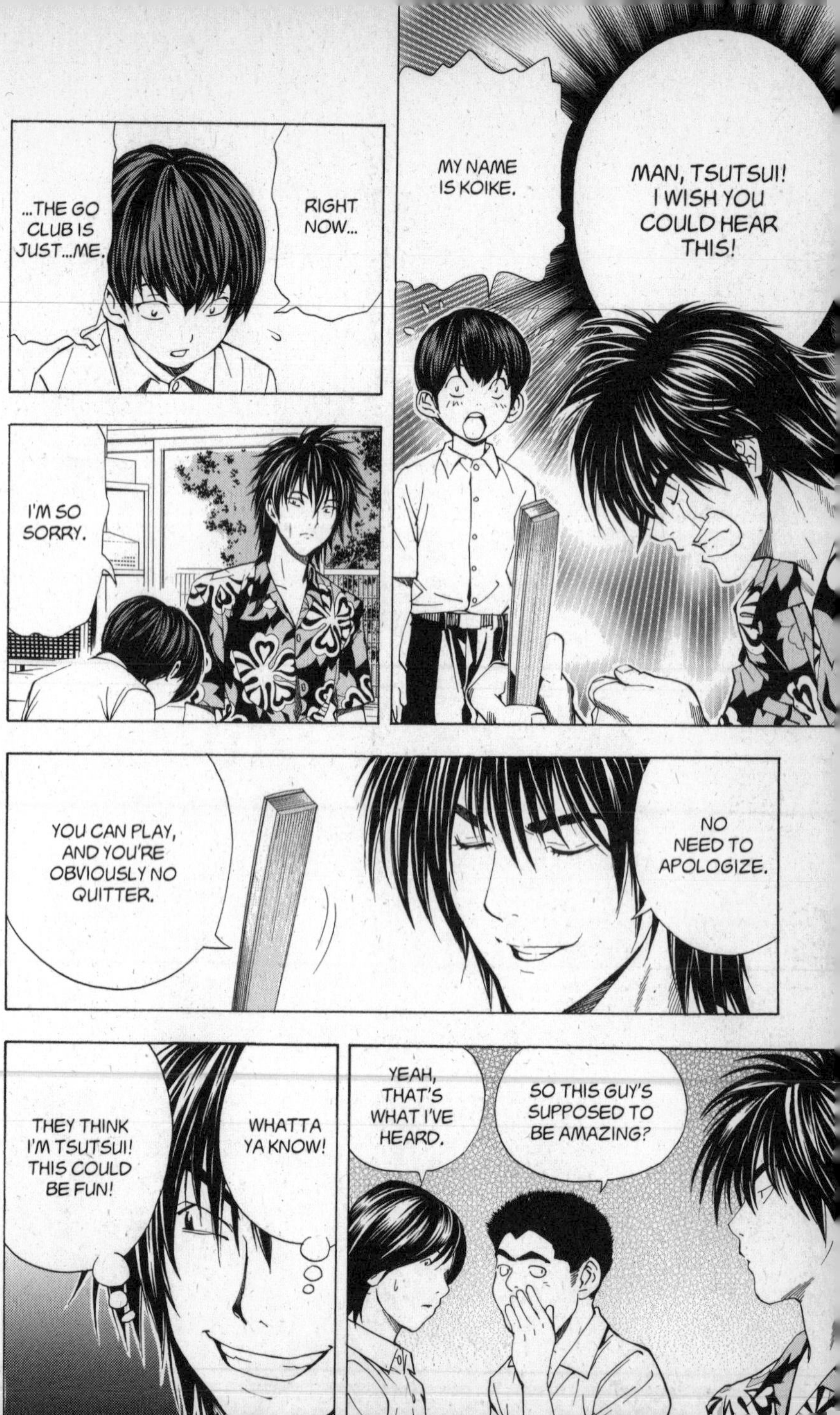
MAN, TSUTSUI! I WISH YOU COULD HEAR THIS!
MY NAME IS KOIKE.
RIGHT NOW...
...THE GO CLUB IS JUST...ME.
I'M SO SORRY.
NO NEED TO APOLOGIZE.
YOU CAN PLAY, AND YOU'RE OBVIOUSLY NO QUITTER.
SO THIS GUY'S SUPPOSED TO BE AMAZING?
YEAH, THAT'S WHAT I'VE HEARD.
WHATTA YA KNOW!
THEY THINK I'M TSUTSUI! THIS COULD BE FUN!

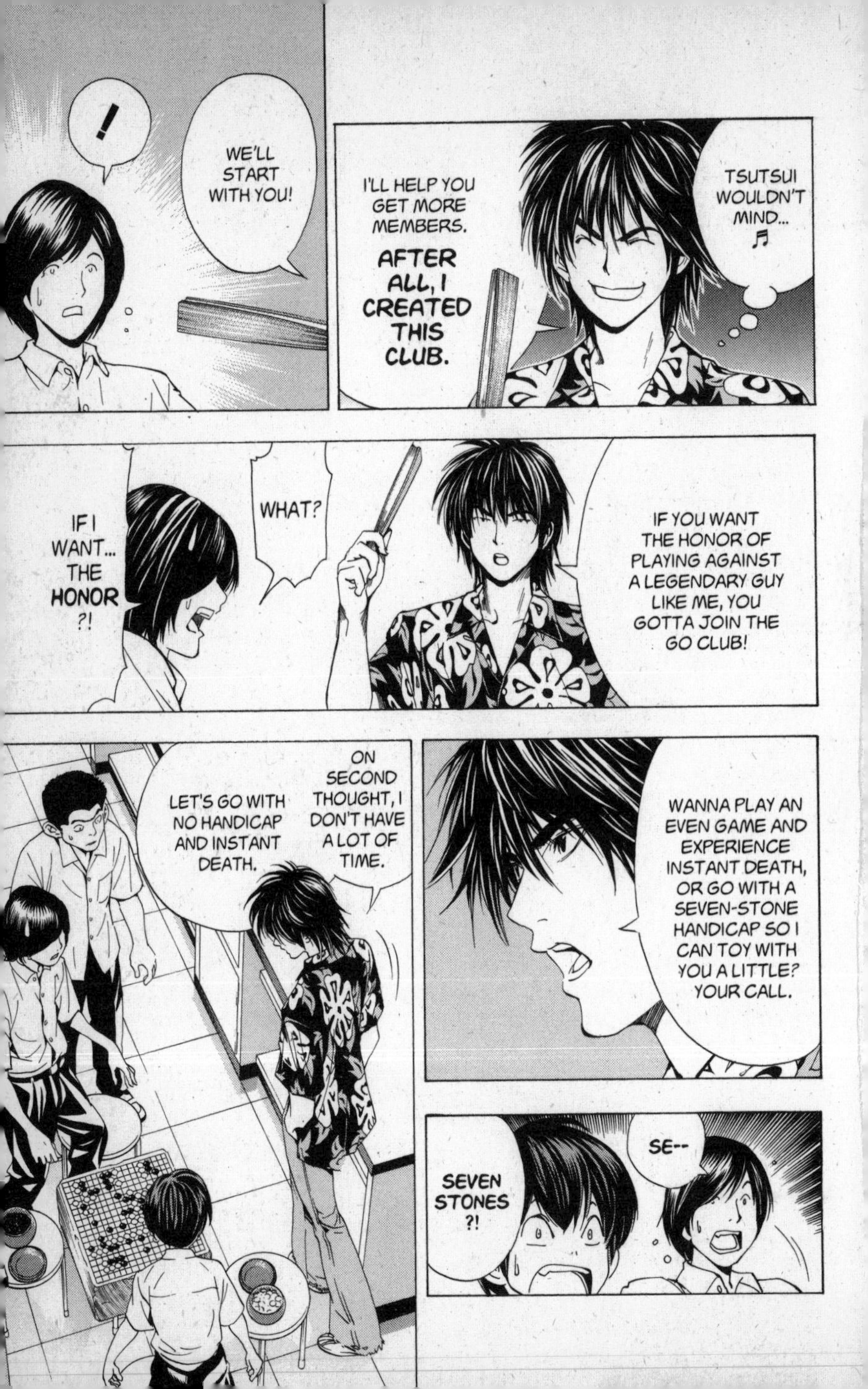
TSUTSUI WOULDN'T MIND... ♬
I'LL HELP YOU GET MORE MEMBERS.
AFTER ALL, I CREATED THIS CLUB.
WE'LL START WITH YOU!
!
IF YOU WANT THE HONOR OF PLAYING AGAINST A LEGENDARY GUY LIKE ME, YOU GOTTA JOIN THE GO CLUB!
WHAT?
IF I WANT... THE HONOR ?!
WANNA PLAY AN EVEN GAME AND EXPERIENCE INSTANT DEATH, OR GO WITH A SEVEN-STONE HANDICAP SO I CAN TOY WITH YOU A LITTLE? YOUR CALL.
SE--
SEVEN STONES ?!
ON SECOND THOUGHT, I DON'T HAVE A LOT OF TIME.
LET'S GO WITH NO HANDICAP AND INSTANT DEATH.

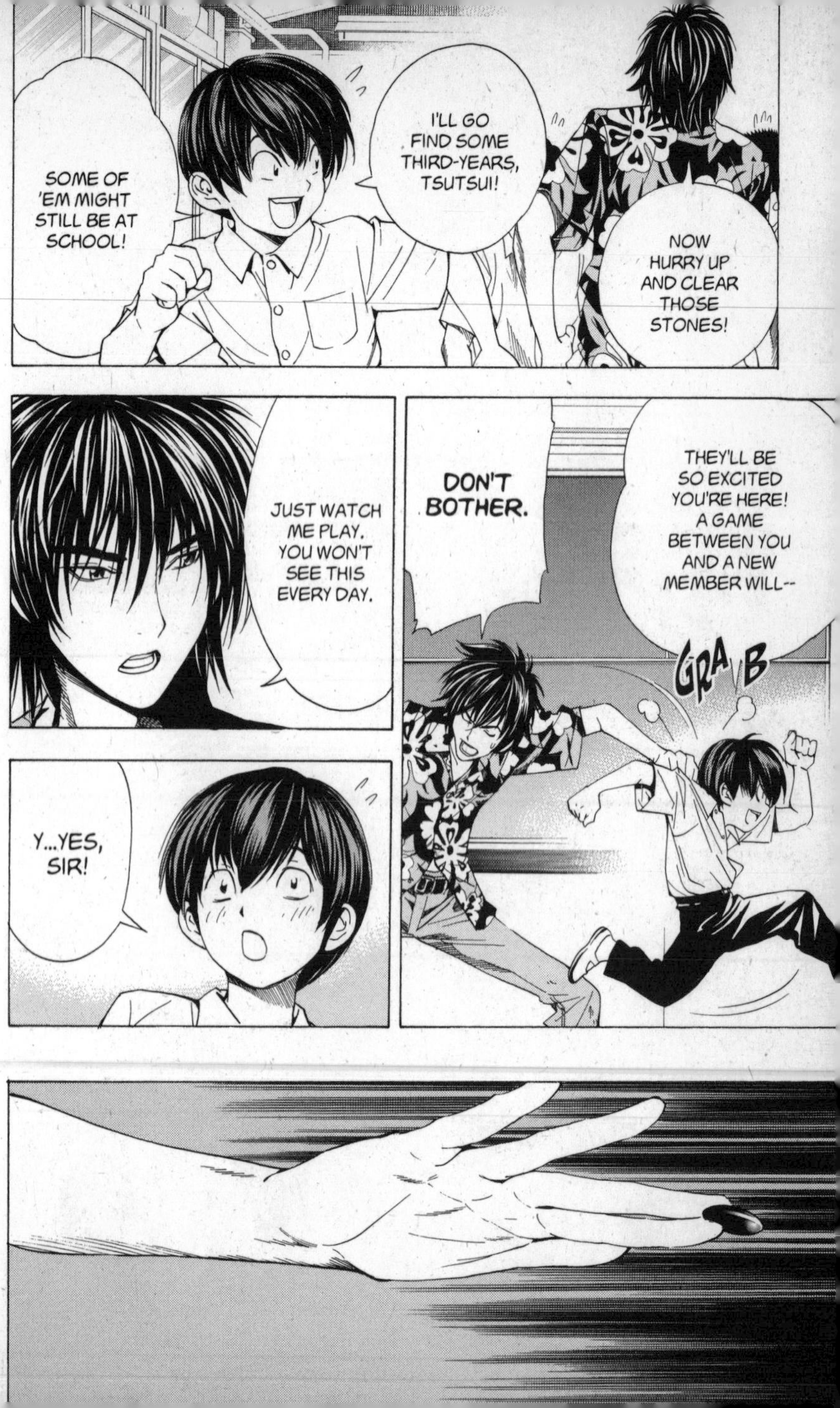
I'LL GO FIND SOME THIRD-YEARS, TSUTSUI!
SOME OF 'EM MIGHT STILL BE AT SCHOOL!
NOW HURRY UP AND CLEAR THOSE STONES!
THEY'LL BE SO EXCITED YOU'RE HERE! A GAME BETWEEN YOU AND A NEW MEMBER WILL--
GRAB
DON'T BOTHER.
JUST WATCH ME PLAY. YOU WON'T SEE THIS EVERY DAY.
Y...YES, SIR!

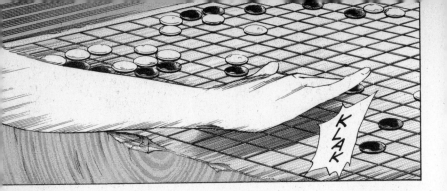

THINKING WON'T HELP YOU. JUST HURRY UP AND PLAY!

...

HUH? ARE YOU IN TROUBLE?

ARE YOU BEHIND?

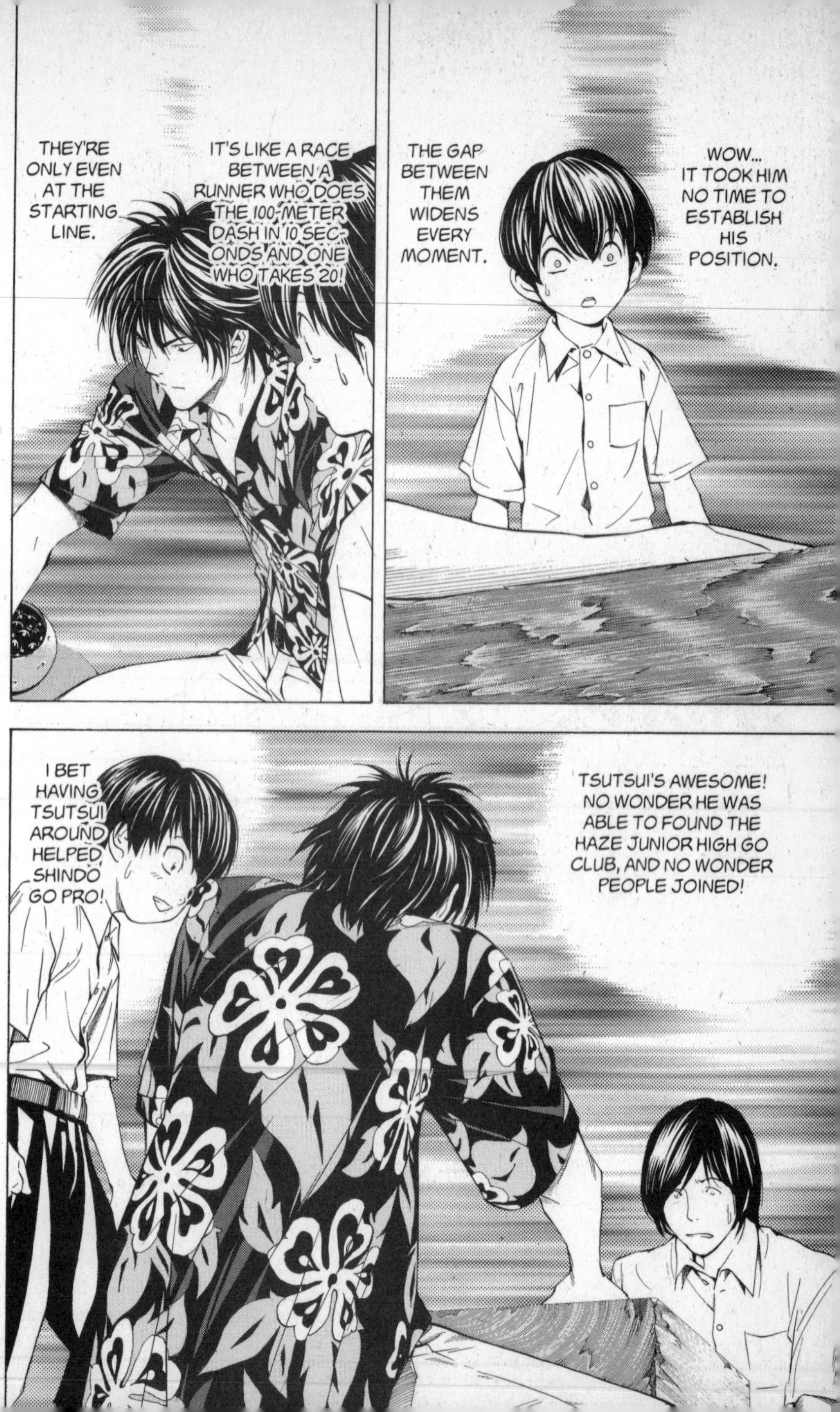
WOW... IT TOOK HIM NO TIME TO ESTABLISH HIS POSITION.
THE GAP BETWEEN THEM WIDENS EVERY MOMENT.
IT'S LIKE A RACE BETWEEN A RUNNER WHO DOES THE 100-METER DASH IN 10 SECONDS AND ONE WHO TAKES 20!
THEY'RE ONLY EVEN AT THE STARTING LINE.
TSUTSUI'S AWESOME! NO WONDER HE WAS ABLE TO FOUND THE HAZE JUNIOR HIGH GO CLUB, AND NO WONDER PEOPLE JOINED!
I BET HAVING TSUTSUI AROUND HELPED SHINDO GO PRO!

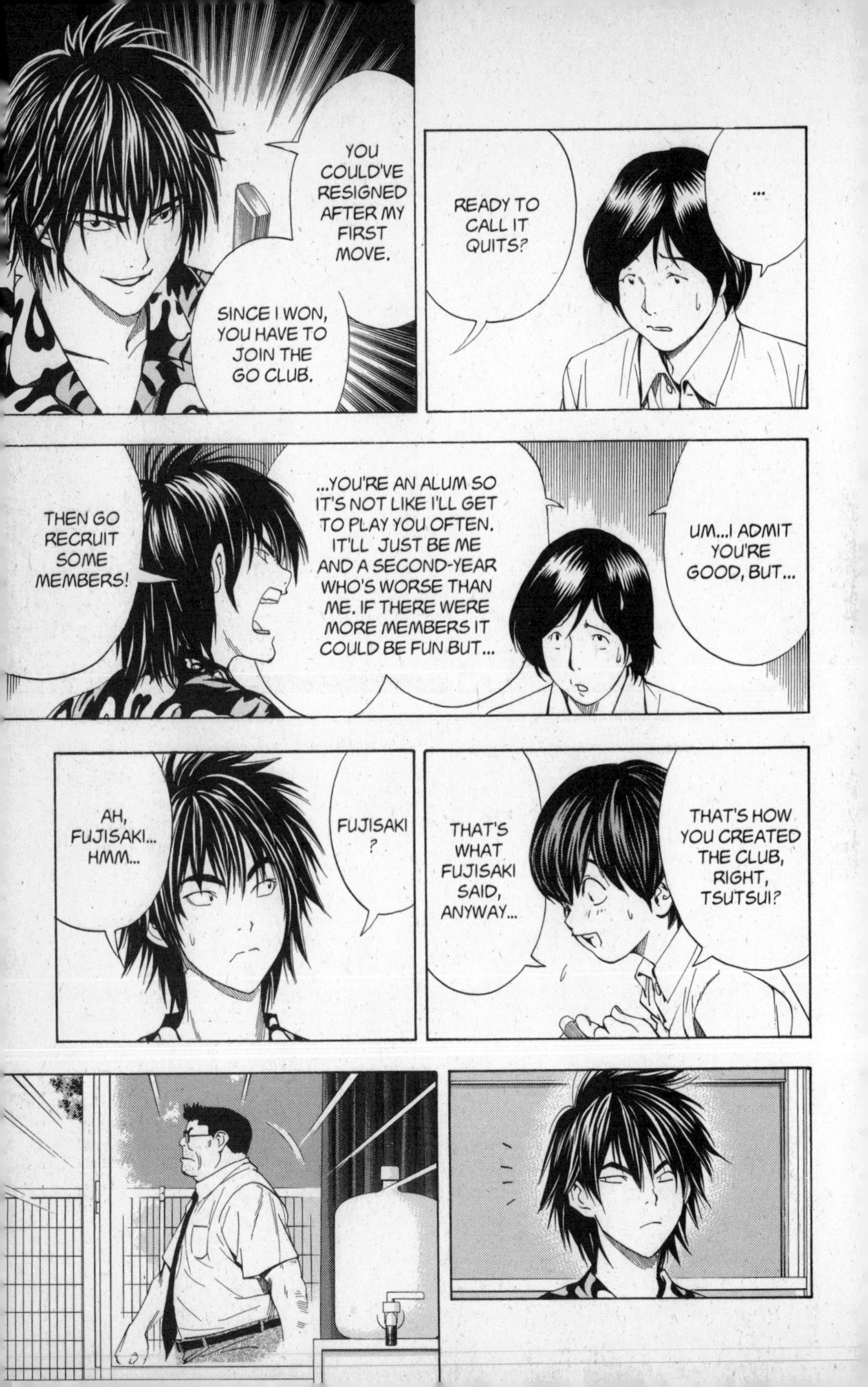
...
READY TO CALL IT QUITS?
YOU COULD'VE RESIGNED AFTER MY FIRST MOVE.
SINCE I WON, YOU HAVE TO JOIN THE GO CLUB.
UM...I ADMIT YOU'RE GOOD, BUT...
...YOU'RE AN ALUM SO IT'S NOT LIKE I'LL GET TO PLAY YOU OFTEN. IT'LL JUST BE ME AND A SECOND-YEAR WHO'S WORSE THAN ME. IF THERE WERE MORE MEMBERS IT COULD BE FUN BUT...
THEN GO RECRUIT SOME MEMBERS!
THAT'S HOW YOU CREATED THE CLUB, RIGHT, TSUTSUI?
THAT'S WHAT FUJISAKI SAID, ANYWAY...
FUJISAKI?
AH, FUJISAKI... HMM...

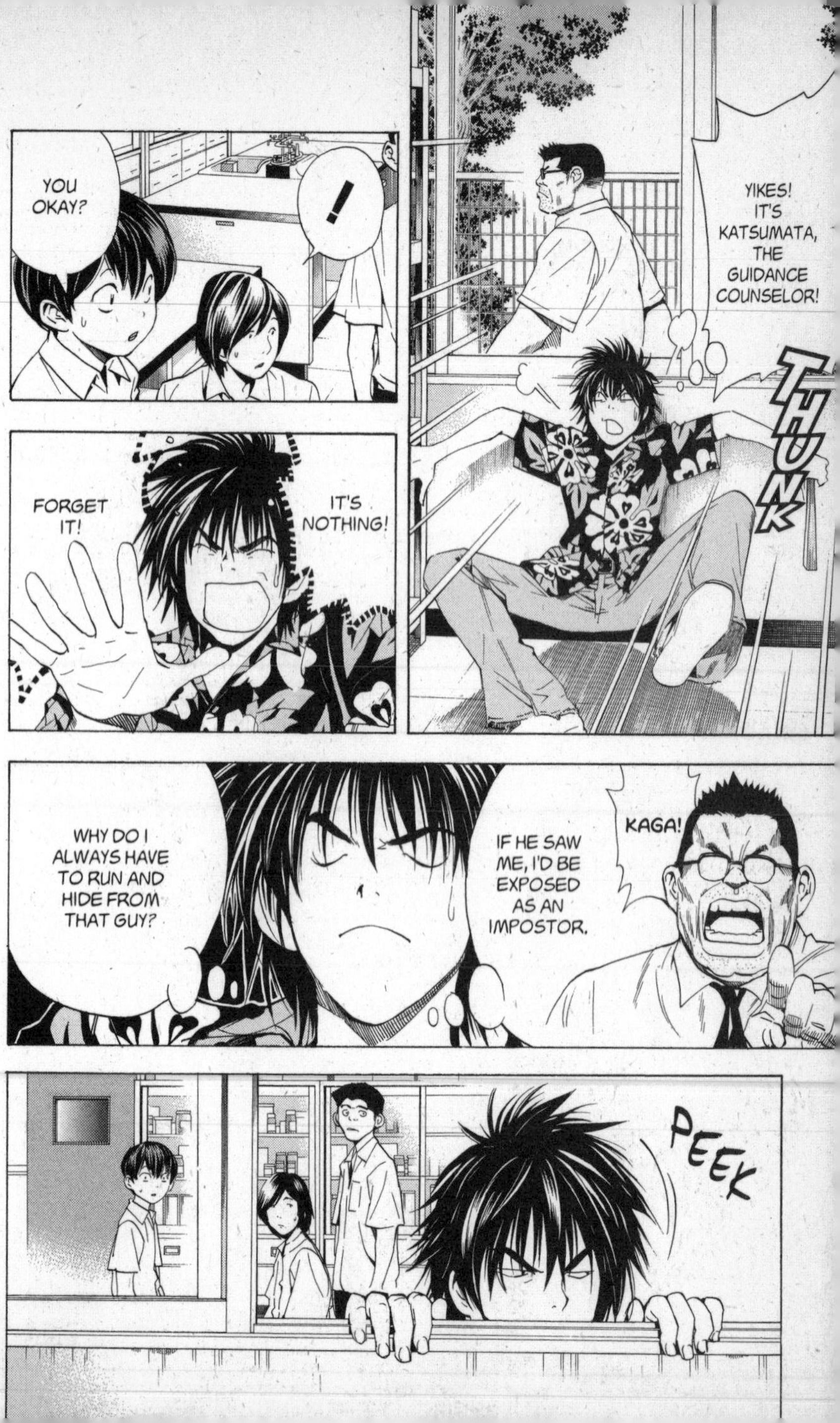
YIKES! IT'S KATSUMATA, THE GUIDANCE COUNSELOR!
THUNK
!
YOU OKAY?
IT'S NOTHING!
FORGET IT!
KAGA!
IF HE SAW ME, I'D BE EXPOSED AS AN IMPOSTOR.
WHY DO I ALWAYS HAVE TO RUN AND HIDE FROM THAT GUY?
PEEK

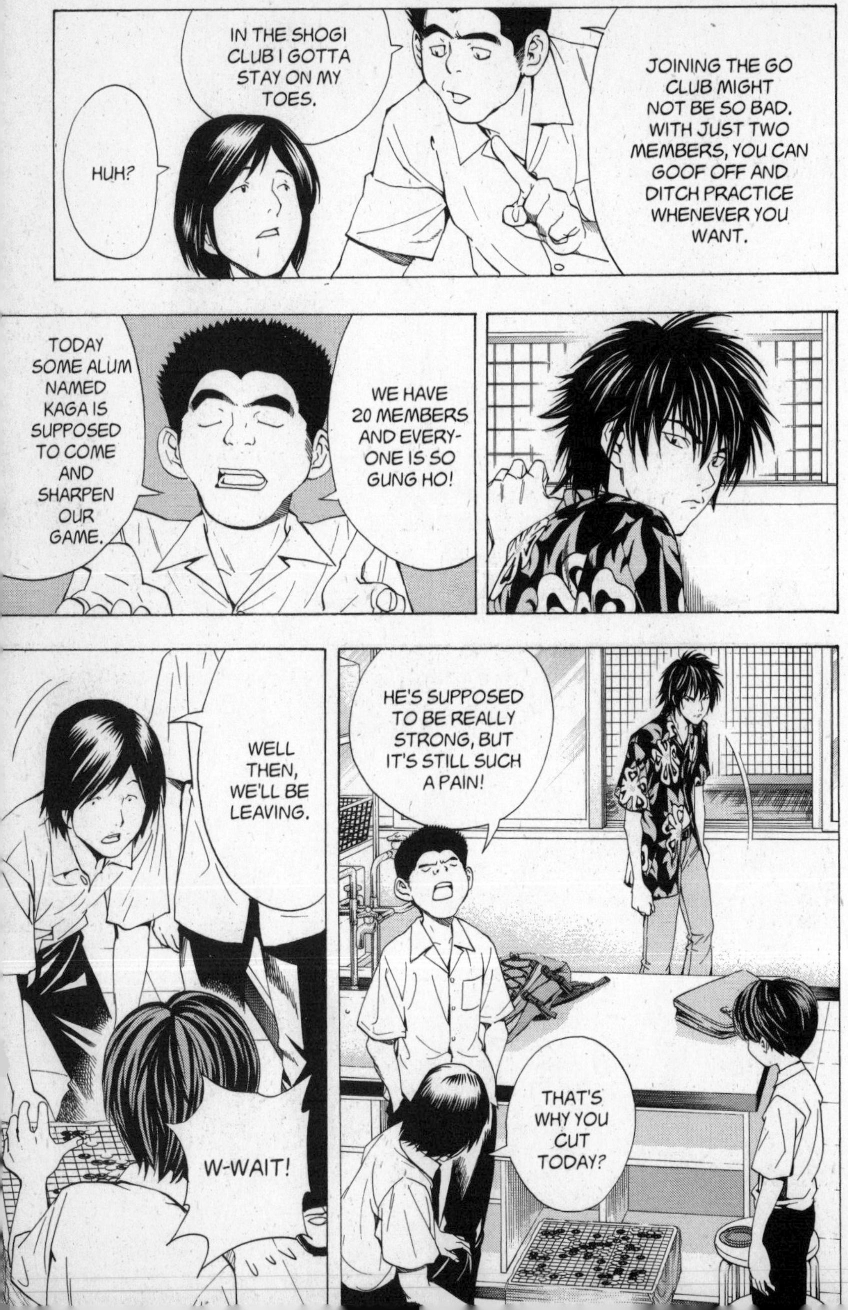
JOINING THE GO CLUB MIGHT NOT BE SO BAD. WITH JUST TWO MEMBERS, YOU CAN GOOF OFF AND DITCH PRACTICE WHENEVER YOU WANT.
IN THE SHOGI CLUB I GOTTA STAY ON MY TOES.
HUH?
WE HAVE 20 MEMBERS AND EVERY-ONE IS SO GUNG HO!
TODAY SOME ALUM NAMED KAGA IS SUPPOSED TO COME AND SHARPEN OUR GAME.
HE'S SUPPOSED TO BE REALLY STRONG, BUT IT'S STILL SUCH A PAIN!
THAT'S WHY YOU CUT TODAY?
WELL THEN, WE'LL BE LEAVING.
W-WAIT!

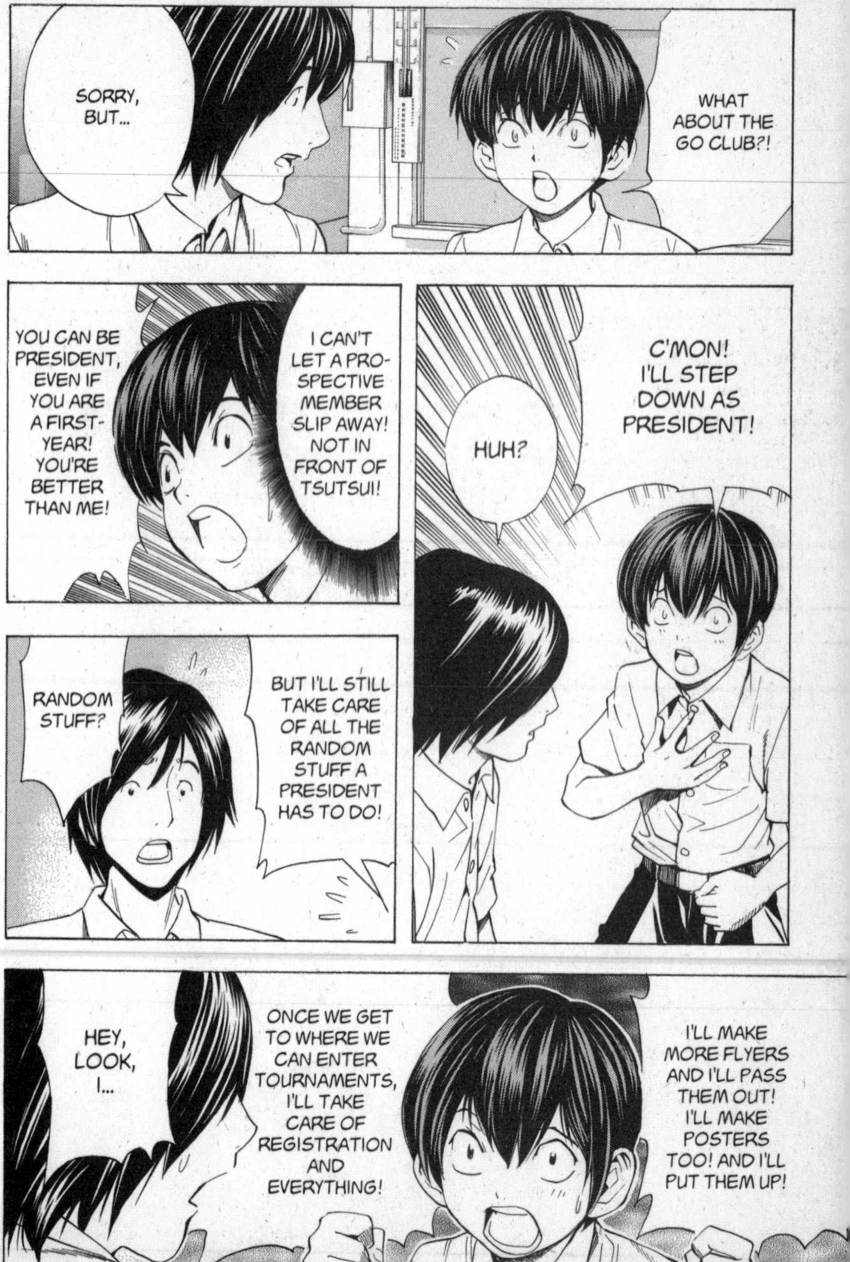
WHAT ABOUT THE GO CLUB?!
SORRY, BUT...
C'MON! I'LL STEP DOWN AS PRESIDENT!
HUH?
I CAN'T LET A PRO-SPECTIVE MEMBER SLIP AWAY! NOT IN FRONT OF TSUTSUI!
YOU CAN BE PRESIDENT, EVEN IF YOU ARE A FIRST-YEAR! YOU'RE BETTER THAN ME!
BUT I'LL STILL TAKE CARE OF ALL THE RANDOM STUFF A PRESIDENT HAS TO DO!
RANDOM STUFF?
I'LL MAKE MORE FLYERS AND I'LL PASS THEM OUT! I'LL MAKE POSTERS TOO! AND I'LL PUT THEM UP!
ONCE WE GET TO WHERE WE CAN ENTER TOURNAMENTS, I'LL TAKE CARE OF REGISTRATION AND EVERYTHING!
HEY, LOOK, I...

READ THIS WAY

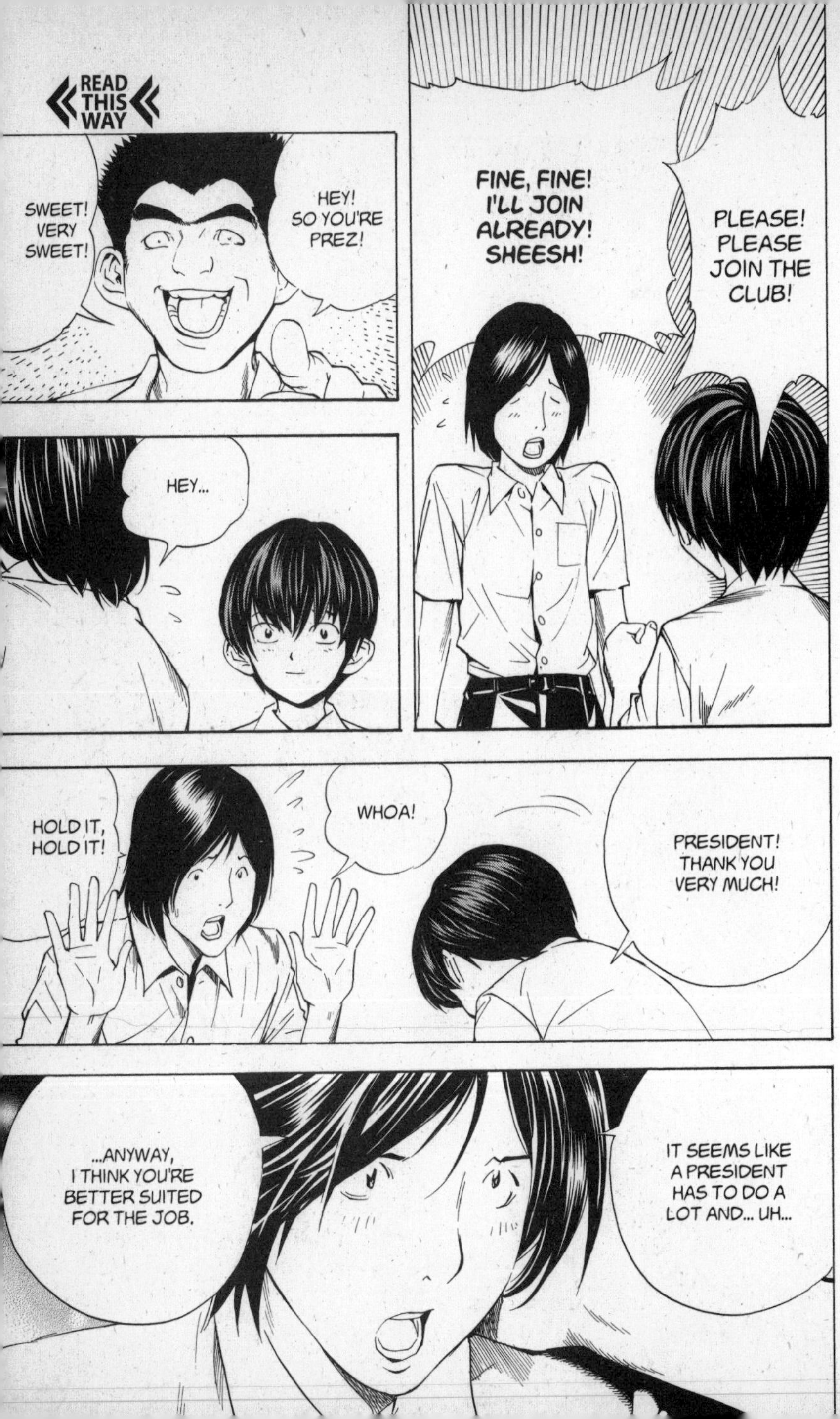
PLEASE! PLEASE JOIN THE CLUB!
FINE, FINE! I'LL JOIN ALREADY! SHEESH!
HEY! SO YOU'RE PREZ!
SWEET! VERY SWEET!
HEY...
PRESIDENT! THANK YOU VERY MUCH!
WHOA!
HOLD IT, HOLD IT!
IT SEEMS LIKE A PRESIDENT HAS TO DO A LOT AND... UH...
...ANYWAY, I THINK YOU'RE BETTER SUITED FOR THE JOB.

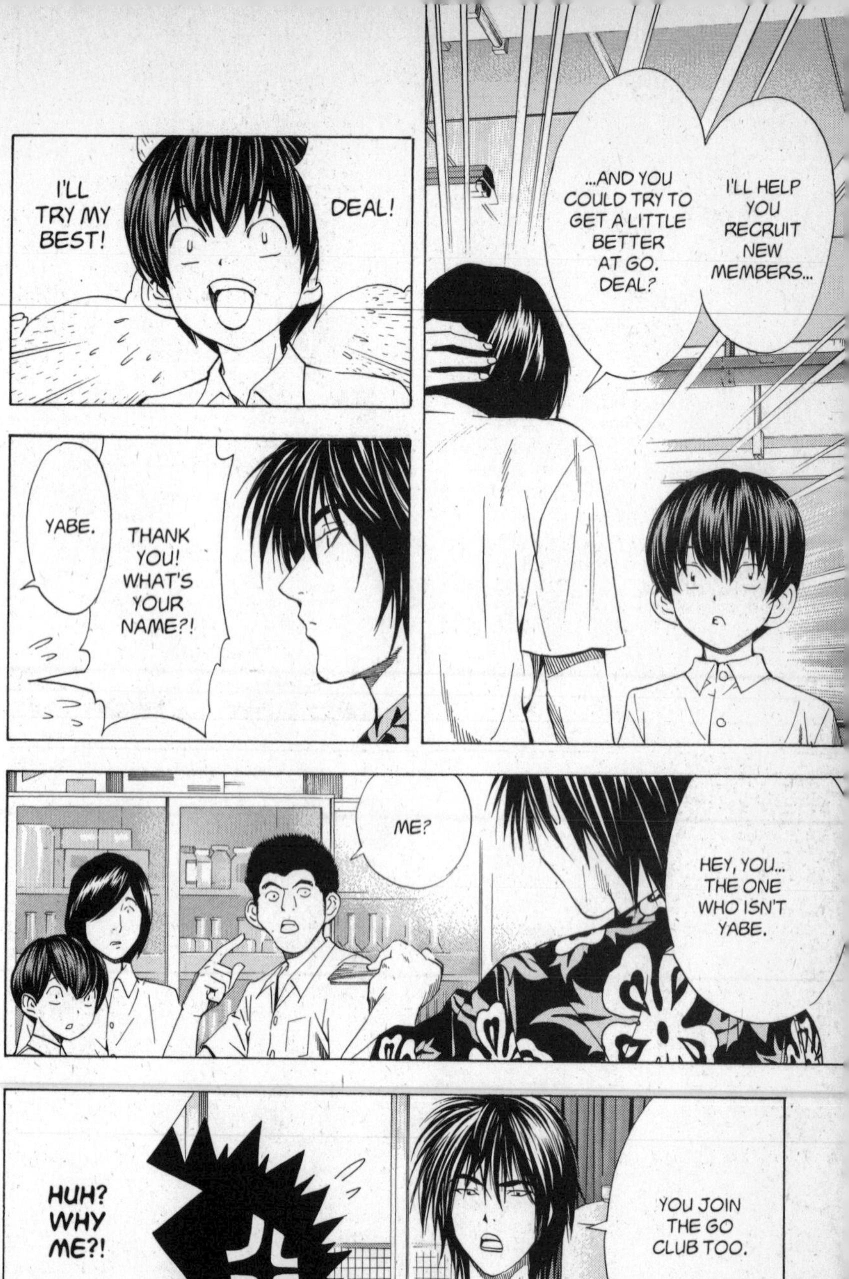
I'LL HELP YOU RECRUIT NEW MEMBERS...
...AND YOU COULD TRY TO GET A LITTLE BETTER AT GO. DEAL?
DEAL!
I'LL TRY MY BEST!
THANK YOU! WHAT'S YOUR NAME?!
YABE.
HEY, YOU... THE ONE WHO ISN'T YABE.
ME?
YOU JOIN THE GO CLUB TOO.
HUH? WHY ME?!

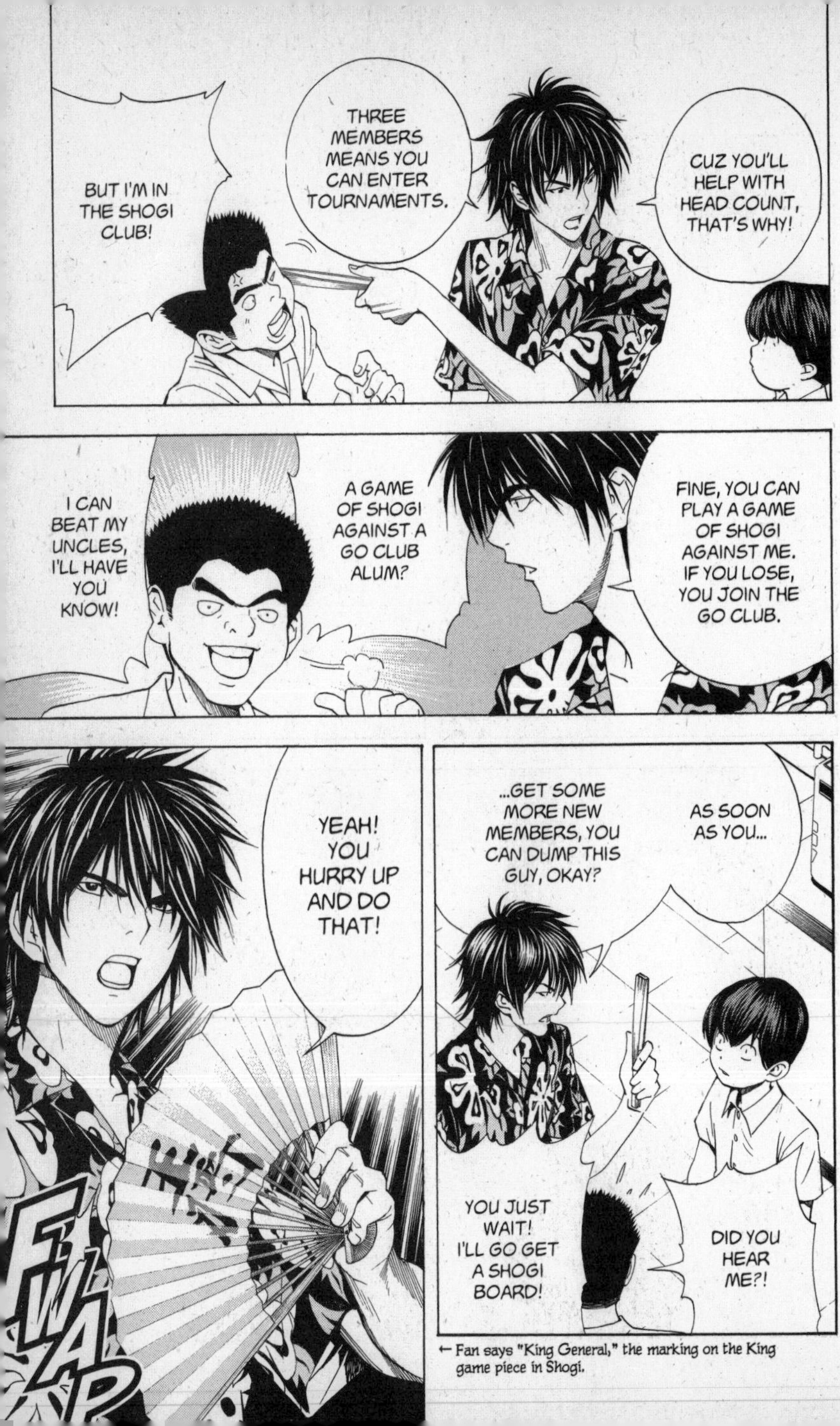
CUZ YOU'LL HELP WITH HEAD COUNT, THAT'S WHY!
THREE MEMBERS MEANS YOU CAN ENTER TOURNAMENTS.
BUT I'M IN THE SHOGI CLUB!
FINE, YOU CAN PLAY A GAME OF SHOGI AGAINST ME. IF YOU LOSE, YOU JOIN THE GO CLUB.
A GAME OF SHOGI AGAINST A GO CLUB ALUM?
I CAN BEAT MY UNCLES, I'LL HAVE YOU KNOW!
AS SOON AS YOU...
...GET SOME MORE NEW MEMBERS, YOU CAN DUMP THIS GUY, OKAY?
DID YOU HEAR ME?!
YOU JUST WAIT! I'LL GO GET A SHOGI BOARD!
YEAH! YOU HURRY UP AND DO THAT!
FWAP

← Fan says "King General," the marking on the King game piece in Shogi.

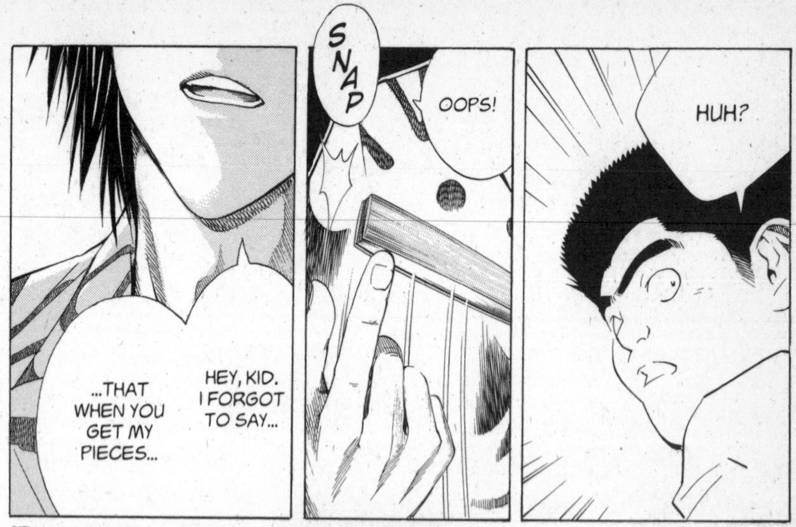
HUH?
SNAP
OOPS!
HEY, KID. I FORGOT TO SAY...
...THAT WHEN YOU GET MY PIECES...

*That means he will play without his rook, bishop, lances or knights.

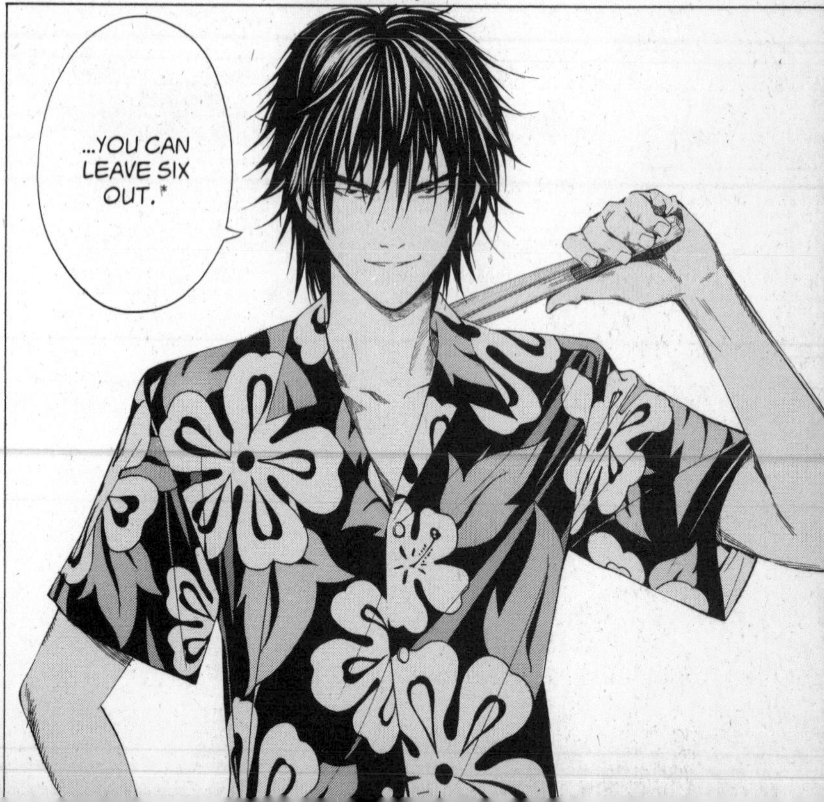
...YOU CAN LEAVE SIX OUT.*

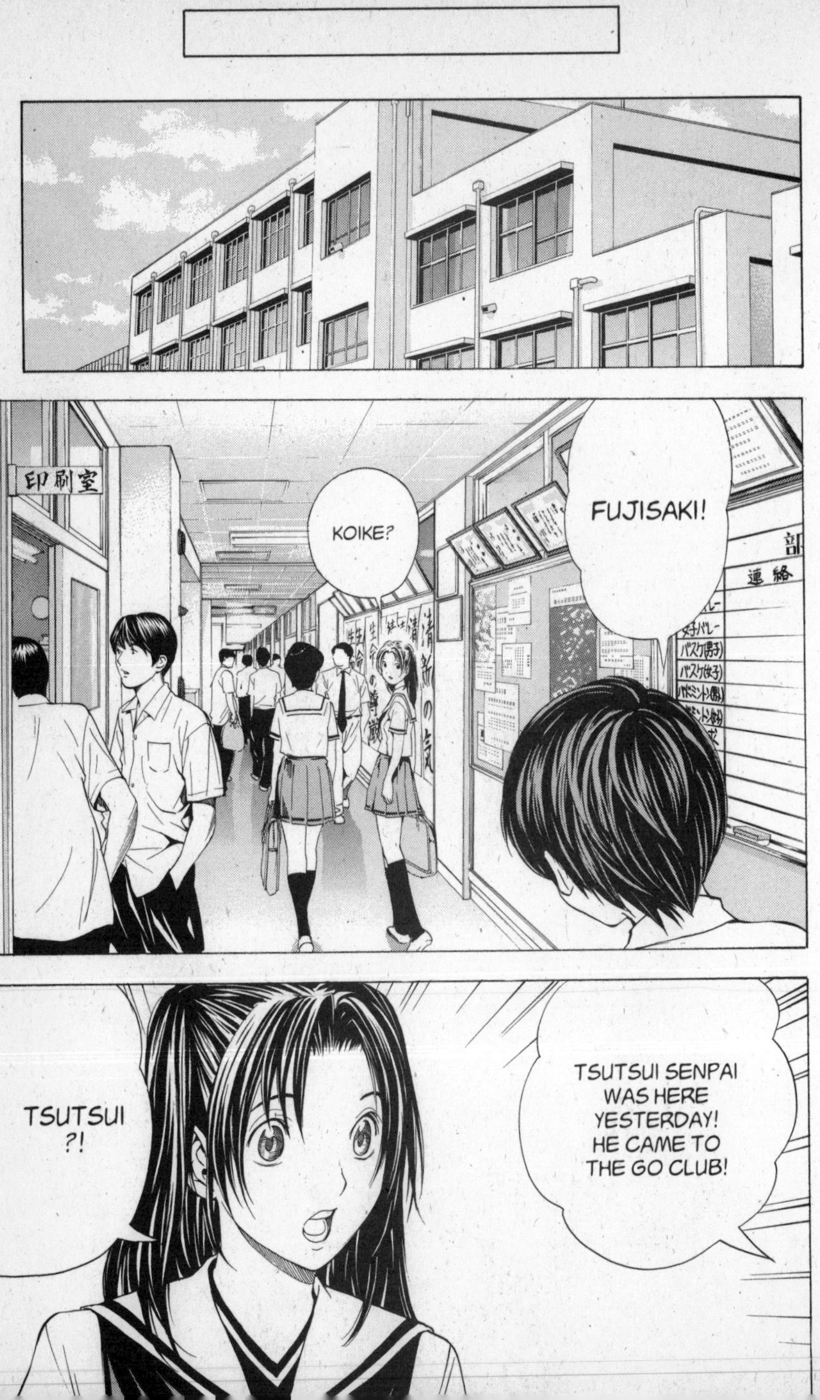
FUJISAKI!
KOIKE?
印刷室
TSUTSUI SENPAI WAS HERE YESTERDAY! HE CAME TO THE GO CLUB!
TSUTSUI ?!

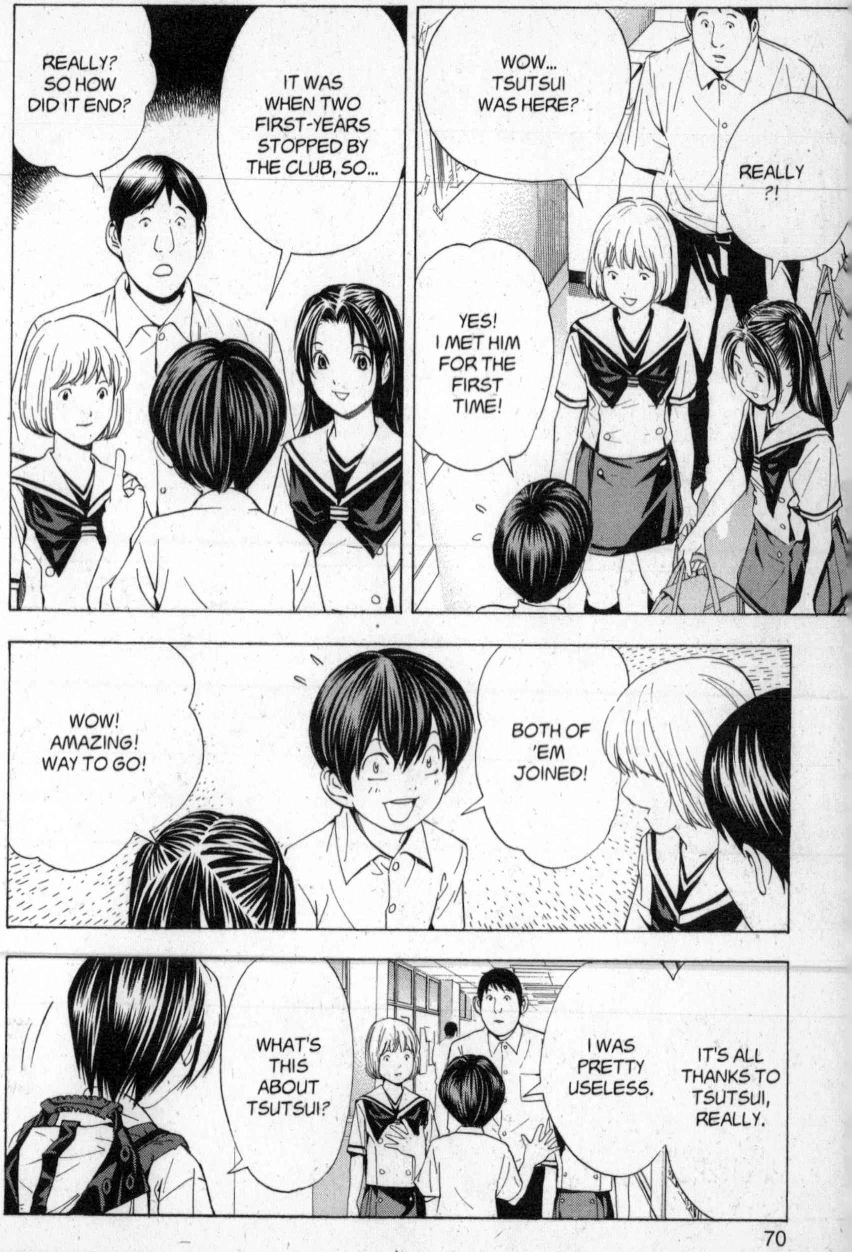
WOW... TSUTSUI WAS HERE?
REALLY ?!
YES! I MET HIM FOR THE FIRST TIME!
IT WAS WHEN TWO FIRST-YEARS STOPPED BY THE CLUB, SO...
REALLY? SO HOW DID IT END?
BOTH OF 'EM JOINED!
WOW! AMAZING! WAY TO GO!
IT'S ALL THANKS TO TSUTSUI, REALLY.
I WAS PRETTY USELESS.
WHAT'S THIS ABOUT TSUTSUI?

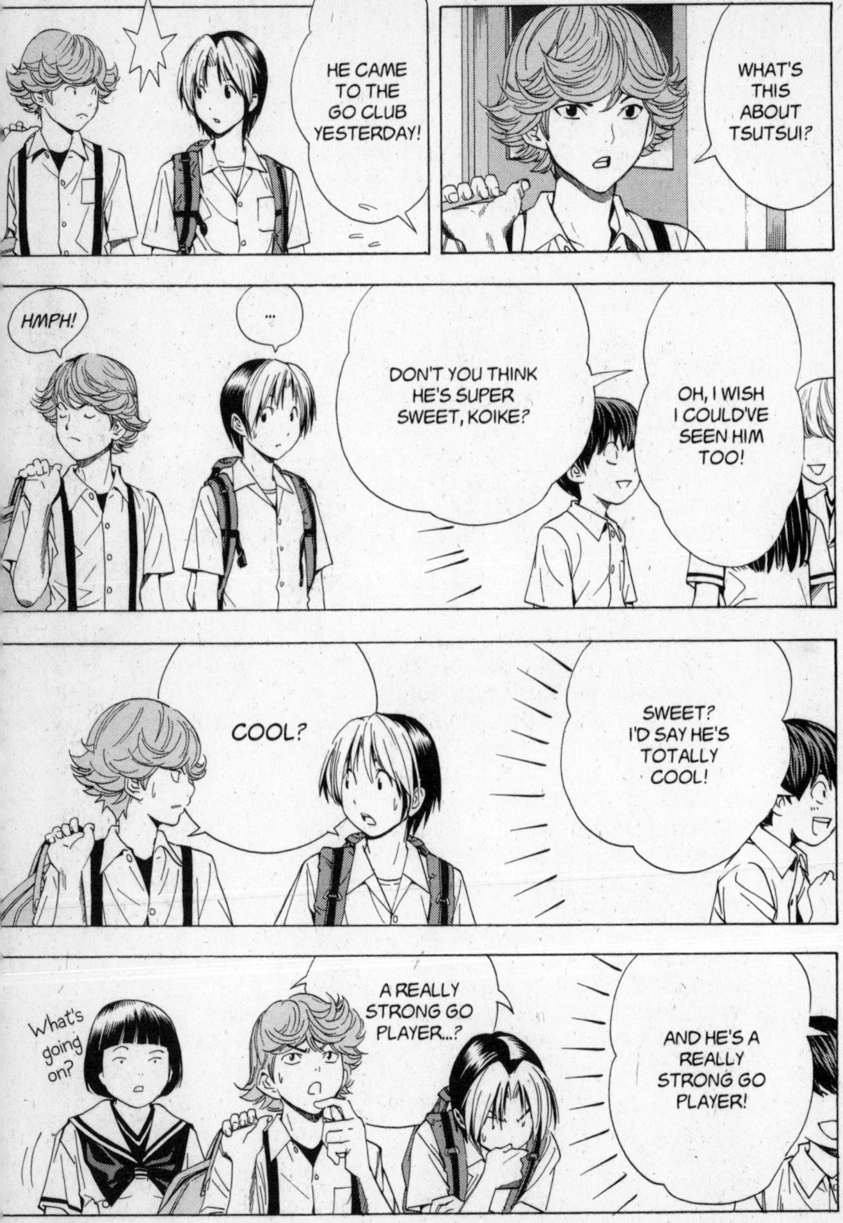
WHAT'S THIS ABOUT TSUTSUI?
HE CAME TO THE GO CLUB YESTERDAY!
OH, I WISH I COULD'VE SEEN HIM TOO!
DON'T YOU THINK HE'S SUPER SWEET, KOIKE?
...
HMPH!
SWEET? I'D SAY HE'S TOTALLY COOL!
COOL?
AND HE'S A REALLY STRONG GO PLAYER!
A REALLY STRONG GO PLAYER...?
What's going on?

YUMI HOTTA'S LONG INTERVIEW WITH TAKESHI OBATA SENSEI: ②

Ⓗ I ENJOYED READING THE PAGE ABOUT HIKARU'S STUFF.

Ⓞ THE BROKEN FRIDGE WAS SOMETHING I ALWAYS HAD IN MIND FROM THE BEGINNING, AS SOMETHING HE'D PICKED UP SOMEWHERE. AFTER ALL, IT'S STRANGE (FOR AN ELEMENTARY SCHOOL KID) TO HAVE A REFRIGERATOR IN HIS ROOM, ISN'T IT?

Ⓗ YES, IT'S STRANGE. SO I ALWAYS THOUGHT HIKARU WAS PRETTY RICH. DO YOU HAVE AN ELECTRIC SKATE-BOARD YOURSELF, OBATA?

Ⓞ YES, I DO. A YELLOW ONE, JUST LIKE THIS.

Ⓗ CAN YOU TELL US ABOUT SOME OTHER ILLUSTRATIONS?

Ⓞ THE ONE I HAD THE MOST FUN DRAWING WAS JUNGLE (PAGE 037). FROM THE ROUGH SKETCH TO THE COLORING, I COULDN'T STOP. USUALLY I TAKE A BREAK AFTER INKING AND BEFORE LAYING ON THE COLOR, BUT I COMPLETED THIS IN ONE GO. I WAS WORKING ON IT 24 HOURS NONSTOP.

Ⓗ I LIKE JUNGLE, AND I ALSO LIKE HALLOWEEN! (PAGE 074)

Ⓞ I HAD FUN DOING HALLOWEEN TOO. IN THE BEGINNING IT WAS JUST FROM THE CHEST UP, BUT THERE WASN'T ANY MOVEMENT IN IT, SO I MADE IT A FULL BODY DRAWING. THERE ARE ACTUALLY A NUMBER OF IMAGES LIKE THIS THAT I'VE WANTED TO DO. BUT I THINK THERE NEEDS TO BE A RELATIONSHIP BETWEEN THE ILLUSTRATION AND THE ISSUE OF THE MANGA IT APPEARS IN... I DON'T REALLY LIKE HAVING AN UPBEAT, LIGHTHEARTED TITLE PAGE FOR A SERIOUS STORY, FOR EXAMPLE. IF I HAVE THE OPPORTUNITY, I'D LIKE TO DO MORE OF THESE.

Ⓗ THE ONE OF HIKARU BITING A TV (PAGE 045), SAI IN FRONT OF A COMPUTER (PAGE 044), AND OTHERS MADE IT ON THE COVER OF *JUMP*, DIDN'T THEY?

Ⓞ THE *JUMP* COVERS ARE ALWAYS DRAWN TO ORDER. THEY EVEN GIVE YOU A ROUGH SKETCH TO FOLLOW.

Ⓗ REALLY?! I DIDN'T KNOW.

(Continued on page 104)

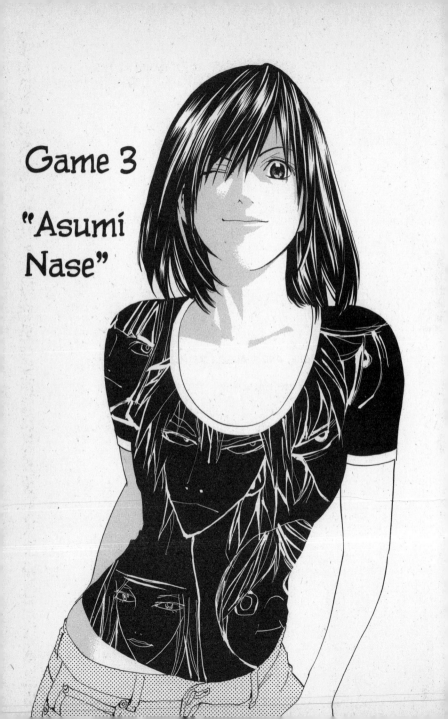

Game 3
"Asumi Nase"

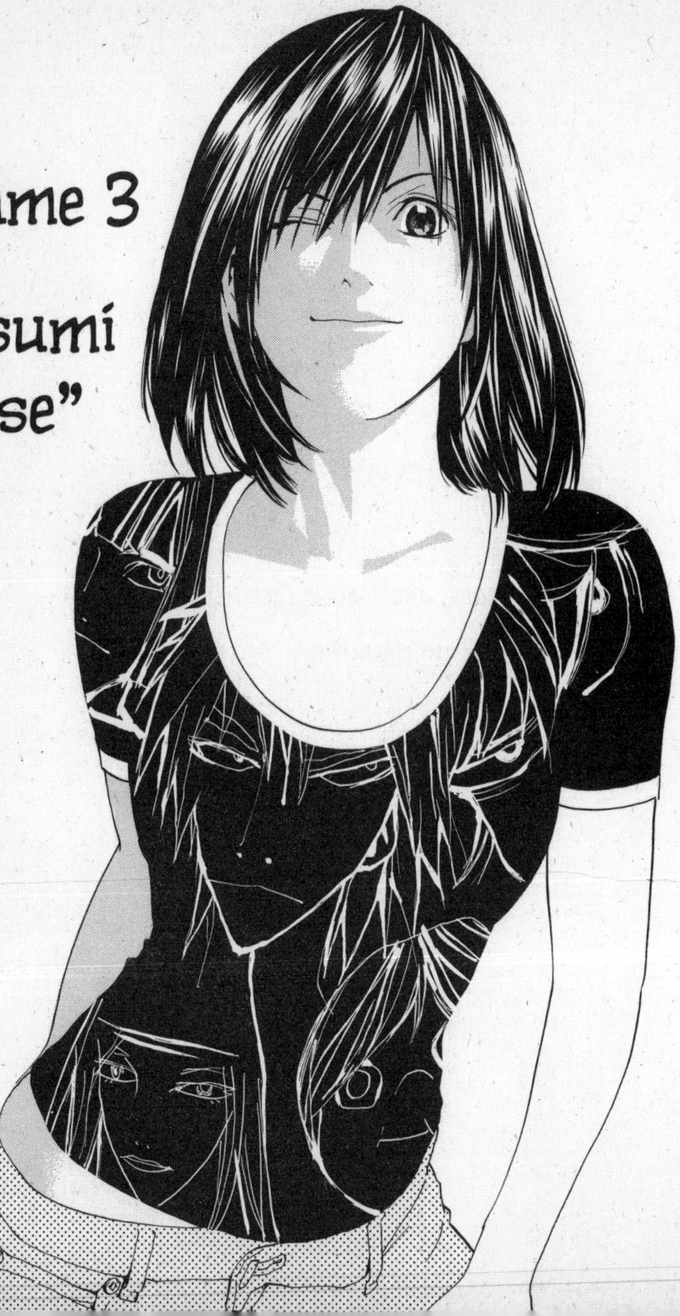

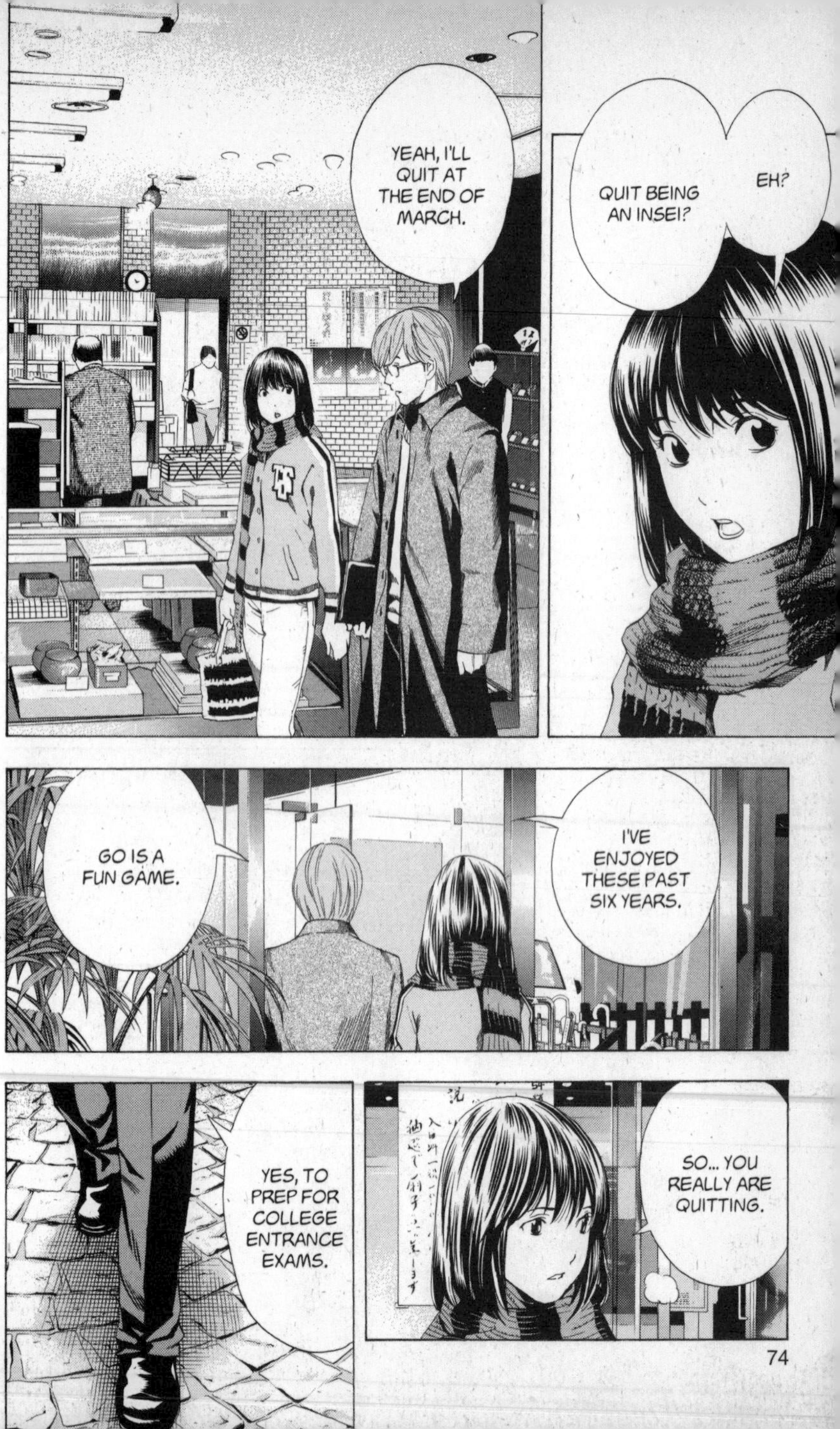
EH?
QUIT BEING AN INSEI?
YEAH, I'LL QUIT AT THE END OF MARCH.
I'VE ENJOYED THESE PAST SIX YEARS.
GO IS A FUN GAME.
SO... YOU REALLY ARE QUITTING.
YES, TO PREP FOR COLLEGE ENTRANCE EXAMS.

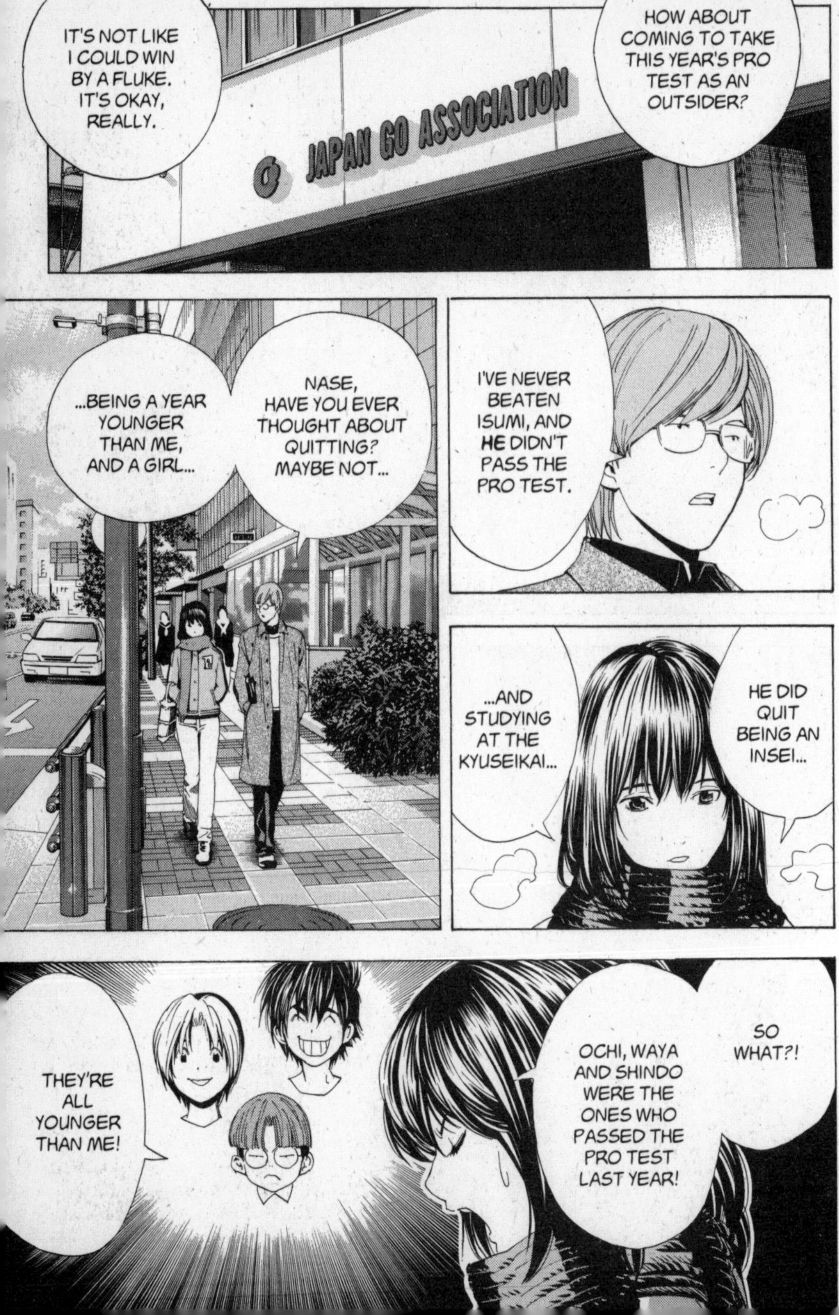
HOW ABOUT COMING TO TAKE THIS YEAR'S PRO TEST AS AN OUTSIDER?
JAPAN GO ASSOCIATION
IT'S NOT LIKE I COULD WIN BY A FLUKE. IT'S OKAY, REALLY.
I'VE NEVER BEATEN ISUMI, AND HE DIDN'T PASS THE PRO TEST.
HE DID QUIT BEING AN INSEI...
...AND STUDYING AT THE KYUSEIKAI...
NASE, HAVE YOU EVER THOUGHT ABOUT QUITTING? MAYBE NOT...
...BEING A YEAR YOUNGER THAN ME, AND A GIRL...
SO WHAT?!
OCHI, WAYA AND SHINDO WERE THE ONES WHO PASSED THE PRO TEST LAST YEAR!
THEY'RE ALL YOUNGER THAN ME!

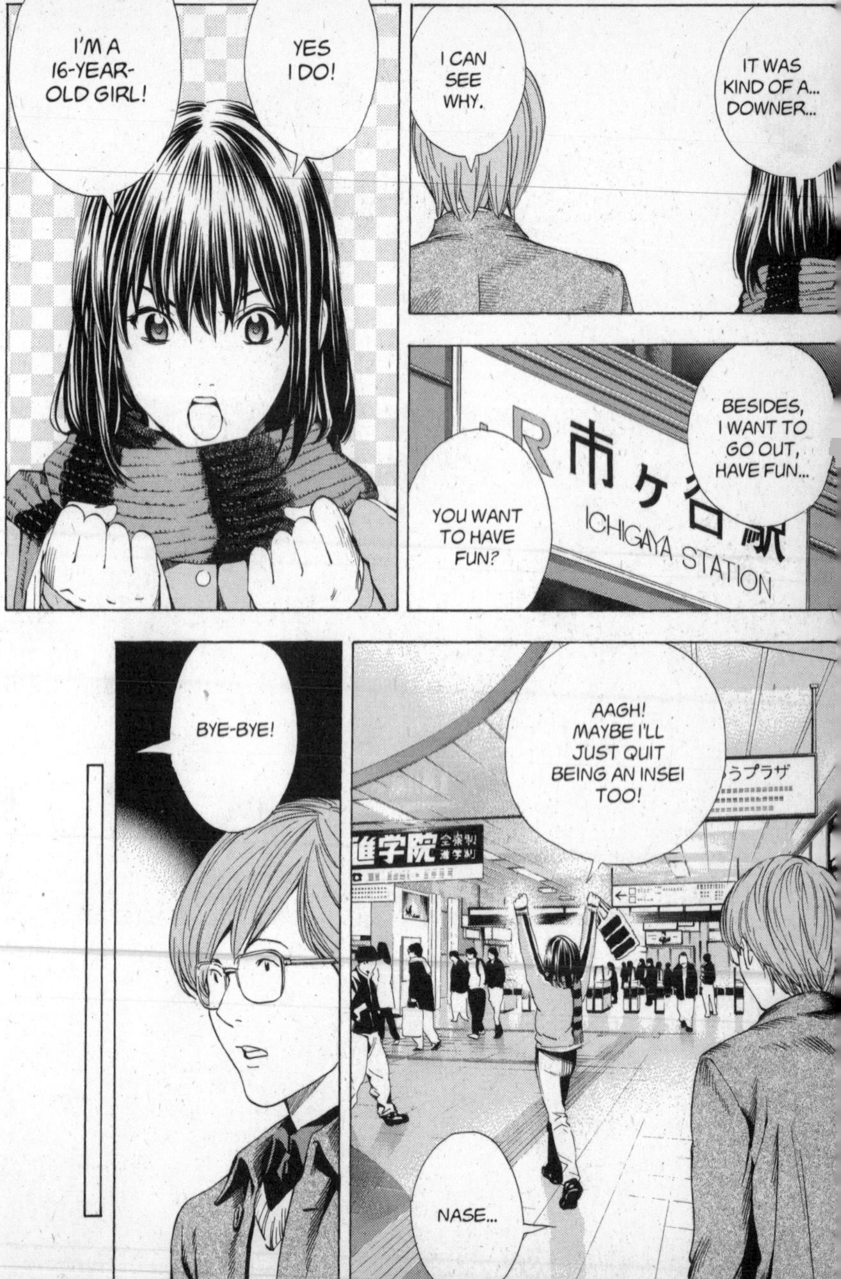
IT WAS KIND OF A... DOWNER...
I CAN SEE WHY.
BESIDES, I WANT TO GO OUT, HAVE FUN...
YOU WANT TO HAVE FUN?
市ヶ谷駅
ICHIGAYA STATION
YES I DO!
I'M A 16-YEAR-OLD GIRL!
AAGH! MAYBE I'LL JUST QUIT BEING AN INSEI TOO!
NASE...
BYE-BYE!

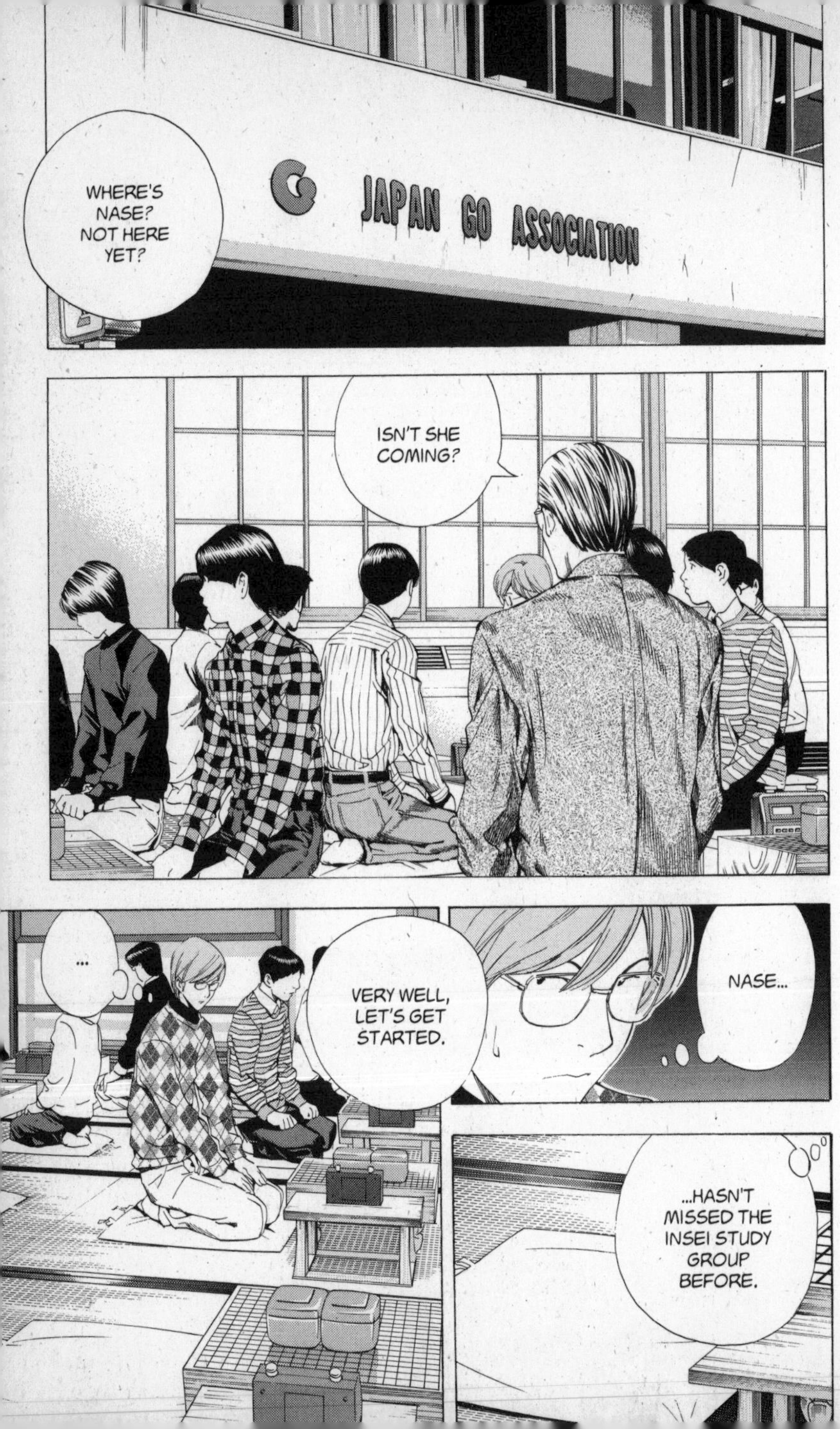
JAPAN GO ASSOCIATION
WHERE'S NASE? NOT HERE YET?
ISN'T SHE COMING?
NASE...
...HASN'T MISSED THE INSEI STUDY GROUP BEFORE.
...
VERY WELL, LET'S GET STARTED.

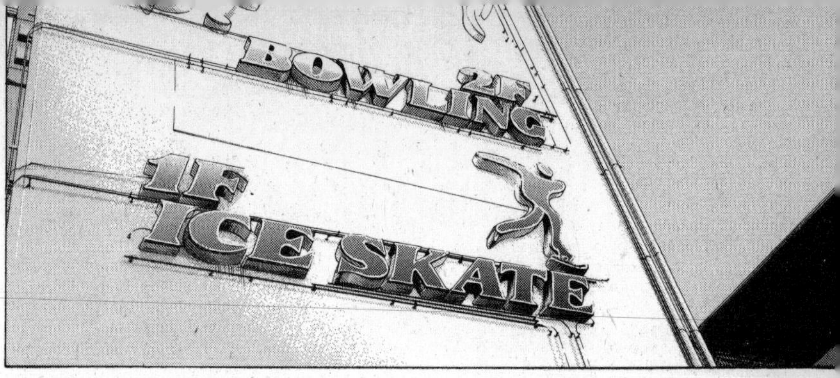
BOWLING 2F
1F ICE SKATE
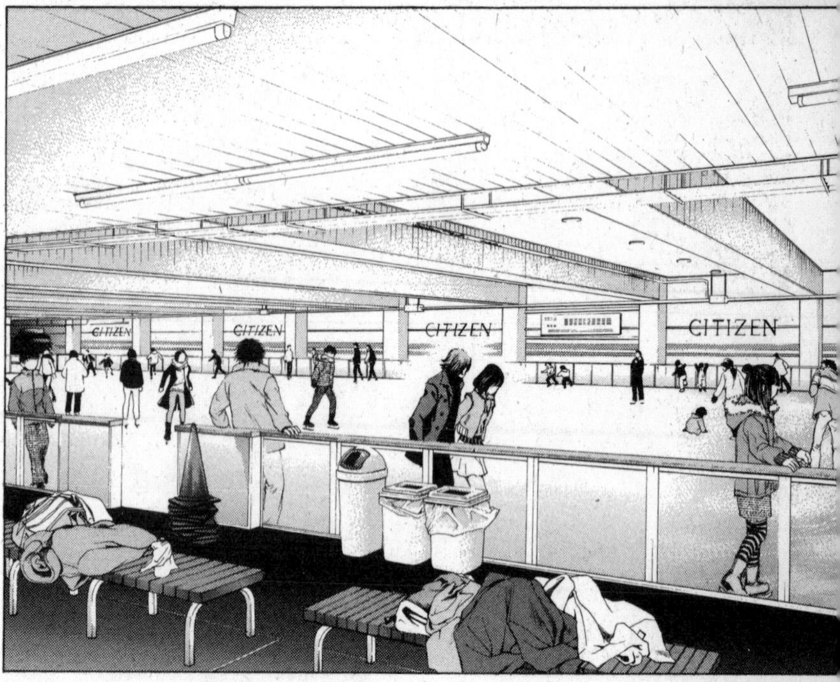
CITIZEN
CITIZEN
CITIZEN
CITIZEN
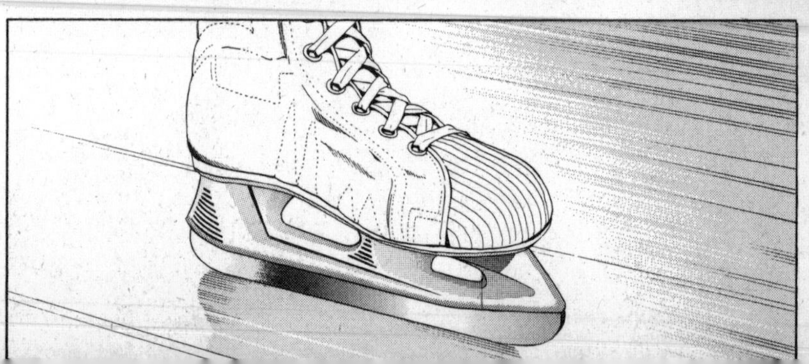

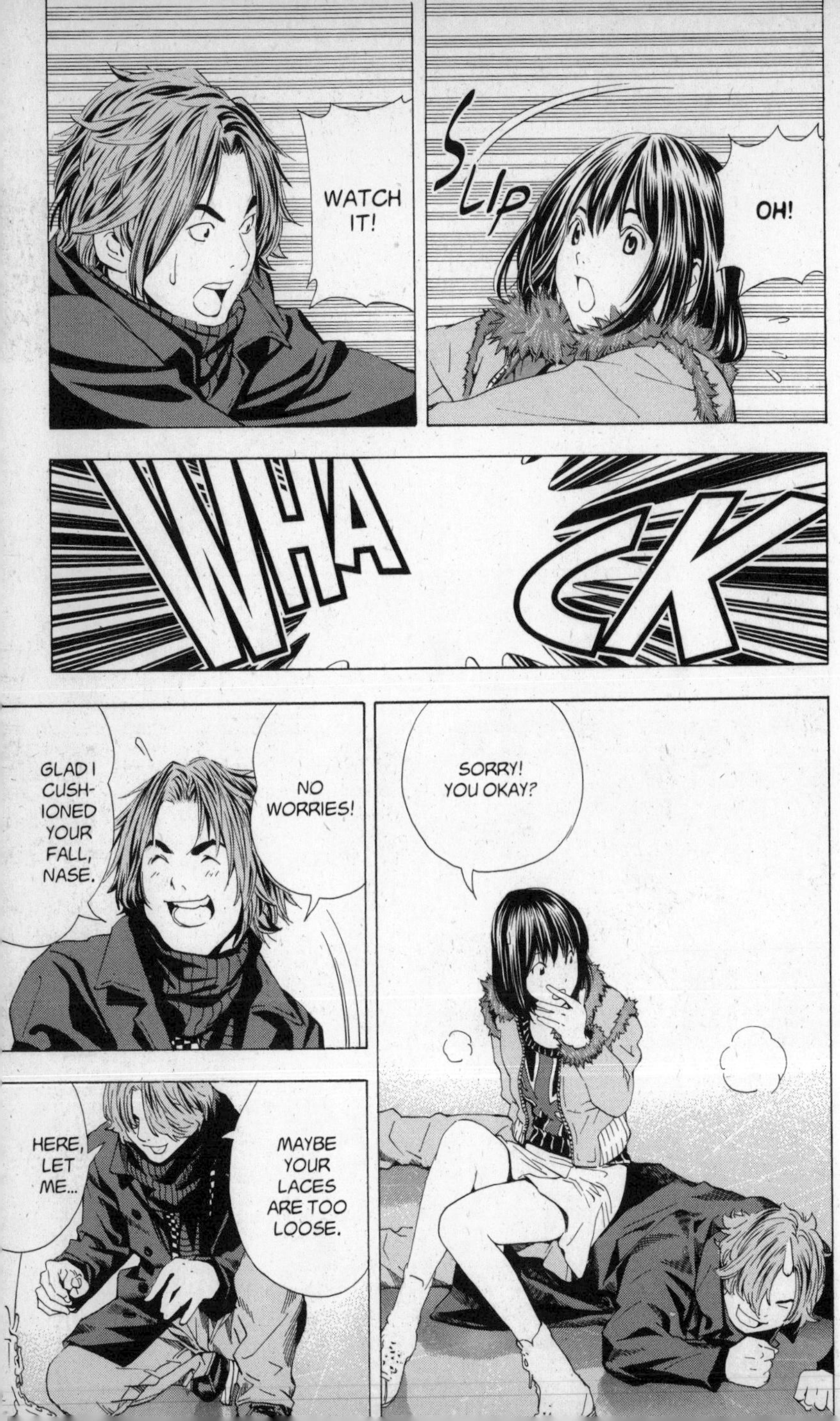
SLIP
OH!
WATCH IT!
WHACK
SORRY! YOU OKAY?
NO WORRIES!
GLAD I CUSHIONED YOUR FALL, NASE.
MAYBE YOUR LACES ARE TOO LOOSE.
HERE, LET ME...

THANKS.

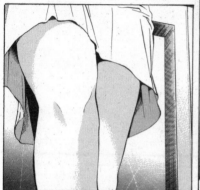

SIGH... I'M ALWAYS AT THE GO ASSOCIATION ON SUNDAYS, NOT OUT PLAYING.

IT FEELS STRANGE. KINDA THROWS ME OFF...

HEH HEH... ♡

ASUMI!

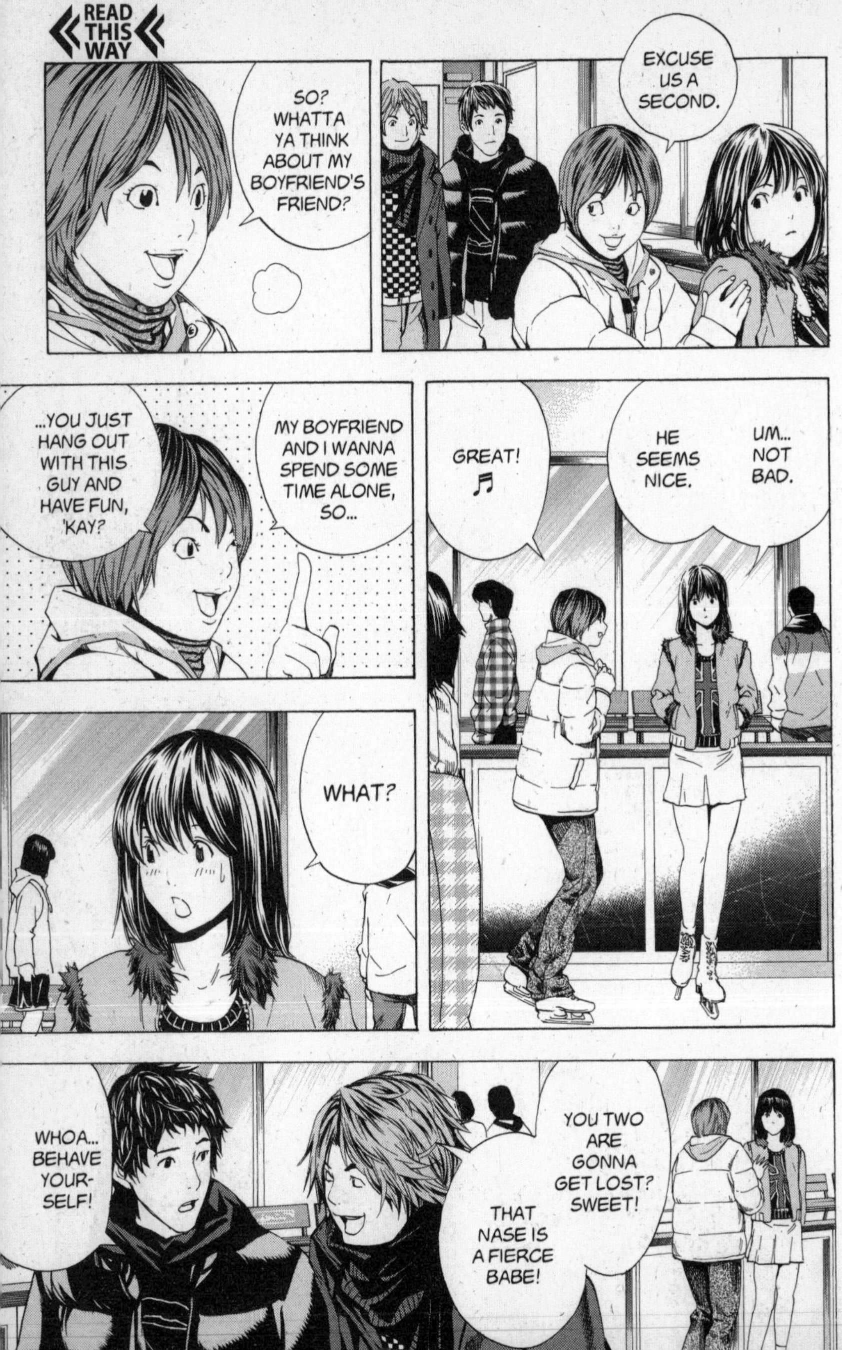
READ THIS WAY
EXCUSE US A SECOND.
SO? WHATTA YA THINK ABOUT MY BOYFRIEND'S FRIEND?
UM... NOT BAD.
HE SEEMS NICE.
GREAT! ♬
MY BOYFRIEND AND I WANNA SPEND SOME TIME ALONE, SO...
...YOU JUST HANG OUT WITH THIS GUY AND HAVE FUN, 'KAY?
WHAT?
YOU TWO ARE GONNA GET LOST? SWEET!
THAT NASE IS A FIERCE BABE!
WHOA... BEHAVE YOURSELF!

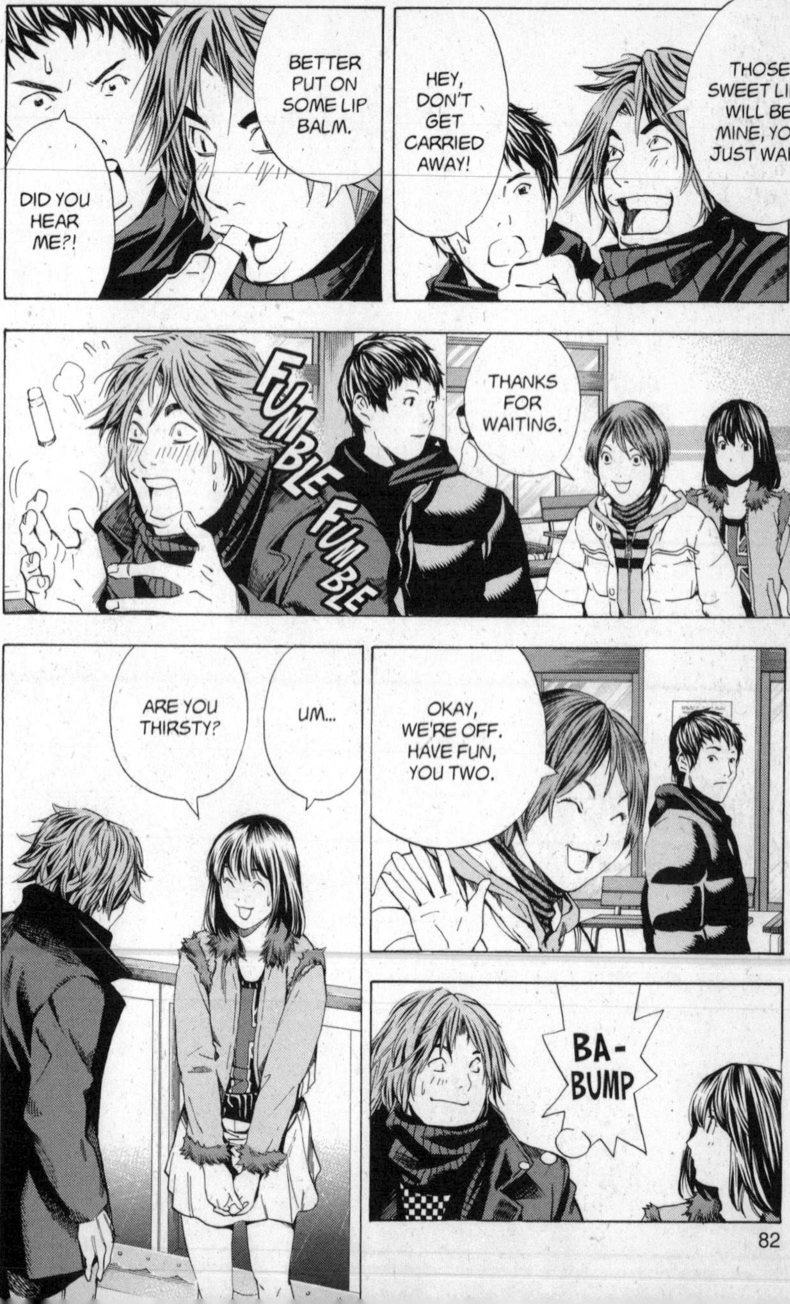
THOSE SWEET LIPS WILL BE MINE, YOU JUST WAIT!
HEY, DON'T GET CARRIED AWAY!
BETTER PUT ON SOME LIP BALM.
DID YOU HEAR ME?!
THANKS FOR WAITING.
FUMBLE FUMBLE
OKAY, WE'RE OFF. HAVE FUN, YOU TWO.
BA-BUMP
UM...
ARE YOU THIRSTY?

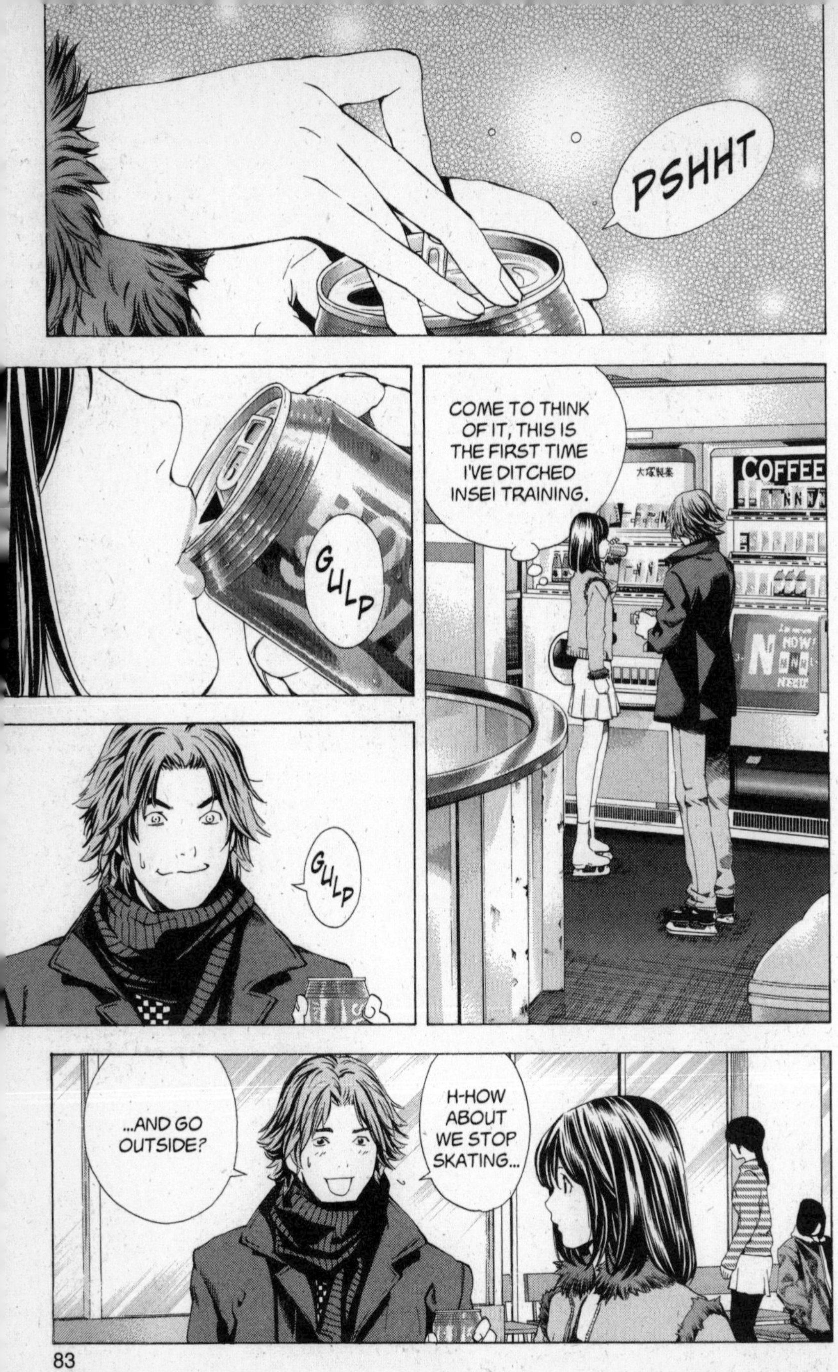
PSHHT
COME TO THINK OF IT, THIS IS THE FIRST TIME I'VE DITCHED INSEI TRAINING.
COFFEE
GULP
GULP
H-HOW ABOUT WE STOP SKATING...
...AND GO OUTSIDE?

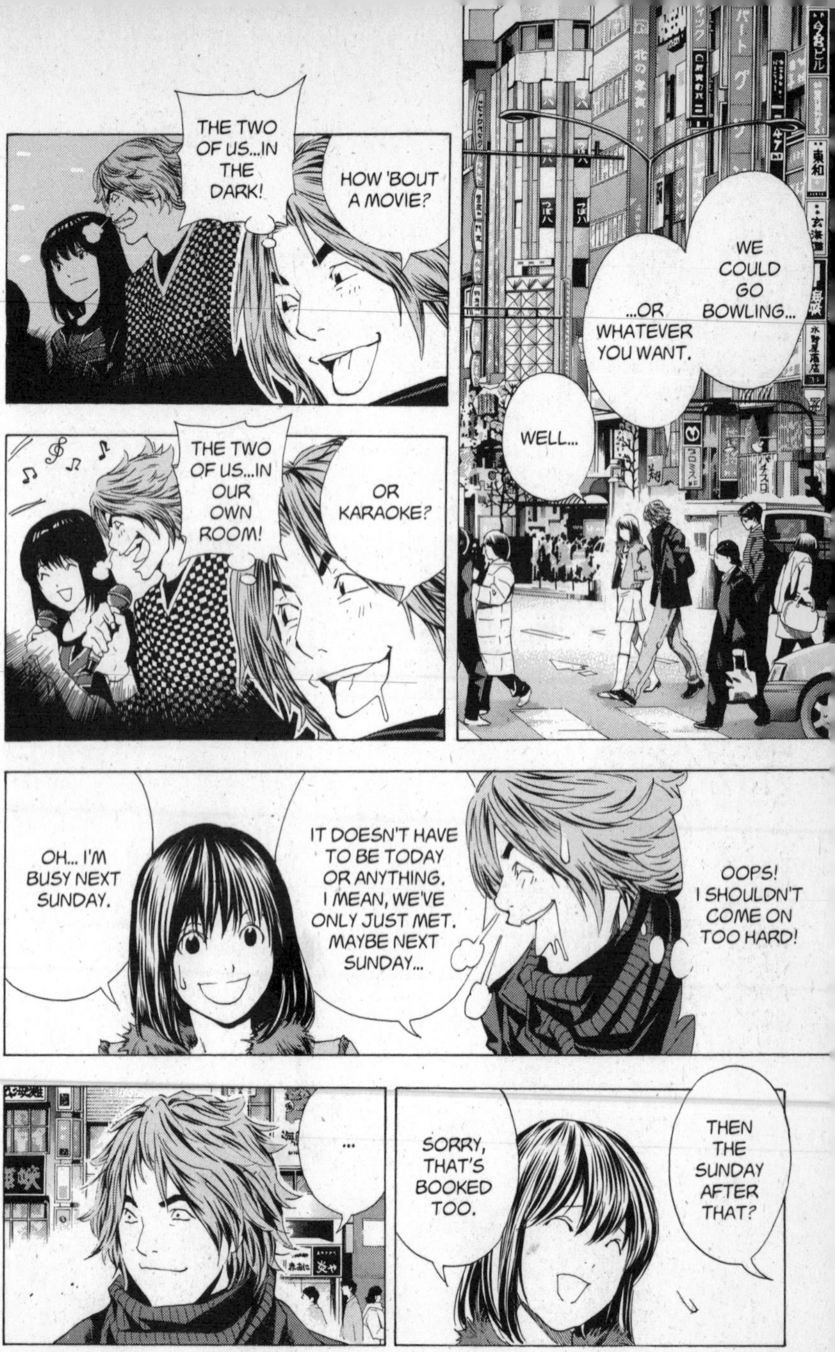
WE COULD GO BOWLING...
...OR WHATEVER YOU WANT.
WELL...
HOW 'BOUT A MOVIE?
THE TWO OF US...IN THE DARK!
OR KARAOKE?
THE TWO OF US...IN OUR OWN ROOM!
OOPS! I SHOULDN'T COME ON TOO HARD!
IT DOESN'T HAVE TO BE TODAY OR ANYTHING. I MEAN, WE'VE ONLY JUST MET. MAYBE NEXT SUNDAY...
OH... I'M BUSY NEXT SUNDAY.
THEN THE SUNDAY AFTER THAT?
SORRY, THAT'S BOOKED TOO.
...

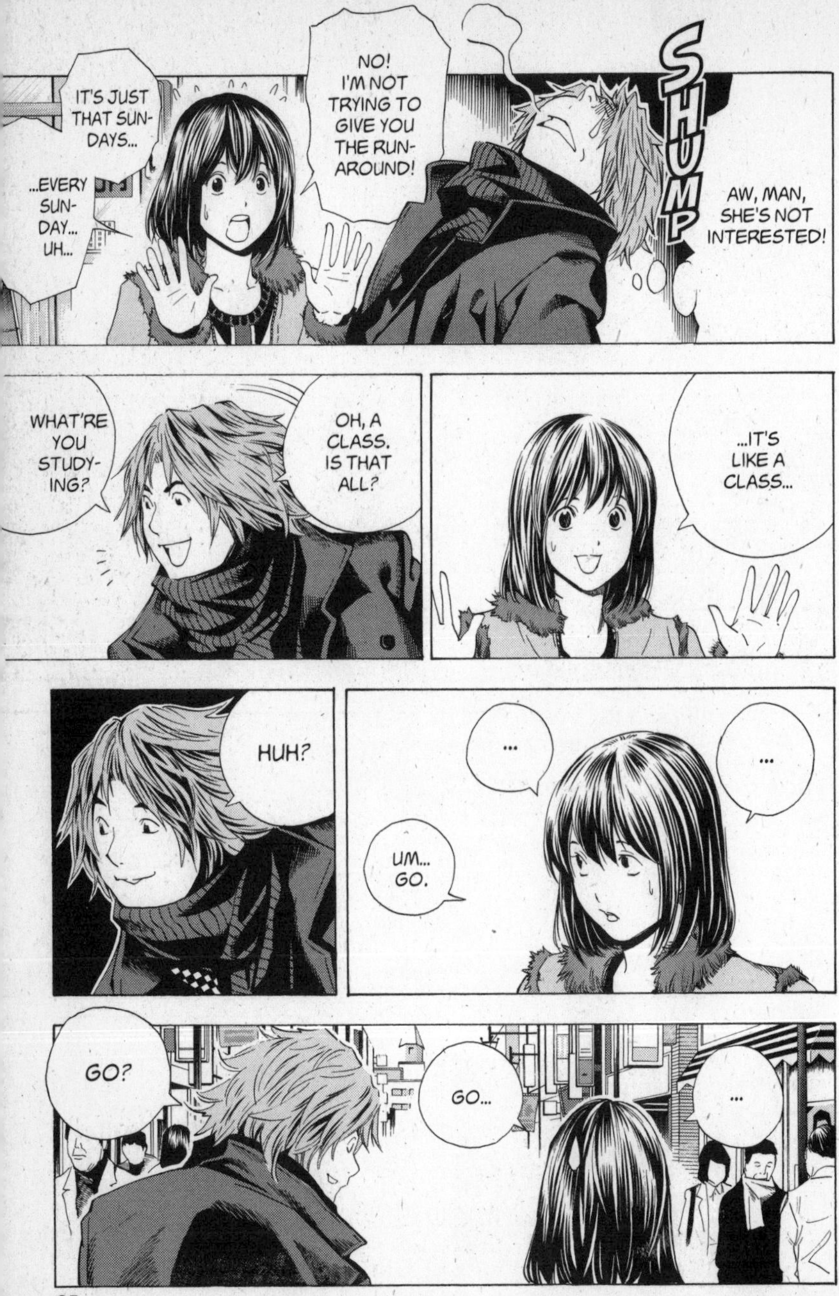
SHUMP
AW, MAN, SHE'S NOT INTERESTED!
NO! I'M NOT TRYING TO GIVE YOU THE RUN-AROUND!
IT'S JUST THAT SUN-DAYS...
...EVERY SUN-DAY... UH...
...IT'S LIKE A CLASS...
OH, A CLASS. IS THAT ALL?
WHAT'RE YOU STUDY-ING?
...
...
UM... GO.
HUH?
...
GO...
GO?

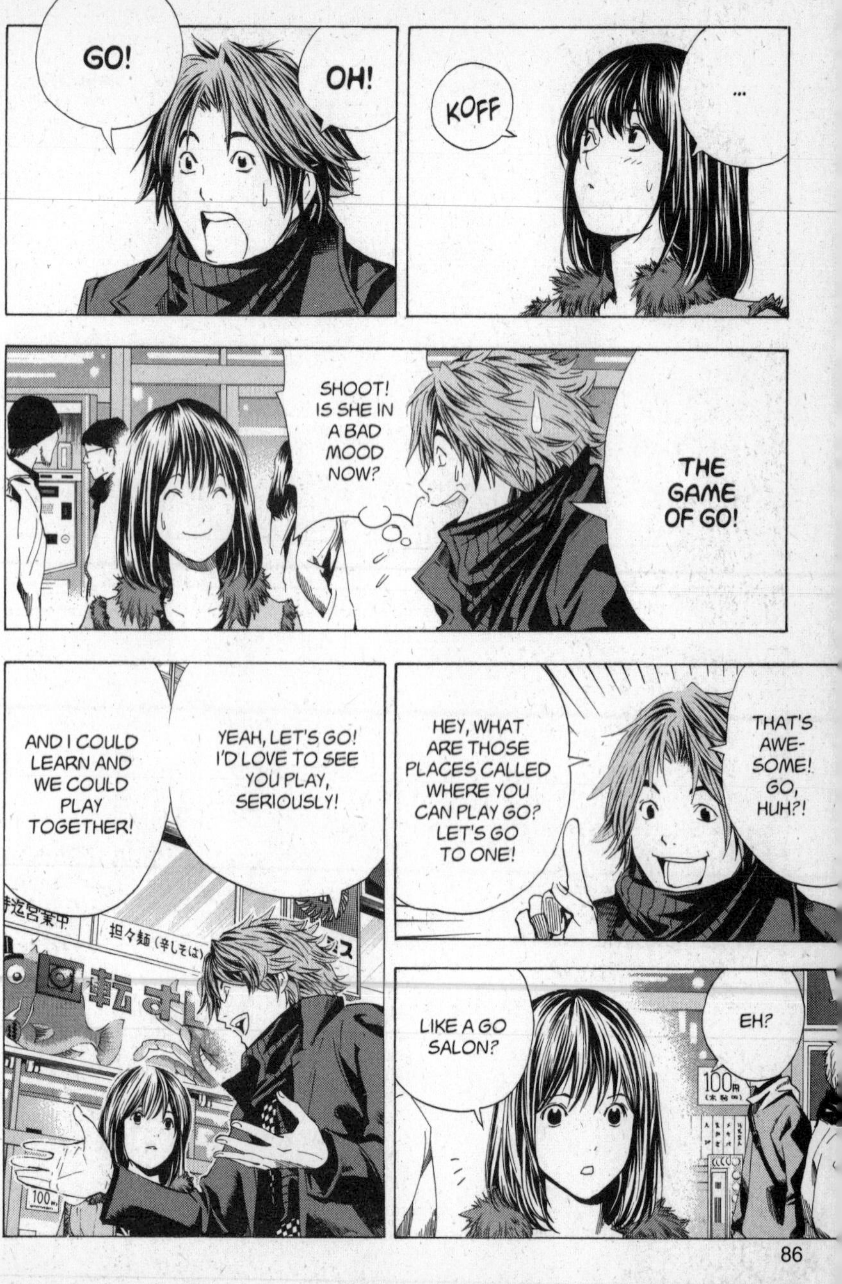
...
KOFF
OH!
GO!
THE GAME OF GO!
SHOOT! IS SHE IN A BAD MOOD NOW?
THAT'S AWE-SOME! GO, HUH?!
HEY, WHAT ARE THOSE PLACES CALLED WHERE YOU CAN PLAY GO? LET'S GO TO ONE!
EH?
LIKE A GO SALON?
YEAH, LET'S GO! I'D LOVE TO SEE YOU PLAY, SERIOUSLY!
AND I COULD LEARN AND WE COULD PLAY TOGETHER!

READ THIS WAY

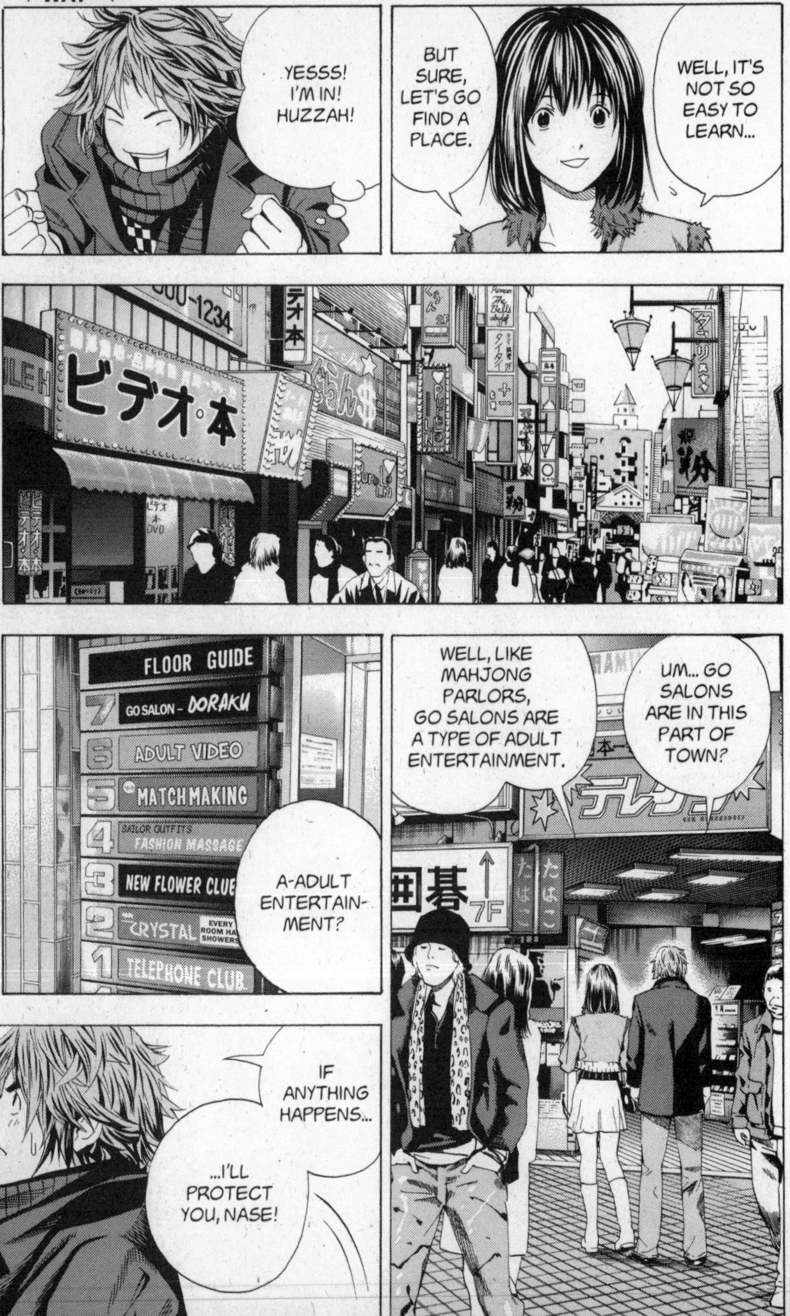

WELL, IT'S NOT SO EASY TO LEARN...
BUT SURE, LET'S GO FIND A PLACE.
YESSS! I'M IN! HUZZAH!
ビデオ・本
UM... GO SALONS ARE IN THIS PART OF TOWN?
WELL, LIKE MAHJONG PARLORS, GO SALONS ARE A TYPE OF ADULT ENTERTAINMENT.
囲碁 7F
FLOOR GUIDE
7 GO SALON - DORAKU
6 ADULT VIDEO
5 MATCHMAKING
4 SAILOR OUTFITS FASHION MASSAGE
3 NEW FLOWER CLUB
2 CRYSTAL EVERY ROOM HAS SHOWERS
1 TELEPHONE CLUB
A-ADULT ENTERTAIN-MENT?
IF ANYTHING HAPPENS...
...I'LL PROTECT YOU, NASE!

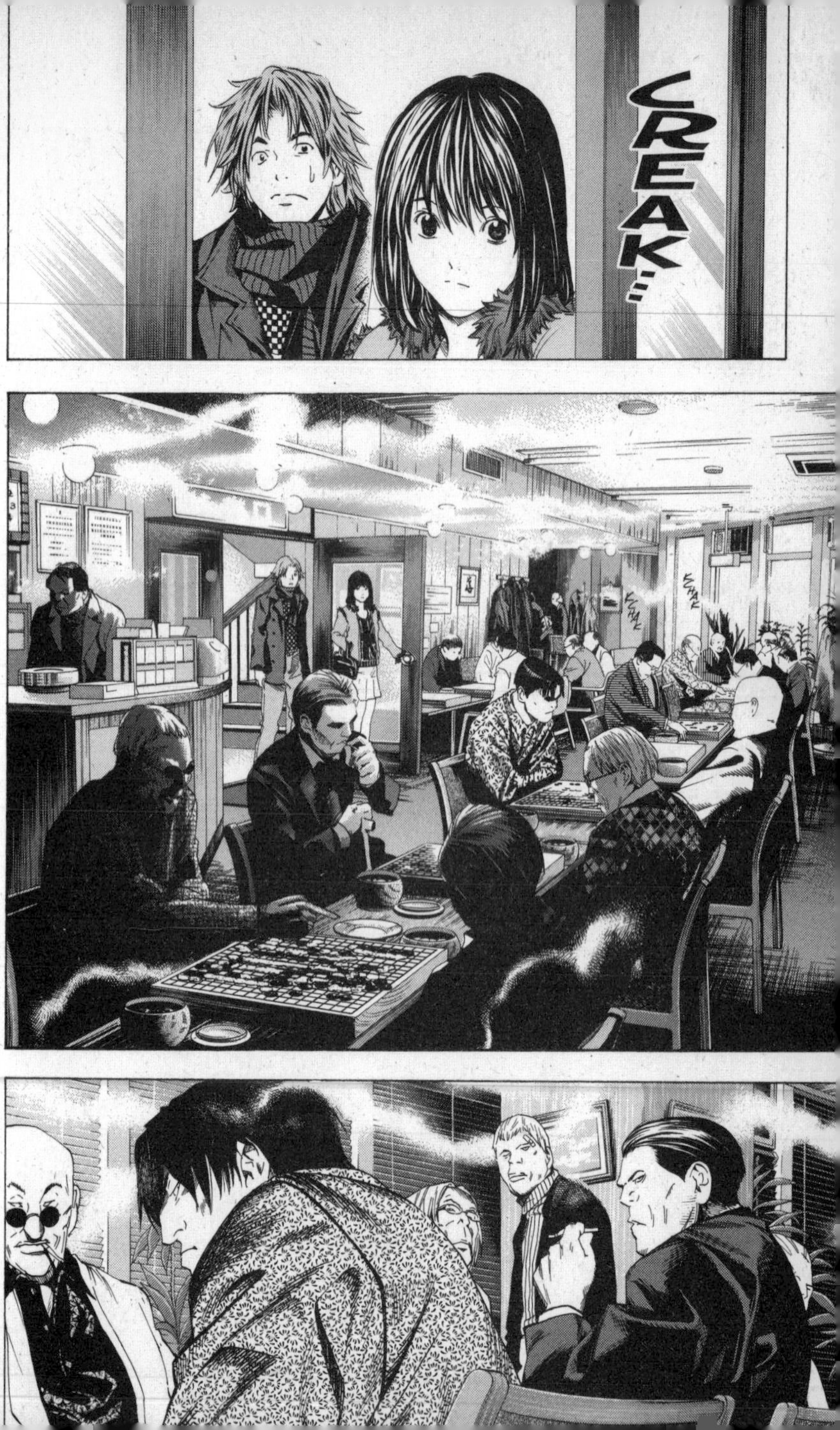
CREAK...
KCHAK
KCHAK

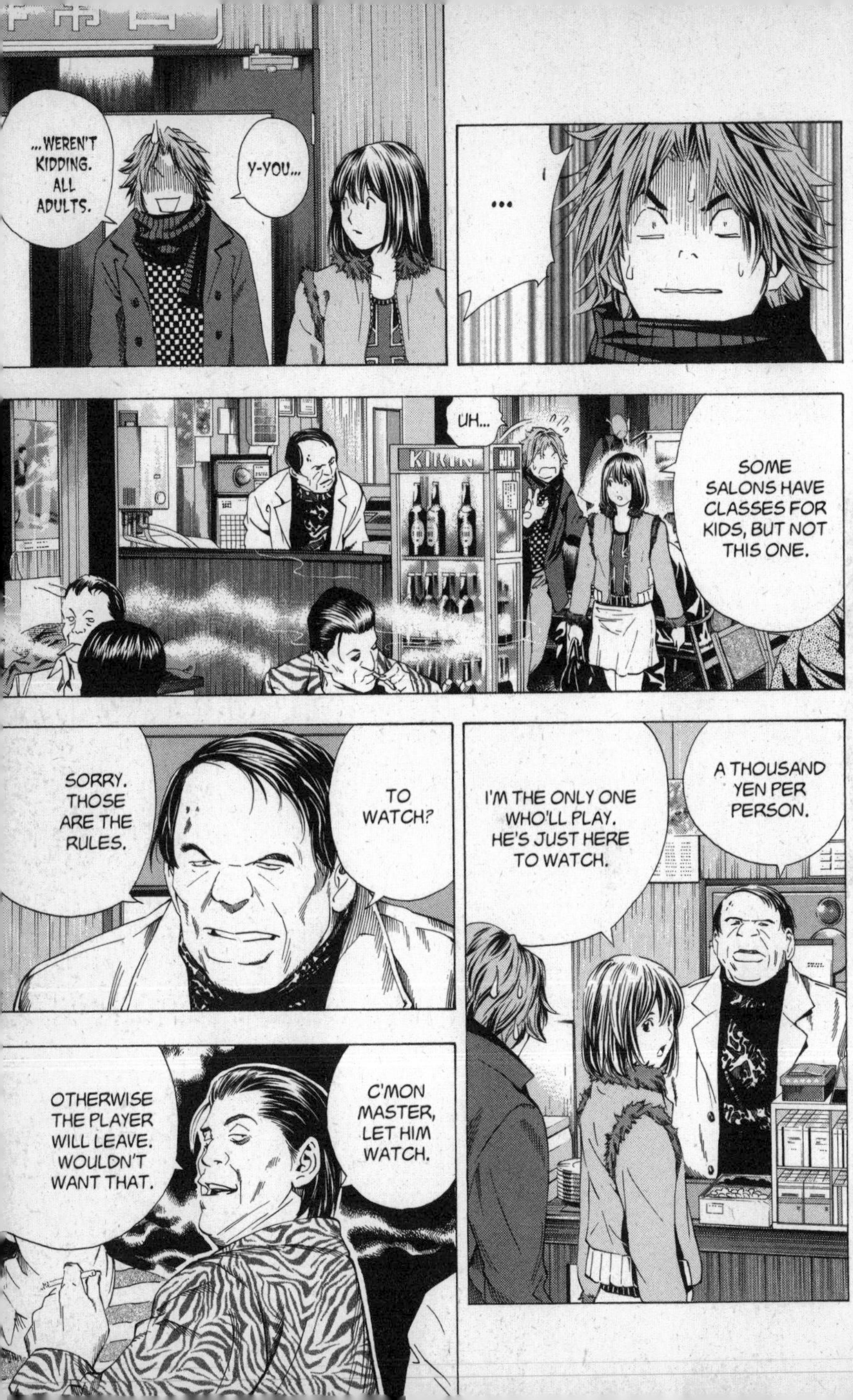
...
Y-YOU...
...WEREN'T KIDDING. ALL ADULTS.
SOME SALONS HAVE CLASSES FOR KIDS, BUT NOT THIS ONE.
UH...
KIRIN
A THOUSAND YEN PER PERSON.
I'M THE ONLY ONE WHO'LL PLAY. HE'S JUST HERE TO WATCH.
TO WATCH?
SORRY. THOSE ARE THE RULES.
C'MON MASTER, LET HIM WATCH.
OTHERWISE THE PLAYER WILL LEAVE. WOULDN'T WANT THAT.

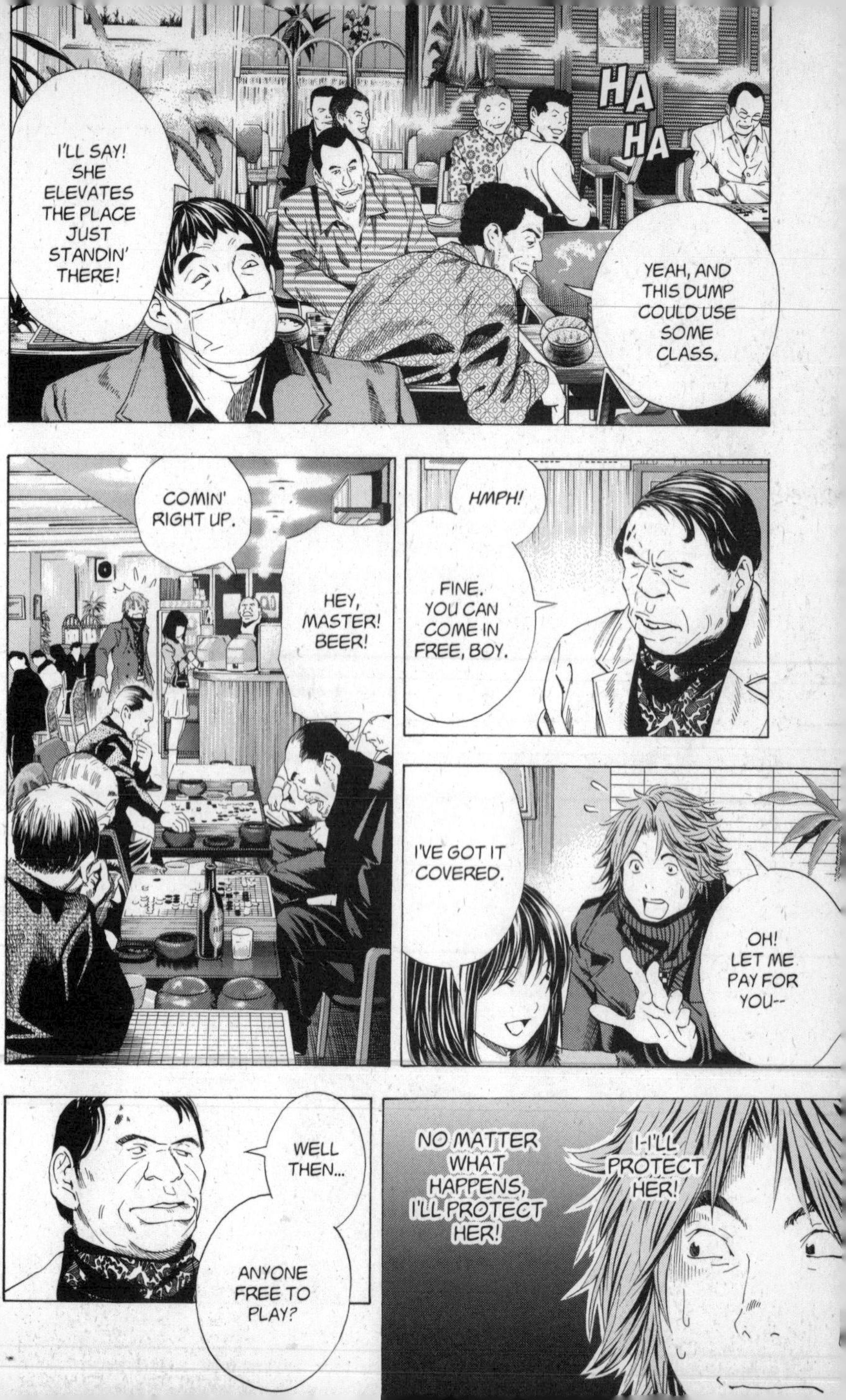
HA HA
YEAH, AND THIS DUMP COULD USE SOME CLASS.
I'LL SAY! SHE ELEVATES THE PLACE JUST STANDIN' THERE!
HMPH!
FINE. YOU CAN COME IN FREE, BOY.
OH! LET ME PAY FOR YOU--
I'VE GOT IT COVERED.
HEY, MASTER! BEER!
COMIN' RIGHT UP.
I-I'LL PROTECT HER!
NO MATTER WHAT HAPPENS, I'LL PROTECT HER!
WELL THEN...
ANYONE FREE TO PLAY?

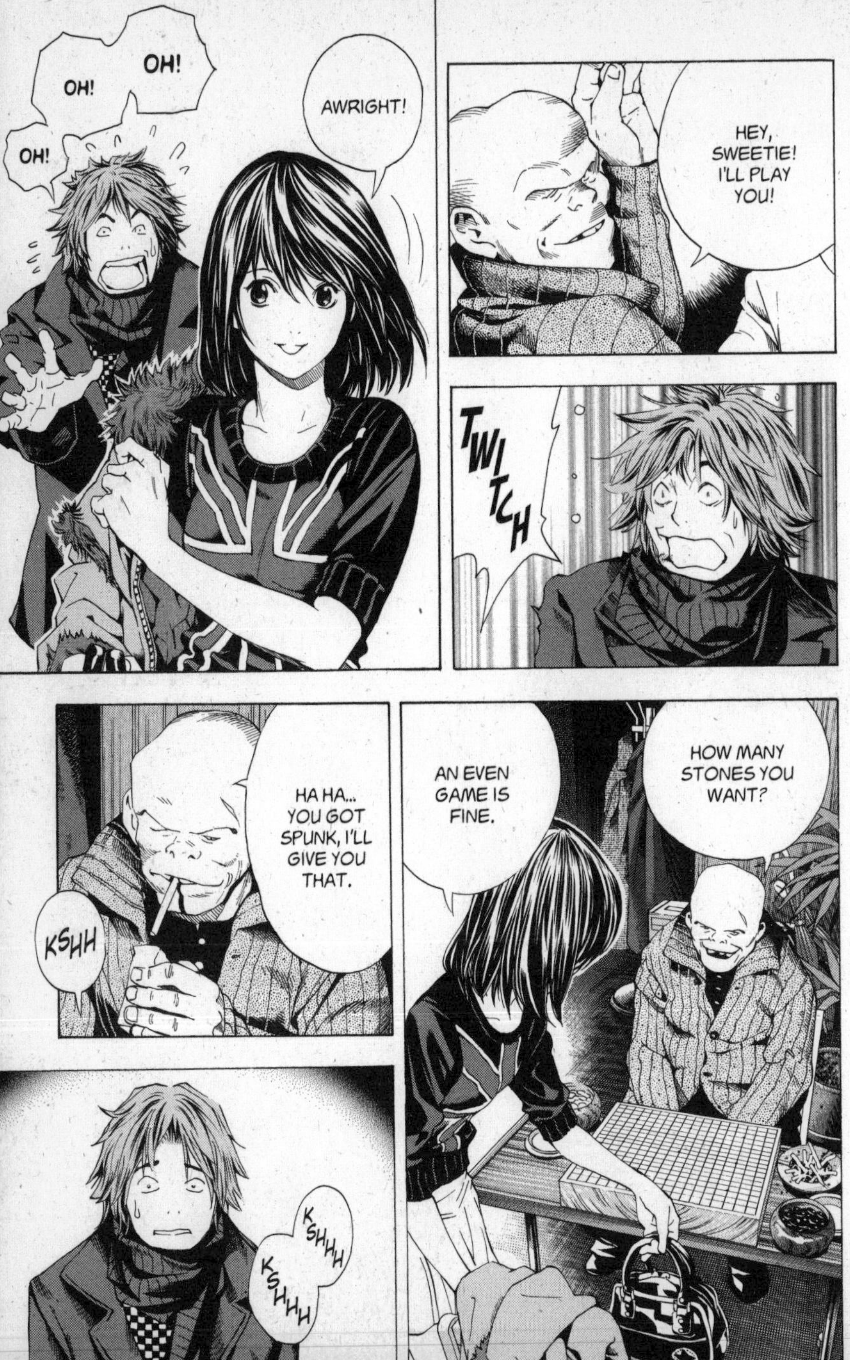
HEY, SWEETIE! I'LL PLAY YOU!
TWITCH
AWRIGHT!
OH!
OH!
OH!
HOW MANY STONES YOU WANT?
AN EVEN GAME IS FINE.
HA HA... YOU GOT SPUNK, I'LL GIVE YOU THAT.
KSHH
KSHHH
KSHHH

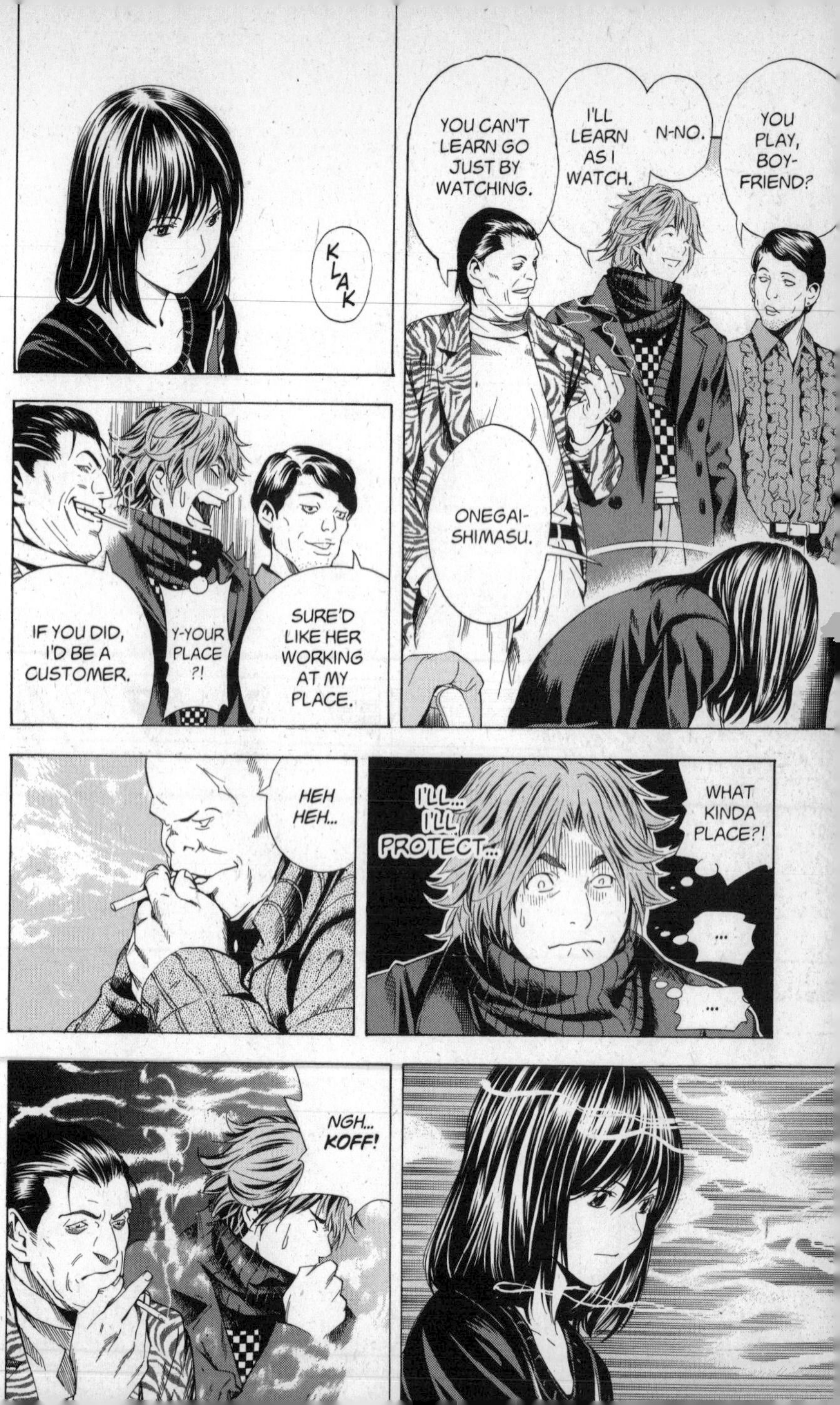
YOU PLAY, BOY-FRIEND?
N-NO.
I'LL LEARN AS I WATCH.
YOU CAN'T LEARN GO JUST BY WATCHING.
ONEGAI-SHIMASU.
KLAK
SURE'D LIKE HER WORKING AT MY PLACE.
Y-YOUR PLACE ?!
IF YOU DID, I'D BE A CUSTOMER.
WHAT KINDA PLACE?!
I'LL... I'LL PROTECT...
...
...
HEH HEH...
NGH... KOFF!

READ THIS WAY

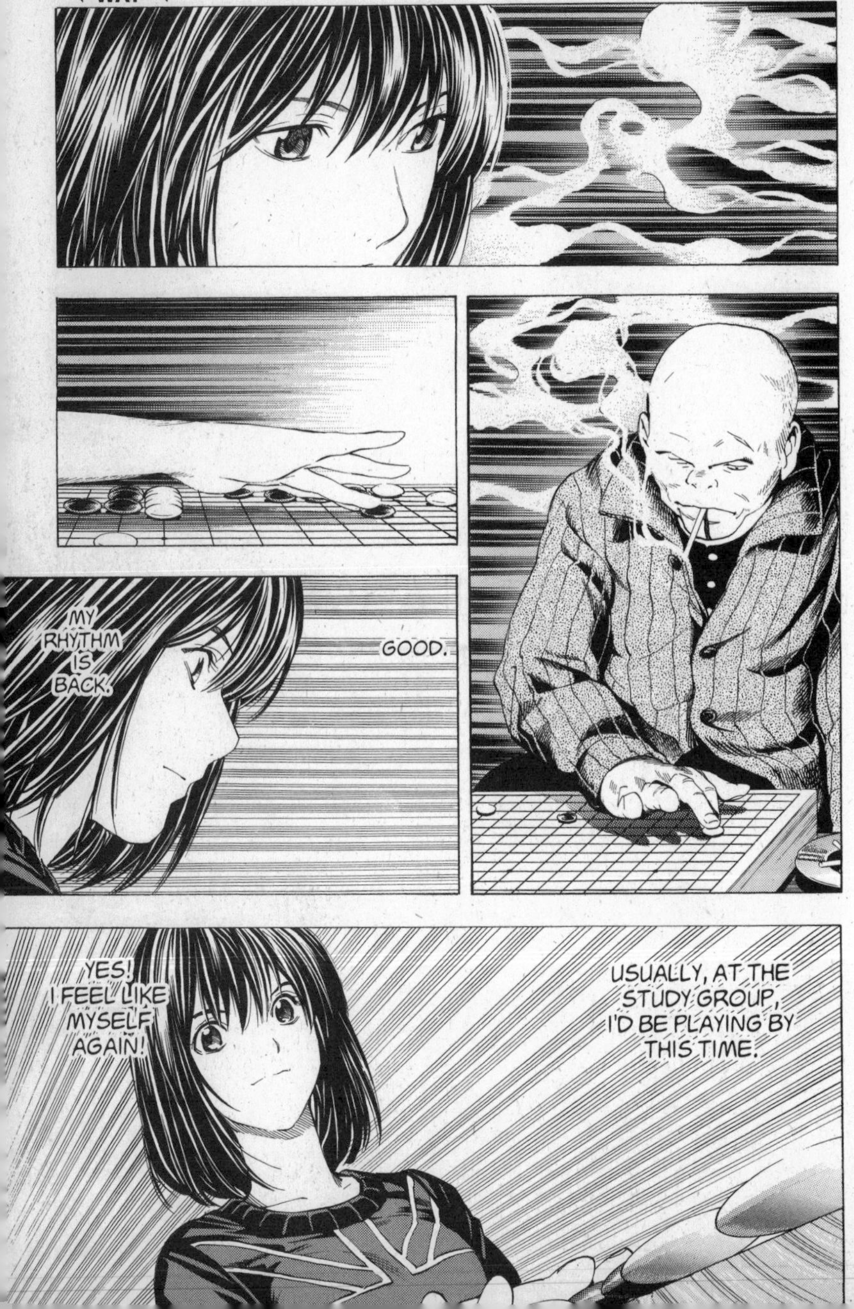
GOOD.
MY RHYTHM IS BACK.
USUALLY, AT THE STUDY GROUP, I'D BE PLAYING BY THIS TIME.
YES! I FEEL LIKE MYSELF AGAIN!

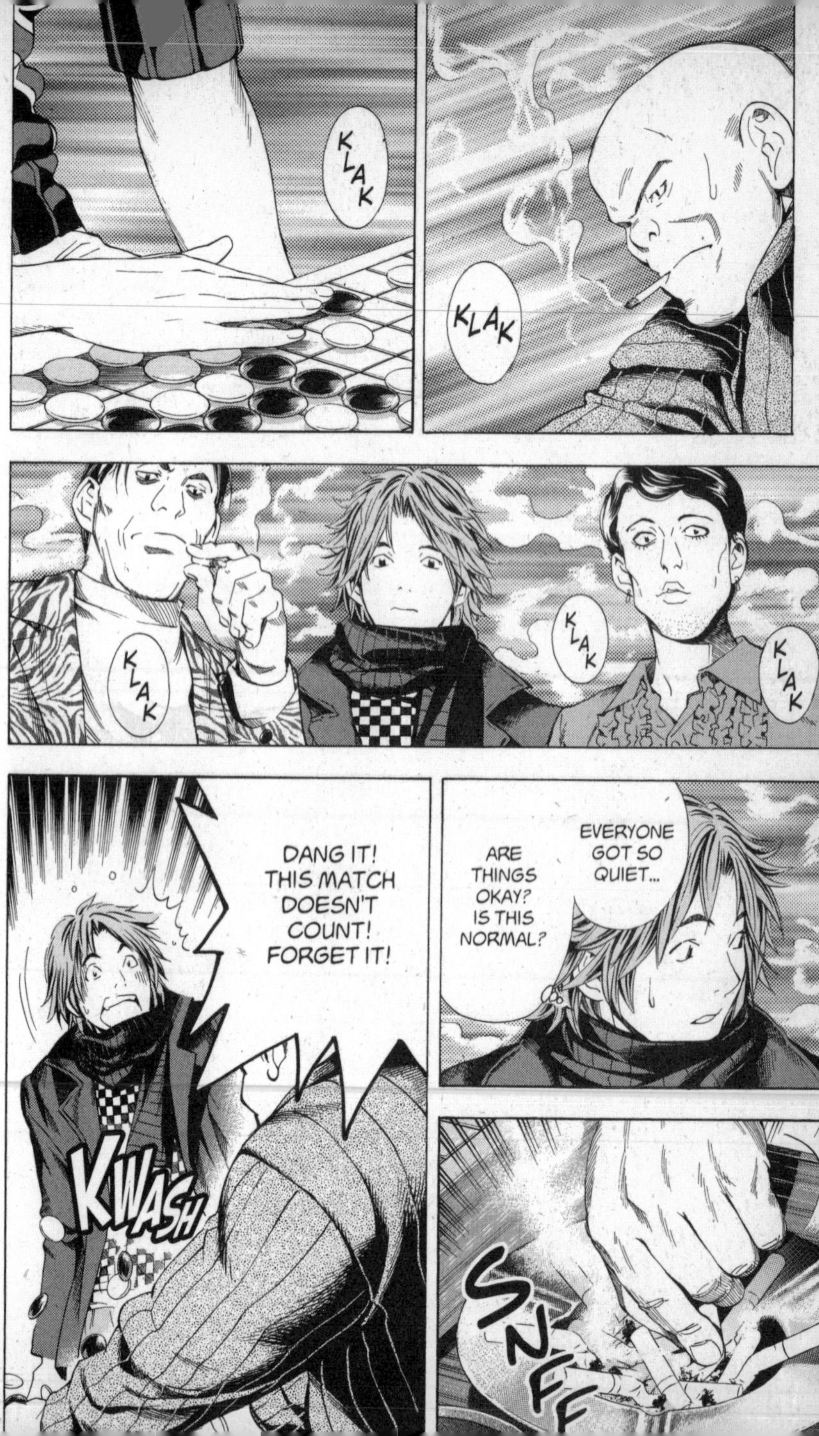
KLAK
KLAK
KLAK
KLAK
KLAK
EVERYONE GOT SO QUIET...
ARE THINGS OKAY? IS THIS NORMAL?
SNFF
DANG IT! THIS MATCH DOESN'T COUNT! FORGET IT!
KWASH

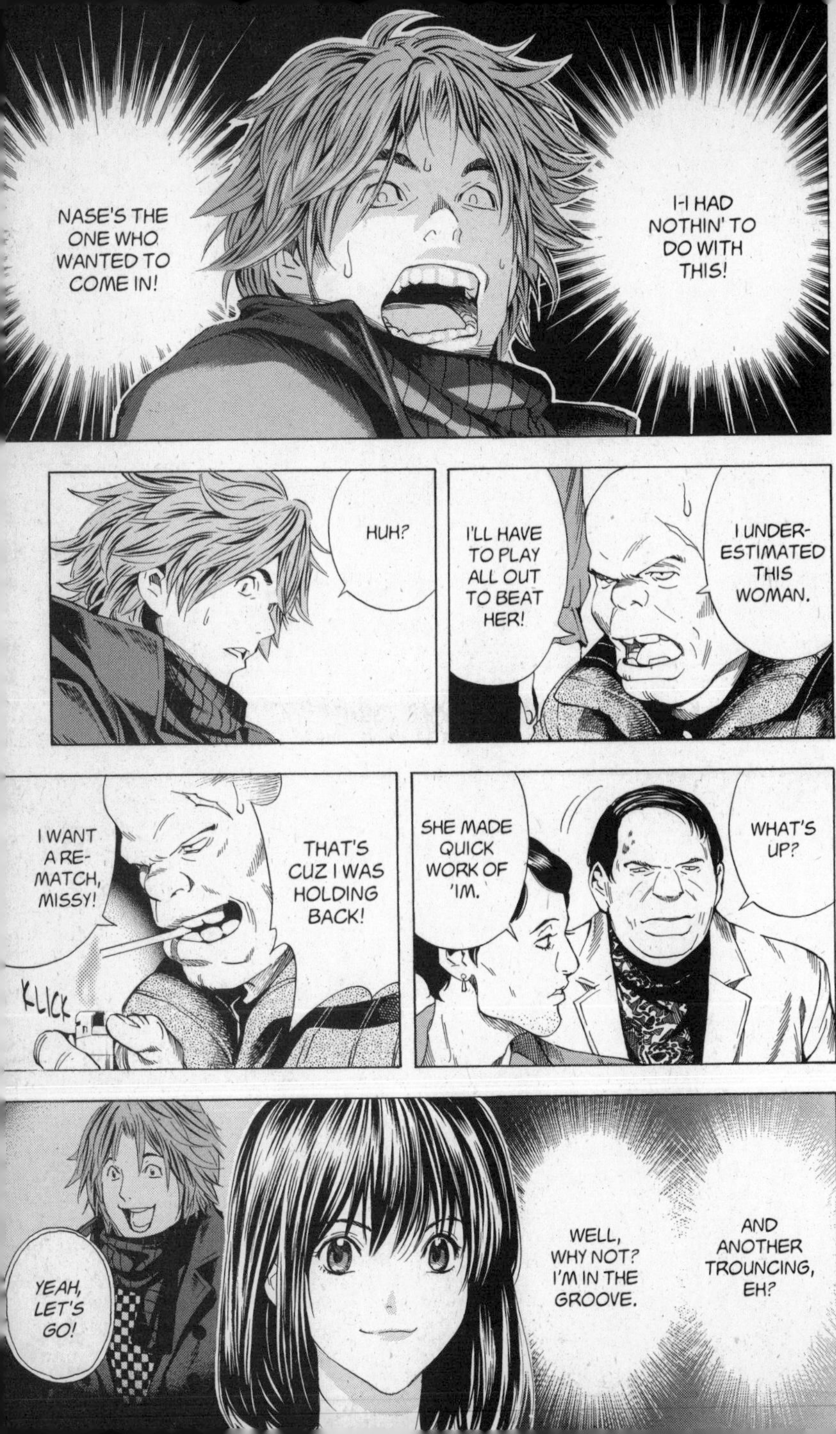
I-I HAD NOTHIN' TO DO WITH THIS!
NASE'S THE ONE WHO WANTED TO COME IN!
I UNDER-ESTIMATED THIS WOMAN.
I'LL HAVE TO PLAY ALL OUT TO BEAT HER!
HUH?
WHAT'S UP?
SHE MADE QUICK WORK OF 'IM.
THAT'S CUZ I WAS HOLDING BACK!
I WANT A RE-MATCH, MISSY!
KLICK
AND ANOTHER TROUNCING, EH?
WELL, WHY NOT? I'M IN THE GROOVE.
YEAH, LET'S GO!

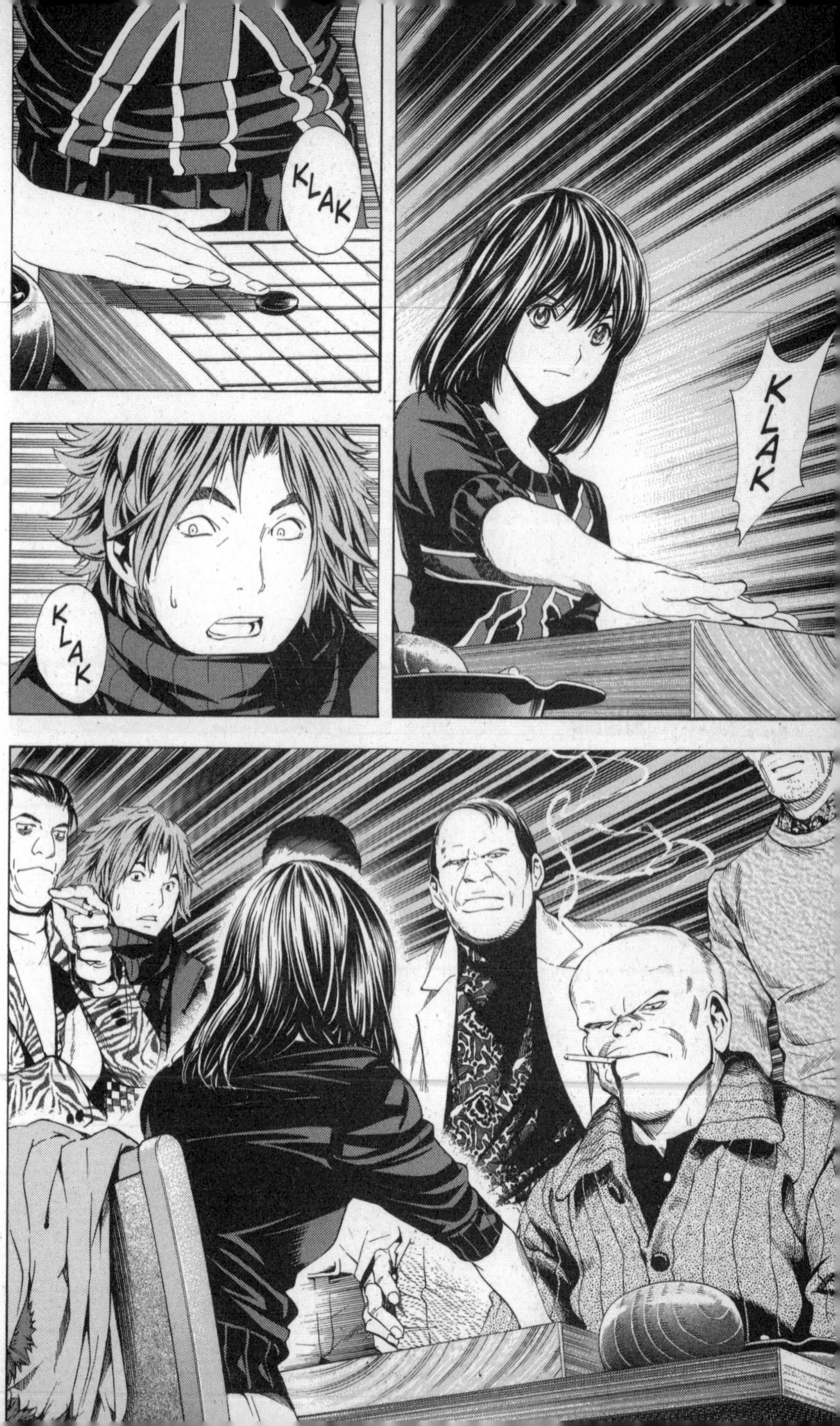
KLAK
KLAK
KLAK

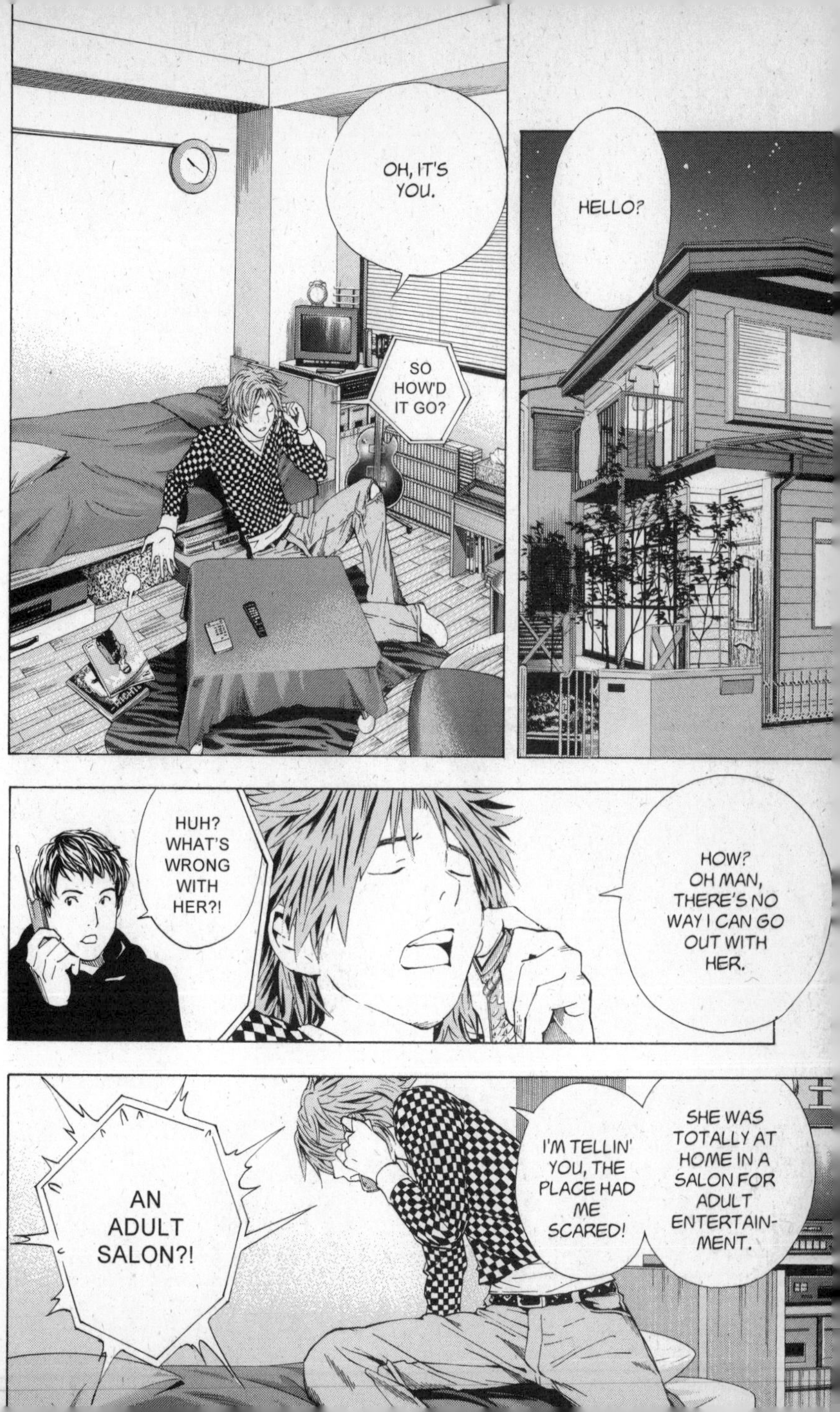
HELLO?
OH, IT'S YOU.
SO HOW'D IT GO?
HOW? OH MAN, THERE'S NO WAY I CAN GO OUT WITH HER.
HUH? WHAT'S WRONG WITH HER?!
SHE WAS TOTALLY AT HOME IN A SALON FOR ADULT ENTERTAIN-MENT.
I'M TELLIN' YOU, THE PLACE HAD ME SCARED!
AN ADULT SALON?!

READ THIS WAY

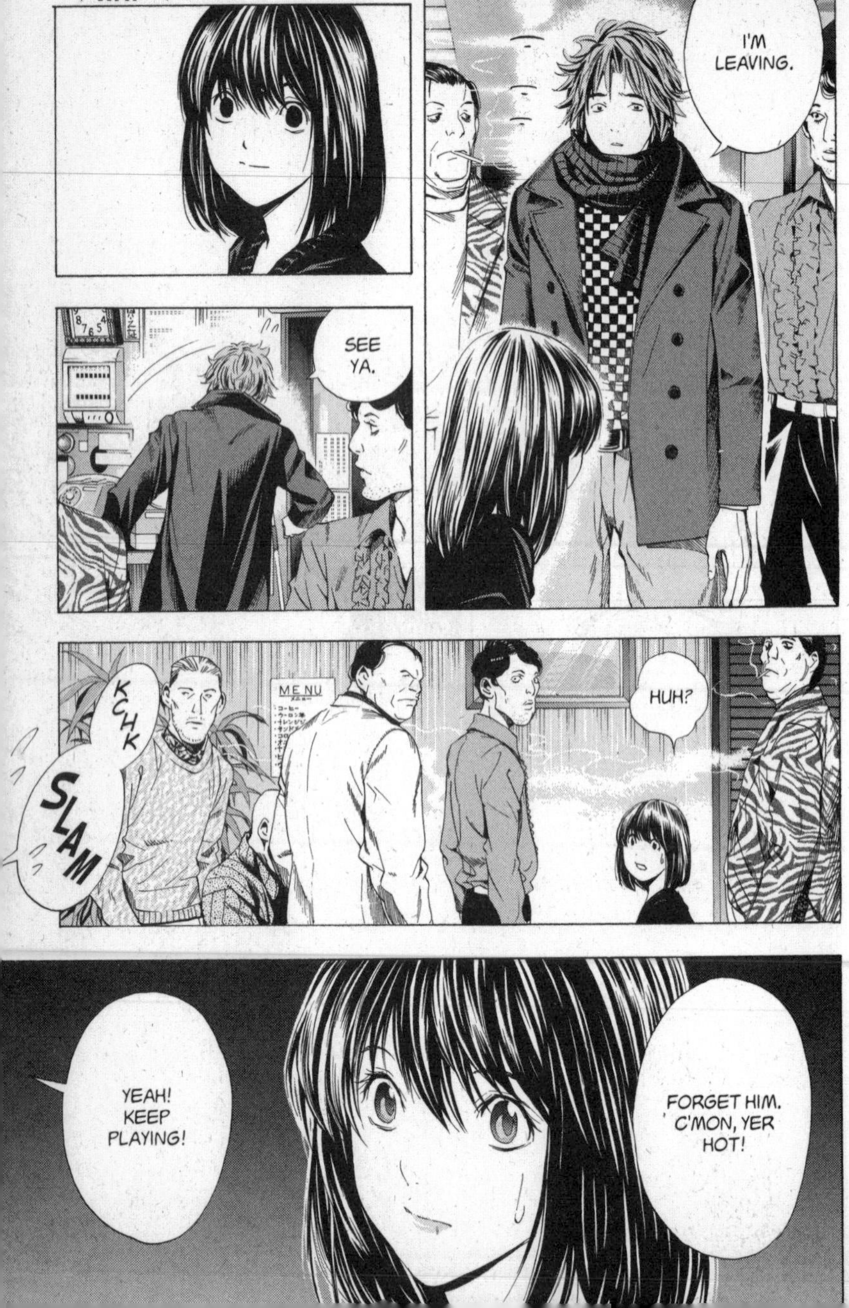
I'M LEAVING.
SEE YA.
HUH?
KCHK
SLAM
FORGET HIM. C'MON, YER HOT!
YEAH! KEEP PLAYING!

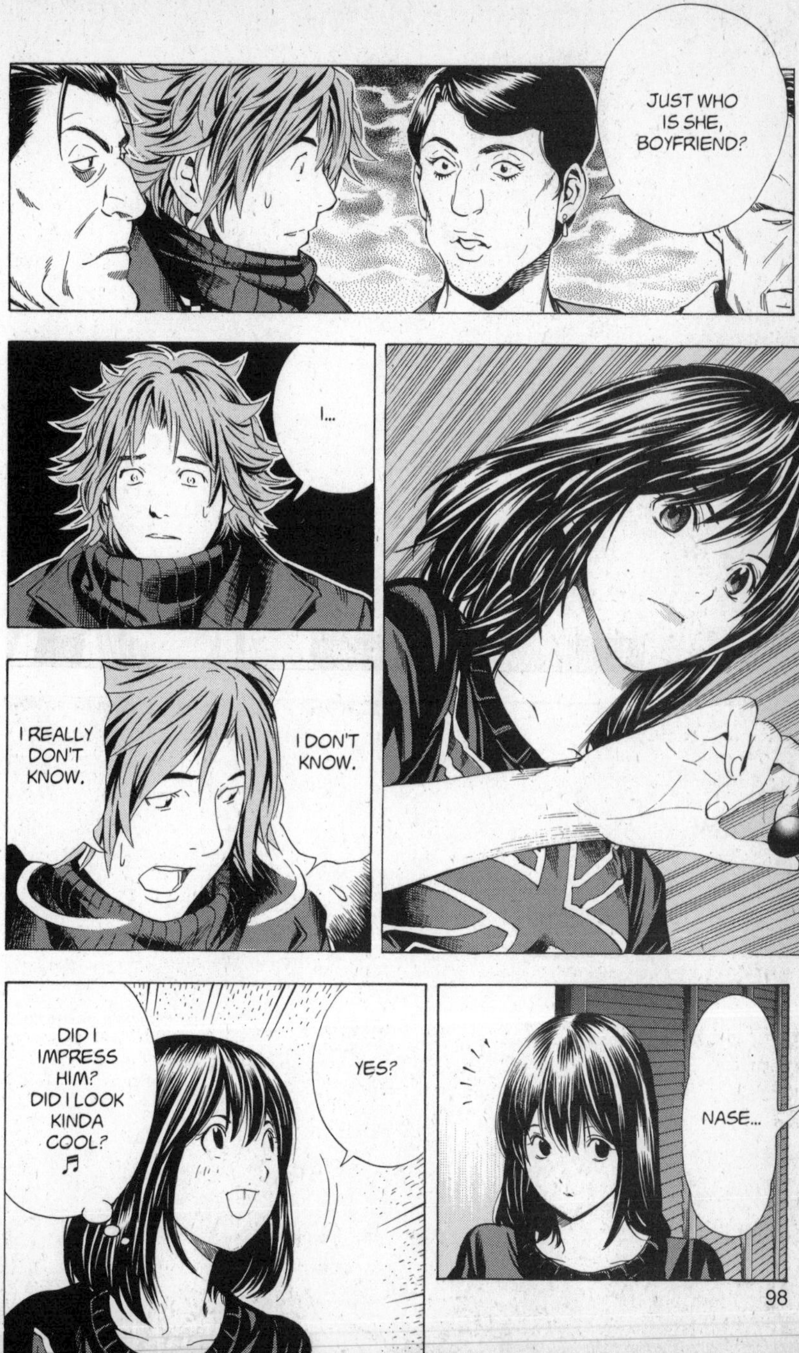
JUST WHO IS SHE, BOYFRIEND?
I...
I DON'T KNOW.
I REALLY DON'T KNOW.
NASE...
YES?
DID I IMPRESS HIM? DID I LOOK KINDA COOL? ♬

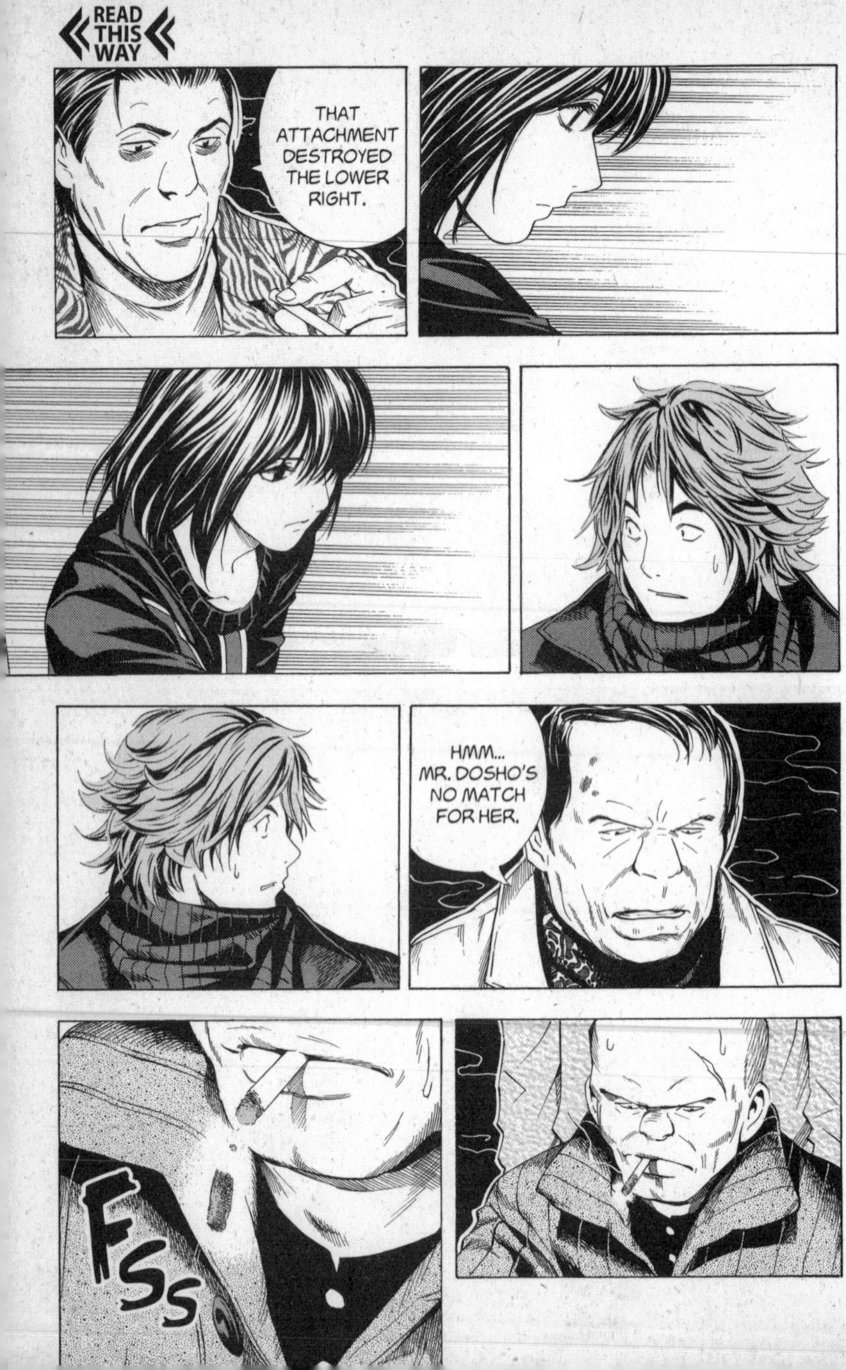
READ THIS WAY
THAT ATTACHMENT DESTROYED THE LOWER RIGHT.
HMM... MR. DOSHO'S NO MATCH FOR HER.
FSS

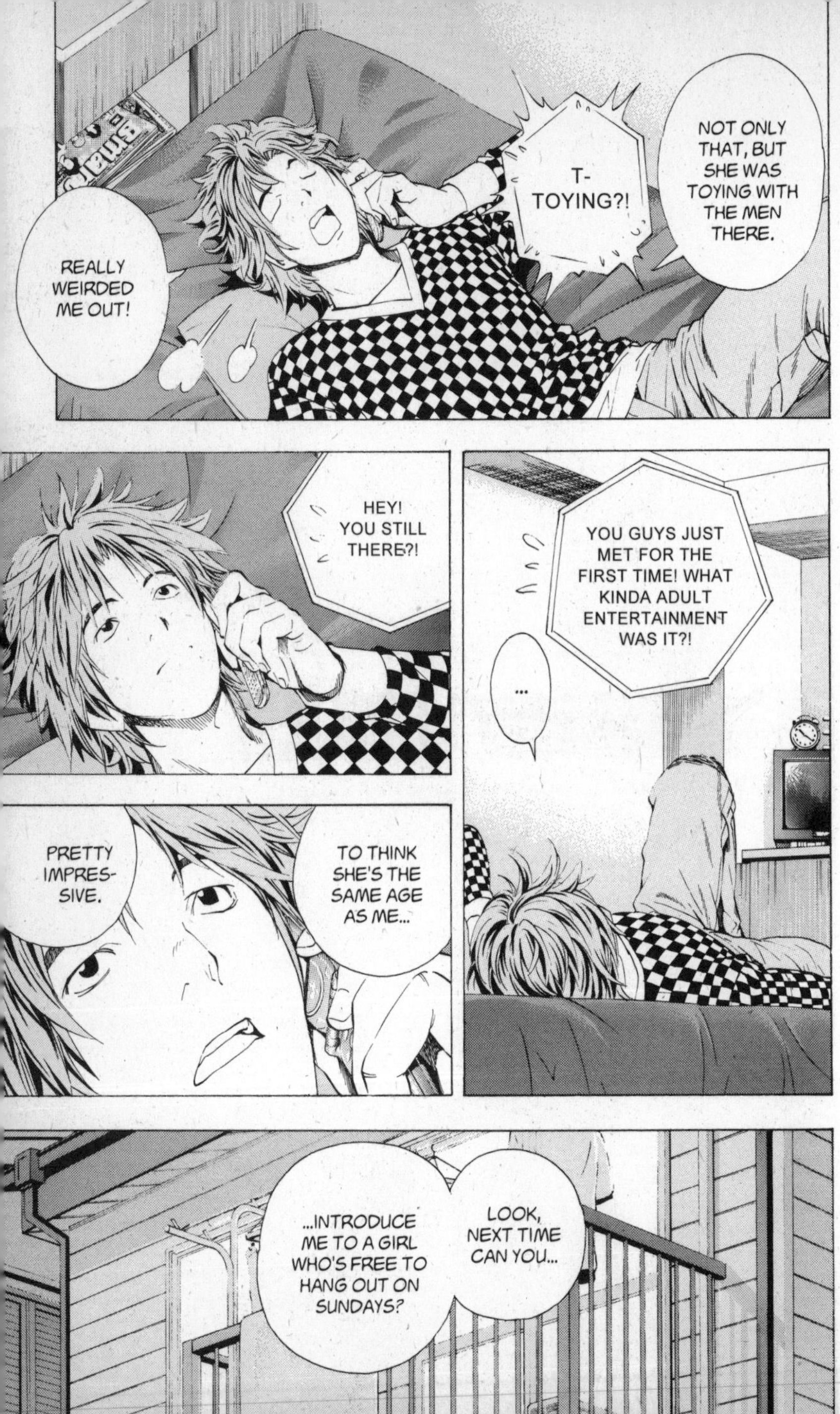
NOT ONLY THAT, BUT SHE WAS TOYING WITH THE MEN THERE.
T-TOYING?!
REALLY WEIRDED ME OUT!
YOU GUYS JUST MET FOR THE FIRST TIME! WHAT KINDA ADULT ENTERTAINMENT WAS IT?!
...
HEY! YOU STILL THERE?!
TO THINK SHE'S THE SAME AGE AS ME...
PRETTY IMPRES-SIVE.
LOOK, NEXT TIME CAN YOU...
...INTRODUCE ME TO A GIRL WHO'S FREE TO HANG OUT ON SUNDAYS?

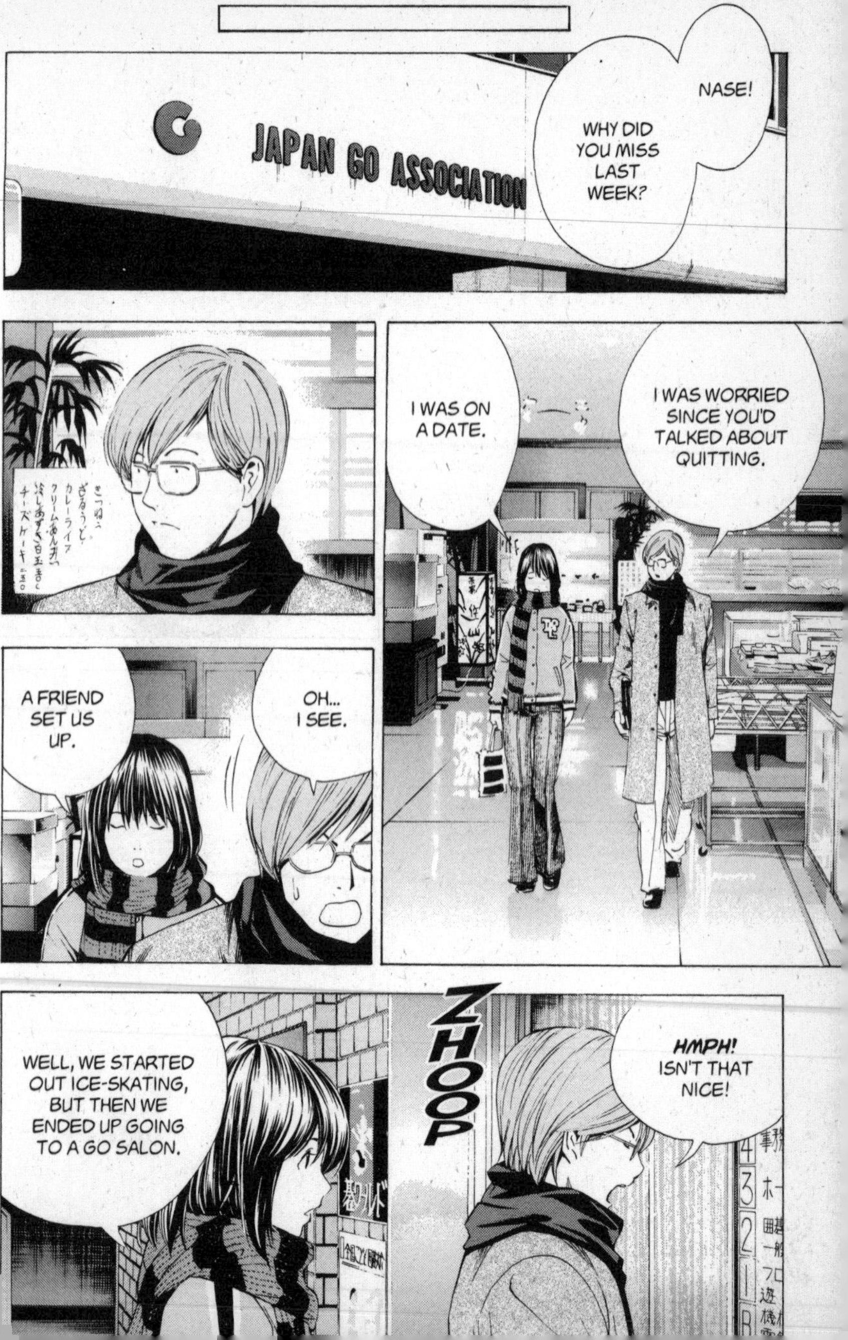
JAPAN GO ASSOCIATION
NASE!
WHY DID YOU MISS LAST WEEK?
I WAS WORRIED SINCE YOU'D TALKED ABOUT QUITTING.
I WAS ON A DATE.
OH... I SEE.
A FRIEND SET US UP.
HMPH! ISN'T THAT NICE!
ZHOOP
WELL, WE STARTED OUT ICE-SKATING, BUT THEN WE ENDED UP GOING TO A GO SALON.

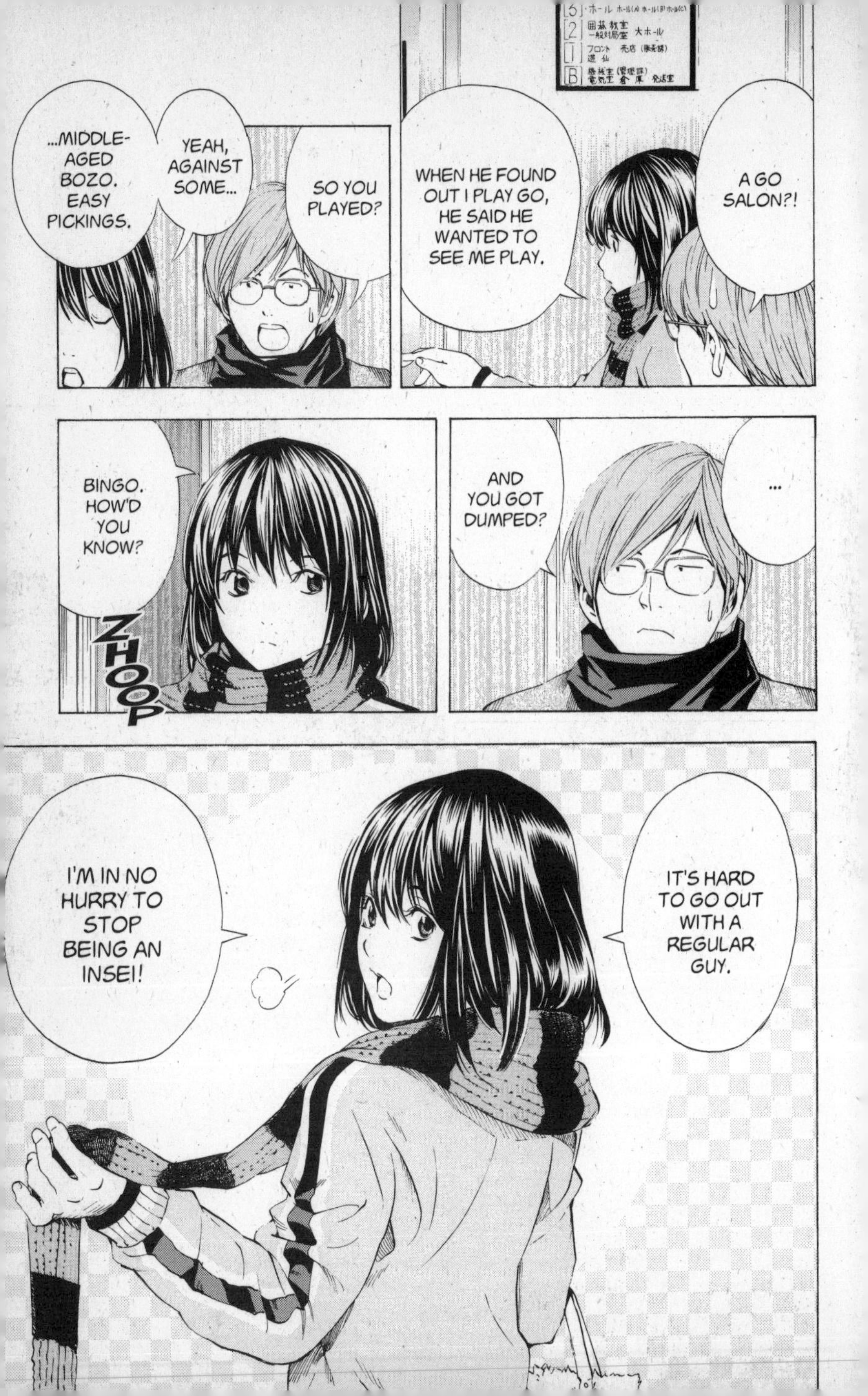
A GO SALON?!
WHEN HE FOUND OUT I PLAY GO, HE SAID HE WANTED TO SEE ME PLAY.
SO YOU PLAYED?
YEAH, AGAINST SOME...
...MIDDLE-AGED BOZO. EASY PICKINGS.
...
AND YOU GOT DUMPED?
BINGO. HOW'D YOU KNOW?
ZHOOP
IT'S HARD TO GO OUT WITH A REGULAR GUY.
I'M IN NO HURRY TO STOP BEING AN INSEI!

YUMI HOTTA'S LONG INTERVIEW WITH TAKESHI OBATA SENSEI: ③

Ⓞ FOR EXAMPLE, FOR THIS ONE (PAGE 045) THE EDITOR IN CHARGE OF COVERS GAVE ME A ROUGH SKETCH OF HIKARU BITING THE TV AND SAI LOOKING WORRIED.

Ⓗ HOW ABOUT (PAGE 069) WHERE SAI AND HIKARU ARE PLAYING GO ABOVE A BLANKET OF AUTUMN LEAVES? WAS THAT A *JUMP* COVER?

Ⓞ WHEN IT'S JUST A ONE-PAGE ILLUSTRATION, I GET INSTRUCTIONS ABOUT THE MOOD, BUT NOT AN ACTUAL SKETCH.

Ⓗ THIS IS A QUESTION ABOUT COLOR. SO FOR THE DRAWING YOU USE COPIC (AN ALCOHOL-BASED MARKER), BUT, FOR EXAMPLE, HOW DO YOU COLOR IN SKIN TONE?

Ⓞ STARTING WITH THE LIGHTEST COLOR, I OVERLAY FIVE OR SIX COLORS BEFORE EACH DRIES. LIKE E000, E00, E09...

Ⓗ E000! SO LIGHT! I USE E21--JUST ONE HUE! (LAUGHTER)

Ⓞ I USE E21 FOR SHADOW. WHEN I'M REALLY TRYING TO GET SAI'S SKIN COLOR, I USE THE R SERIES. WHEN I'M IN A HURRY I USE THE E SERIES (THAT I USE FOR HIKARU).

Ⓗ HOW LONG DOES THE COLORING TAKE? YOU SAID JUNGLE (PAGE 037) TOOK 24 HOURS.

Ⓞ THE COVER OF VOLUME 15, WHERE SAI IS DANCING (PAGE 080) TOOK 9 HOURS JUST FOR THE COLORING. THE ONE WHERE HIKARU AND AKIRA ARE STANDING TOGETHER (PAGE 066) WAS QUICK--3 TO 4 HOURS FROM PENCILING TO COMPLETION.

(Continued on page 136)

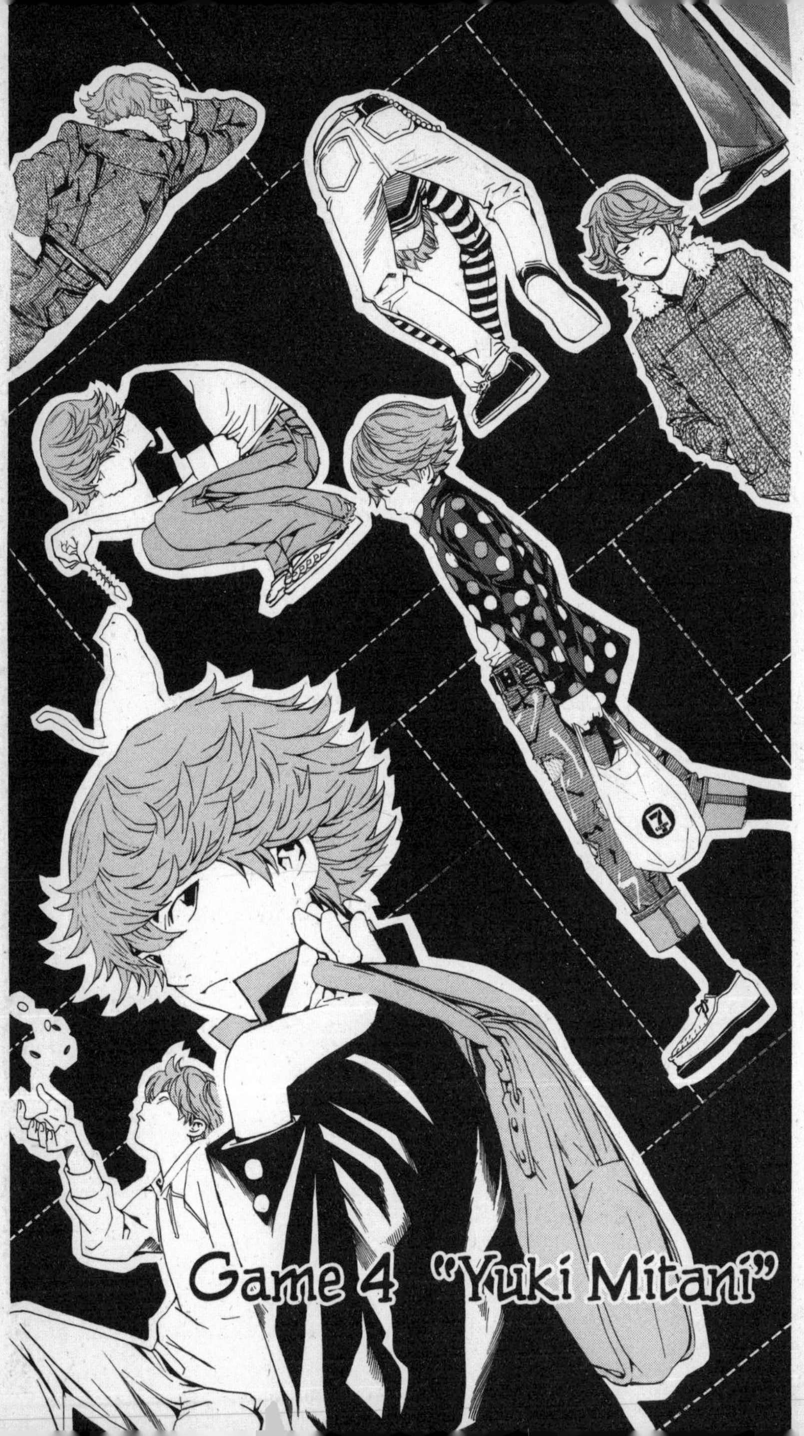
Game 4 "Yuki Mitani"

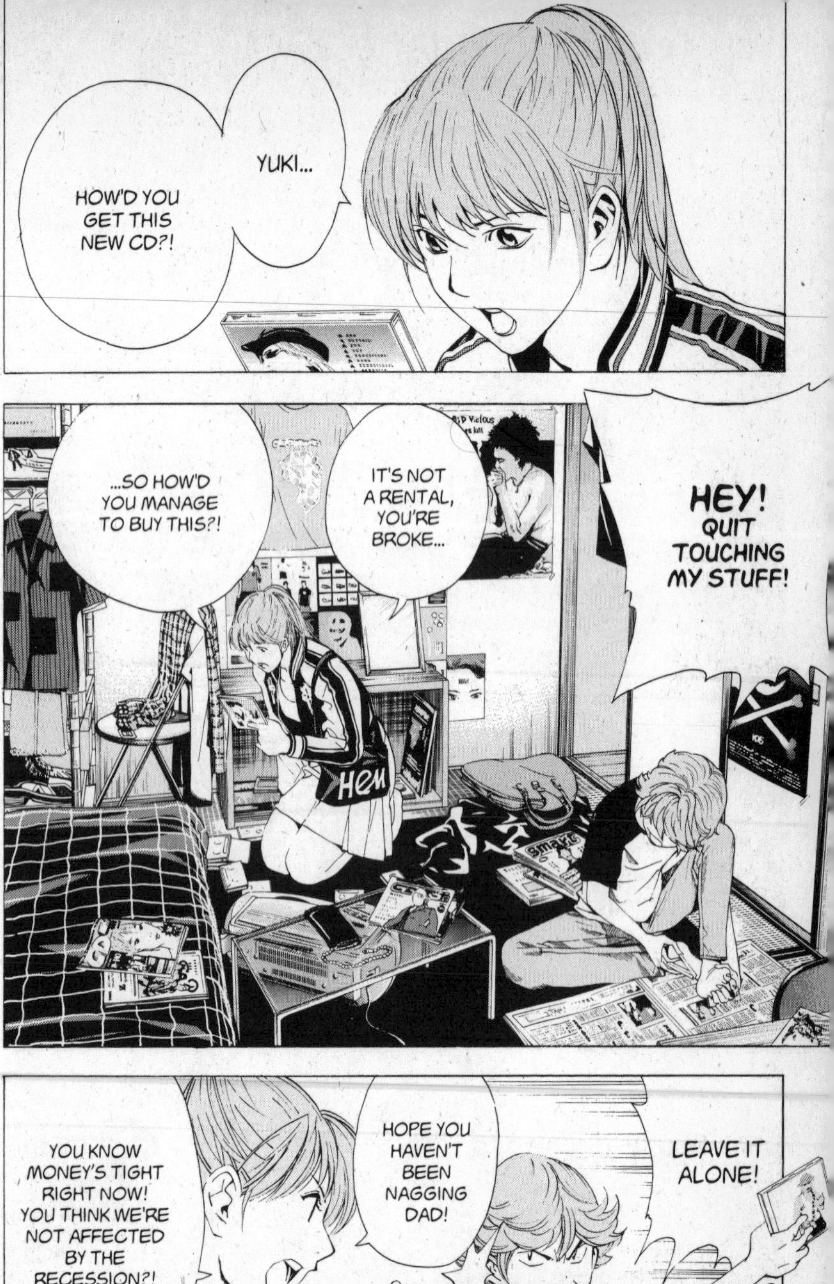
YUKI...
HOW'D YOU GET THIS NEW CD?!
HEY! QUIT TOUCHING MY STUFF!
IT'S NOT A RENTAL, YOU'RE BROKE...
...SO HOW'D YOU MANAGE TO BUY THIS?!
LEAVE IT ALONE!
HOPE YOU HAVEN'T BEEN NAGGING DAD!
YOU KNOW MONEY'S TIGHT RIGHT NOW! YOU THINK WE'RE NOT AFFECTED BY THE RECESSION?!

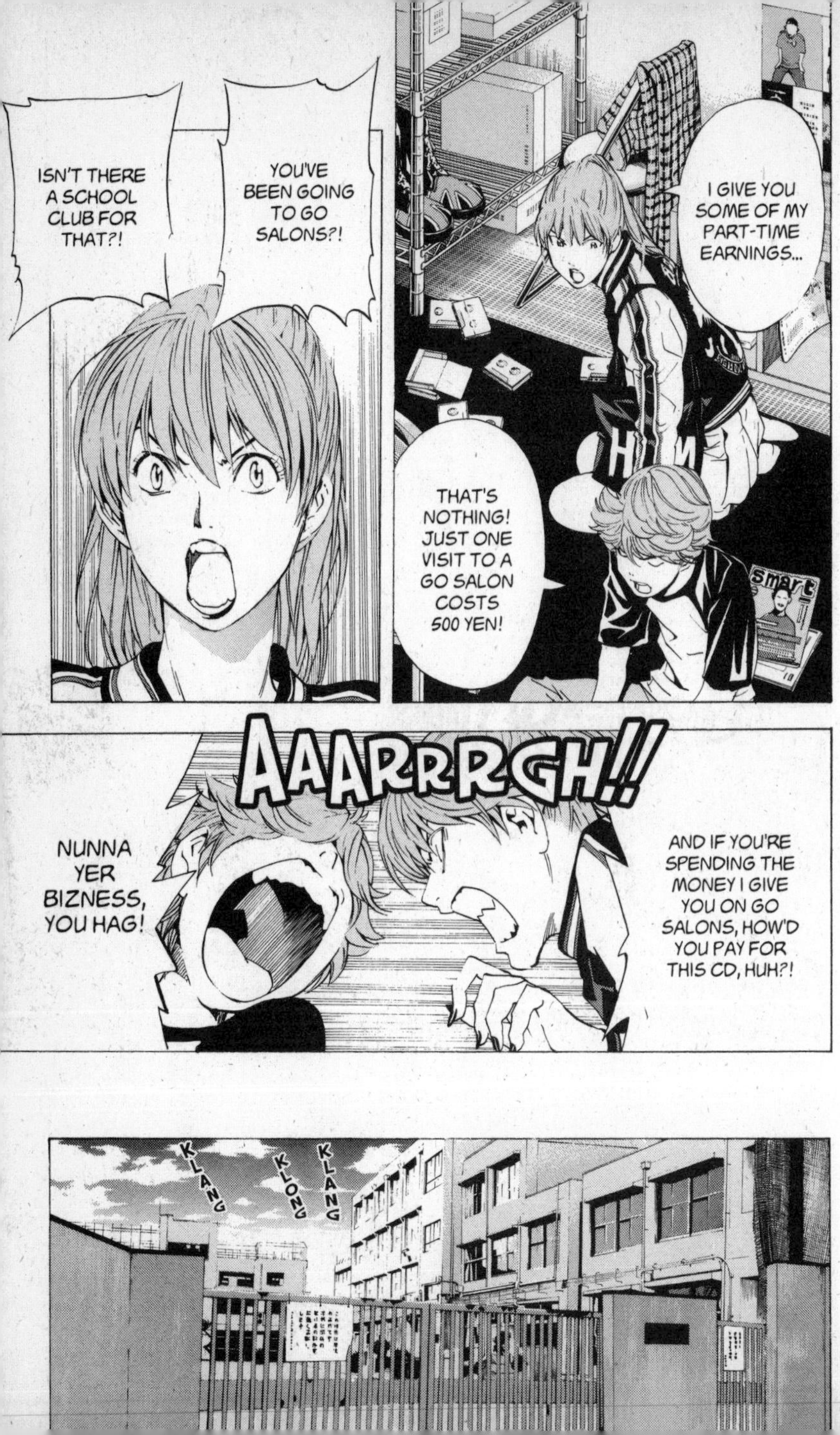
I GIVE YOU SOME OF MY PART-TIME EARNINGS...
THAT'S NOTHING! JUST ONE VISIT TO A GO SALON COSTS 500 YEN!
smart
YOU'VE BEEN GOING TO GO SALONS?!
ISN'T THERE A SCHOOL CLUB FOR THAT?!
AAARRRGH!!
AND IF YOU'RE SPENDING THE MONEY I GIVE YOU ON GO SALONS, HOW'D YOU PAY FOR THIS CD, HUH?!
NUNNA YER BIZNESS, YOU HAG!
KLANG
KLONG
KLANG

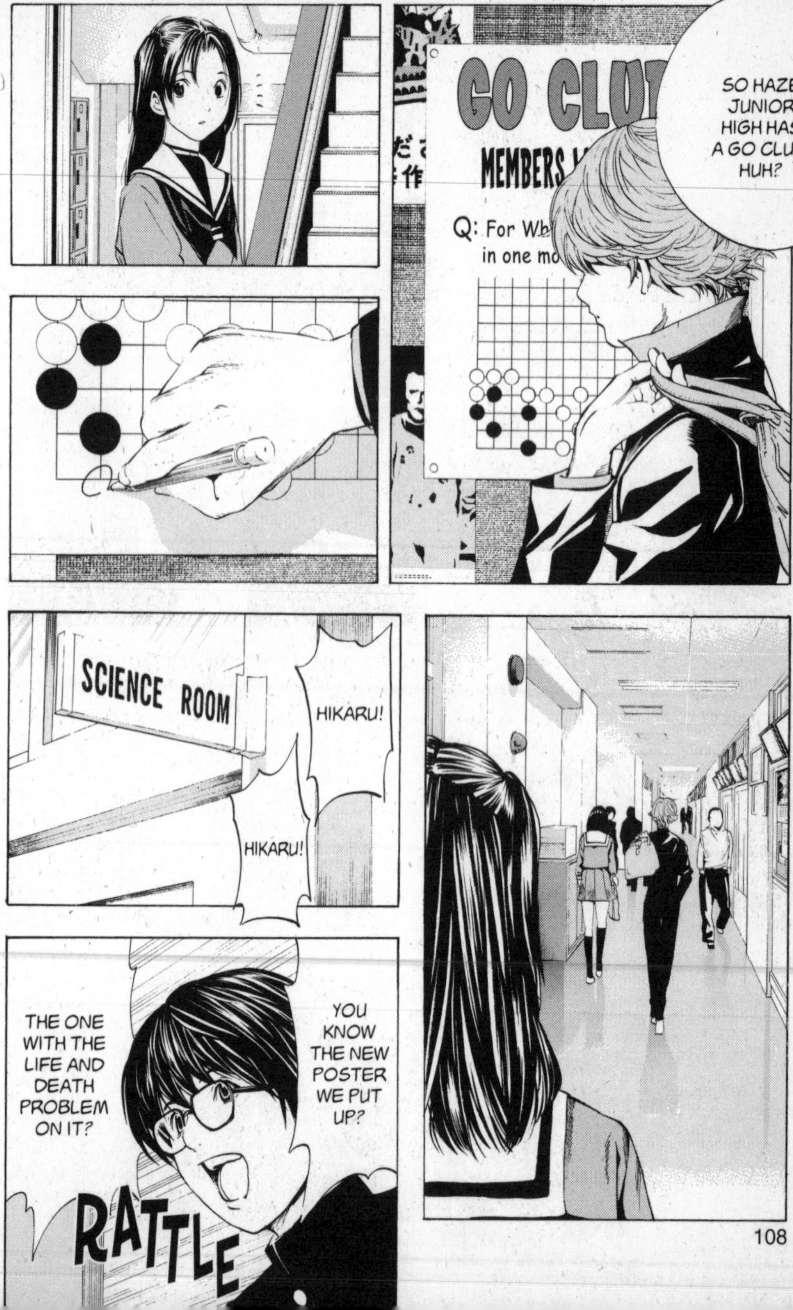

SO HAZE JUNIOR HIGH HAS A GO CLUB, HUH?
SCIENCE ROOM
HIKARU!
HIKARU!
YOU KNOW THE NEW POSTER WE PUT UP?
THE ONE WITH THE LIFE AND DEATH PROBLEM ON IT?
RATTLE

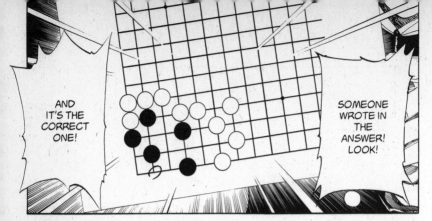

SOMEONE WROTE IN THE ANSWER! LOOK!
AND IT'S THE CORRECT ONE!
IT'S AN ADVANCED PROBLEM. THIS GUY MUST BE SHARP!
WE GOTTA FIND WHO DID IT!
I KNOW WHO IT IS.
WHO?!
AND HOW DO YOU KNOW?!
WELL, I SAW HIM.
IT WAS MITANI, IN ROOM 3.

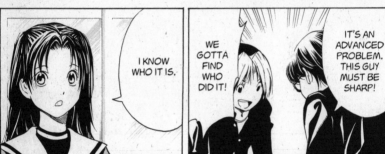

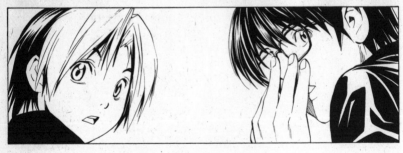

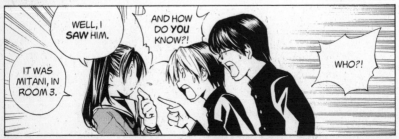

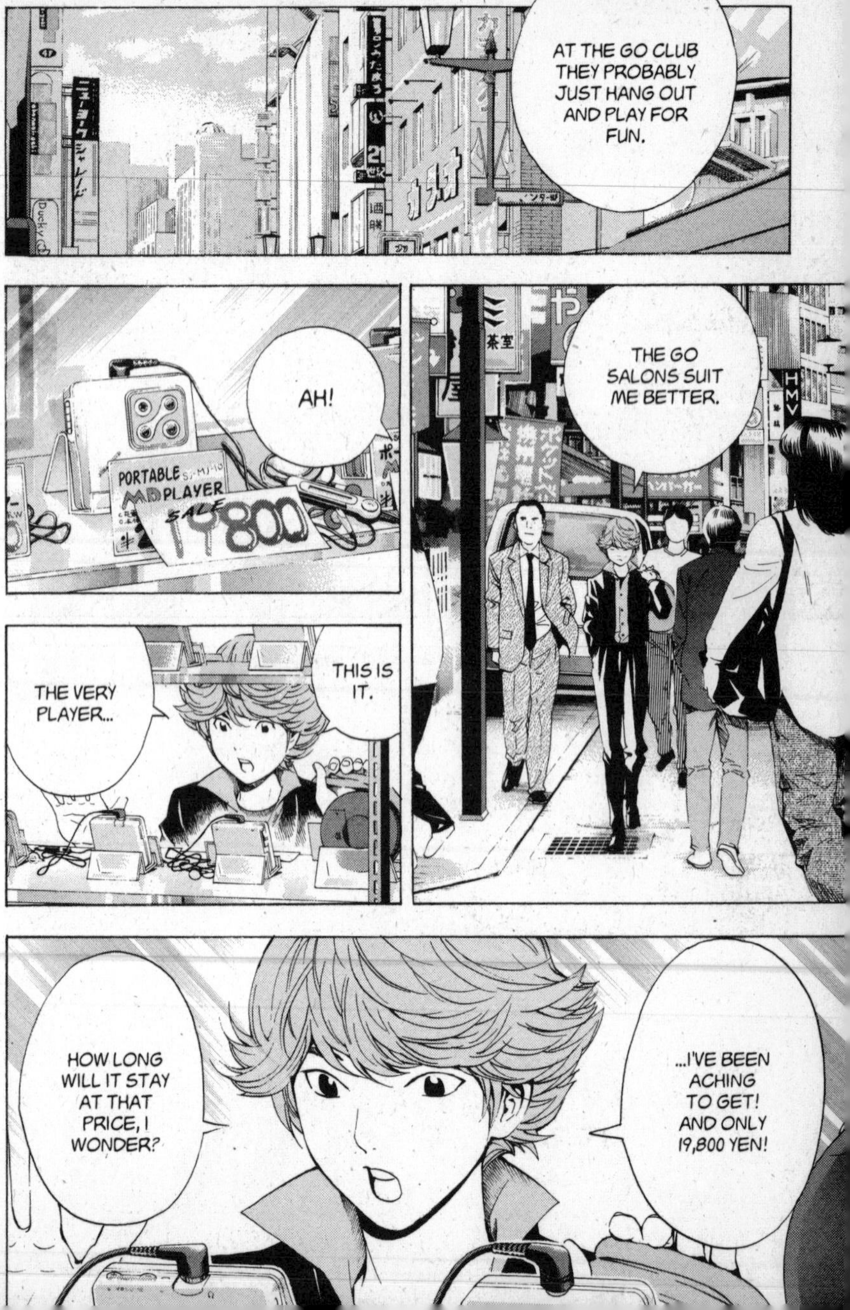
AT THE GO CLUB THEY PROBABLY JUST HANG OUT AND PLAY FOR FUN.
THE GO SALONS SUIT ME BETTER.
AH!
PORTABLE MD PLAYER
SALE 19800
THIS IS IT.
THE VERY PLAYER...
...I'VE BEEN ACHING TO GET! AND ONLY 19,800 YEN!
HOW LONG WILL IT STAY AT THAT PRICE, I WONDER?

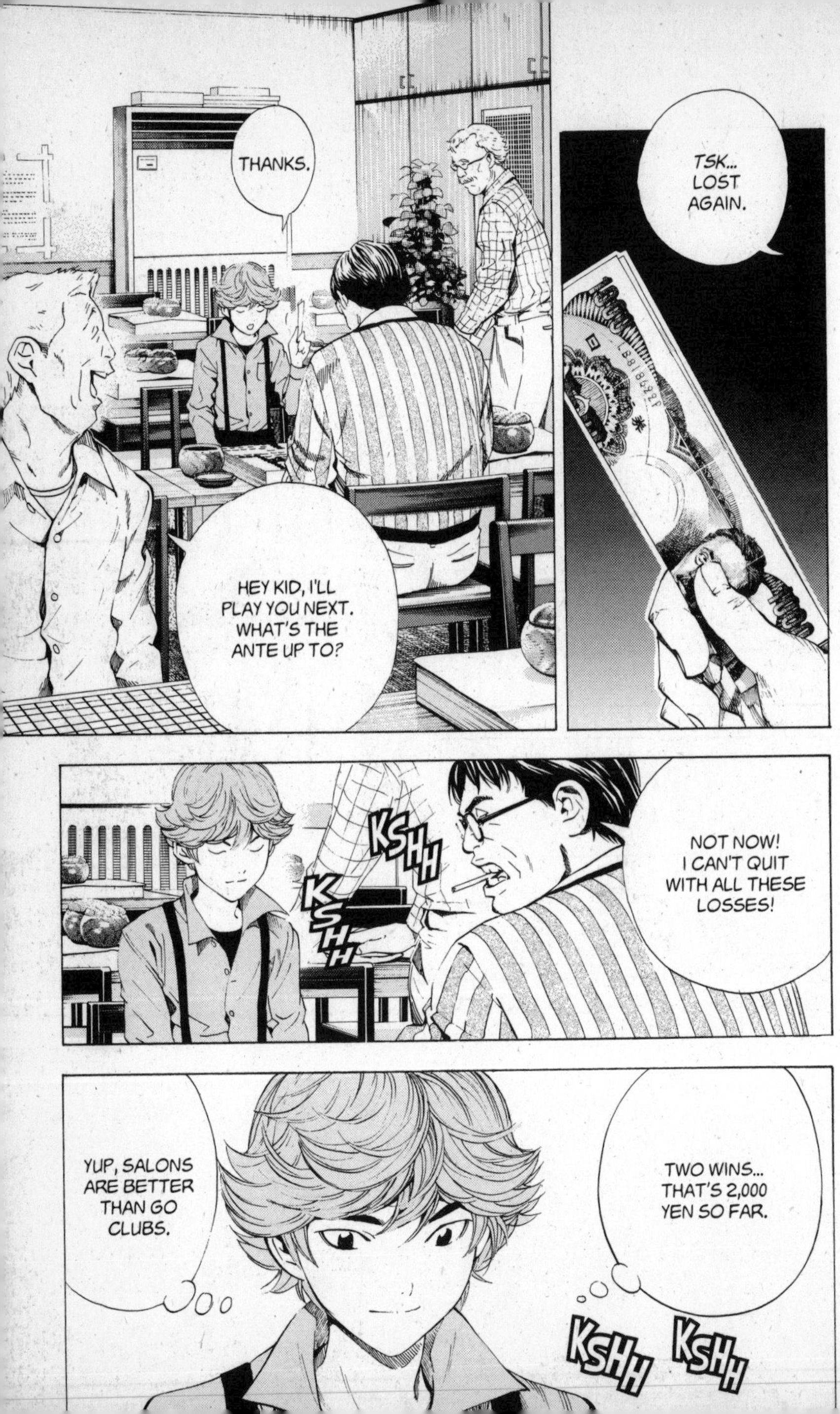
TSK... LOST AGAIN.
THANKS.
HEY KID, I'LL PLAY YOU NEXT. WHAT'S THE ANTE UP TO?
NOT NOW! I CAN'T QUIT WITH ALL THESE LOSSES!
KSHH
KSHH
TWO WINS... THAT'S 2,000 YEN SO FAR.
YUP, SALONS ARE BETTER THAN GO CLUBS.
KSHH
KSHH

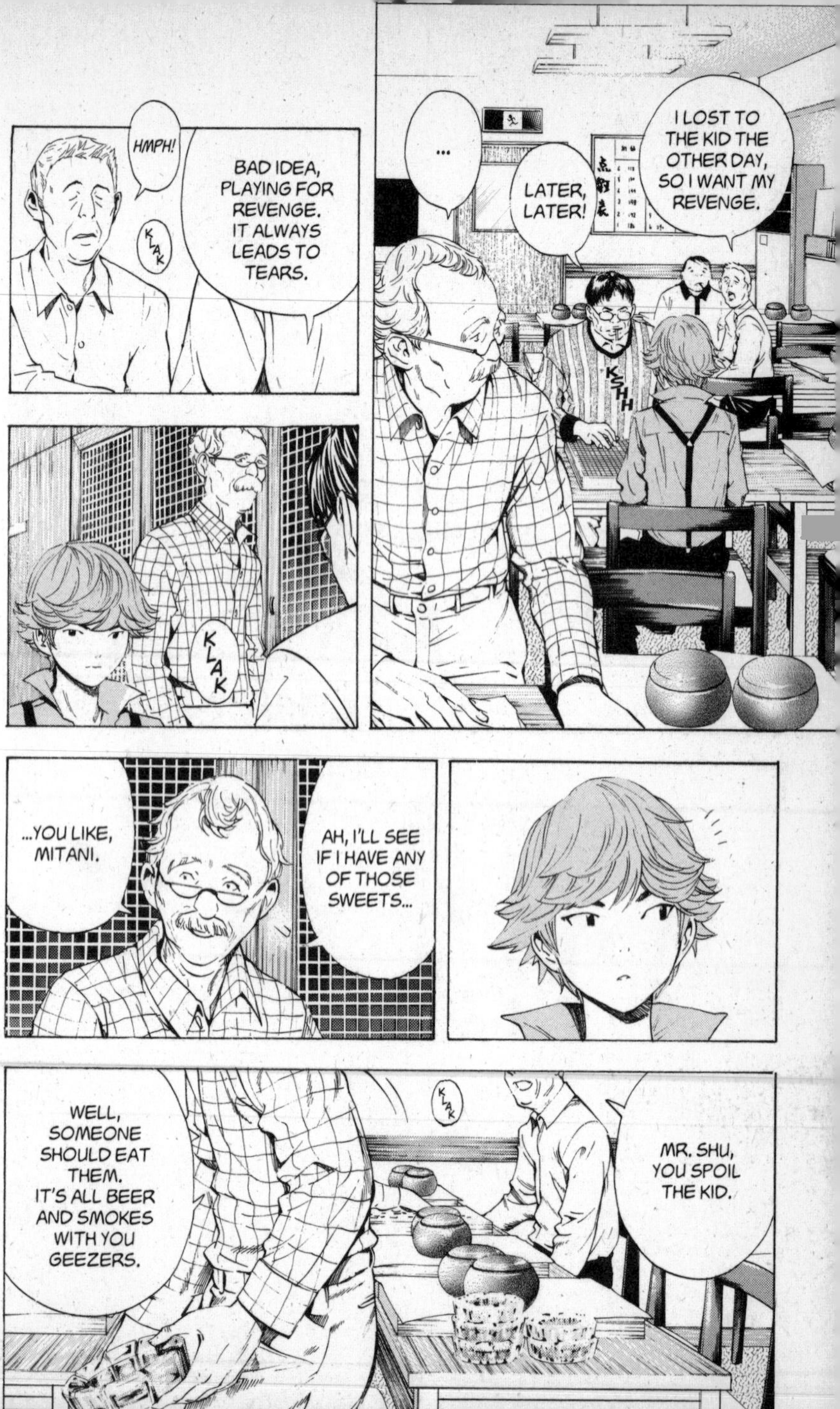
I LOST TO THE KID THE OTHER DAY, SO I WANT MY REVENGE.
LATER, LATER!
...
KSHH
BAD IDEA, PLAYING FOR REVENGE. IT ALWAYS LEADS TO TEARS.
HMPH!
KLAK
KLAK
AH, I'LL SEE IF I HAVE ANY OF THOSE SWEETS...
...YOU LIKE, MITANI.
MR. SHU, YOU SPOIL THE KID.
KLAK
WELL, SOMEONE SHOULD EAT THEM. IT'S ALL BEER AND SMOKES WITH YOU GEEZERS.

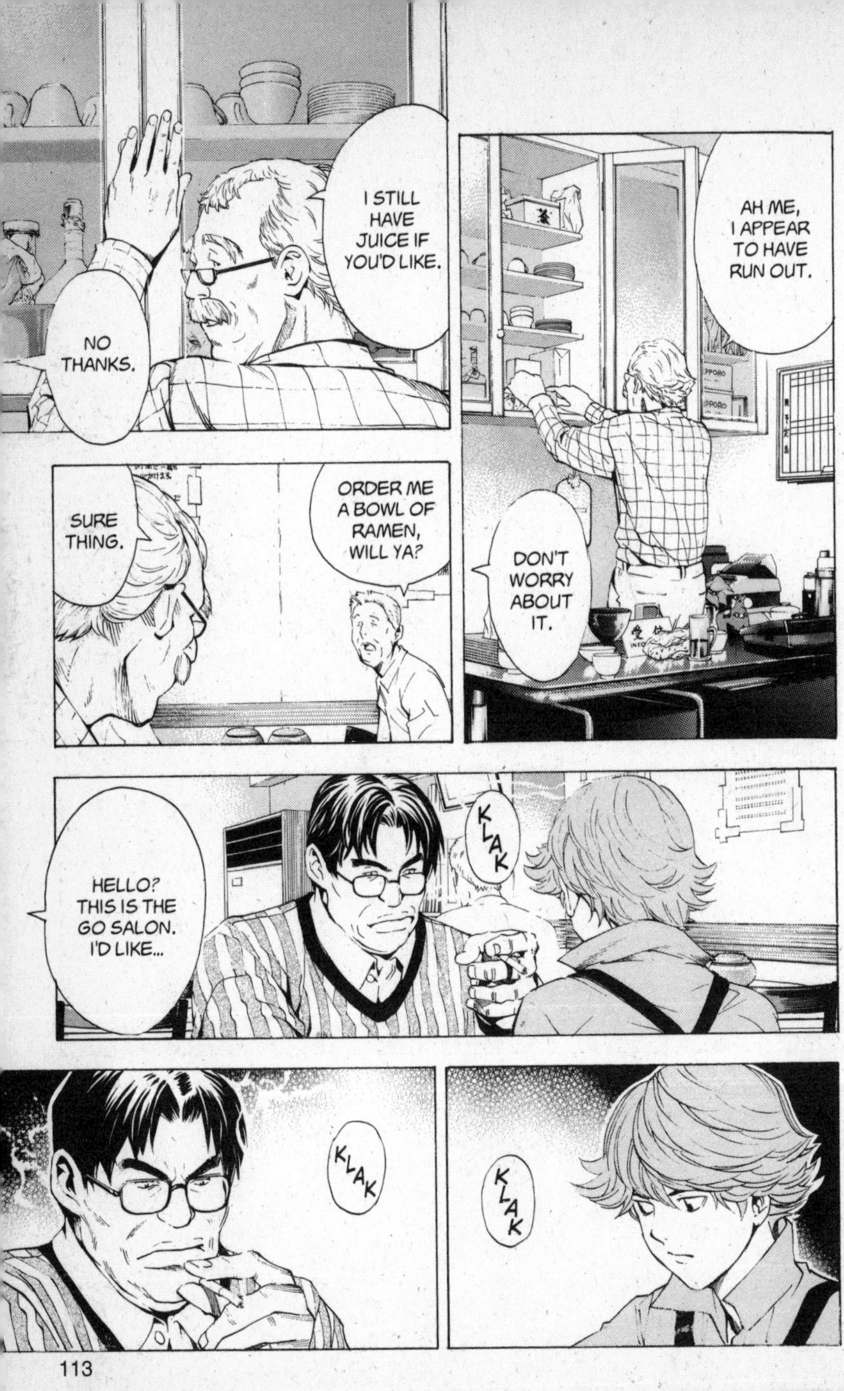
AH ME, I APPEAR TO HAVE RUN OUT.
DON'T WORRY ABOUT IT.
I STILL HAVE JUICE IF YOU'D LIKE.
NO THANKS.
ORDER ME A BOWL OF RAMEN, WILL YA?
SURE THING.
KLAK
HELLO? THIS IS THE GO SALON. I'D LIKE...
KLAK
KLAK

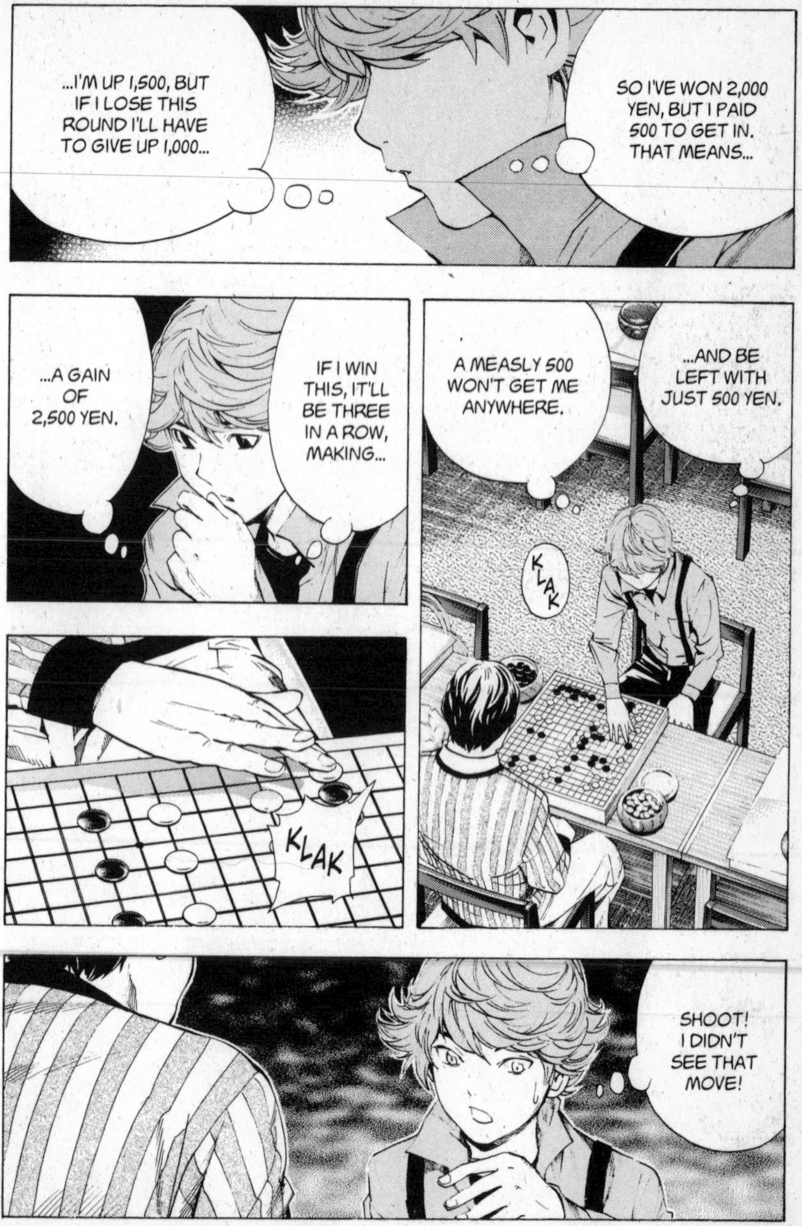
SO I'VE WON 2,000 YEN, BUT I PAID 500 TO GET IN. THAT MEANS...
...I'M UP 1,500, BUT IF I LOSE THIS ROUND I'LL HAVE TO GIVE UP 1,000...
...AND BE LEFT WITH JUST 500 YEN.
A MEASLY 500 WON'T GET ME ANYWHERE.
KLAK
IF I WIN THIS, IT'LL BE THREE IN A ROW, MAKING...
...A GAIN OF 2,500 YEN.
KLAK
SHOOT! I DIDN'T SEE THAT MOVE!

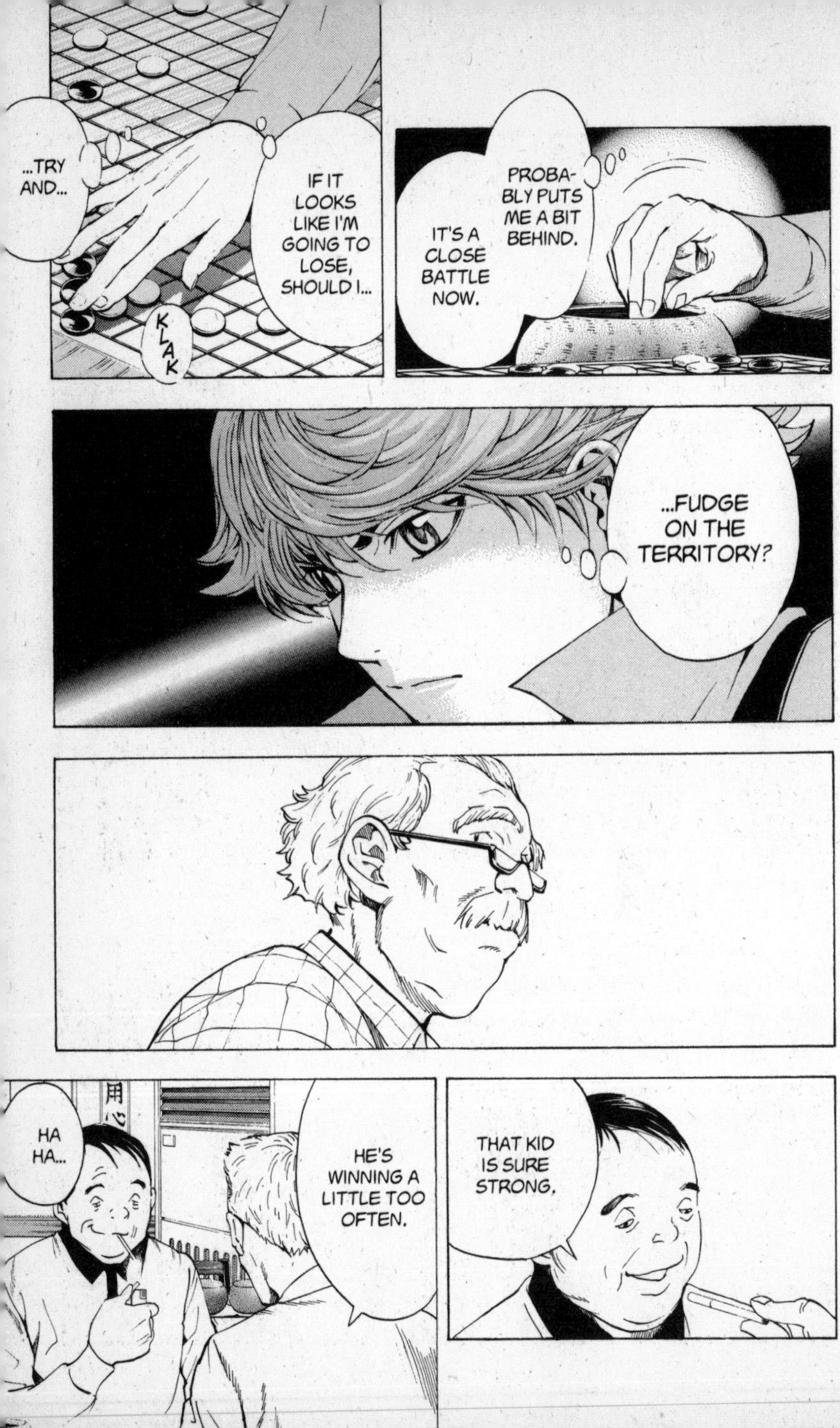
PROBA-BLY PUTS ME A BIT BEHIND.
IT'S A CLOSE BATTLE NOW.
IF IT LOOKS LIKE I'M GOING TO LOSE, SHOULD I...
...TRY AND...
KLAK
...FUDGE ON THE TERRITORY?
THAT KID IS SURE STRONG.
HE'S WINNING A LITTLE TOO OFTEN.
HA HA...

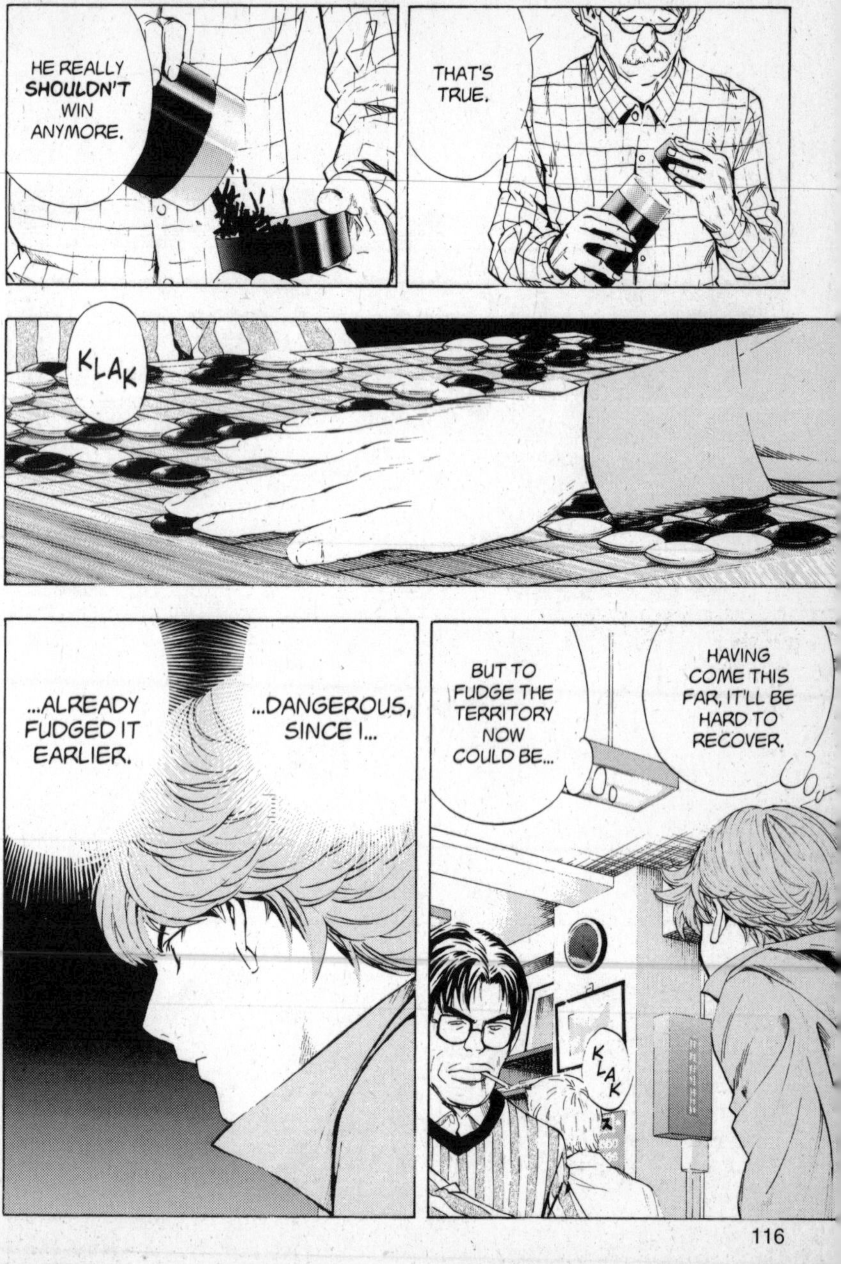
THAT'S TRUE.
HE REALLY SHOULDN'T WIN ANYMORE.
KLAK
HAVING COME THIS FAR, IT'LL BE HARD TO RECOVER.
BUT TO FUDGE THE TERRITORY NOW COULD BE...
KLAK
...DANGEROUS, SINCE I...
...ALREADY FUDGED IT EARLIER.

READ THIS WAY

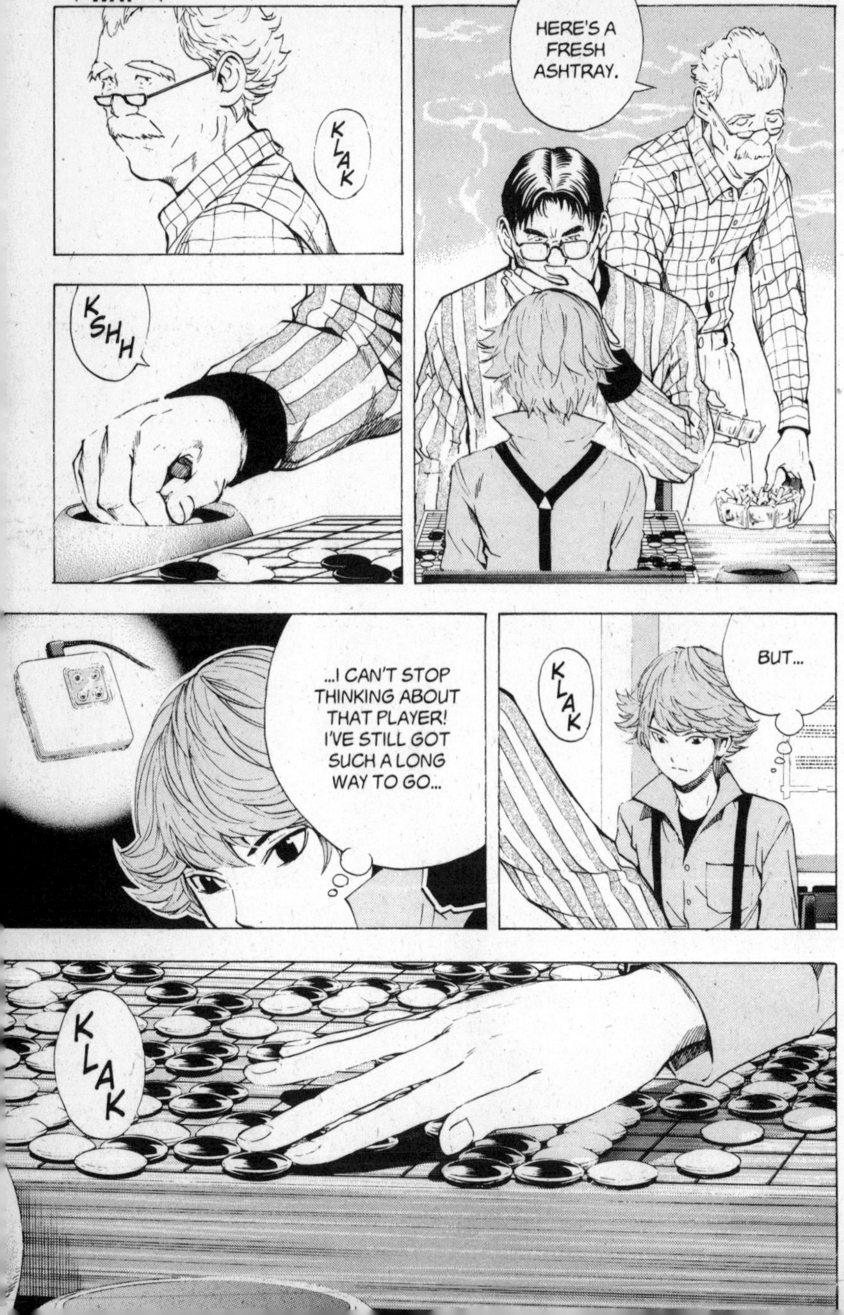
HERE'S A FRESH ASHTRAY.
KLAK
KSHH
KLAK
BUT...
...I CAN'T STOP THINKING ABOUT THAT PLAYER! I'VE STILL GOT SUCH A LONG WAY TO GO...
KLAK

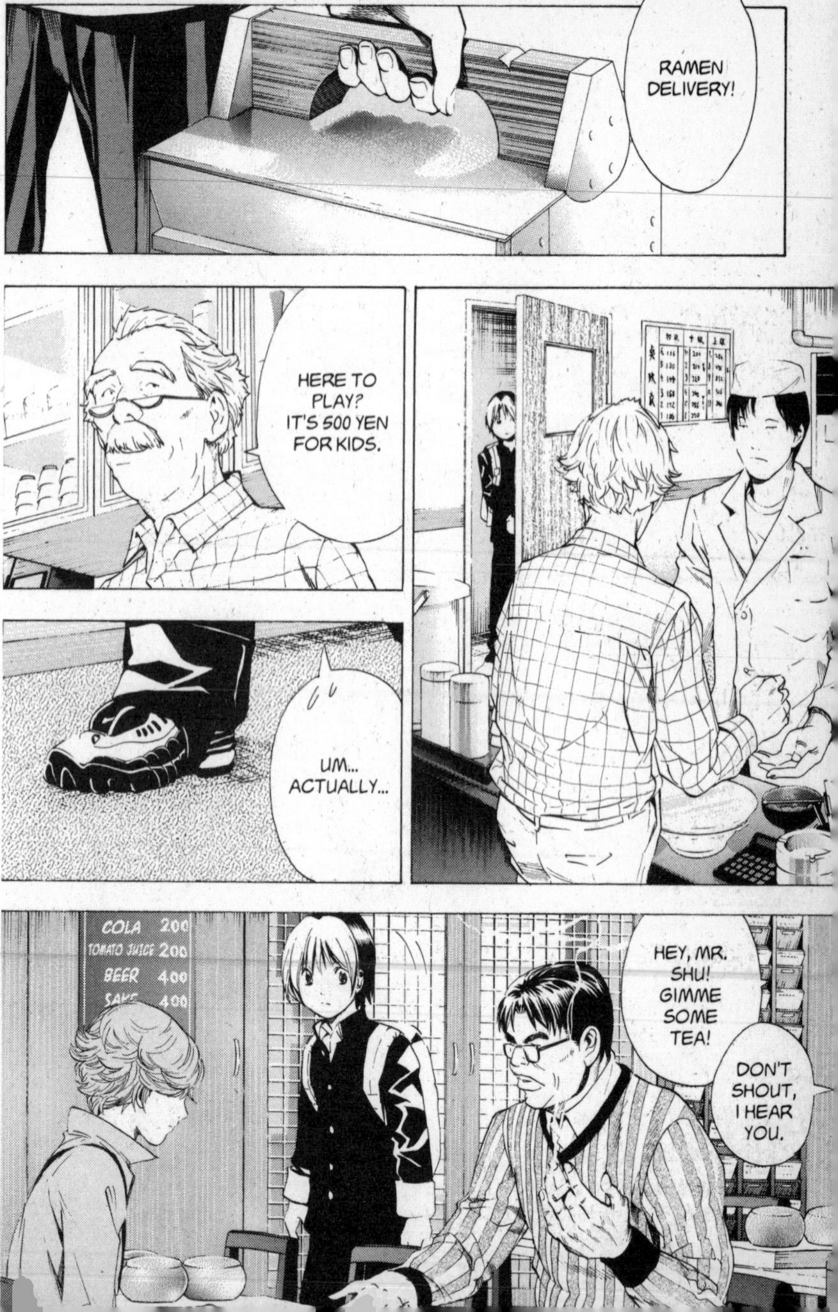
RAMEN DELIVERY!
HERE TO PLAY? IT'S 500 YEN FOR KIDS.
UM... ACTUALLY...
HEY, MR. SHU! GIMME SOME TEA!
DON'T SHOUT, I HEAR YOU.
COLA 200
TOMATO JUICE 200
BEER 400

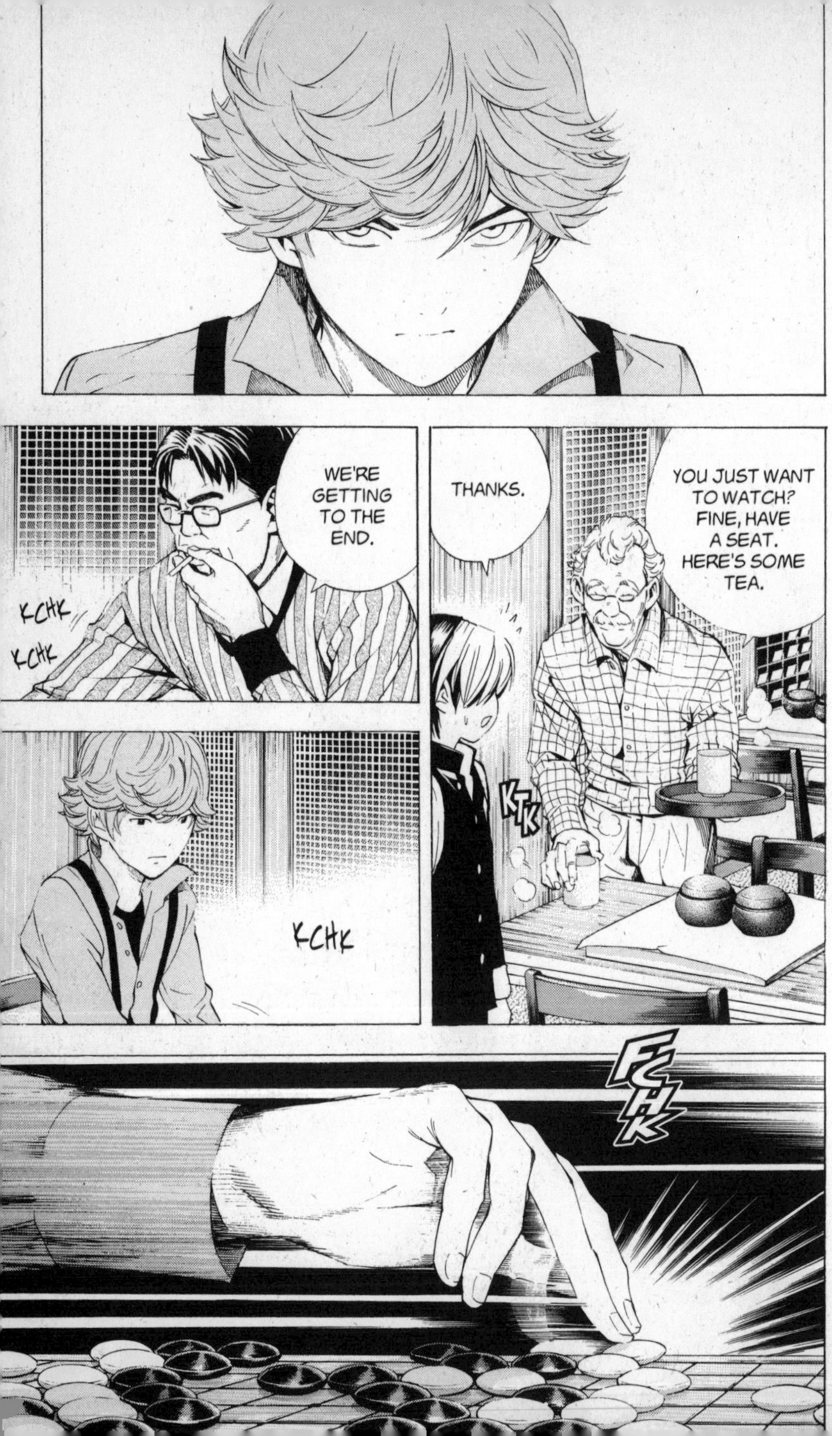
YOU JUST WANT TO WATCH? FINE, HAVE A SEAT. HERE'S SOME TEA.
THANKS.
KTK
WE'RE GETTING TO THE END.
KCHK
KCHK
KCHK
FCHK

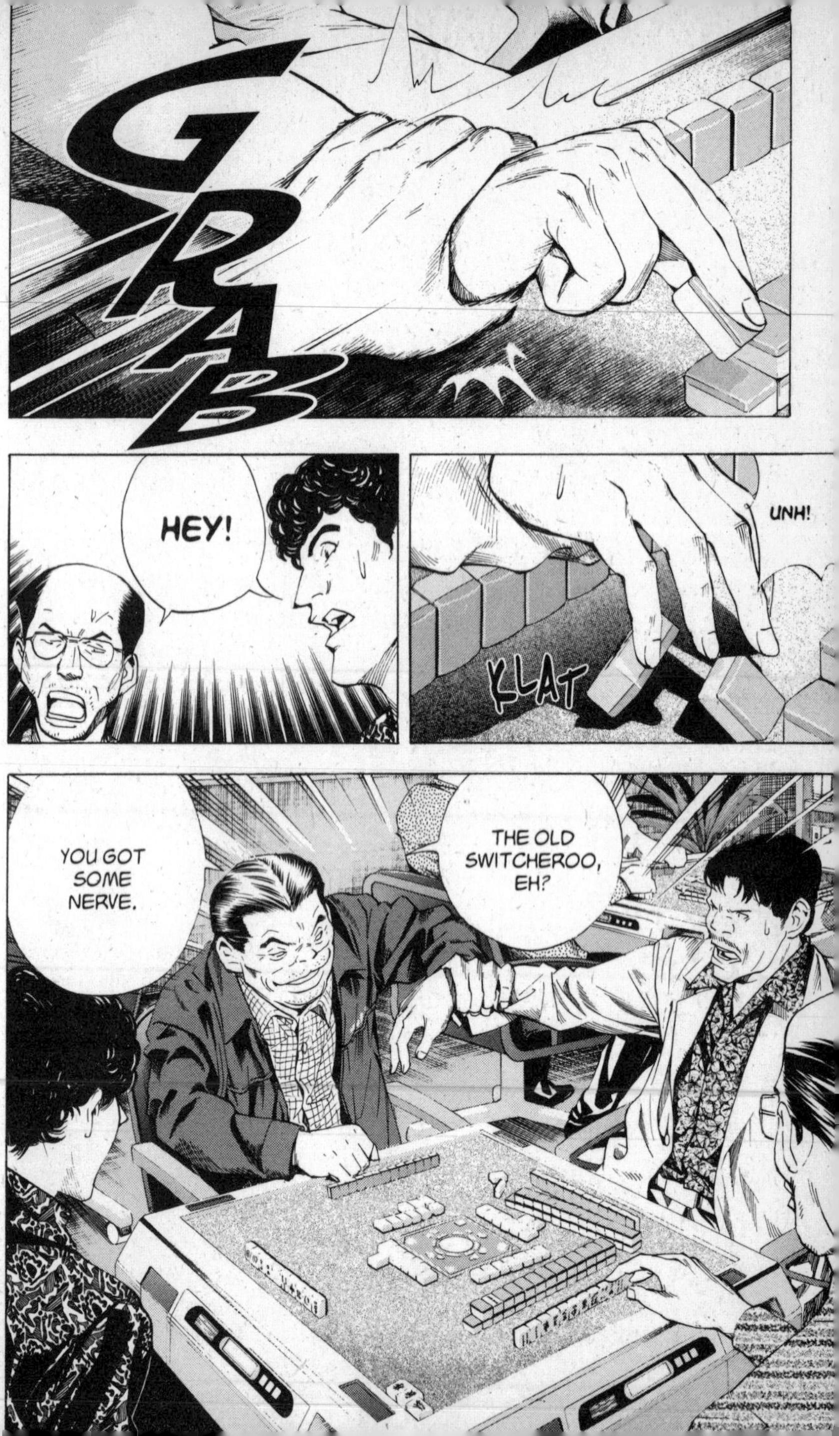
GRAB
UNH!
KLAT
HEY!
THE OLD SWITCHEROO, EH?
YOU GOT SOME NERVE.

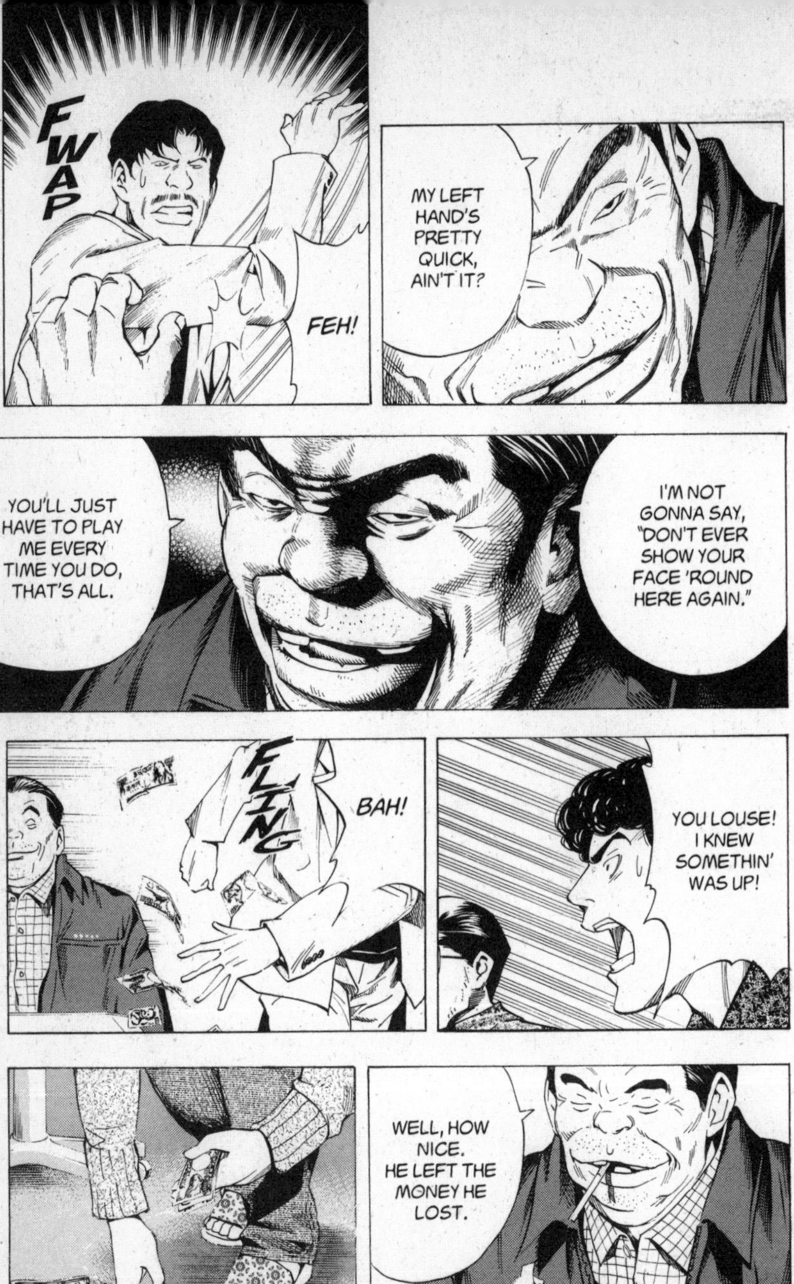
MY LEFT HAND'S PRETTY QUICK, AIN'T IT?
FWAP
FEH!
I'M NOT GONNA SAY, "DON'T EVER SHOW YOUR FACE 'ROUND HERE AGAIN."
YOU'LL JUST HAVE TO PLAY ME EVERY TIME YOU DO, THAT'S ALL.
YOU LOUSE! I KNEW SOMETHIN' WAS UP!
FLING
BAH!
WELL, HOW NICE. HE LEFT THE MONEY HE LOST.

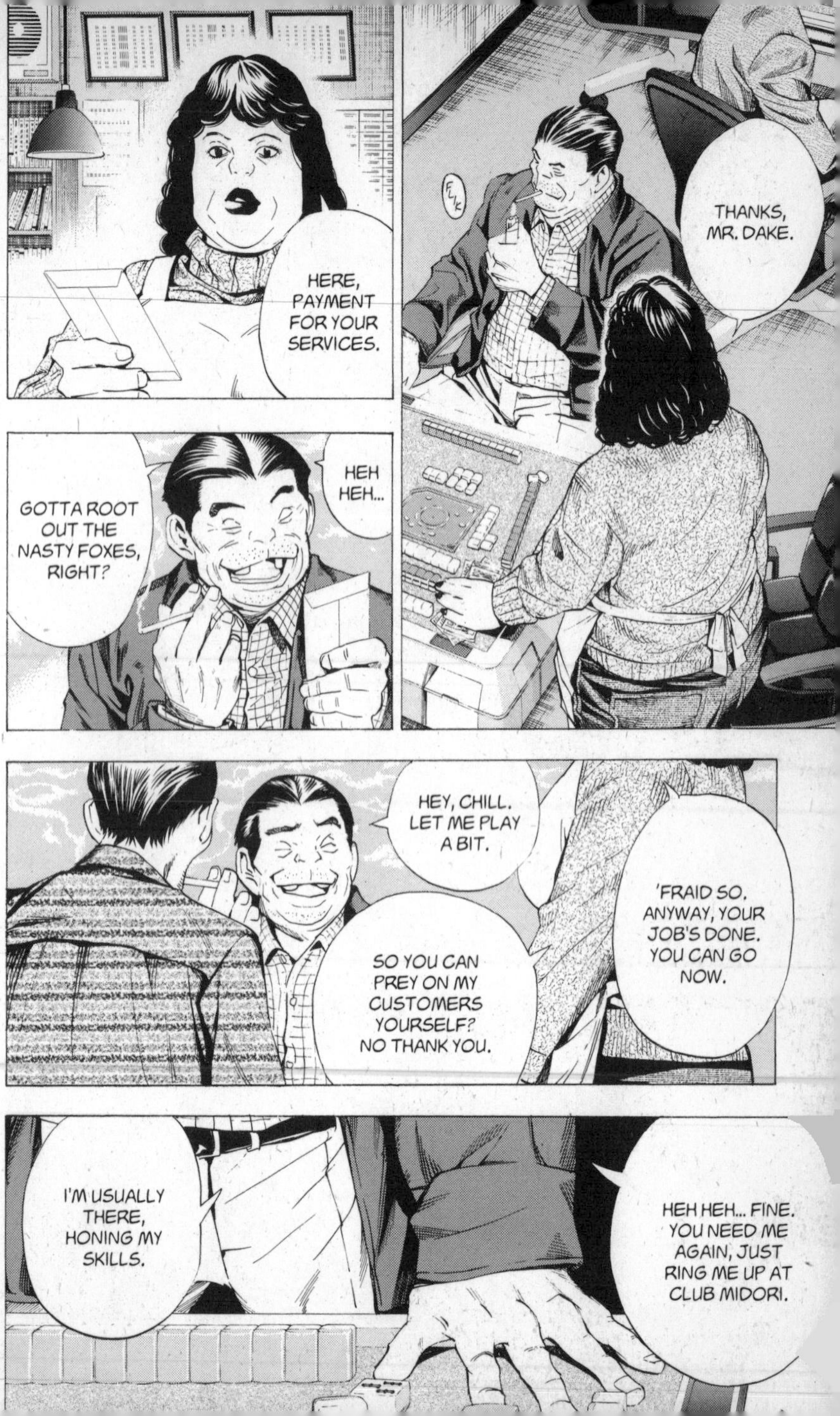
FLIK
THANKS, MR. DAKE.
HERE, PAYMENT FOR YOUR SERVICES.
HEH HEH...
GOTTA ROOT OUT THE NASTY FOXES, RIGHT?
'FRAID SO. ANYWAY, YOUR JOB'S DONE. YOU CAN GO NOW.
HEY, CHILL. LET ME PLAY A BIT.
SO YOU CAN PREY ON MY CUSTOMERS YOURSELF? NO THANK YOU.
HEH HEH... FINE. YOU NEED ME AGAIN, JUST RING ME UP AT CLUB MIDORI.
I'M USUALLY THERE, HONING MY SKILLS.

SHHK

HUH?
NOT QUITE
ENOUGH?
I THOUGHT I'D
DONE A LITTLE
BETTER THAN
YOU.

HERE.

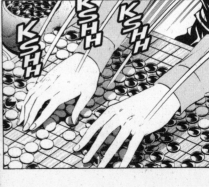

KSHH KSHH KSHH

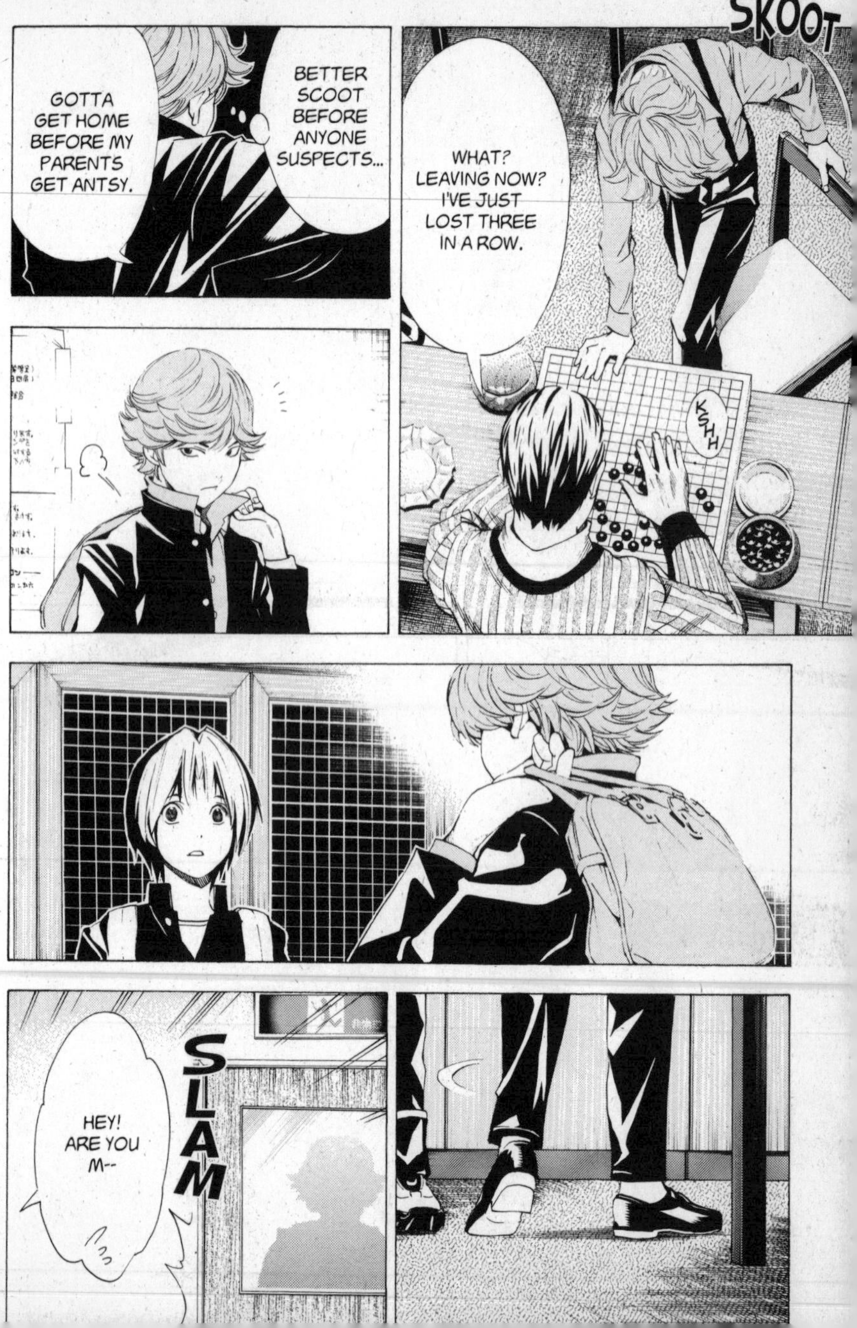
SKOOT
WHAT? LEAVING NOW? I'VE JUST LOST THREE IN A ROW.
KSHH
BETTER SCOOT BEFORE ANYONE SUSPECTS...
GOTTA GET HOME BEFORE MY PARENTS GET ANTSY.
SLAM
HEY! ARE YOU M--

READ THIS WAY

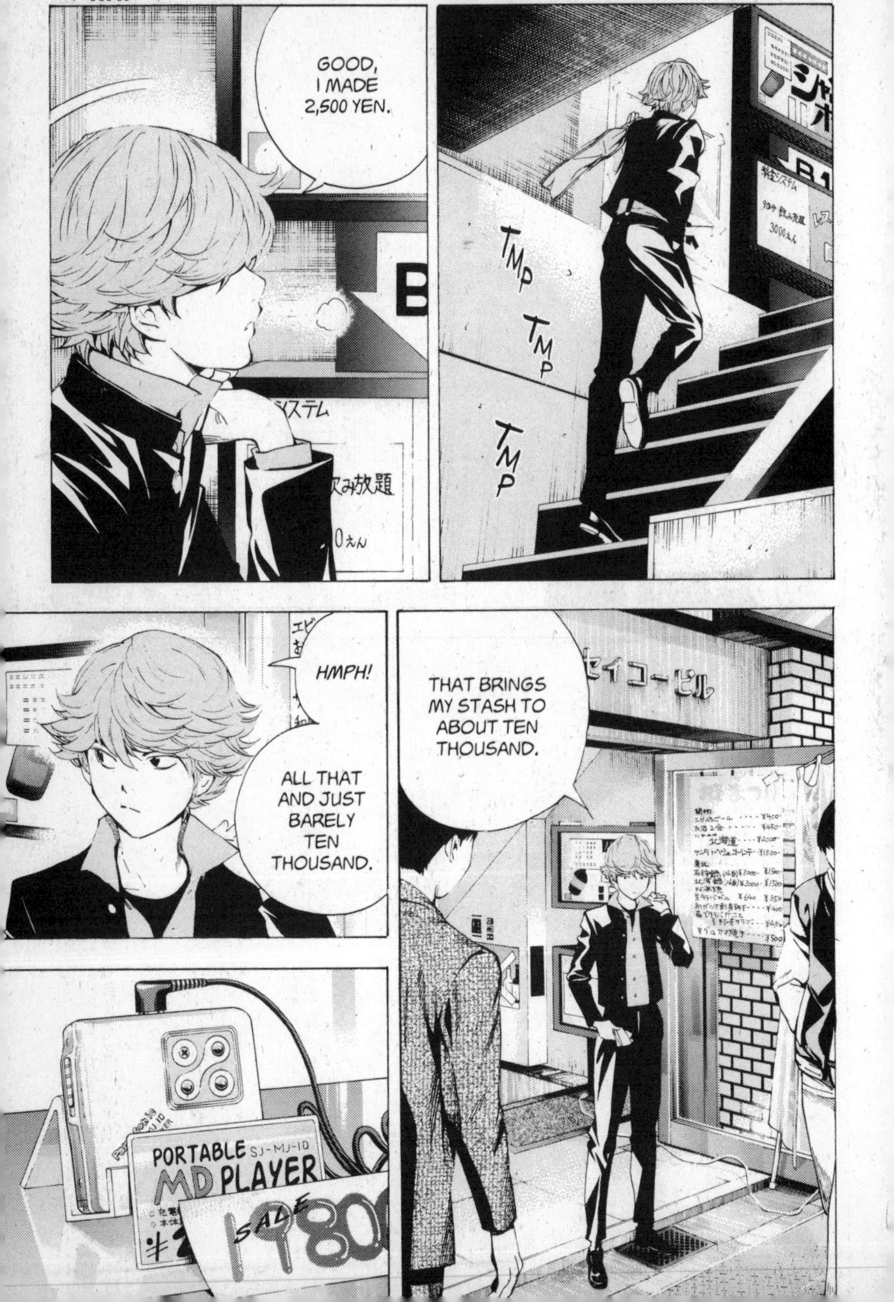
TMP
TMP
TMP
GOOD, I MADE 2,500 YEN.
THAT BRINGS MY STASH TO ABOUT TEN THOUSAND.
HMPH!
ALL THAT AND JUST BARELY TEN THOUSAND.
PORTABLE SJ-MJ-10
MD PLAYER
SALE

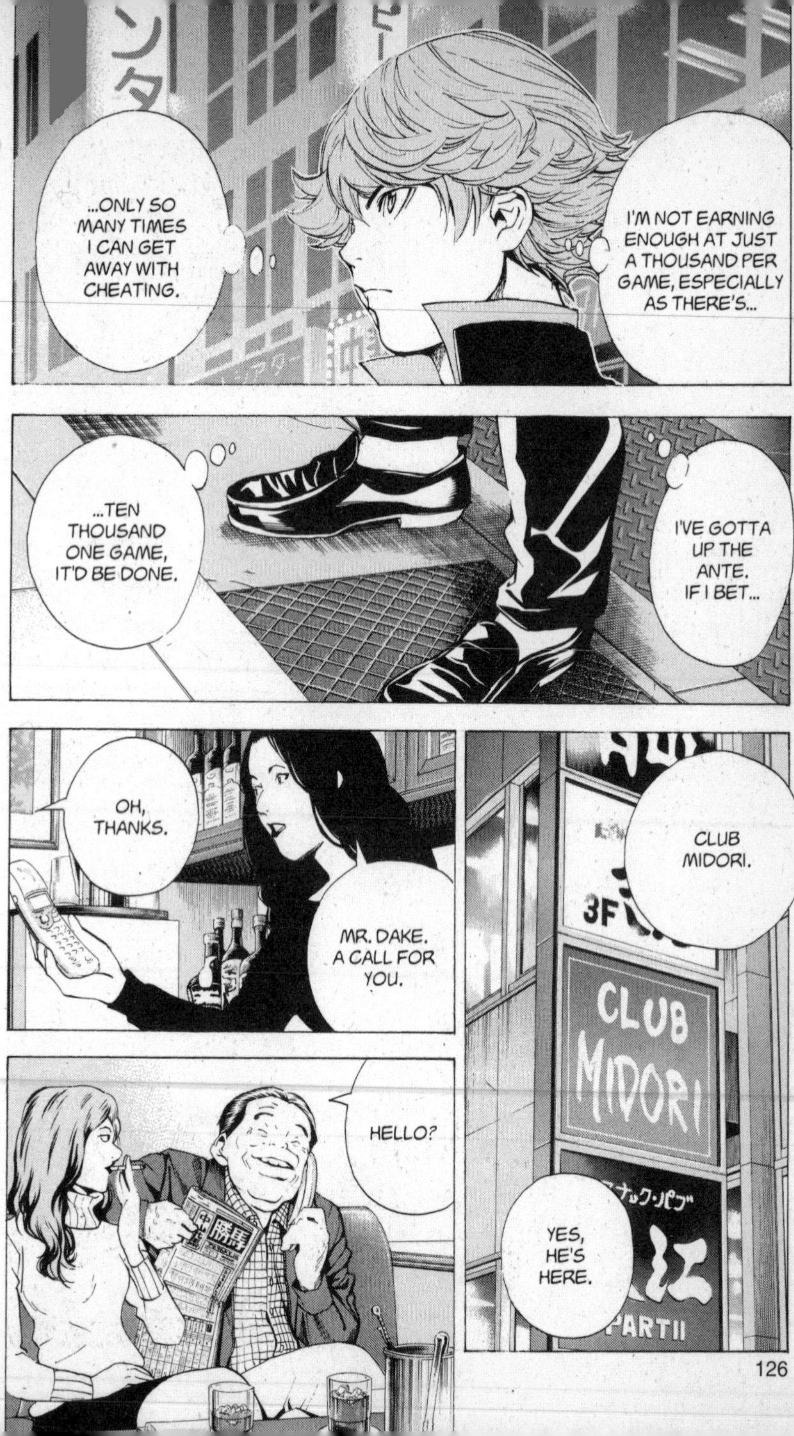
I'M NOT EARNING ENOUGH AT JUST A THOUSAND PER GAME, ESPECIALLY AS THERE'S...
...ONLY SO MANY TIMES I CAN GET AWAY WITH CHEATING.
I'VE GOTTA UP THE ANTE. IF I BET...
...TEN THOUSAND ONE GAME, IT'D BE DONE.
CLUB MIDORI.
3F
CLUB MIDORI
YES, HE'S HERE.
PART II
MR. DAKE. A CALL FOR YOU.
OH, THANKS.
HELLO?

READ THIS WAY

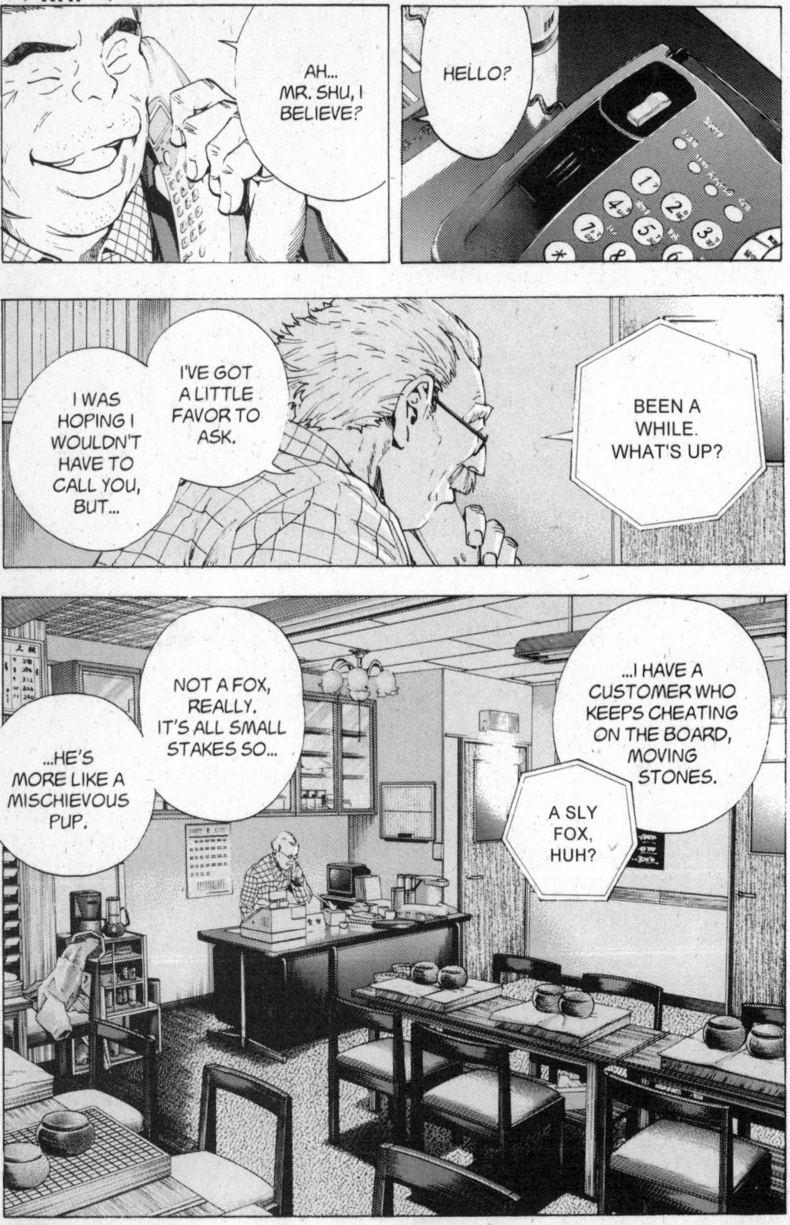
HELLO?
AH... MR. SHU, I BELIEVE?
BEEN A WHILE. WHAT'S UP?
I'VE GOT A LITTLE FAVOR TO ASK.
I WAS HOPING I WOULDN'T HAVE TO CALL YOU, BUT...
...I HAVE A CUSTOMER WHO KEEPS CHEATING ON THE BOARD, MOVING STONES.
A SLY FOX, HUH?
NOT A FOX, REALLY. IT'S ALL SMALL STAKES SO...
...HE'S MORE LIKE A MISCHIEVOUS PUP.

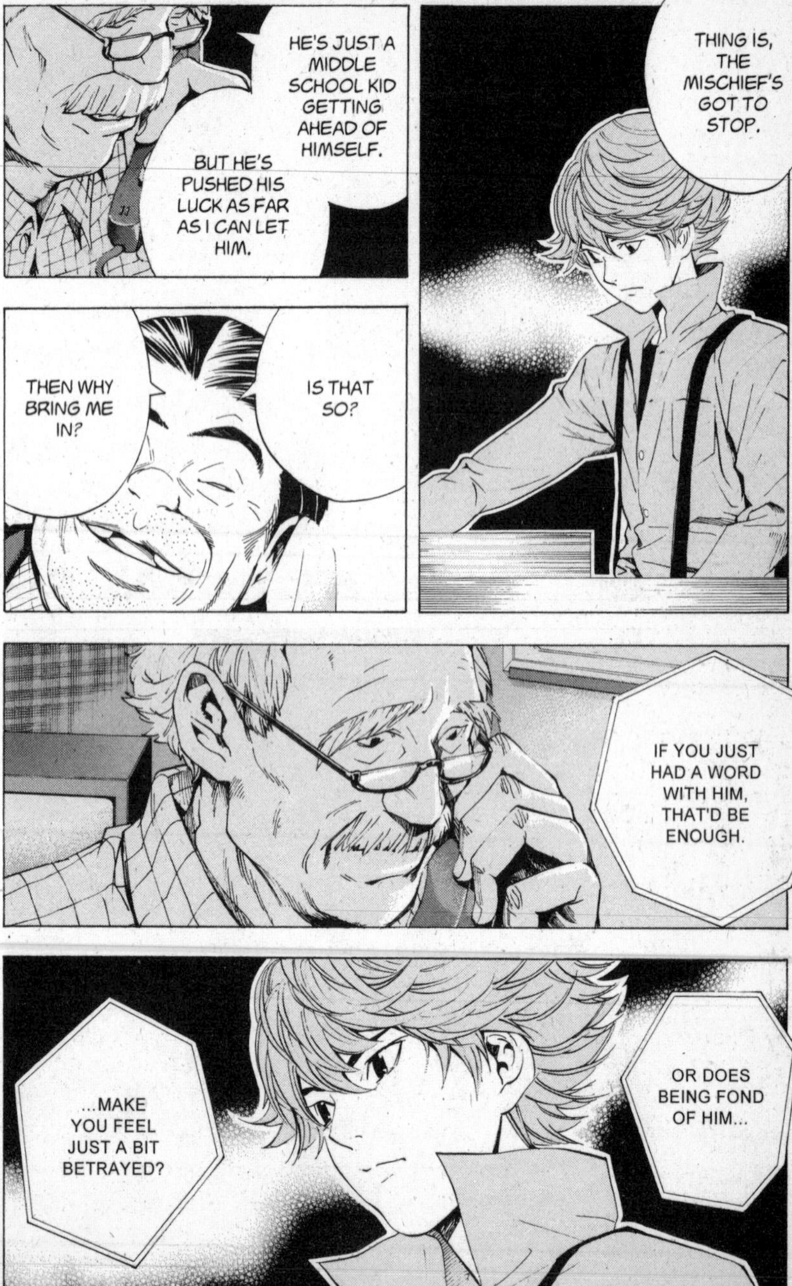
THING IS, THE MISCHIEF'S GOT TO STOP.
HE'S JUST A MIDDLE SCHOOL KID GETTING AHEAD OF HIMSELF.
BUT HE'S PUSHED HIS LUCK AS FAR AS I CAN LET HIM.
IS THAT SO?
THEN WHY BRING ME IN?
IF YOU JUST HAD A WORD WITH HIM, THAT'D BE ENOUGH.
OR DOES BEING FOND OF HIM...
...MAKE YOU FEEL JUST A BIT BETRAYED?

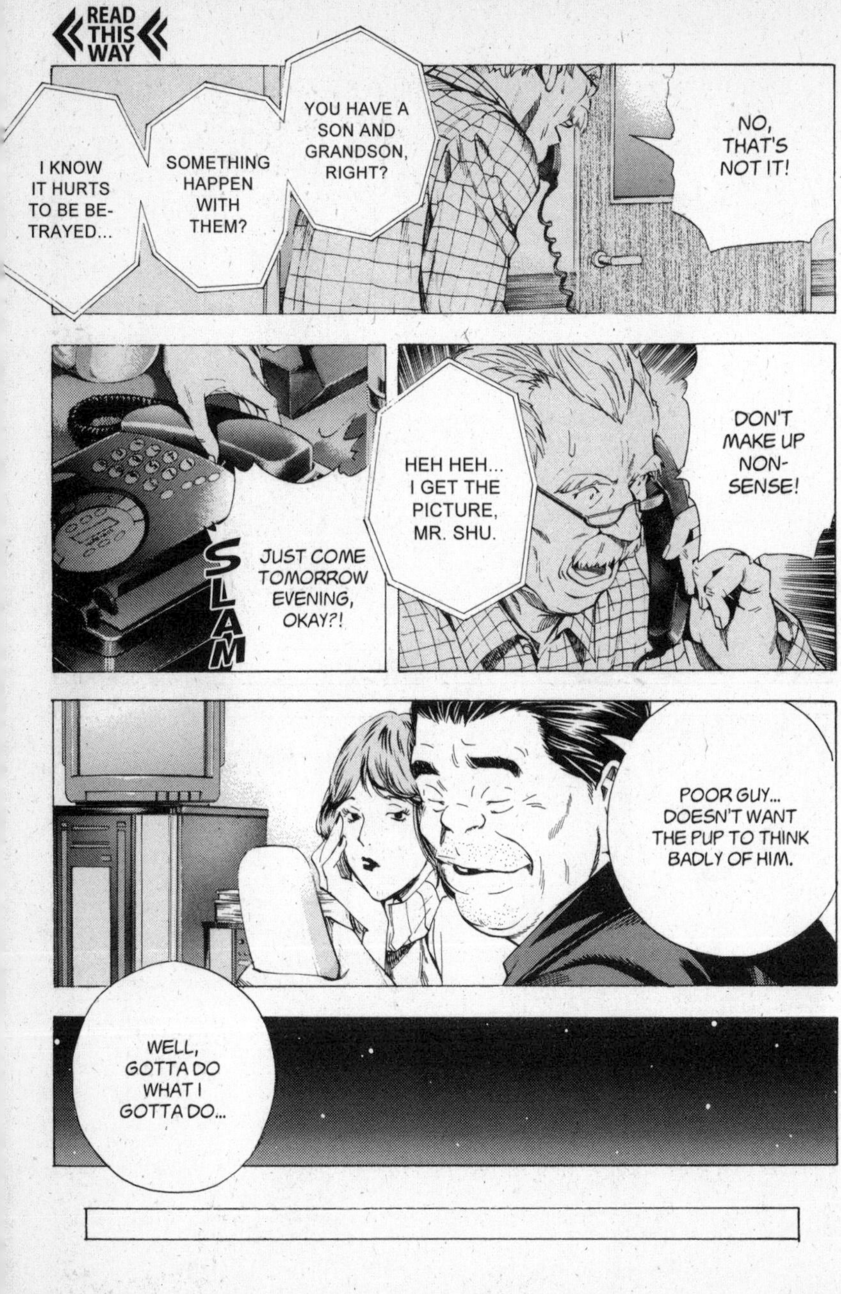
READ THIS WAY
NO, THAT'S NOT IT!
YOU HAVE A SON AND GRANDSON, RIGHT?
SOMETHING HAPPEN WITH THEM?
I KNOW IT HURTS TO BE BE-TRAYED...
DON'T MAKE UP NON-SENSE!
HEH HEH... I GET THE PICTURE, MR. SHU.
JUST COME TOMORROW EVENING, OKAY?!
SLAM
POOR GUY... DOESN'T WANT THE PUP TO THINK BADLY OF HIM.
WELL, GOTTA DO WHAT I GOTTA DO...

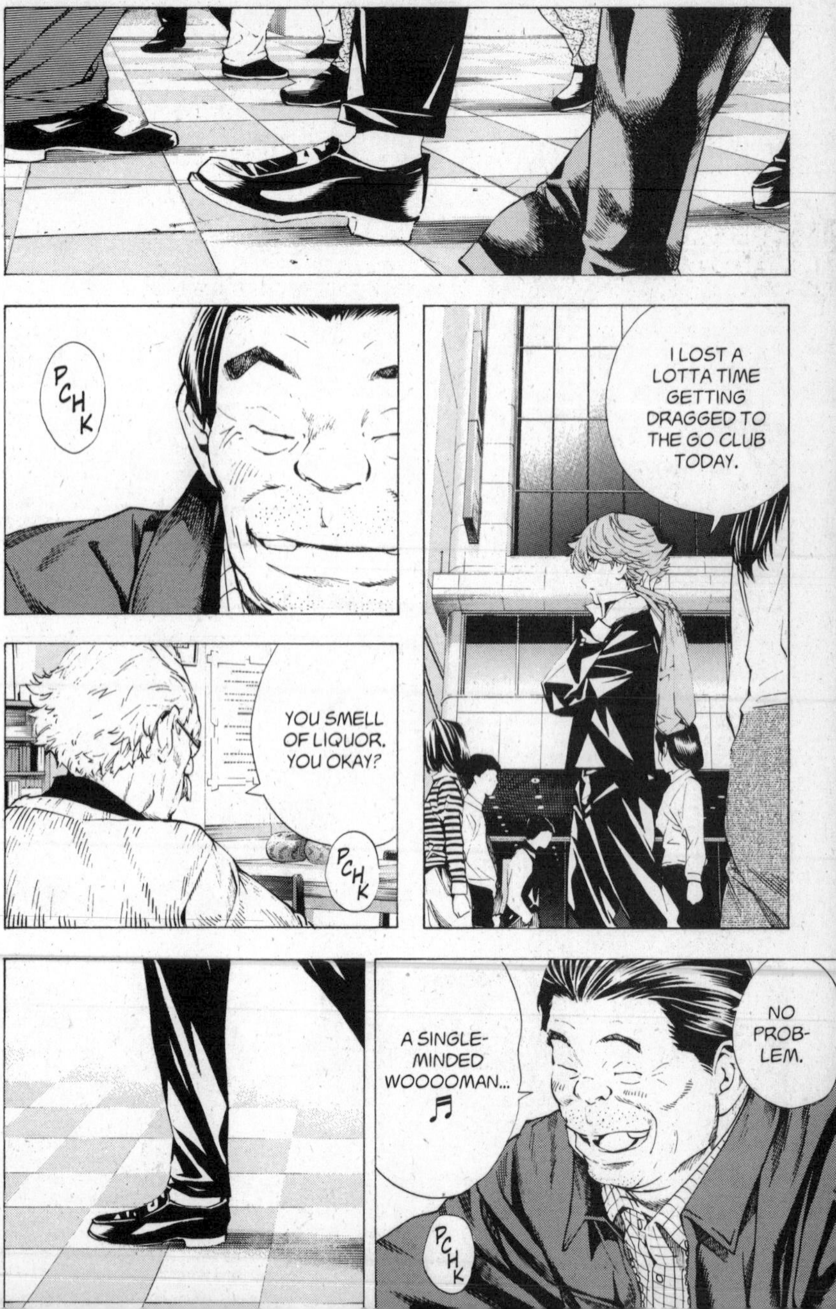
I LOST A LOTTA TIME GETTING DRAGGED TO THE GO CLUB TODAY.
PCHK
YOU SMELL OF LIQUOR. YOU OKAY?
PCHK
NO PROB-LEM.
A SINGLE-MINDED WOOOOMAN... ♫
PCHK

READ THIS WAY

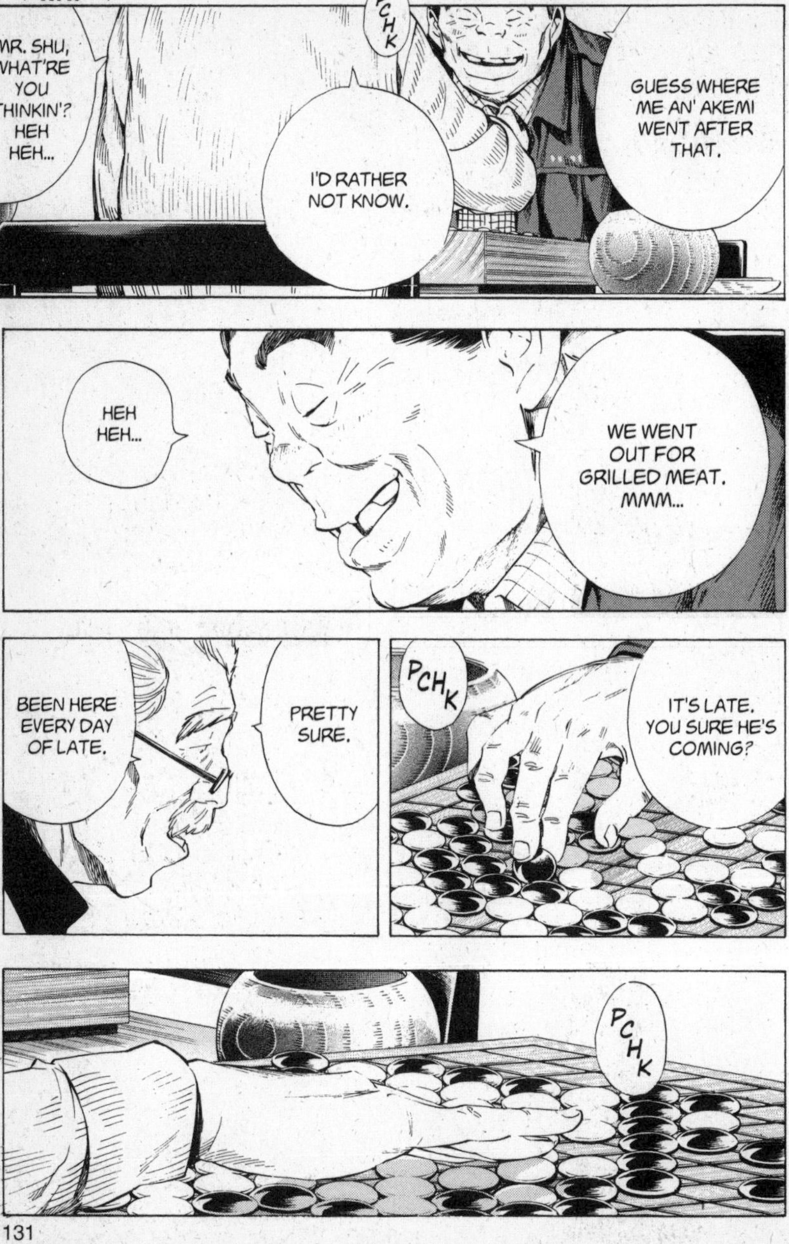
GUESS WHERE ME AN' AKEMI WENT AFTER THAT.
PCHK
I'D RATHER NOT KNOW.
MR. SHU, WHAT'RE YOU THINKIN'? HEH HEH...
WE WENT OUT FOR GRILLED MEAT. MMM...
HEH HEH...
IT'S LATE. YOU SURE HE'S COMING?
PCHK
PRETTY SURE.
BEEN HERE EVERY DAY OF LATE.
PCHK

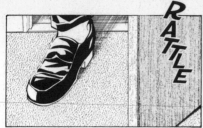

RATTLE

TMP
TMP
TMP

HEY, MITANI.

I'M JUST ABOUT DONE HERE.

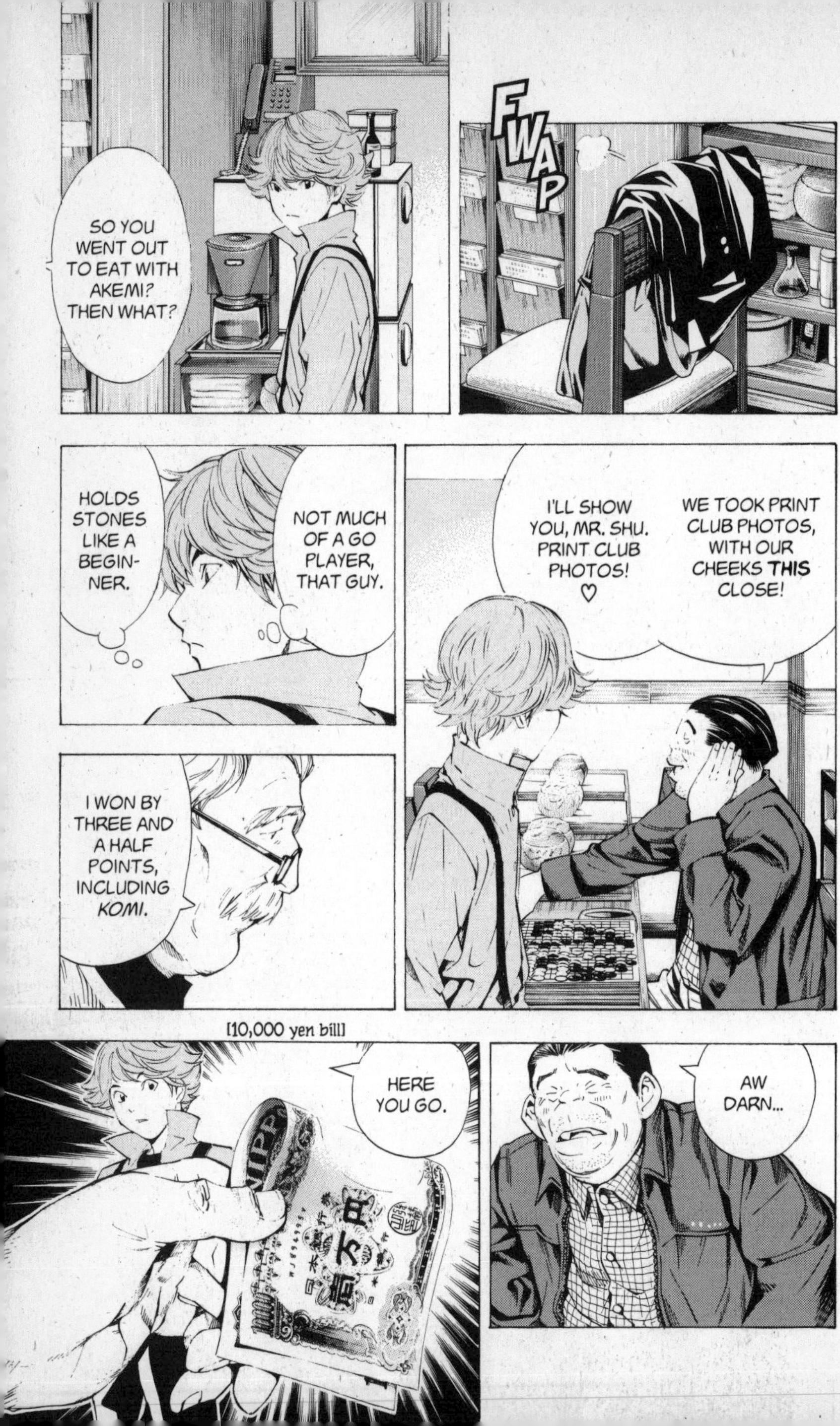
FWAP
SO YOU WENT OUT TO EAT WITH AKEMI? THEN WHAT?
WE TOOK PRINT CLUB PHOTOS, WITH OUR CHEEKS **THIS** CLOSE!
I'LL SHOW YOU, MR. SHU. PRINT CLUB PHOTOS! ♡
NOT MUCH OF A GO PLAYER, THAT GUY.
HOLDS STONES LIKE A BEGIN-NER.
I WON BY THREE AND A HALF POINTS, INCLUDING *KOMI*.
AW DARN...
[10,000 yen bill]
HERE YOU GO.

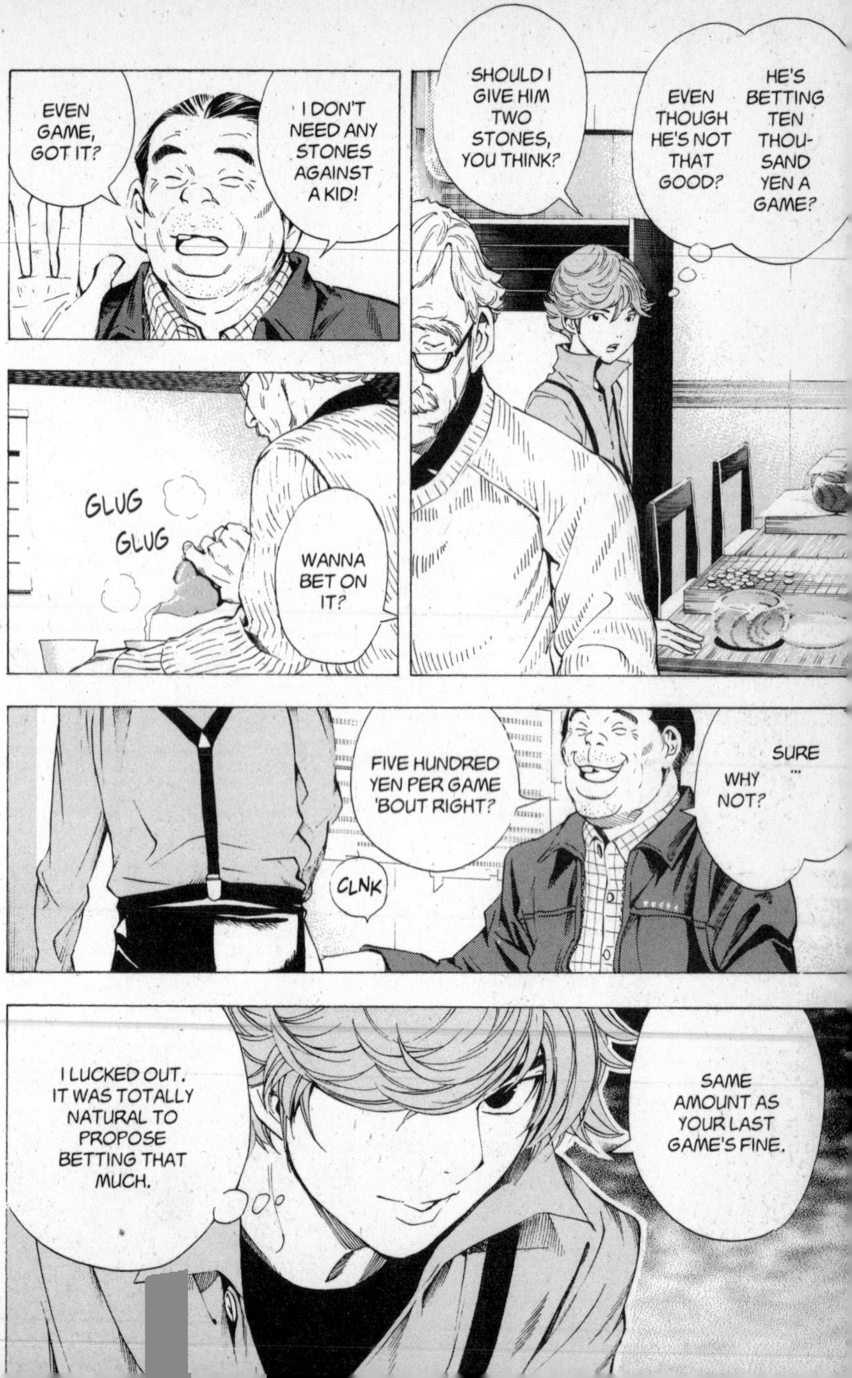
HE'S BETTING TEN THOUSAND YEN A GAME?
EVEN THOUGH HE'S NOT THAT GOOD?
SHOULD I GIVE HIM TWO STONES, YOU THINK?
I DON'T NEED ANY STONES AGAINST A KID!
EVEN GAME, GOT IT?
WANNA BET ON IT?
GLUG GLUG
SURE... WHY NOT?
FIVE HUNDRED YEN PER GAME 'BOUT RIGHT?
CLNK
SAME AMOUNT AS YOUR LAST GAME'S FINE.
I LUCKED OUT. IT WAS TOTALLY NATURAL TO PROPOSE BETTING THAT MUCH.

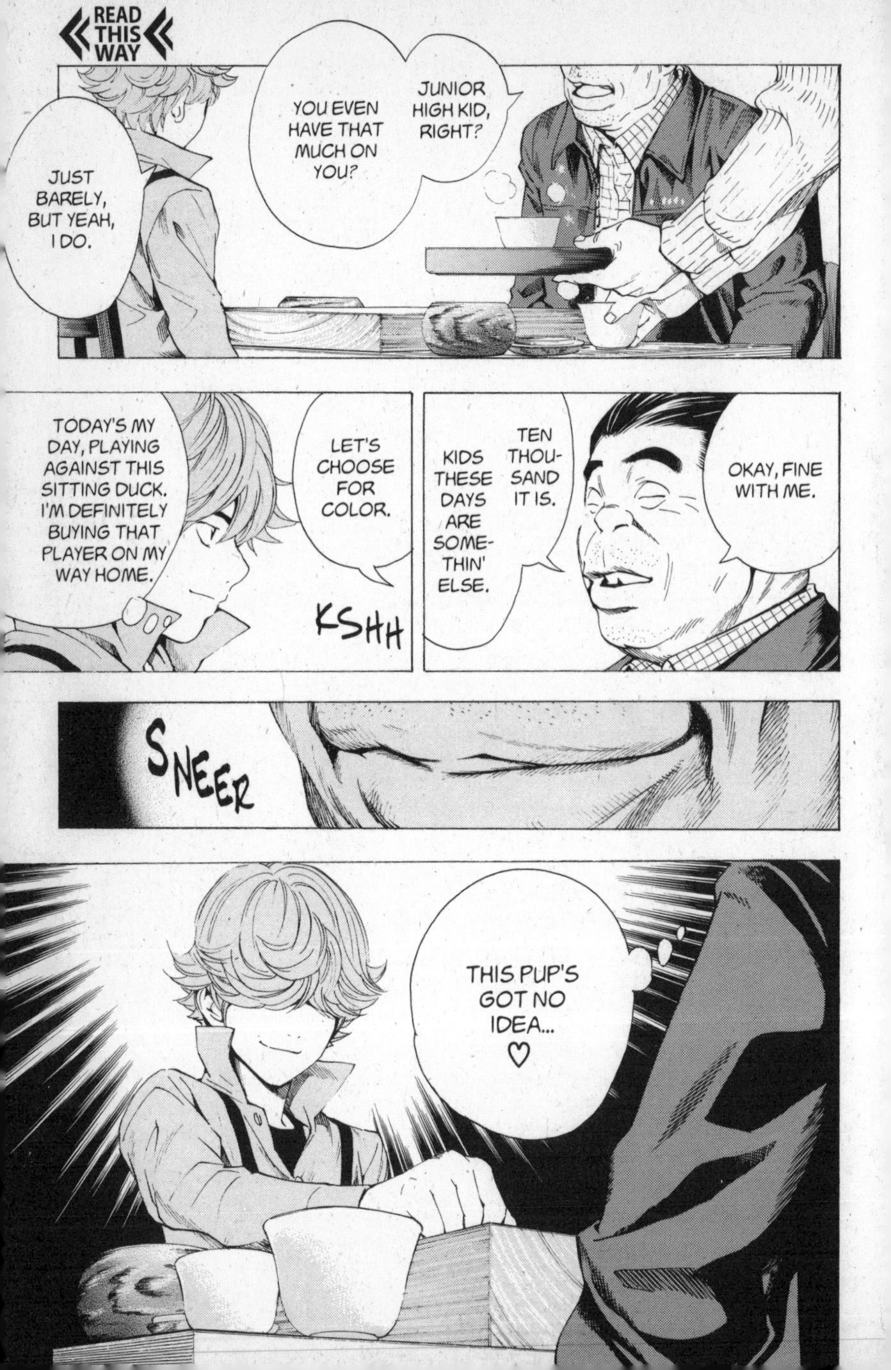
READ THIS WAY
JUNIOR HIGH KID, RIGHT?
YOU EVEN HAVE THAT MUCH ON YOU?
JUST BARELY, BUT YEAH, I DO.
OKAY, FINE WITH ME.
TEN THOUSAND IT IS.
KIDS THESE DAYS ARE SOMETHIN' ELSE.
LET'S CHOOSE FOR COLOR.
KSHH
TODAY'S MY DAY, PLAYING AGAINST THIS SITTING DUCK. I'M DEFINITELY BUYING THAT PLAYER ON MY WAY HOME.
SNEER
THIS PUP'S GOT NO IDEA... ♡

YUMI HOTTA'S LONG INTERVIEW WITH TAKESHI OBATA SENSEI: ④

● SIDE STORIES ON THE CHARACTERS

Ⓗ I WROTE THESE JUST AS I LIKED, INCLUDING MAH-JONG, HORSE BETTING AND EVERYTHING. ACCORDING TO POLLS, ALL SIX STORIES WERE WELL RECEIVED BY READERS. I WAS RELIEVED TO FIND THAT READERS OF *JUMP* ARE WILLING TO ACCEPT A WIDE RANGE OF MANGA.

Ⓞ I HAD MORE FUN THAN EXPECTED, DRAWING THE MEN IN THE *GO* SALON IN THE NASE STORY. IN FACT, I WORRIED THAT I GOT SO INTO IT THAT I MIGHT HAVE GONE OVER THE TOP.

Ⓗ THERE ARE A LOT OF OLDER MEN IN THE MITANI STORY TOO.

Ⓞ I REALLY GOT INTO THAT ONE. I LIKE MITANI. I WANTED TO DRAW MITANI IN STREET CLOTHES, SO I WENT ALL OUT ON THE TITLE PAGE OF THAT ONE. ON THE OTHER HAND, KAGA'S FASHION WAS TOUGH. THE ALOHA SHIRT WAS A GOOD IDEA (I THINK). I DEBATED ABOUT HIS MOTORCYCLE. AFTERWARDS I WONDERED IF A PASSOL WOULD HAVE BEEN BETTER THAN A CUB.

Ⓗ DO YOU LIKE MOTORCYCLES TOO?

Ⓞ YES. THE ONE I RIDE NOW IS A SCOOTER. AT ANY RATE, FOR THESE SIDE STORIES, I WAS LUCKY THAT I HAD ASSISTANTS WHO KNEW A LOT ABOUT MAHJONG, HORSE RACING AND MOTORCYCLES.

● WORK AND SELF

Ⓗ HOW MANY ASSISTANTS DO YOU HAVE RIGHT NOW?

Ⓞ WE MANAGE WITH NINE--FIVE MEN, FOUR WOMEN. THERE ARE ABOUT FIVE OR SIX WHO WORK IN THE OFFICE. OUR WORKPLACE IS NONSMOKING. WE ASK THE SMOKERS TO SMOKE ON THE BALCONY.

(Continued on page 168)

Game 5 "Atsushi Kurata"

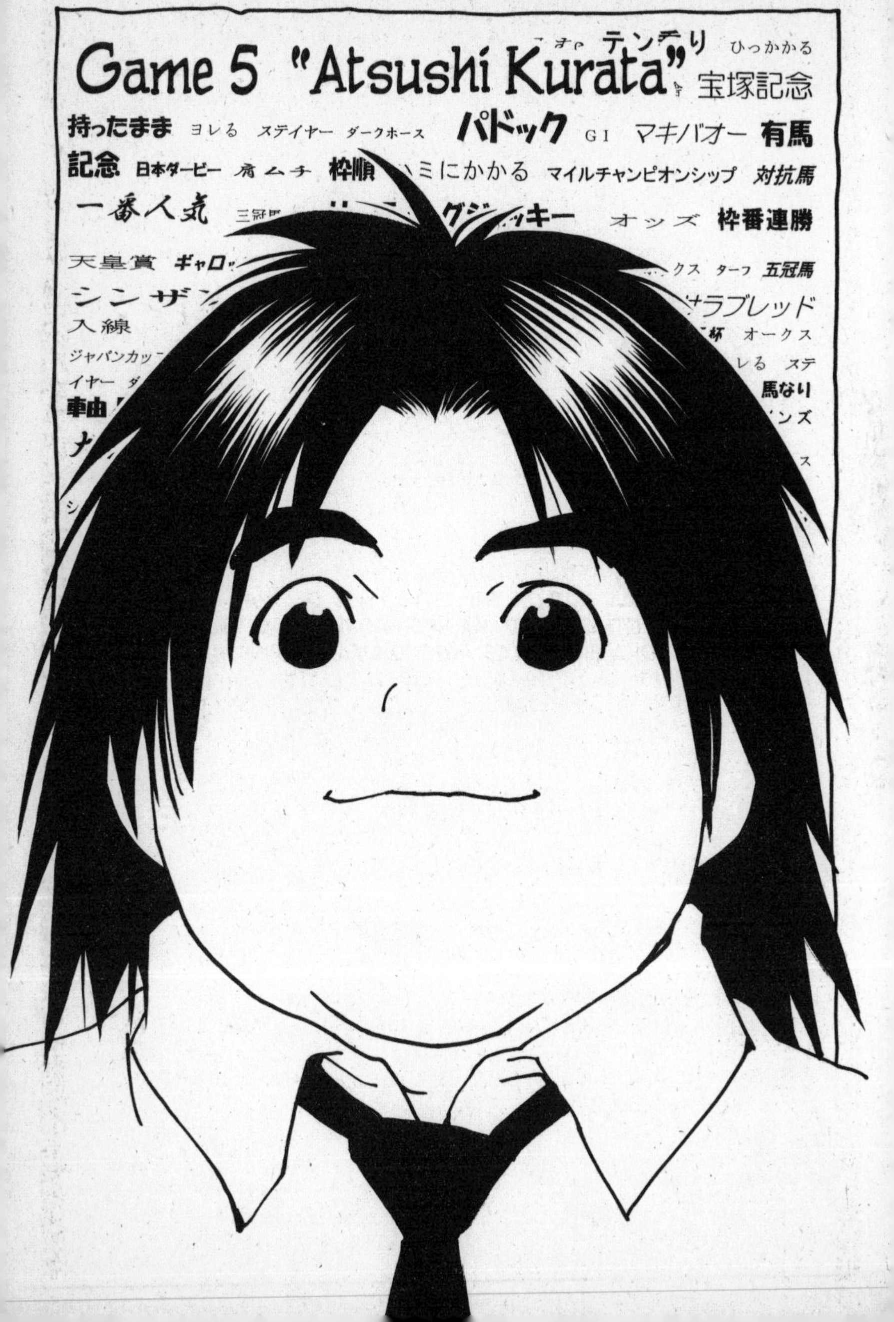

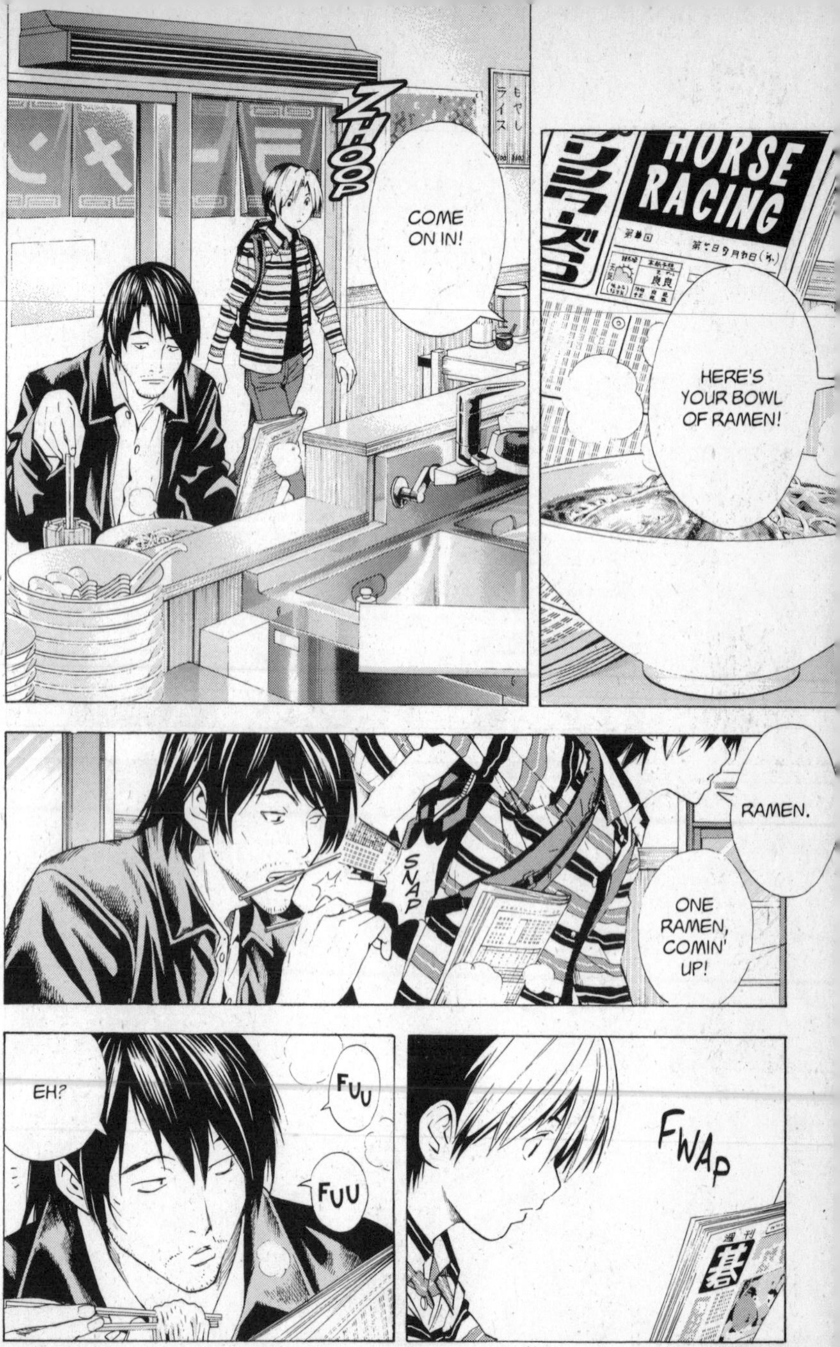
HORSE RACING
HERE'S YOUR BOWL OF RAMEN!
ZHOOP
COME ON IN!
RAMEN.
ONE RAMEN, COMIN' UP!
SNAP
FWAP
EH?
FUU
FUU

READ THIS WAY

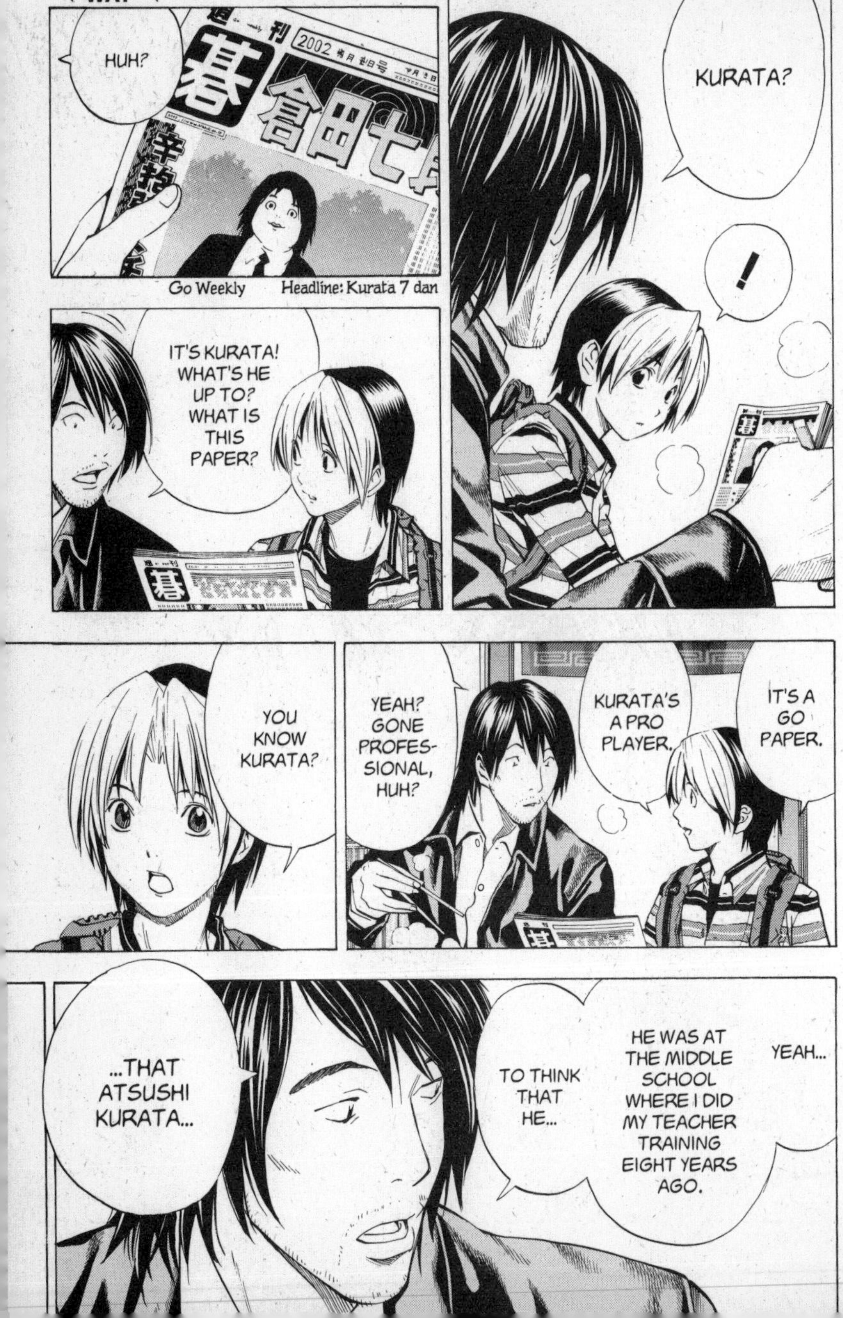
KURATA?
!
HUH?
Go Weekly
Headline: Kurata 7 dan
IT'S KURATA! WHAT'S HE UP TO? WHAT IS THIS PAPER?
IT'S A GO PAPER.
KURATA'S A PRO PLAYER.
YEAH? GONE PROFES-SIONAL, HUH?
YOU KNOW KURATA?
YEAH...
HE WAS AT THE MIDDLE SCHOOL WHERE I DID MY TEACHER TRAINING EIGHT YEARS AGO.
TO THINK THAT HE...
...THAT ATSUSHI KURATA...

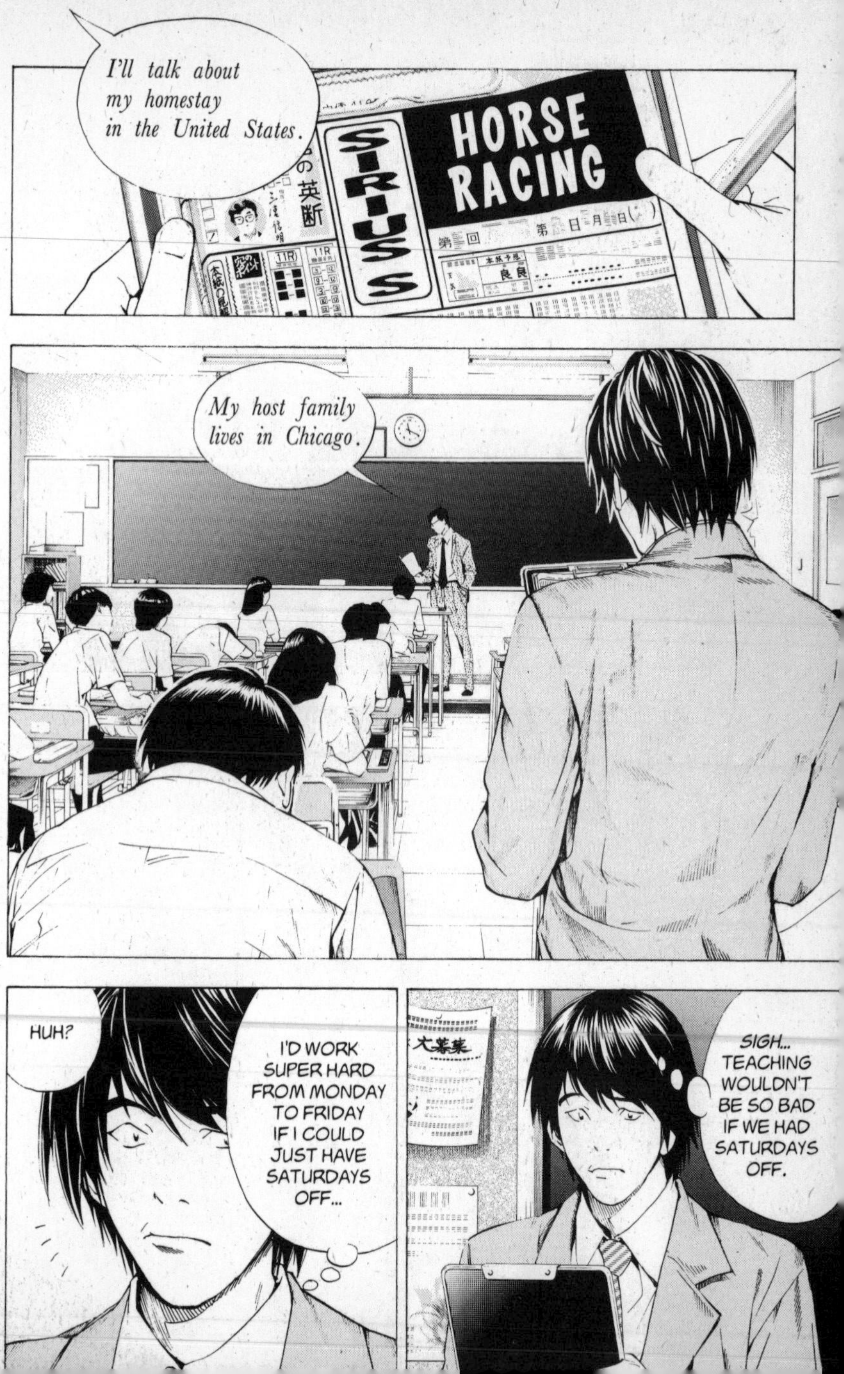
I'll talk about my homestay in the United States.
SIRIUS S
HORSE RACING
My host family lives in Chicago.
SIGH... TEACHING WOULDN'T BE SO BAD IF WE HAD SATURDAYS OFF.
I'D WORK SUPER HARD FROM MONDAY TO FRIDAY IF I COULD JUST HAVE SATURDAYS OFF...
HUH?

READ THIS WAY

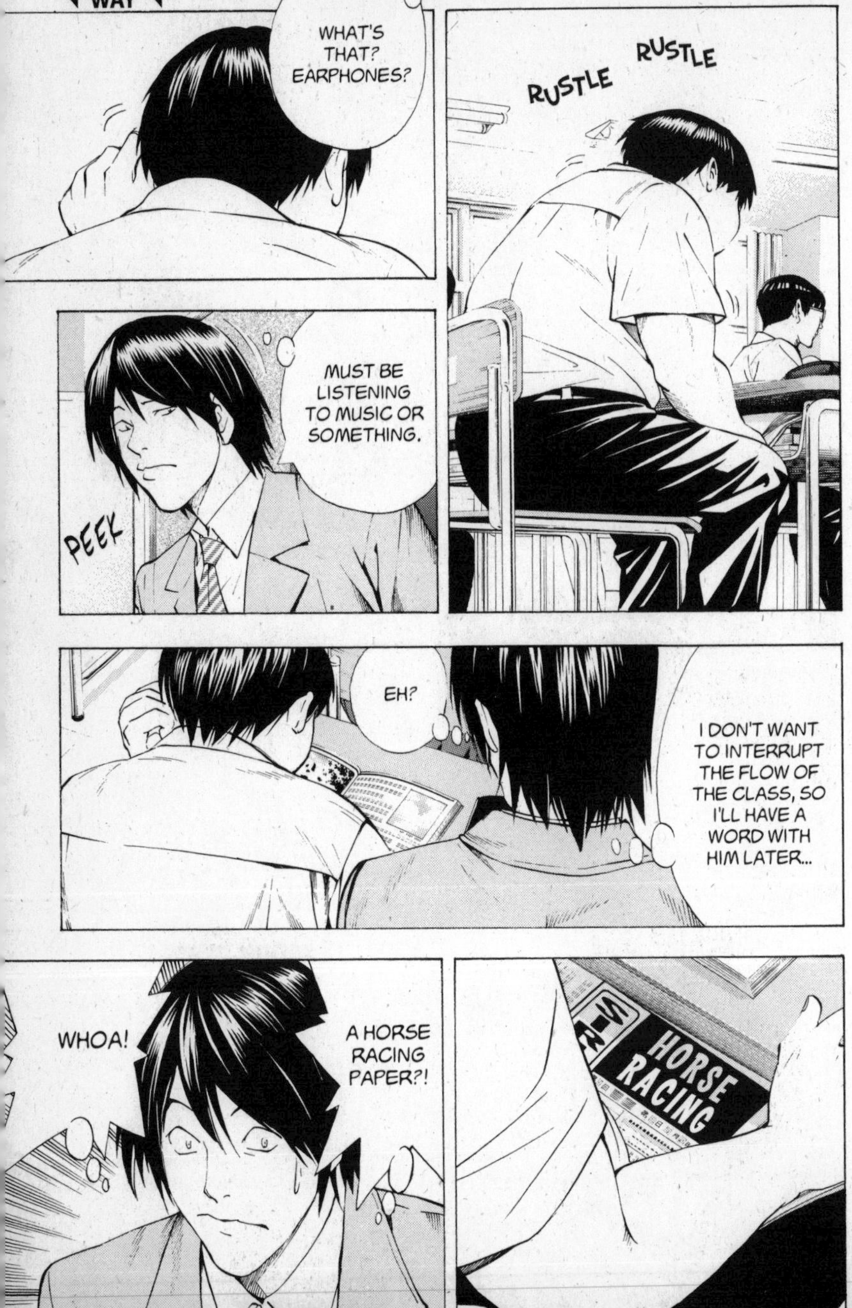

RUSTLE
RUSTLE
WHAT'S THAT? EARPHONES?
MUST BE LISTENING TO MUSIC OR SOMETHING.
PEEK
I DON'T WANT TO INTERRUPT THE FLOW OF THE CLASS, SO I'LL HAVE A WORD WITH HIM LATER...
EH?
HORSE RACING
A HORSE RACING PAPER?!
WHOA!

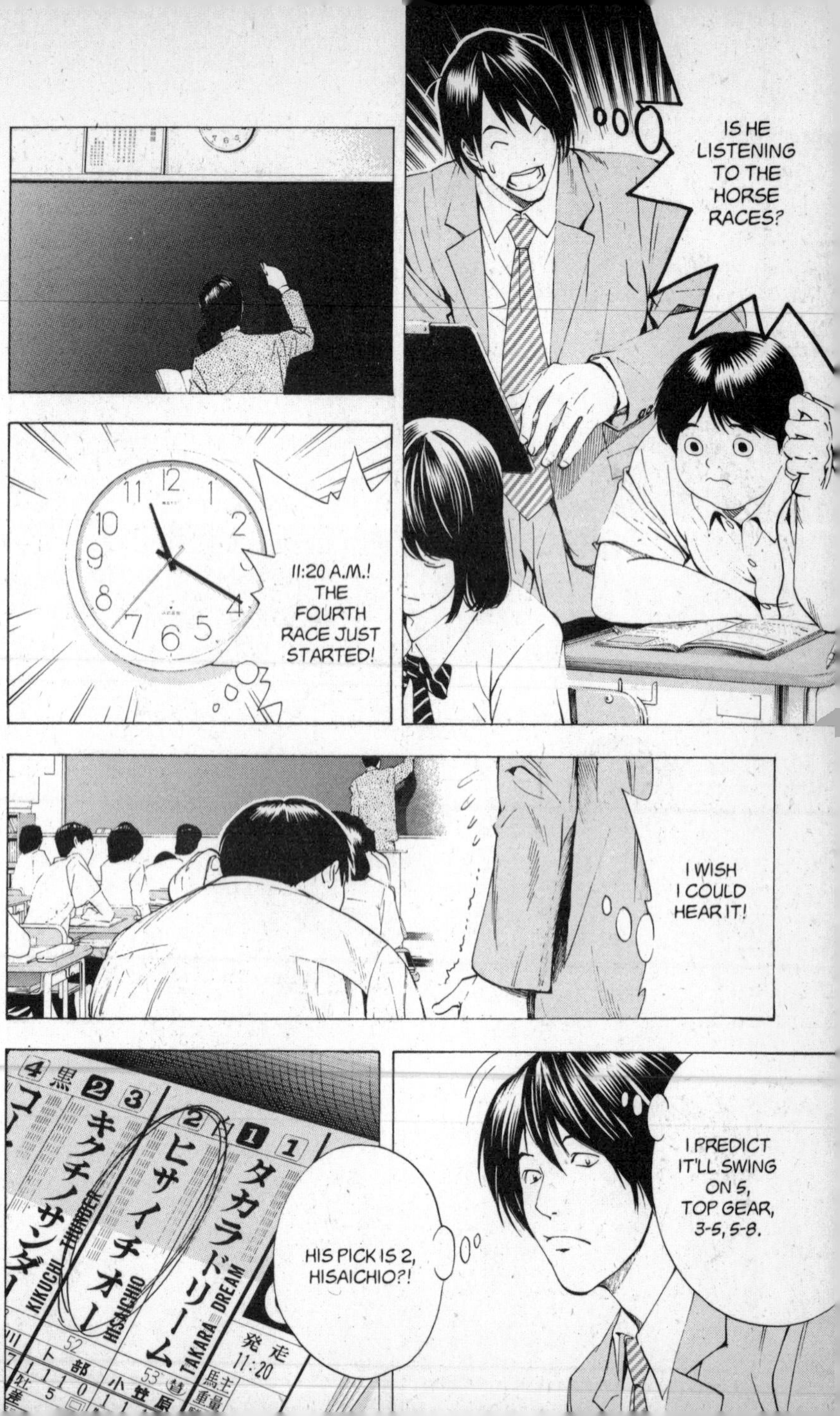
IS HE LISTENING TO THE HORSE RACES?
11:20 A.M.! THE FOURTH RACE JUST STARTED!
I WISH I COULD HEAR IT!
I PREDICT IT'LL SWING ON 5, TOP GEAR, 3-5, 5-8.
HIS PICK IS 2, HISAICHIO?!
発走 11:20
タカラドリーム
TAKARA DREAM
ヒサイチオー
HISAICHIO
キクチノサンダー
KIKUCHI THUNDER

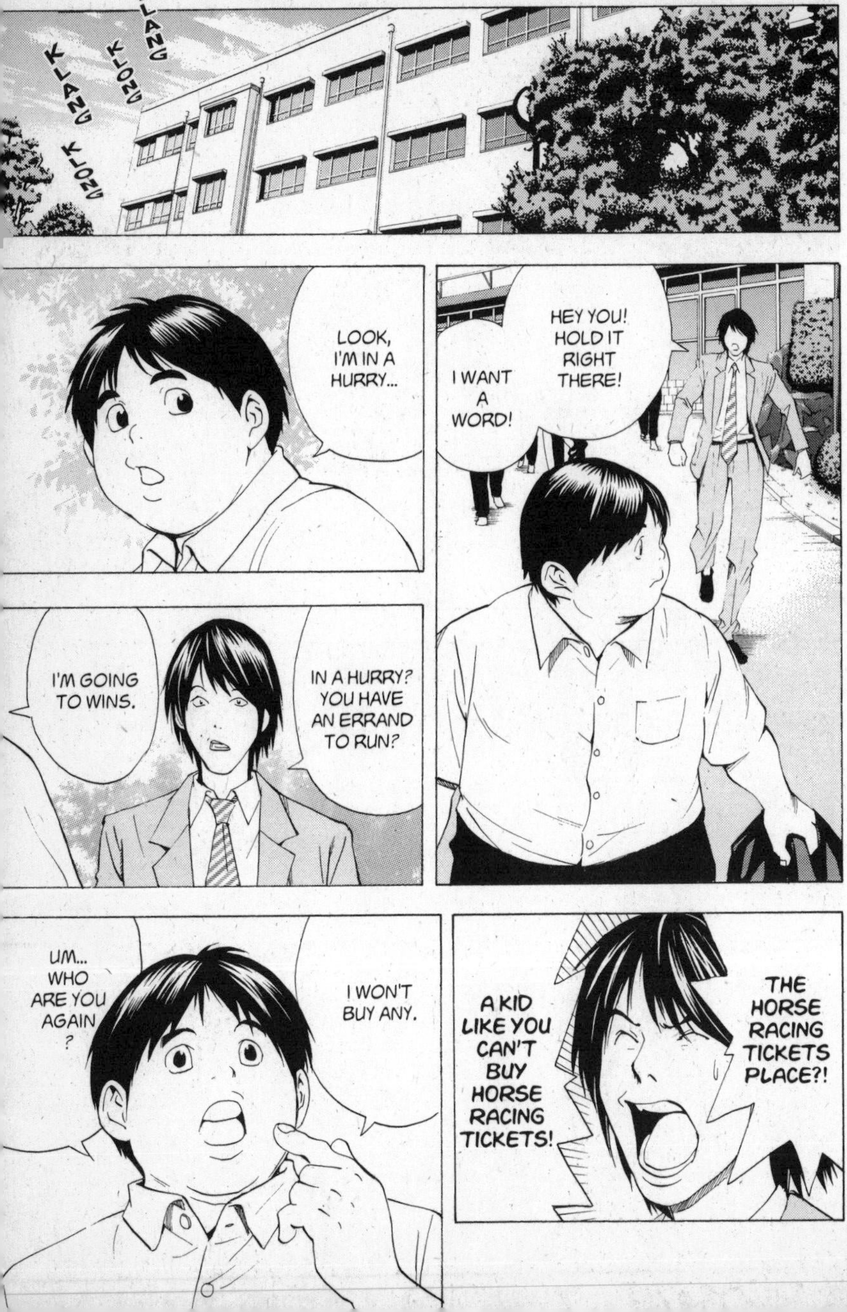
KLANG
KLONG
KLANG
KLONG
HEY YOU! HOLD IT RIGHT THERE!
I WANT A WORD!
LOOK, I'M IN A HURRY...
IN A HURRY? YOU HAVE AN ERRAND TO RUN?
I'M GOING TO WINS.
THE HORSE RACING TICKETS PLACE?!
A KID LIKE YOU CAN'T BUY HORSE RACING TICKETS!
I WON'T BUY ANY.
UM... WHO ARE YOU AGAIN?

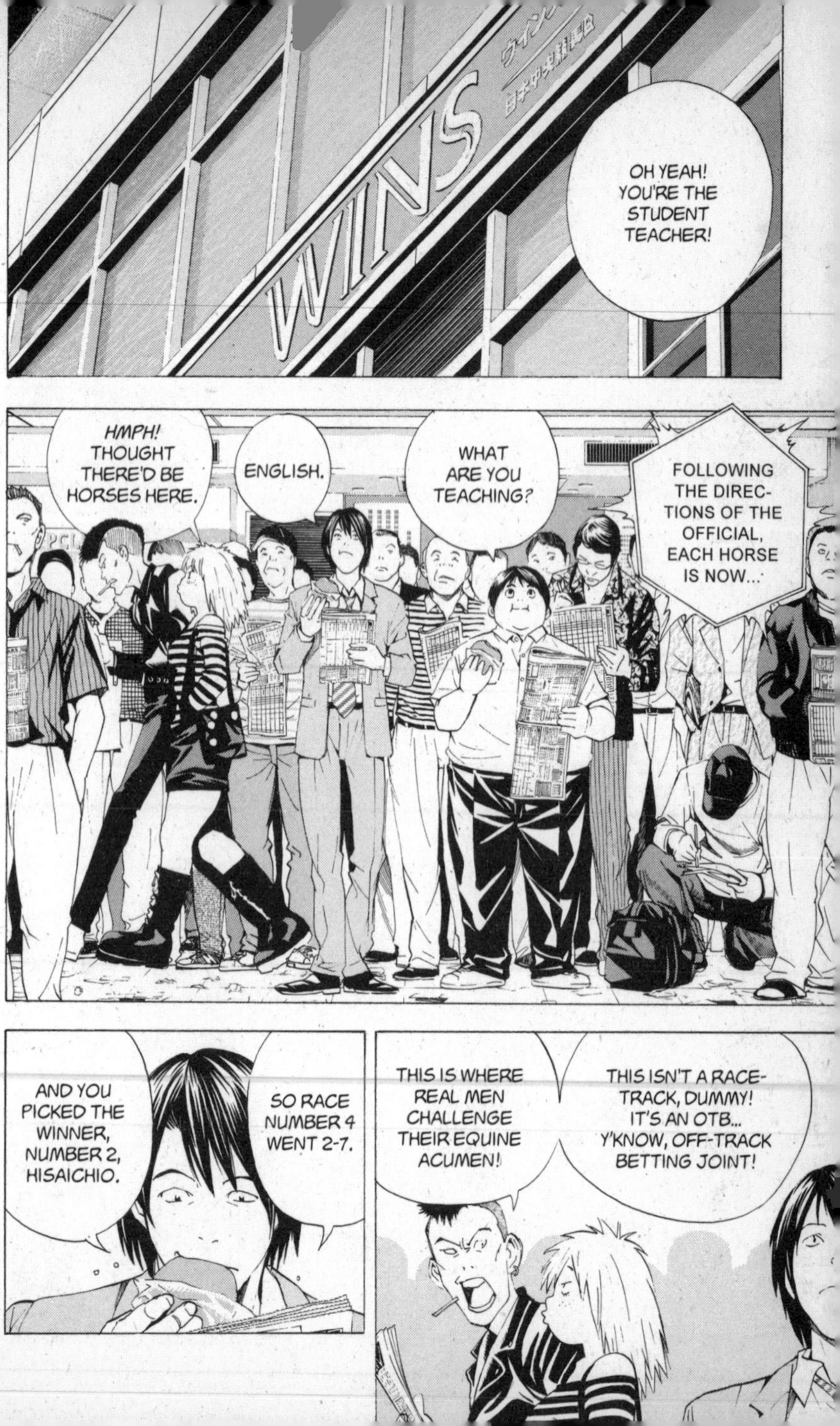
WINS
OH YEAH! YOU'RE THE STUDENT TEACHER!
FOLLOWING THE DIRECTIONS OF THE OFFICIAL, EACH HORSE IS NOW...
WHAT ARE YOU TEACHING?
ENGLISH.
HMPH! THOUGHT THERE'D BE HORSES HERE.
THIS ISN'T A RACE-TRACK, DUMMY! IT'S AN OTB... Y'KNOW, OFF-TRACK BETTING JOINT!
THIS IS WHERE REAL MEN CHALLENGE THEIR EQUINE ACUMEN!
SO RACE NUMBER 4 WENT 2-7.
AND YOU PICKED THE WINNER, NUMBER 2, HISAICHIO.

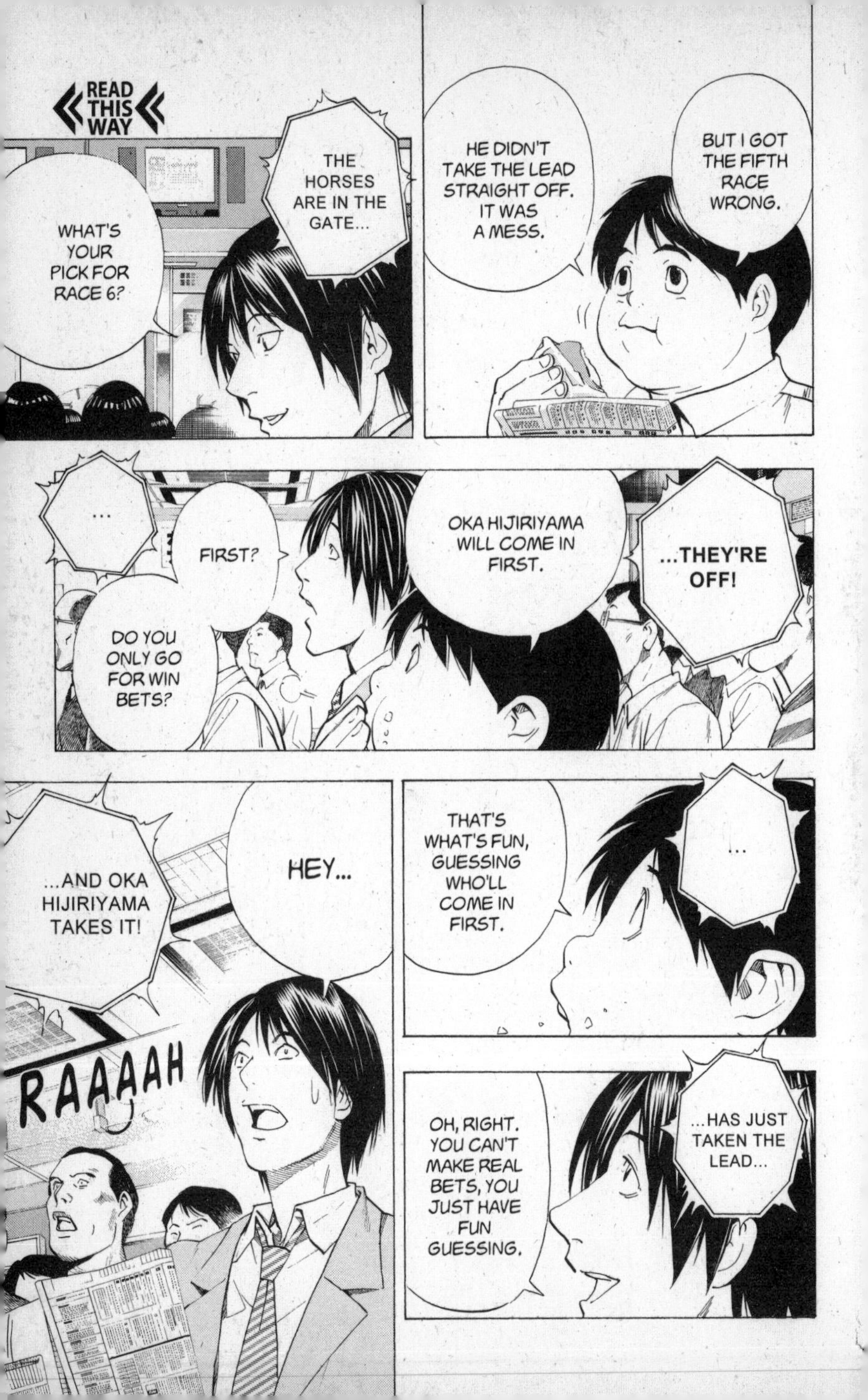
READ THIS WAY
BUT I GOT THE FIFTH RACE WRONG.
HE DIDN'T TAKE THE LEAD STRAIGHT OFF. IT WAS A MESS.
THE HORSES ARE IN THE GATE...
WHAT'S YOUR PICK FOR RACE 6?
...THEY'RE OFF!
OKA HIJIRIYAMA WILL COME IN FIRST.
FIRST?
...
DO YOU ONLY GO FOR WIN BETS?
...
THAT'S WHAT'S FUN, GUESSING WHO'LL COME IN FIRST.
...HAS JUST TAKEN THE LEAD...
OH, RIGHT. YOU CAN'T MAKE REAL BETS, YOU JUST HAVE FUN GUESSING.
HEY...
...AND OKA HIJIRIYAMA TAKES IT!
RAAAAH

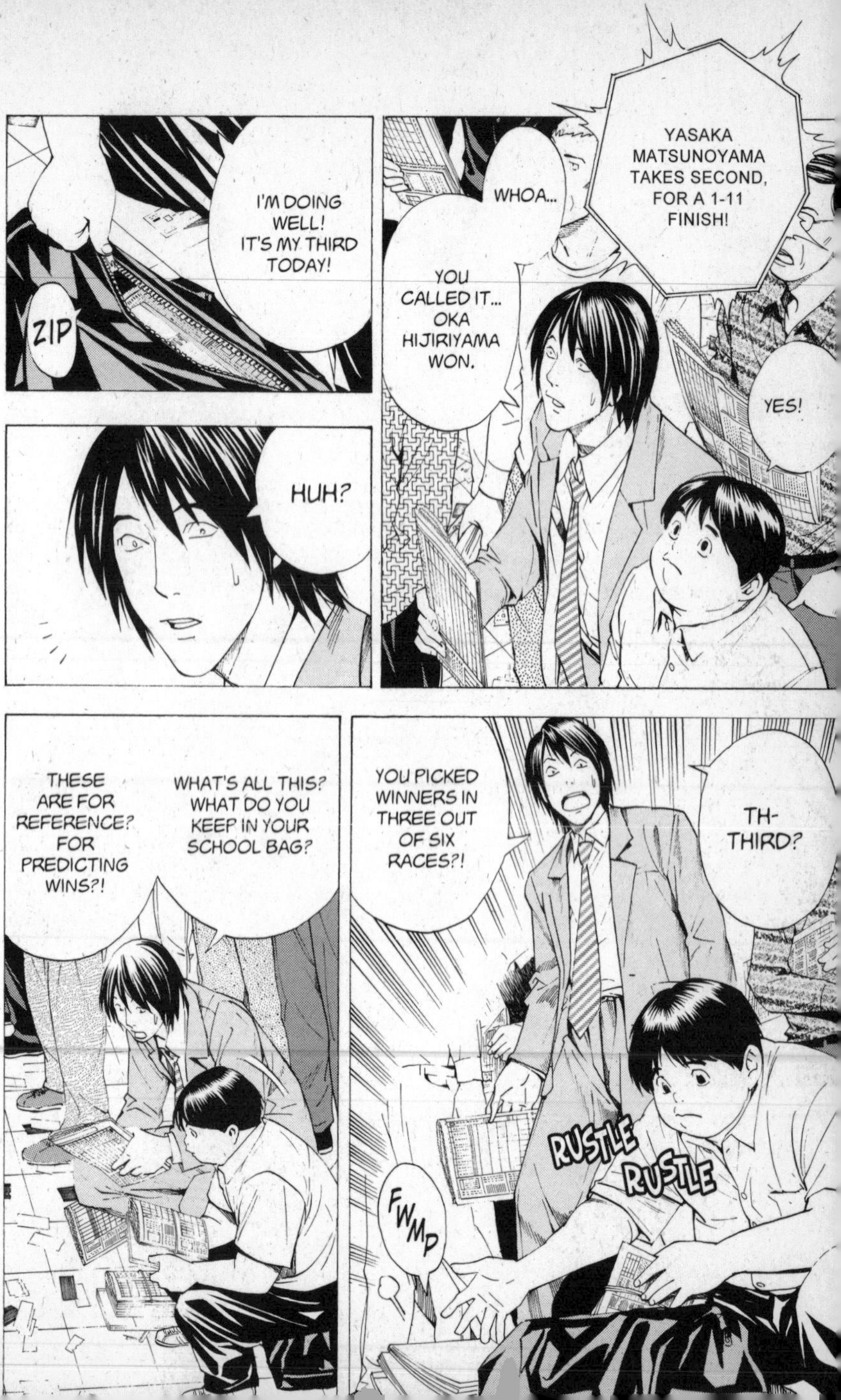
YASAKA MATSUNOYAMA TAKES SECOND, FOR A 1-11 FINISH!
WHOA...
YOU CALLED IT... OKA HIJIRIYAMA WON.
YES!
I'M DOING WELL! IT'S MY THIRD TODAY!
ZIP
HUH?
TH-THIRD?
YOU PICKED WINNERS IN THREE OUT OF SIX RACES?!
RUSTLE
RUSTLE
FWMP
WHAT'S ALL THIS? WHAT DO YOU KEEP IN YOUR SCHOOL BAG?
THESE ARE FOR REFERENCE? FOR PREDICTING WINS?!

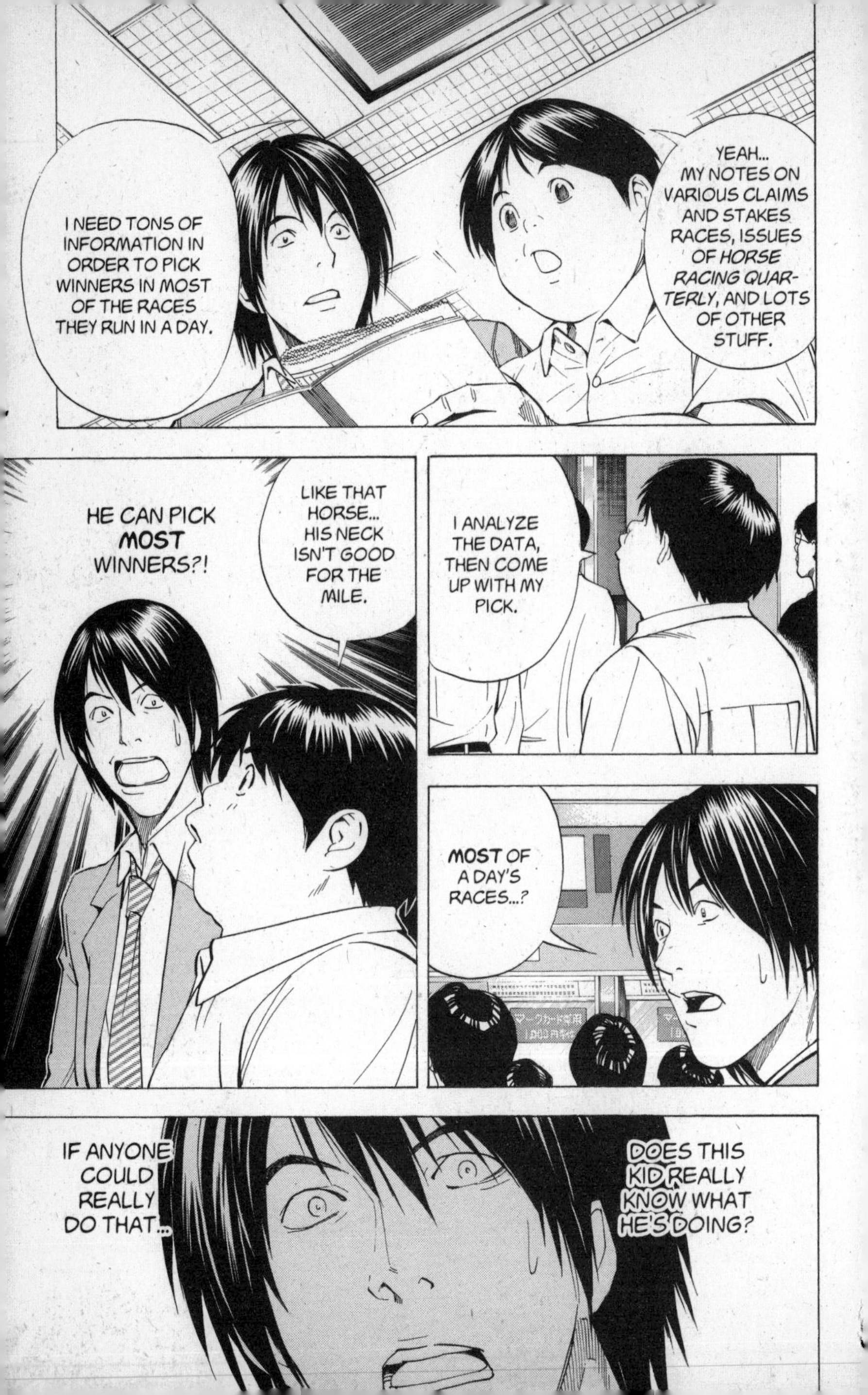
YEAH... MY NOTES ON VARIOUS CLAIMS AND STAKES RACES, ISSUES OF *HORSE RACING QUARTERLY*, AND LOTS OF OTHER STUFF.
I NEED TONS OF INFORMATION IN ORDER TO PICK WINNERS IN MOST OF THE RACES THEY RUN IN A DAY.
I ANALYZE THE DATA, THEN COME UP WITH MY PICK.
MOST OF A DAY'S RACES...?
LIKE THAT HORSE... HIS NECK ISN'T GOOD FOR THE MILE.
HE CAN PICK **MOST** WINNERS?!
DOES THIS KID REALLY KNOW WHAT HE'S DOING?
IF ANYONE COULD REALLY DO THAT...

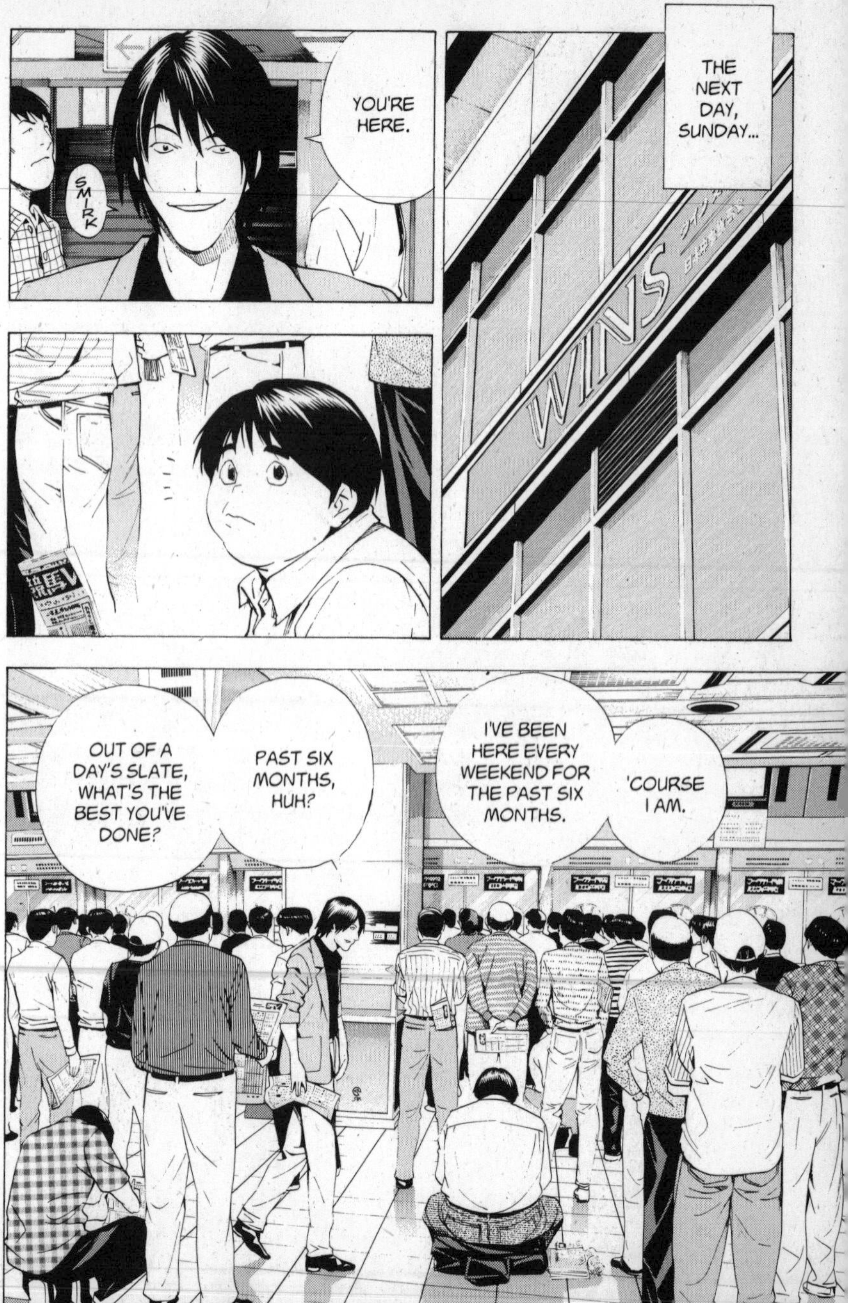
THE NEXT DAY, SUNDAY...
WINS
YOU'RE HERE.
SMIRK
'COURSE I AM.
I'VE BEEN HERE EVERY WEEKEND FOR THE PAST SIX MONTHS.
PAST SIX MONTHS, HUH?
OUT OF A DAY'S SLATE, WHAT'S THE BEST YOU'VE DONE?

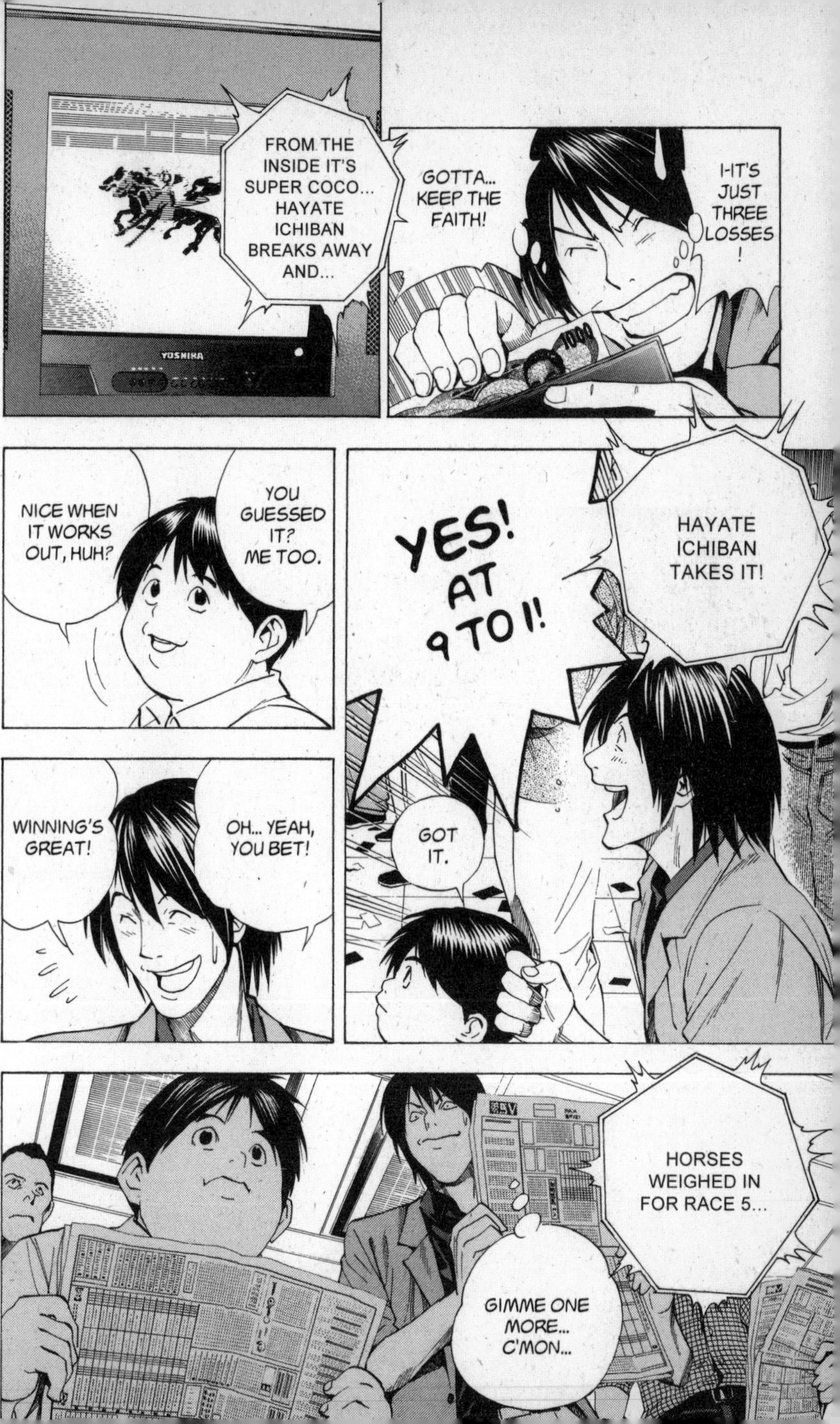
I-IT'S JUST THREE LOSSES!
GOTTA... KEEP THE FAITH!
FROM THE INSIDE IT'S SUPER COCO... HAYATE ICHIBAN BREAKS AWAY AND...
YOSHIRA
HAYATE ICHIBAN TAKES IT!
YES! AT 9 TO 1!
GOT IT.
YOU GUESSED IT? ME TOO.
NICE WHEN IT WORKS OUT, HUH?
OH... YEAH, YOU BET!
WINNING'S GREAT!
HORSES WEIGHED IN FOR RACE 5...
GIMME ONE MORE... C'MON...

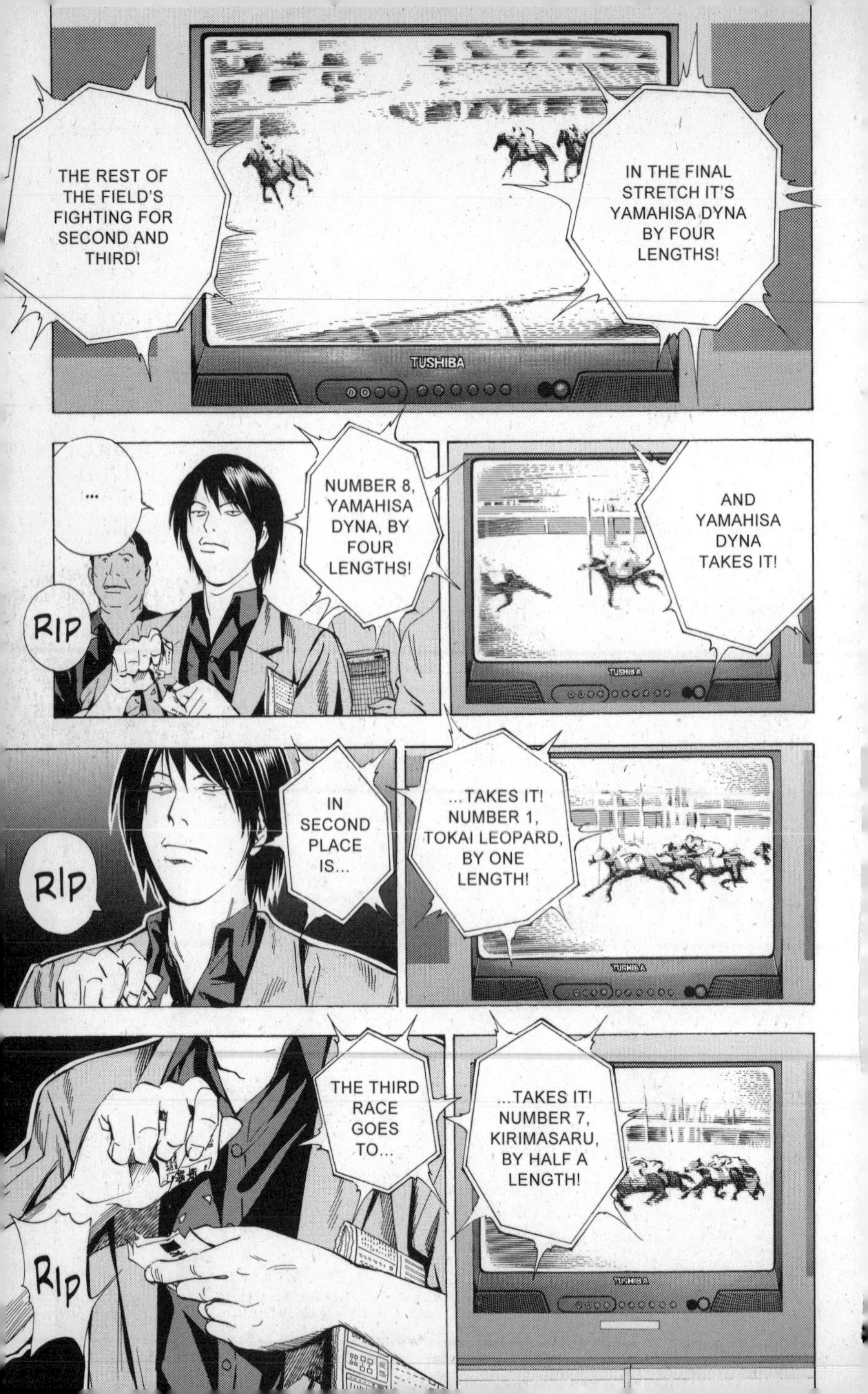
THE REST OF THE FIELD'S FIGHTING FOR SECOND AND THIRD!
IN THE FINAL STRETCH IT'S YAMAHISA DYNA BY FOUR LENGTHS!
TUSHIBA
...
RIP
NUMBER 8, YAMAHISA DYNA, BY FOUR LENGTHS!
AND YAMAHISA DYNA TAKES IT!
TUSHIBA
RIP
IN SECOND PLACE IS...
...TAKES IT! NUMBER 1, TOKAI LEOPARD, BY ONE LENGTH!
TUSHIBA
RIP
THE THIRD RACE GOES TO...
...TAKES IT! NUMBER 7, KIRIMASARU, BY HALF A LENGTH!
TUSHIBA

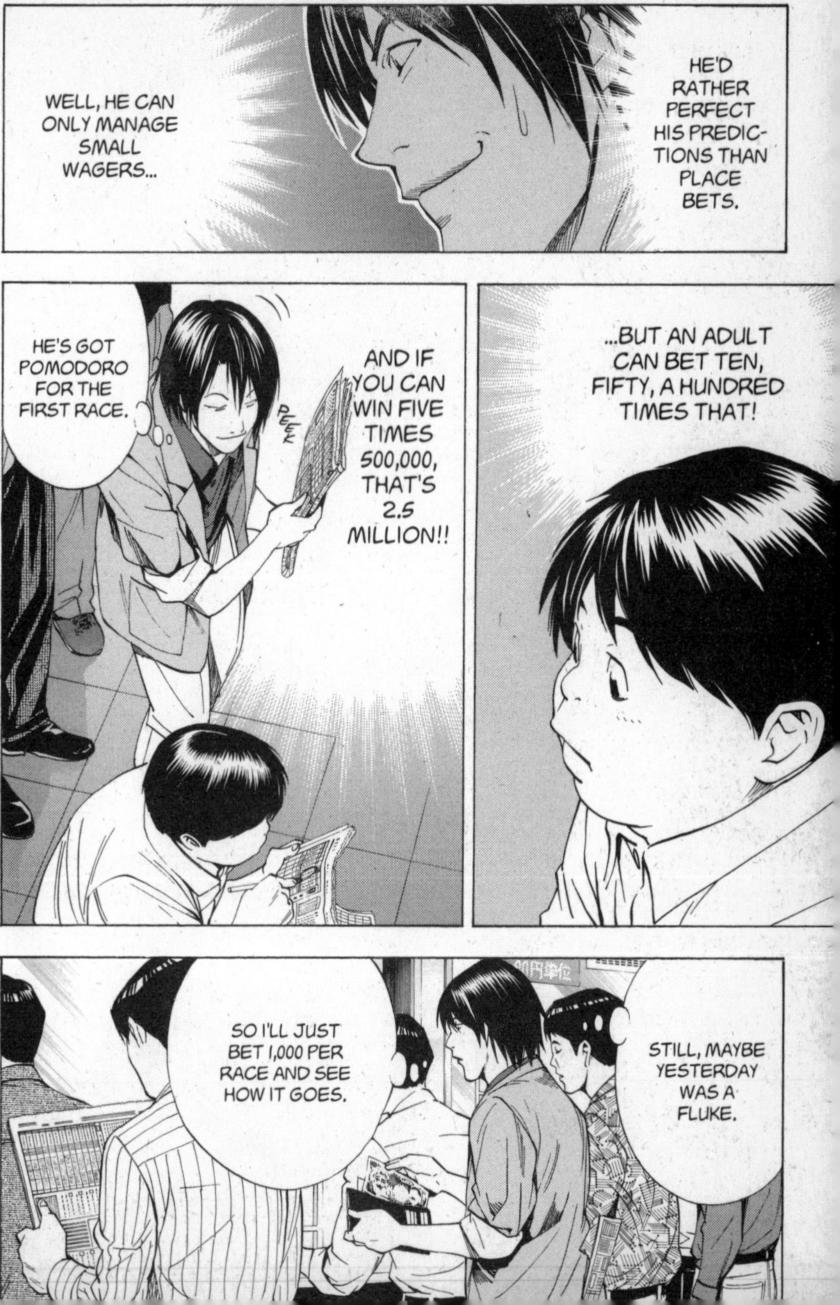
HE'D RATHER PERFECT HIS PREDIC- TIONS THAN PLACE BETS.
WELL, HE CAN ONLY MANAGE SMALL WAGERS...
...BUT AN ADULT CAN BET TEN, FIFTY, A HUNDRED TIMES THAT!
AND IF YOU CAN WIN FIVE TIMES 500,000, THAT'S 2.5 MILLION!!
HE'S GOT POMODORO FOR THE FIRST RACE.
PEEK
STILL, MAYBE YESTERDAY WAS A FLUKE.
SO I'LL JUST BET 1,000 PER RACE AND SEE HOW IT GOES.

READ THIS WAY

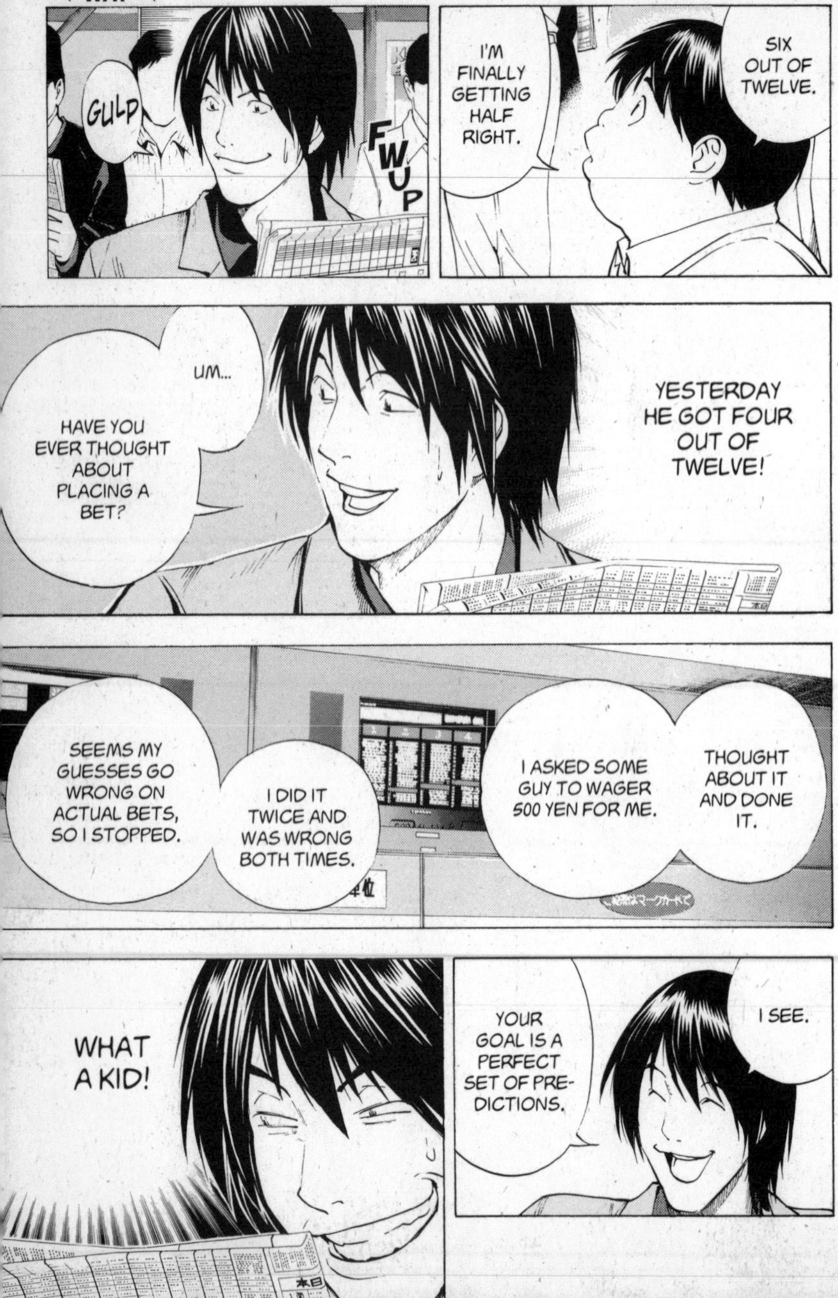
SIX OUT OF TWELVE.
I'M FINALLY GETTING HALF RIGHT.
FWUP
GULP
YESTERDAY HE GOT FOUR OUT OF TWELVE!
UM...
HAVE YOU EVER THOUGHT ABOUT PLACING A BET?
THOUGHT ABOUT IT AND DONE IT.
I ASKED SOME GUY TO WAGER 500 YEN FOR ME.
I DID IT TWICE AND WAS WRONG BOTH TIMES.
SEEMS MY GUESSES GO WRONG ON ACTUAL BETS, SO I STOPPED.
I SEE.
YOUR GOAL IS A PERFECT SET OF PREDICTIONS.
WHAT A KID!

READ THIS WAY

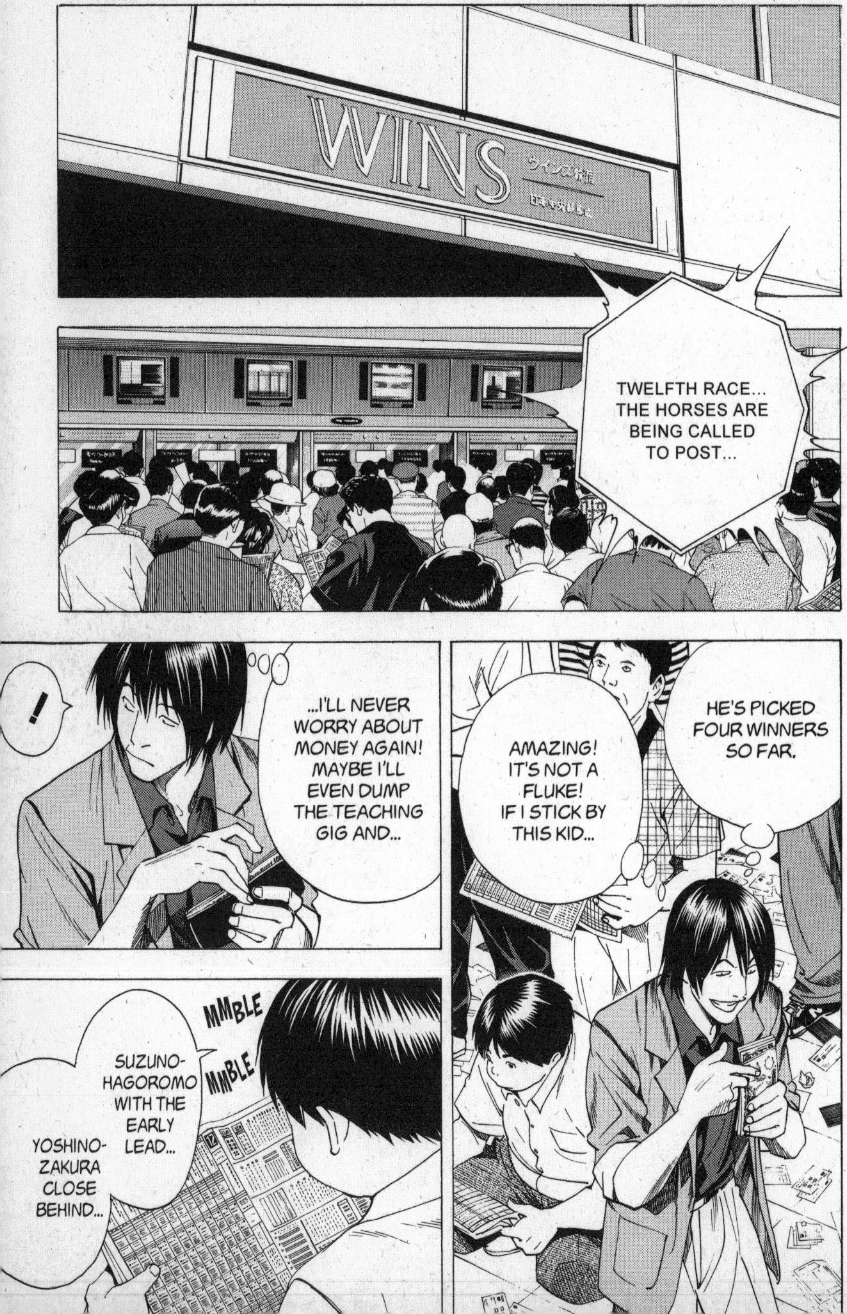
WINS
TWELFTH RACE... THE HORSES ARE BEING CALLED TO POST...
HE'S PICKED FOUR WINNERS SO FAR.
AMAZING! IT'S NOT A FLUKE! IF I STICK BY THIS KID...
!
...I'LL NEVER WORRY ABOUT MONEY AGAIN! MAYBE I'LL EVEN DUMP THE TEACHING GIG AND...
MMBLE
MMBLE
SUZUNO-HAGOROMO WITH THE EARLY LEAD...
YOSHINO-ZAKURA CLOSE BEHIND...

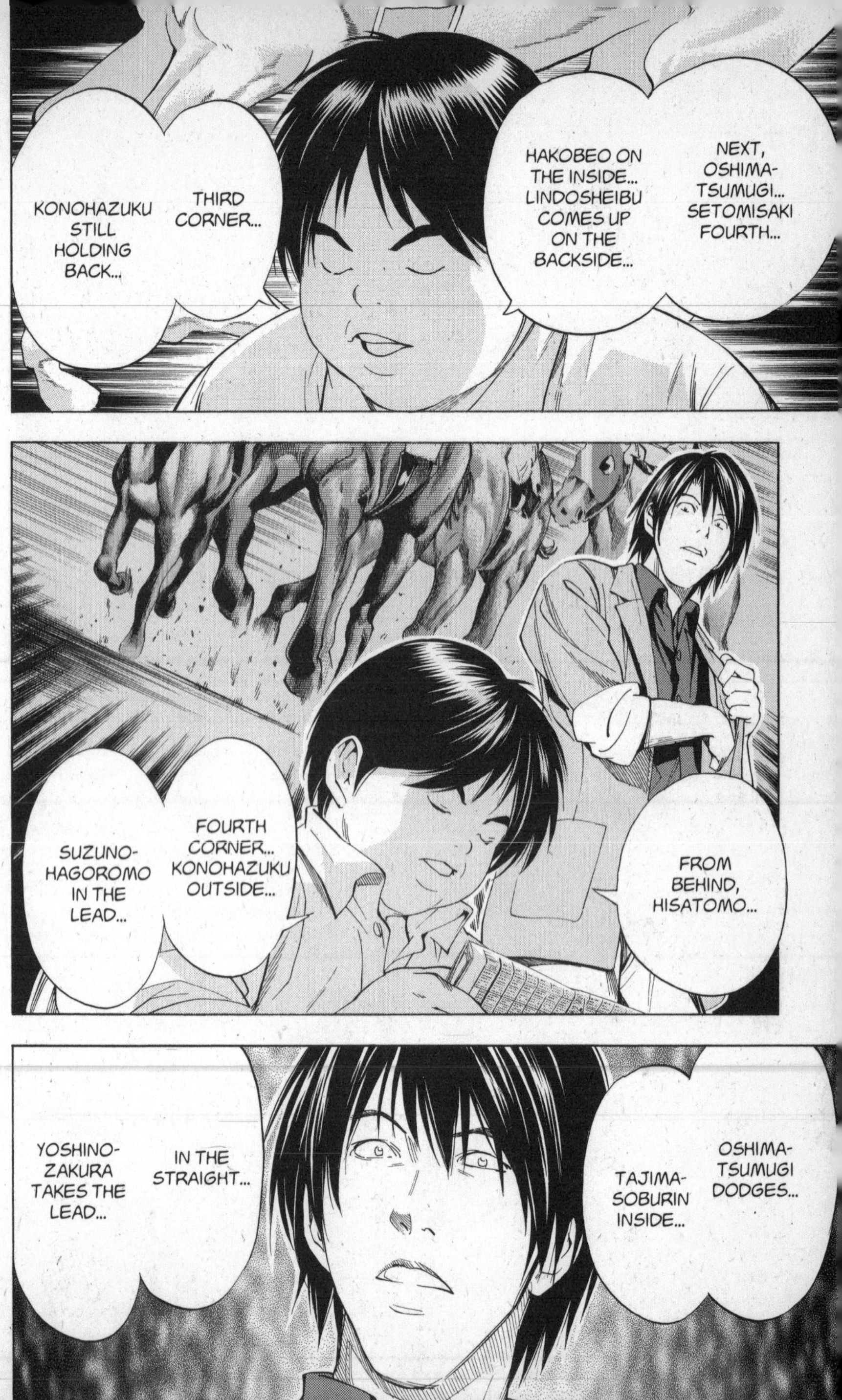
NEXT, OSHIMA-TSUMUGI... SETOMISAKI FOURTH...
HAKOBEO ON THE INSIDE... LINDOSHEIBU COMES UP ON THE BACKSIDE...
THIRD CORNER...
KONOHAZUKU STILL HOLDING BACK...
FROM BEHIND, HISATOMO...
FOURTH CORNER... KONOHAZUKU OUTSIDE...
SUZUNO-HAGOROMO IN THE LEAD...
OSHIMA-TSUMUGI DODGES...
TAJIMA-SOBURIN INSIDE...
IN THE STRAIGHT...
YOSHINO-ZAKURA TAKES THE LEAD...

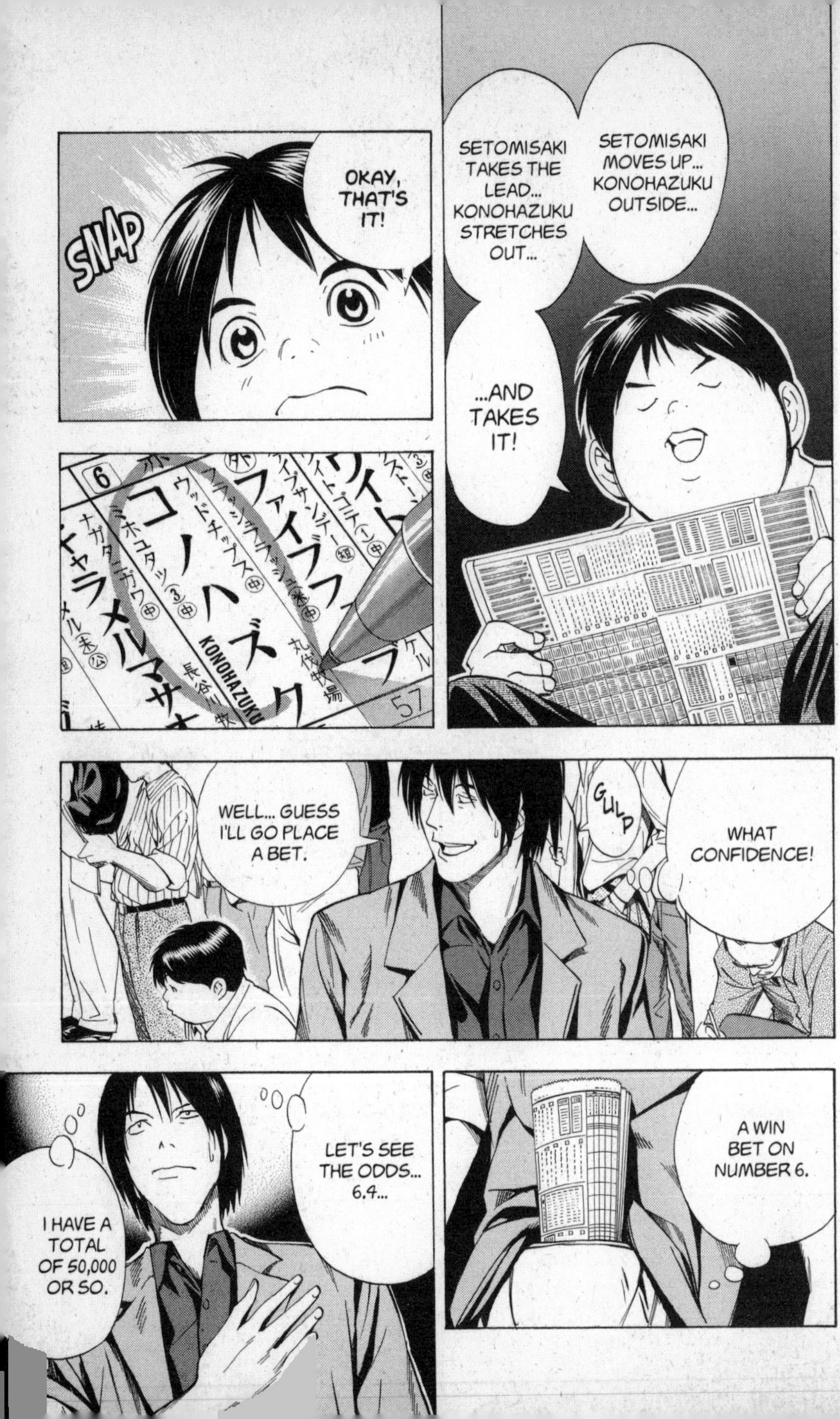
SETOMISAKI MOVES UP... KONOHAZUKU OUTSIDE...
SETOMISAKI TAKES THE LEAD... KONOHAZUKU STRETCHES OUT...
...AND TAKES IT!
OKAY, THAT'S IT!
SNAP
KONOHAZUKU
WHAT CONFIDENCE!
GULP
WELL... GUESS I'LL GO PLACE A BET.
A WIN BET ON NUMBER 6.
LET'S SEE THE ODDS... 6.4...
I HAVE A TOTAL OF 50,000 OR SO.

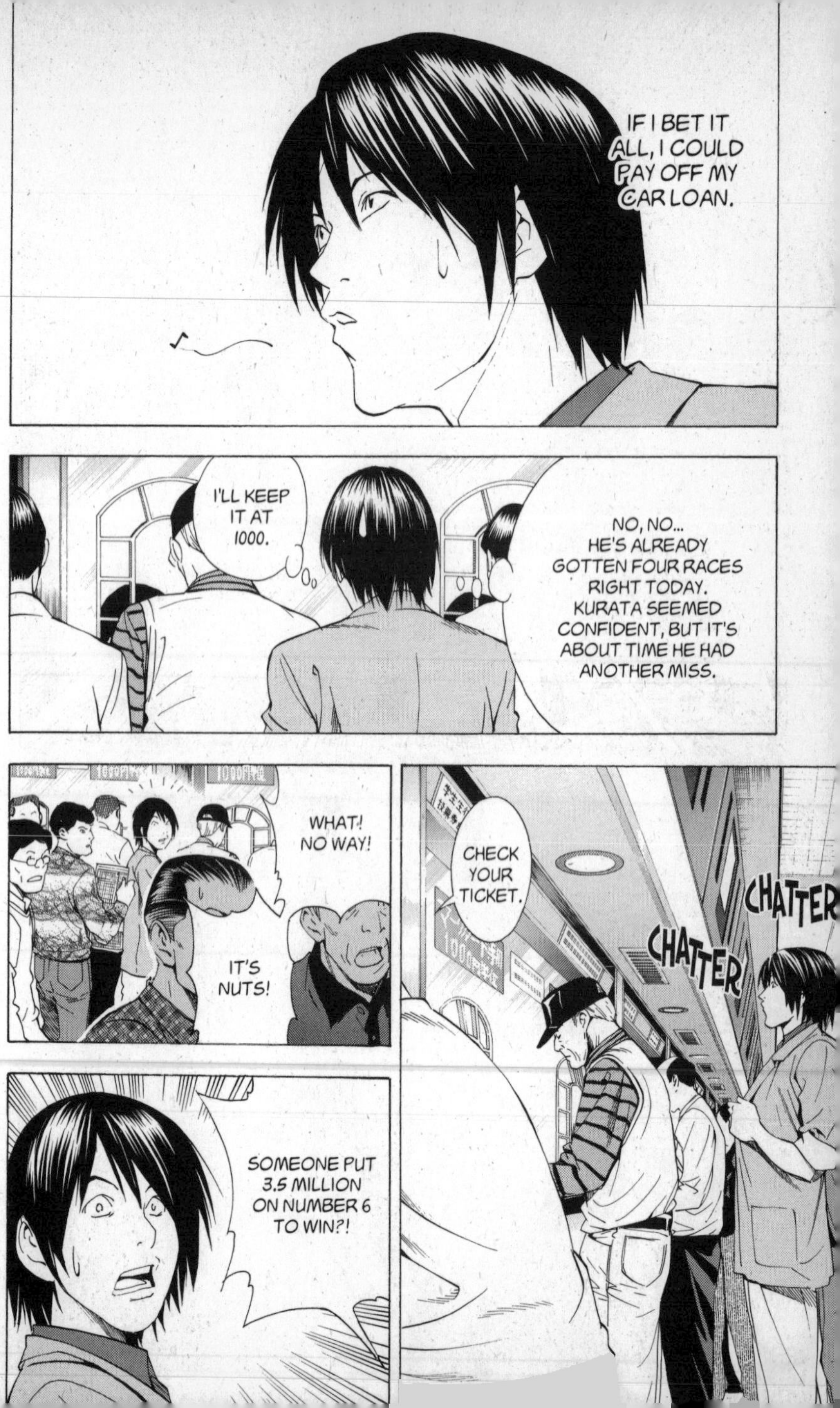
IF I BET IT ALL, I COULD PAY OFF MY CAR LOAN.
NO, NO... HE'S ALREADY GOTTEN FOUR RACES RIGHT TODAY. KURATA SEEMED CONFIDENT, BUT IT'S ABOUT TIME HE HAD ANOTHER MISS.
I'LL KEEP IT AT 1000.
CHATTER
CHATTER
CHECK YOUR TICKET.
WHAT! NO WAY!
IT'S NUTS!
SOMEONE PUT 3.5 MILLION ON NUMBER 6 TO WIN?!

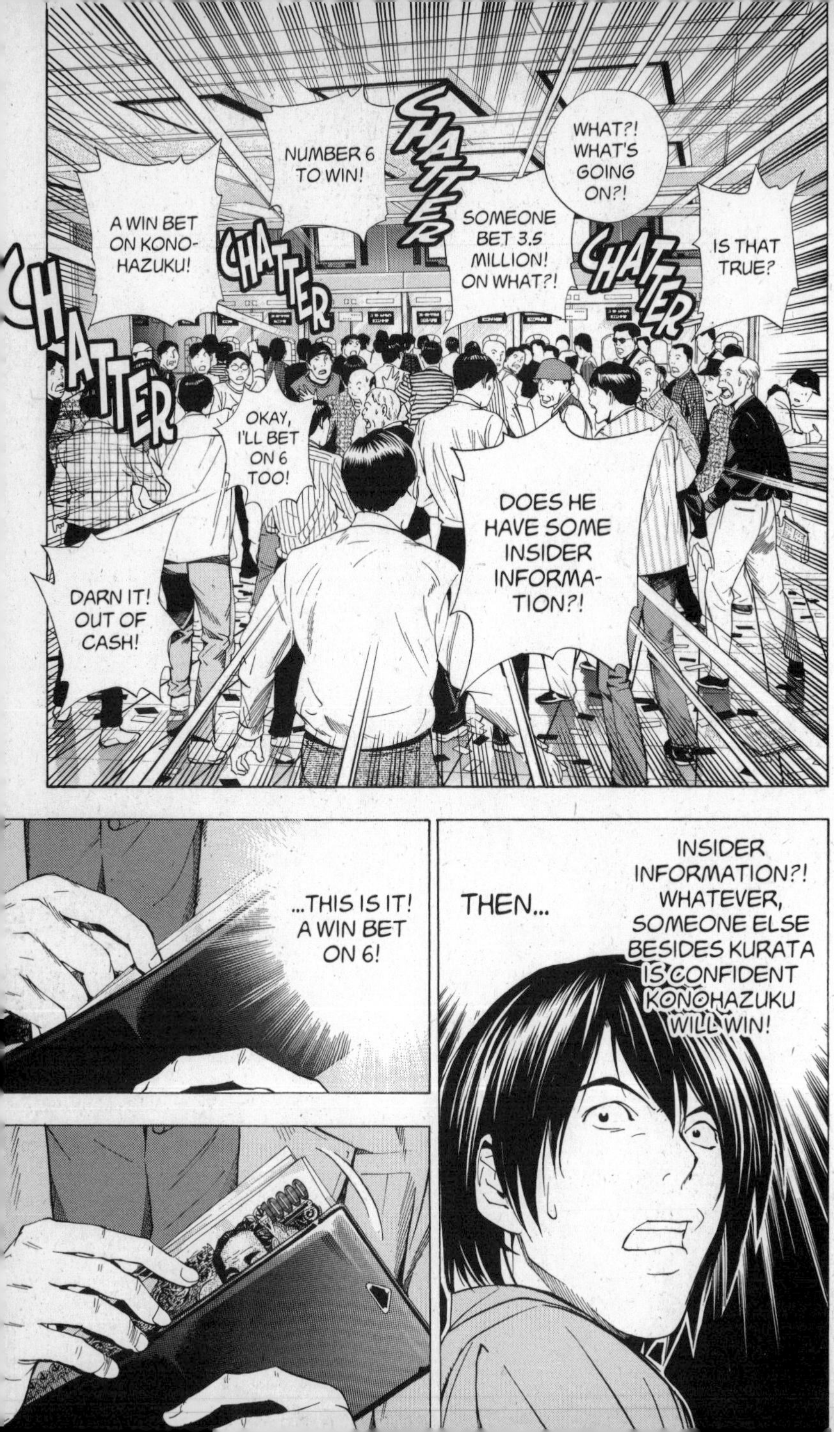
IS THAT TRUE?
WHAT?! WHAT'S GOING ON?!
CHATTER
CHATTER
SOMEONE BET 3.5 MILLION! ON WHAT?!
NUMBER 6 TO WIN!
CHATTER
A WIN BET ON KONO-HAZUKU!
CHATTER
DOES HE HAVE SOME INSIDER INFORMATION?!
OKAY, I'LL BET ON 6 TOO!
DARN IT! OUT OF CASH!
INSIDER INFORMATION?! WHATEVER, SOMEONE ELSE BESIDES KURATA IS CONFIDENT KONOHAZUKU WILL WIN!
THEN...
...THIS IS IT! A WIN BET ON 6!

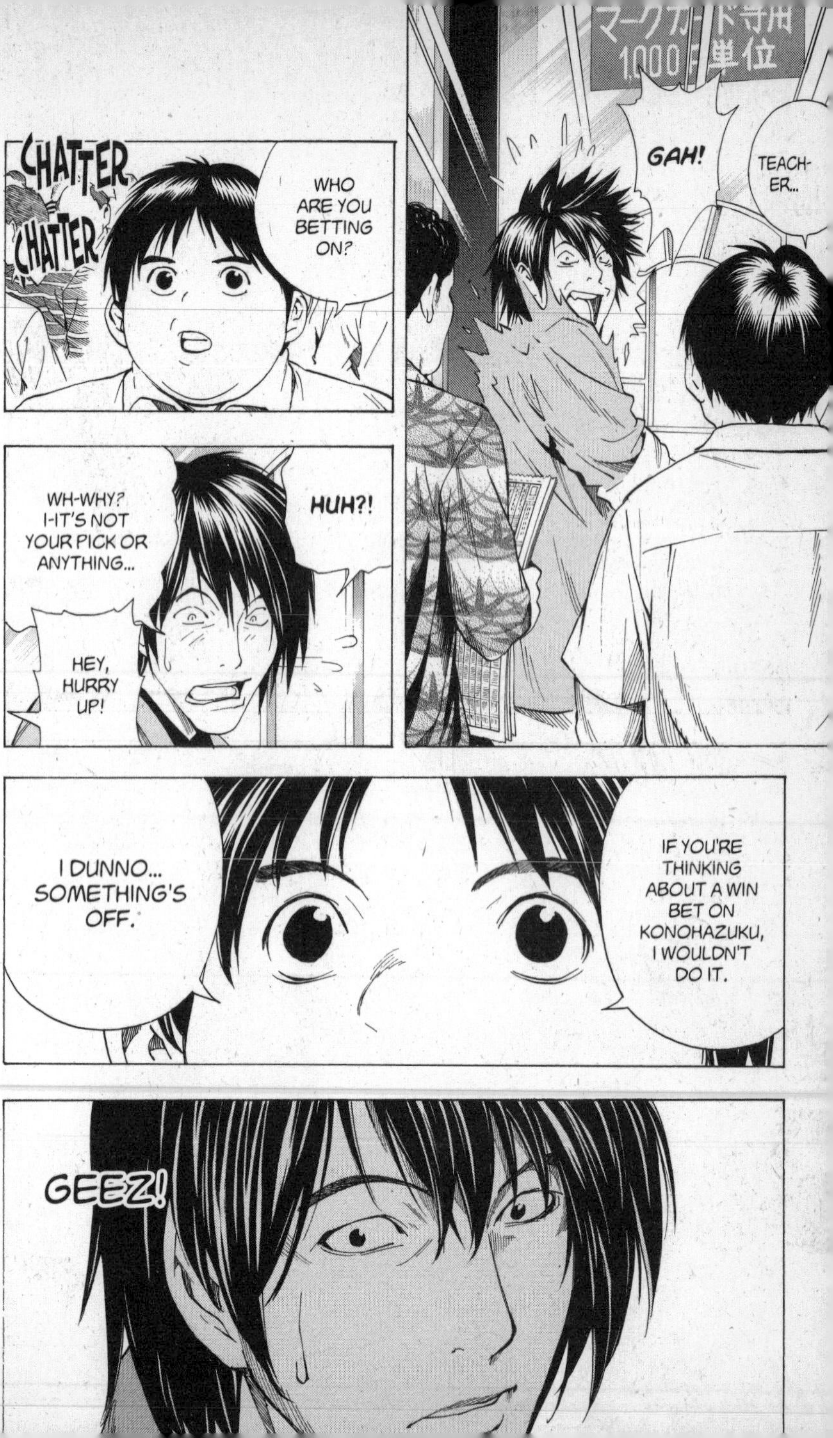

マークカード専用
1,000 単位
TEACHER...
GAH!
WHO ARE YOU BETTING ON?
CHATTER CHATTER
HUH?!
WH-WHY? I-IT'S NOT YOUR PICK OR ANYTHING...
HEY, HURRY UP!
IF YOU'RE THINKING ABOUT A WIN BET ON KONOHAZUKU, I WOULDN'T DO IT.
I DUNNO... SOMETHING'S OFF.
GEEZ!

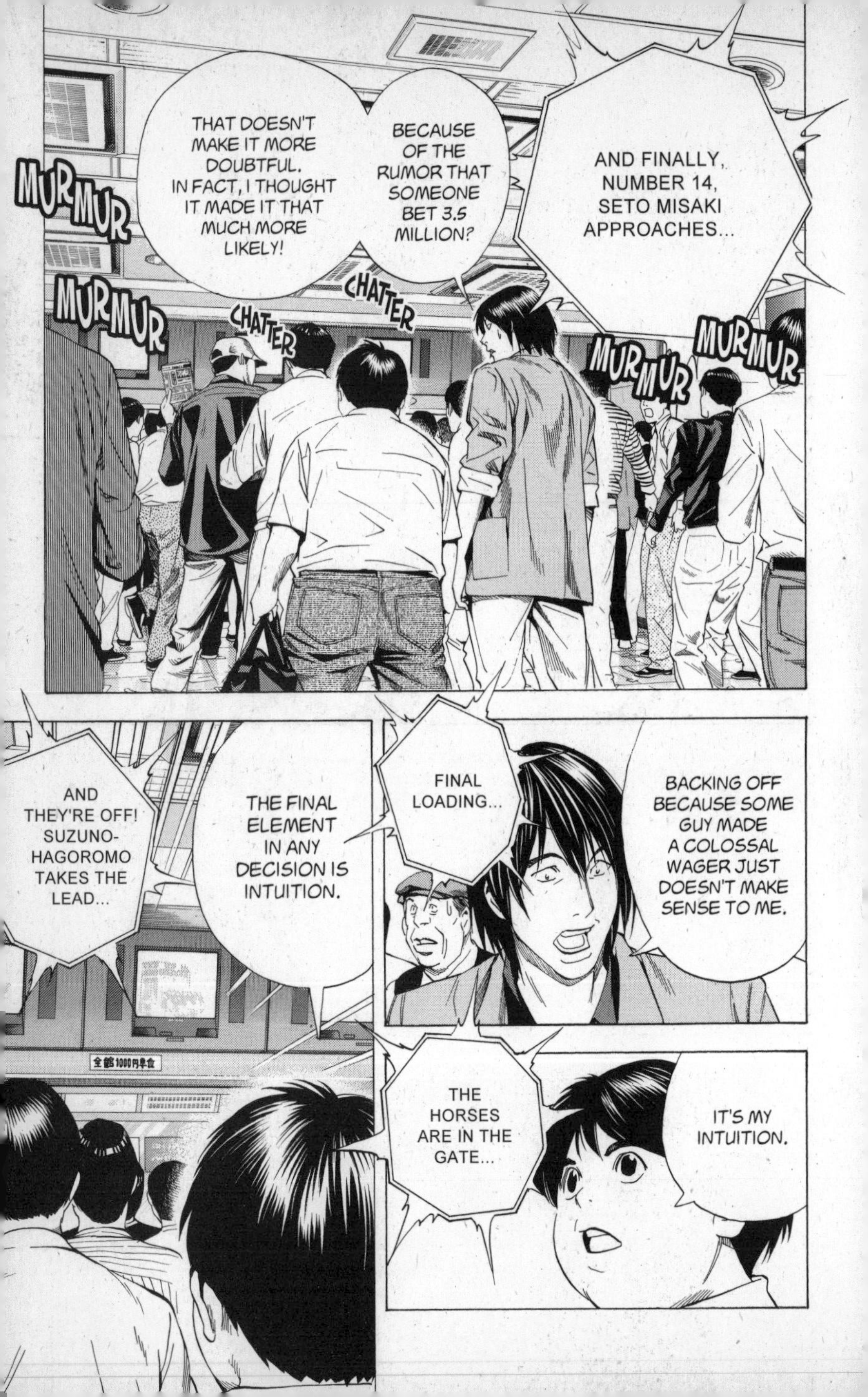
AND FINALLY, NUMBER 14, SETO MISAKI APPROACHES...
BECAUSE OF THE RUMOR THAT SOMEONE BET 3.5 MILLION?
THAT DOESN'T MAKE IT MORE DOUBTFUL. IN FACT, I THOUGHT IT MADE IT THAT MUCH MORE LIKELY!
MURMUR
MURMUR
MURMUR
MURMUR
CHATTER
CHATTER
BACKING OFF BECAUSE SOME GUY MADE A COLOSSAL WAGER JUST DOESN'T MAKE SENSE TO ME.
FINAL LOADING...
IT'S MY INTUITION.
THE HORSES ARE IN THE GATE...
THE FINAL ELEMENT IN ANY DECISION IS INTUITION.
AND THEY'RE OFF! SUZUNO-HAGOROMO TAKES THE LEAD...
全館1000円単位

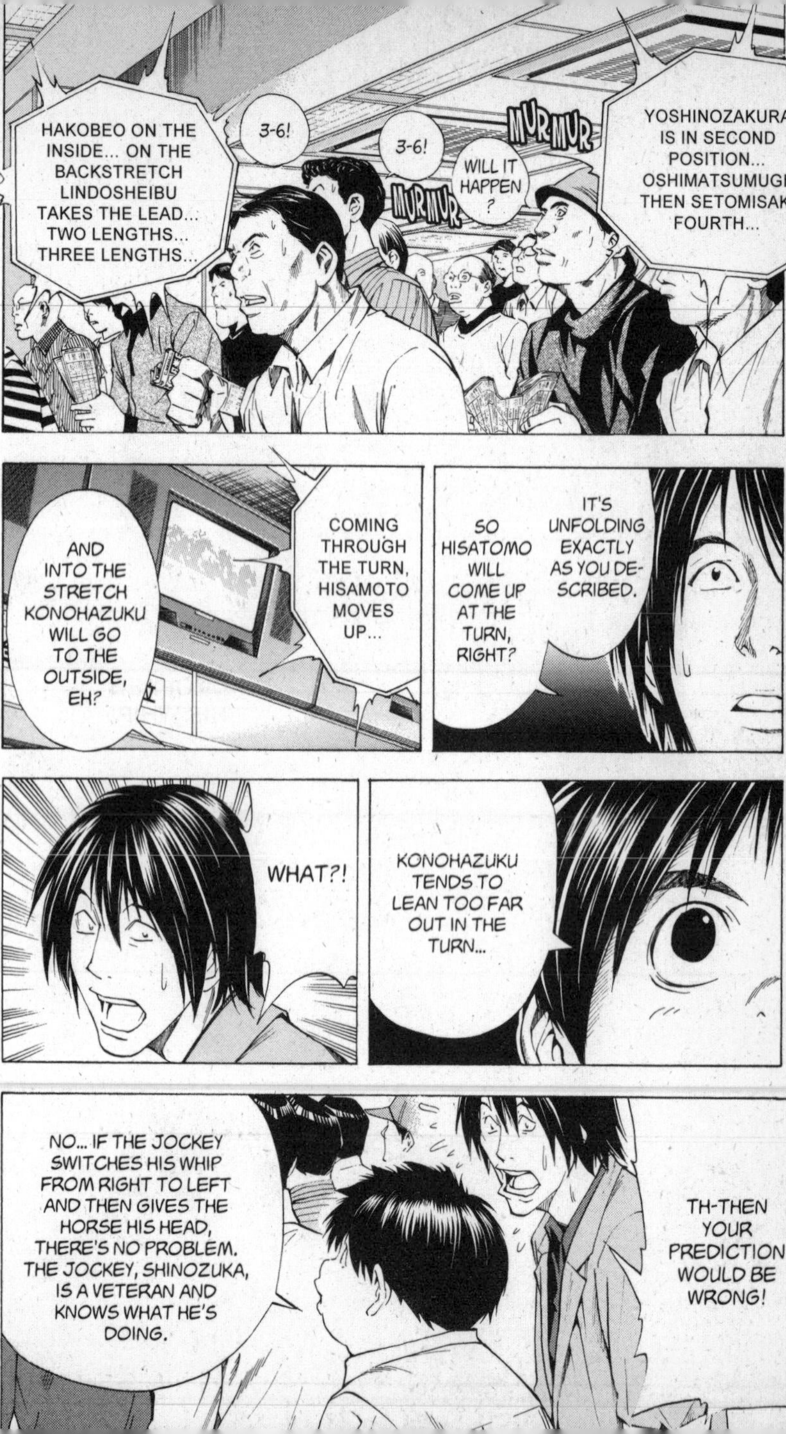
YOSHINOZAKURA IS IN SECOND POSITION... OSHIMATSUMUGI, THEN SETOMISAKI FOURTH...
MURMUR
WILL IT HAPPEN?
3-6!
3-6!
MURMUR
HAKOBEO ON THE INSIDE... ON THE BACKSTRETCH LINDOSHEIBU TAKES THE LEAD... TWO LENGTHS... THREE LENGTHS...
IT'S UNFOLDING EXACTLY AS YOU DESCRIBED.
SO HISATOMO WILL COME UP AT THE TURN, RIGHT?
COMING THROUGH THE TURN, HISAMOTO MOVES UP...
AND INTO THE STRETCH KONOHAZUKU WILL GO TO THE OUTSIDE, EH?
KONOHAZUKU TENDS TO LEAN TOO FAR OUT IN THE TURN...
WHAT?!
TH-THEN YOUR PREDICTION WOULD BE WRONG!
NO... IF THE JOCKEY SWITCHES HIS WHIP FROM RIGHT TO LEFT AND THEN GIVES THE HORSE HIS HEAD, THERE'S NO PROBLEM. THE JOCKEY, SHINOZUKA, IS A VETERAN AND KNOWS WHAT HE'S DOING.

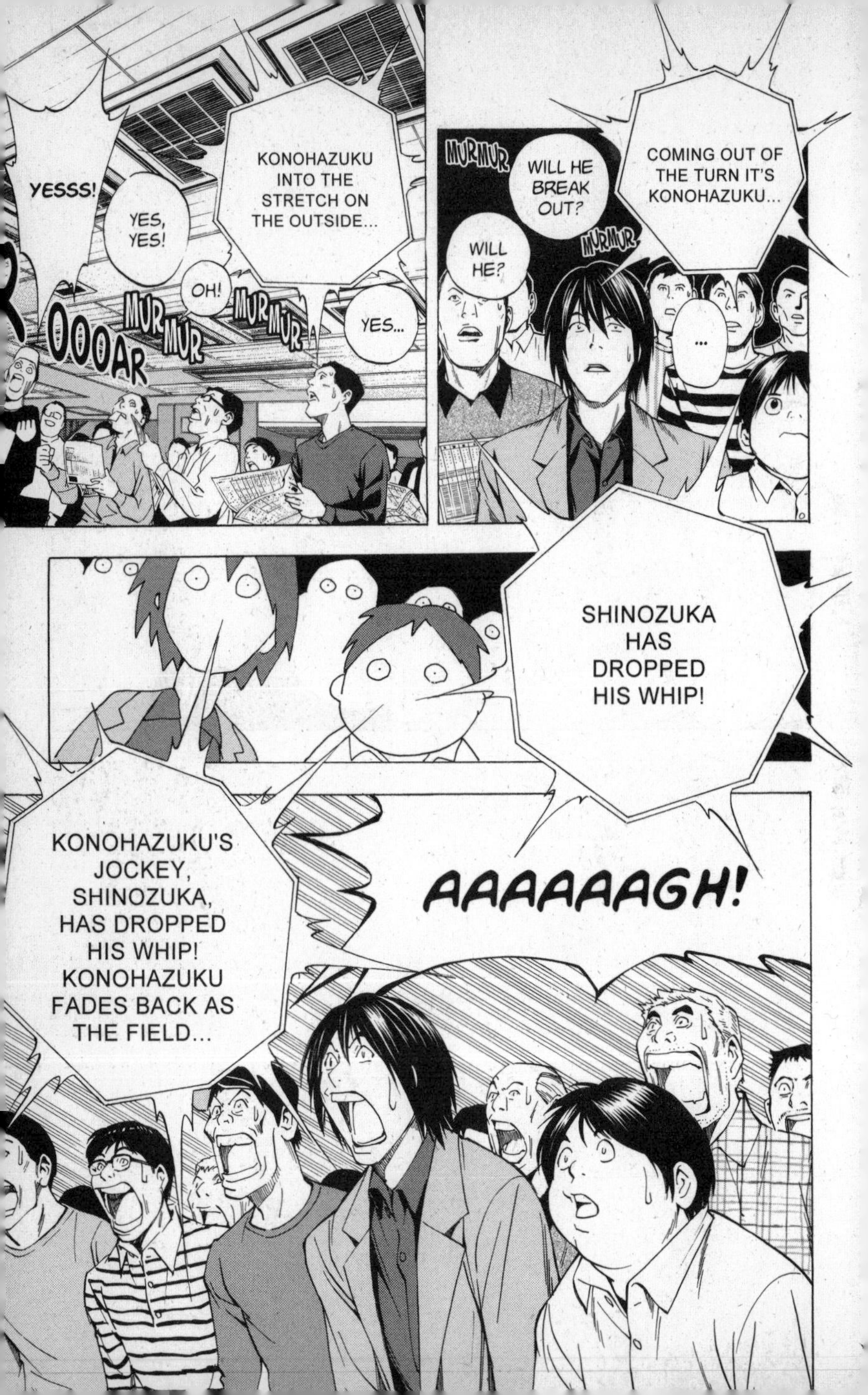

COMING OUT OF THE TURN IT'S KONOHAZUKU...
MURMUR
WILL HE BREAK OUT?
WILL HE?
MURMUR
...
KONOHAZUKU INTO THE STRETCH ON THE OUTSIDE...
YES...
YES, YES!
OH!
MURMUR
MURMUR
YESSS!
ROOOAR
SHINOZUKA HAS DROPPED HIS WHIP!
KONOHAZUKU'S JOCKEY, SHINOZUKA, HAS DROPPED HIS WHIP! KONOHAZUKU FADES BACK AS THE FIELD...
AAAAAAGH!

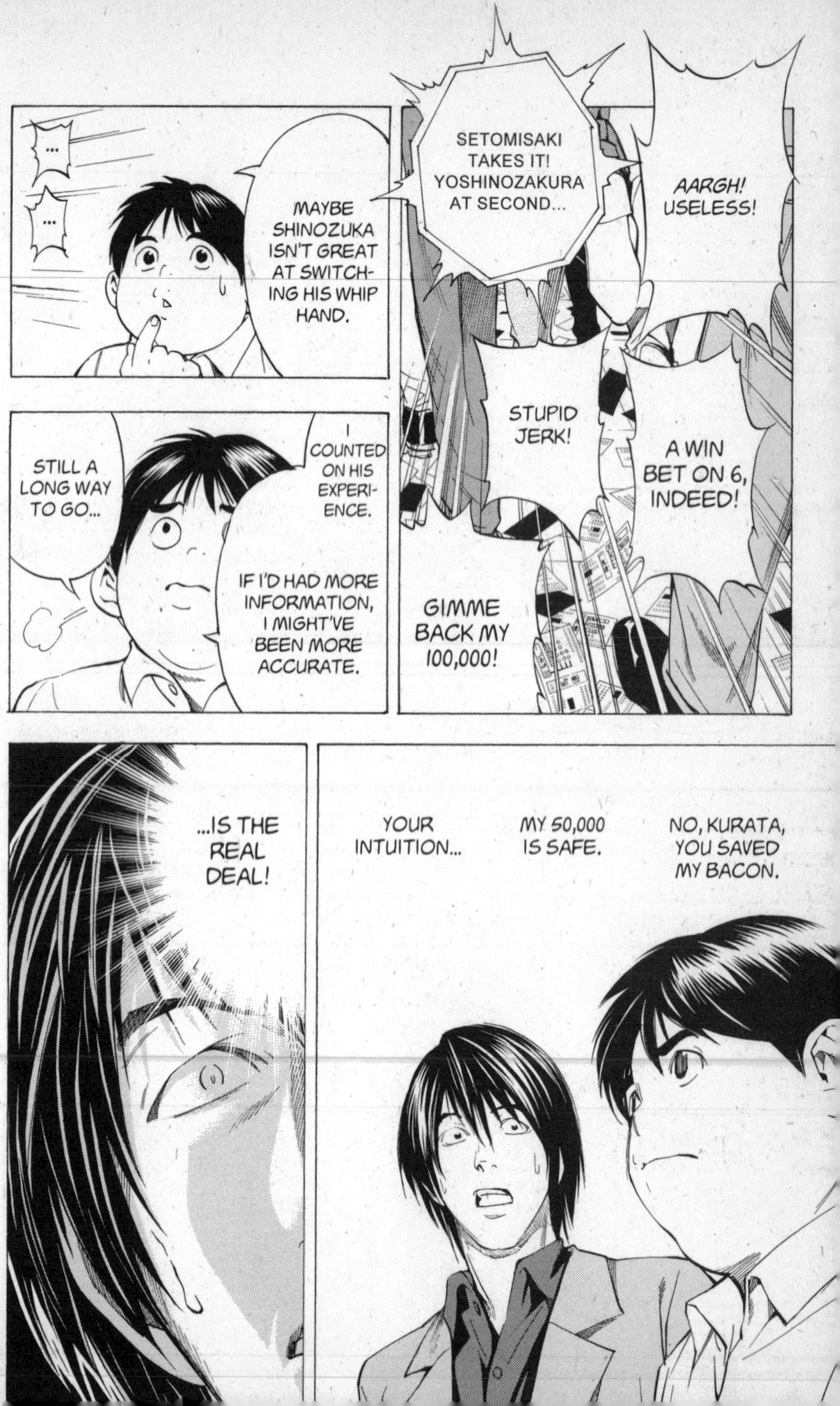
SETOMISAKI TAKES IT! YOSHINOZAKURA AT SECOND...
AARGH! USELESS!
A WIN BET ON 6, INDEED!
STUPID JERK!
GIMME BACK MY 100,000!
MAYBE SHINOZUKA ISN'T GREAT AT SWITCHING HIS WHIP HAND.
...
...
I COUNTED ON HIS EXPERIENCE.
IF I'D HAD MORE INFORMATION, I MIGHT'VE BEEN MORE ACCURATE.
STILL A LONG WAY TO GO...
NO, KURATA, YOU SAVED MY BACON.
MY 50,000 IS SAFE.
YOUR INTUITION...
...IS THE REAL DEAL!

READ THIS WAY

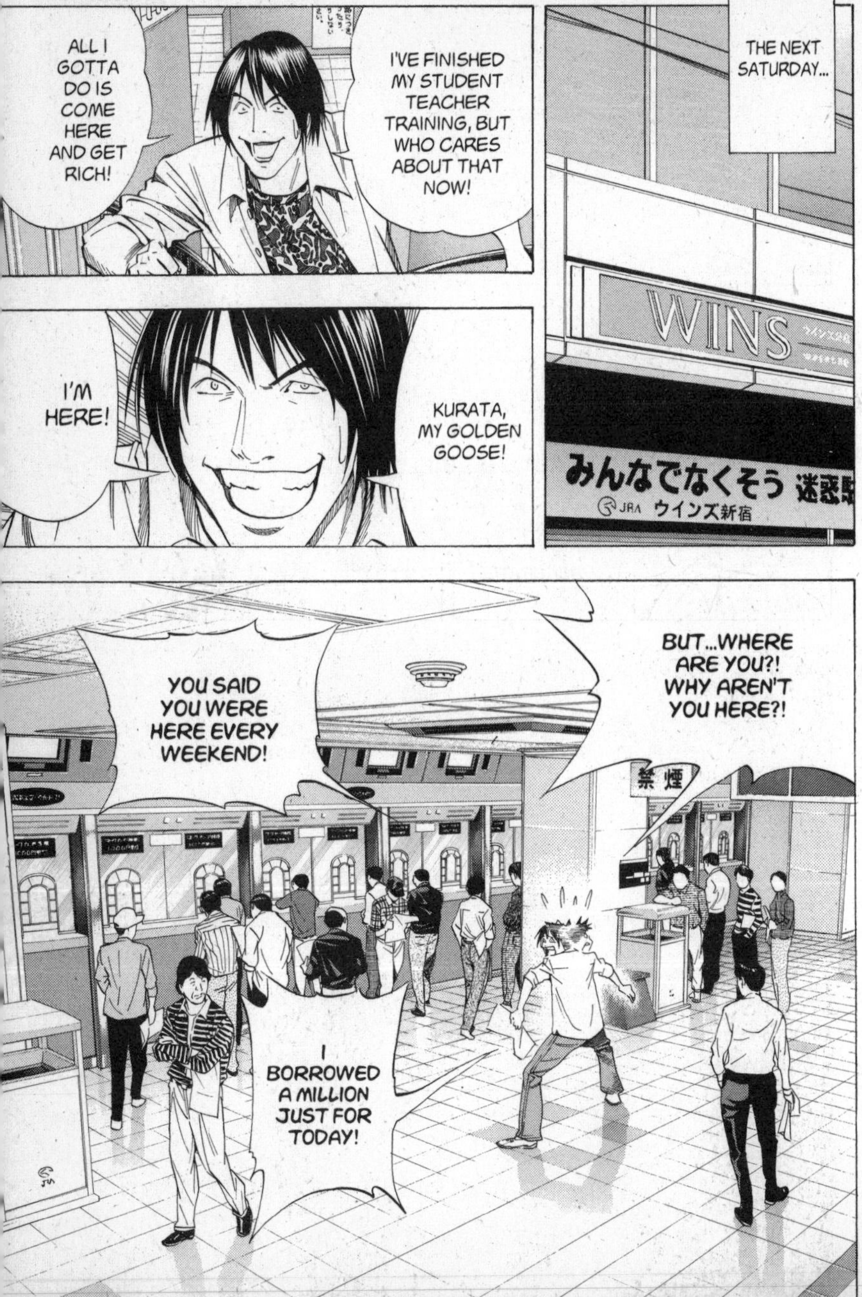
THE NEXT SATURDAY...
WINS
みんなでなくそう 迷惑駐
JRA ウインズ新宿
I'VE FINISHED MY STUDENT TEACHER TRAINING, BUT WHO CARES ABOUT THAT NOW!
ALL I GOTTA DO IS COME HERE AND GET RICH!
KURATA, MY GOLDEN GOOSE!
I'M HERE!
BUT...WHERE ARE YOU?! WHY AREN'T YOU HERE?!
禁煙
YOU SAID YOU WERE HERE EVERY WEEKEND!
I BORROWED A MILLION JUST FOR TODAY!

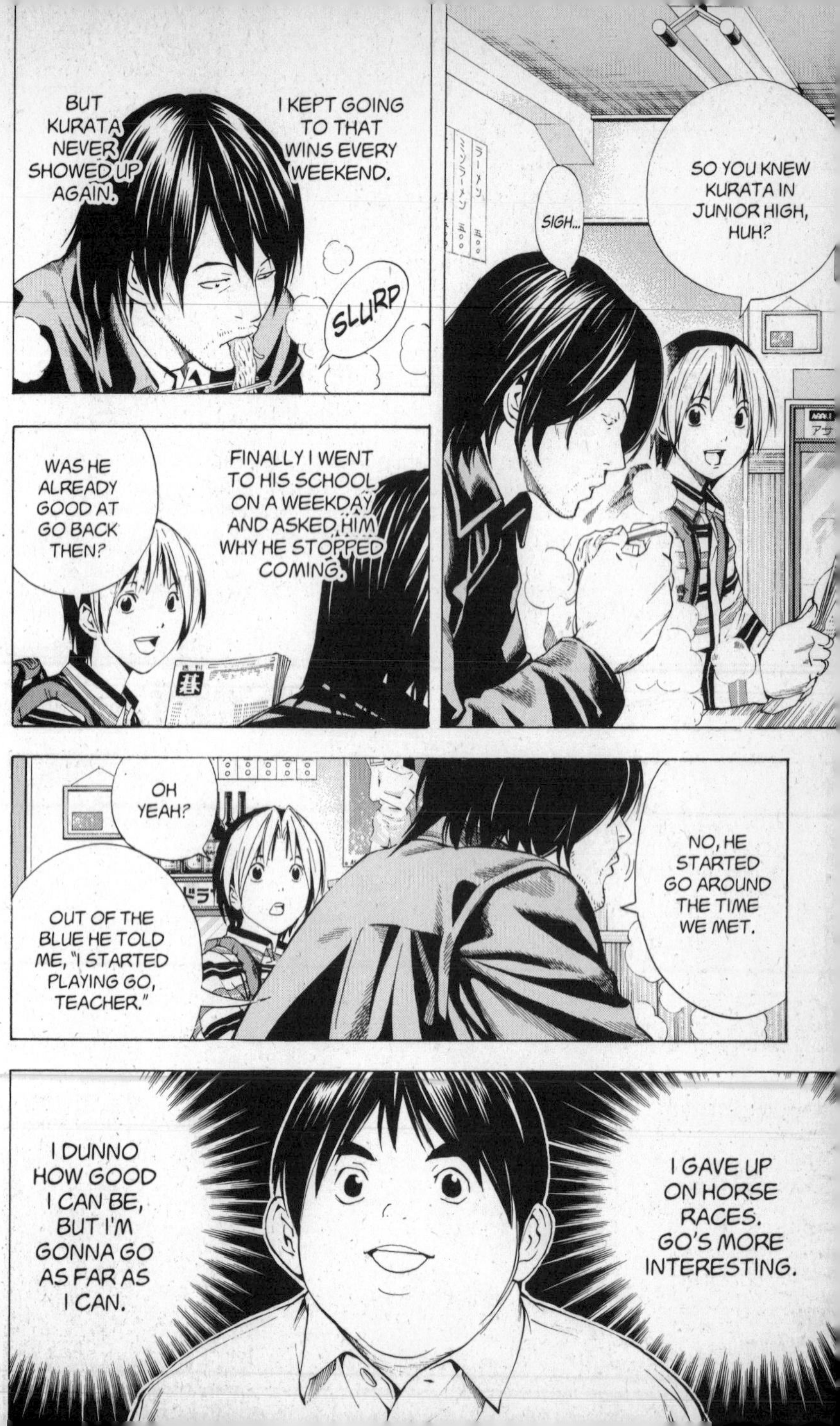
SO YOU KNEW KURATA IN JUNIOR HIGH, HUH?
SIGH...
I KEPT GOING TO THAT WINS EVERY WEEKEND.
BUT KURATA NEVER SHOWED UP AGAIN.
SLURP
FINALLY I WENT TO HIS SCHOOL ON A WEEKDAY AND ASKED HIM WHY HE STOPPED COMING.
WAS HE ALREADY GOOD AT GO BACK THEN?
NO, HE STARTED GO AROUND THE TIME WE MET.
OH YEAH?
OUT OF THE BLUE HE TOLD ME, "I STARTED PLAYING GO, TEACHER."
I GAVE UP ON HORSE RACES. GO'S MORE INTERESTING.
I DUNNO HOW GOOD I CAN BE, BUT I'M GONNA GO AS FAR AS I CAN.

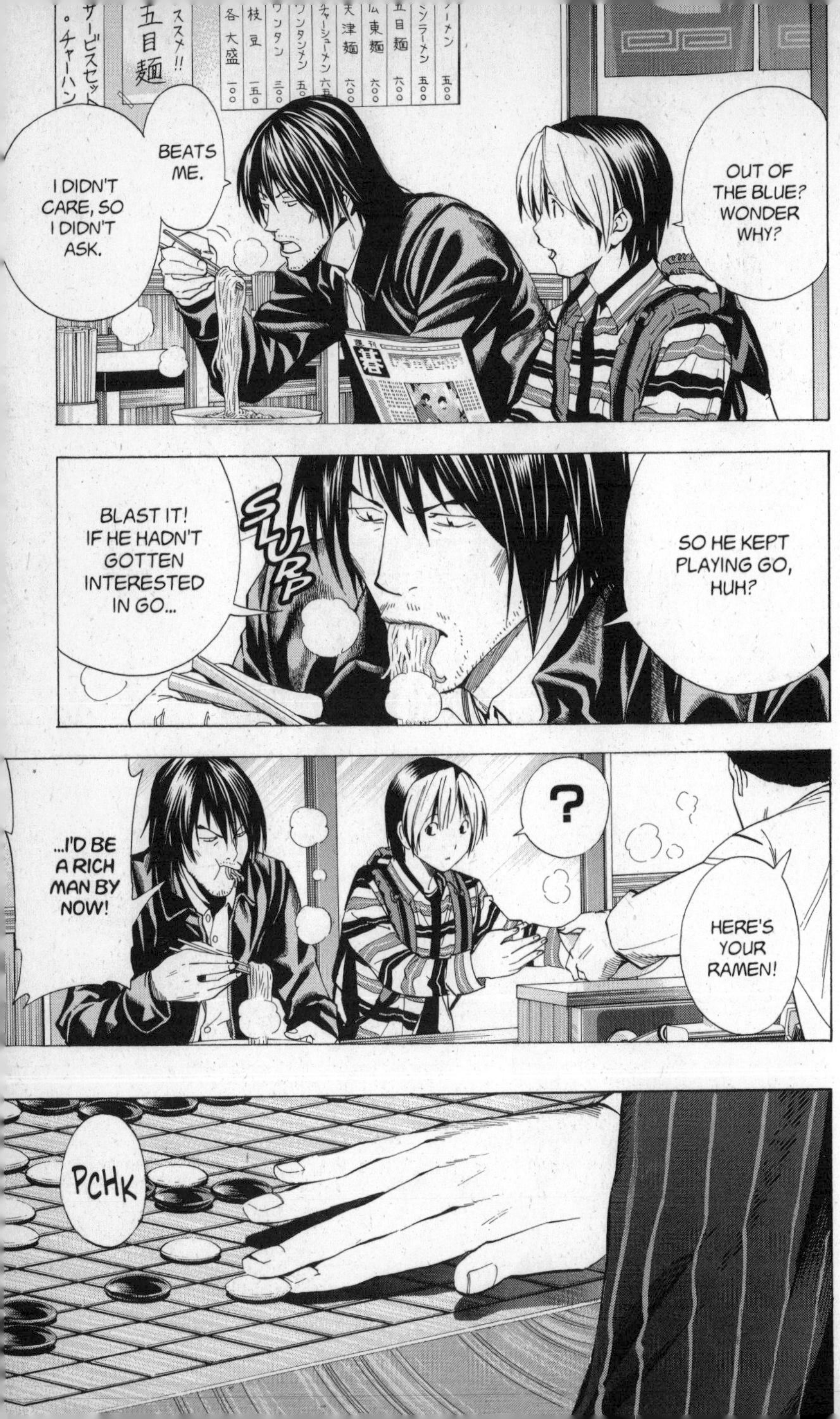
五目麺 六〇〇
広東麺 六〇〇
天津麺 六〇〇
ワンタン 三〇〇
枝豆 一五〇
各大盛 一〇〇
五目麺
OUT OF THE BLUE? WONDER WHY?
BEATS ME.
I DIDN'T CARE, SO I DIDN'T ASK.
SO HE KEPT PLAYING GO, HUH?
SLURP
BLAST IT! IF HE HADN'T GOTTEN INTERESTED IN GO...
HERE'S YOUR RAMEN!
?
...I'D BE A RICH MAN BY NOW!
PCHK

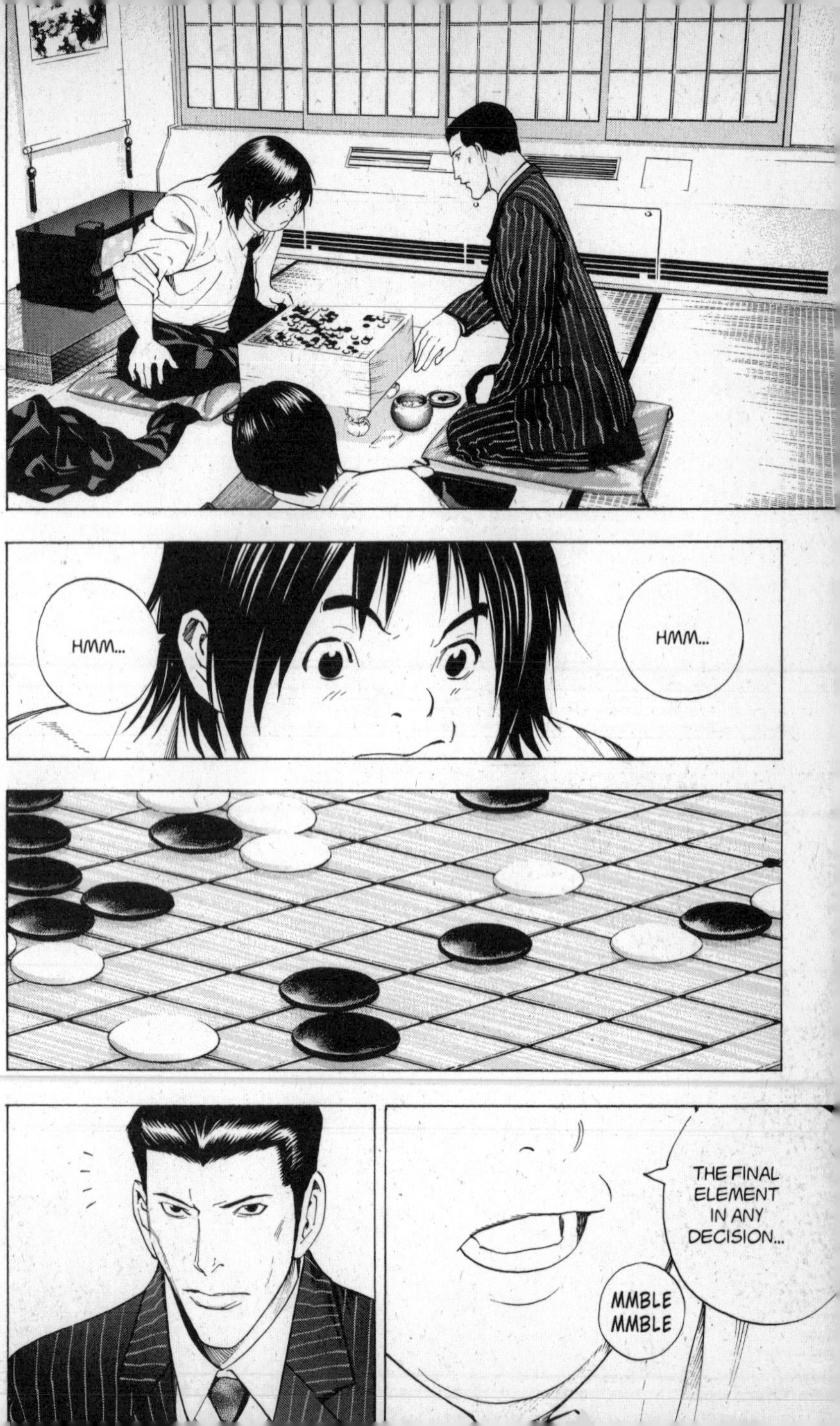
HMM...
HMM...
THE FINAL ELEMENT IN ANY DECISION...
MMBLE MMBLE

READ THIS WAY

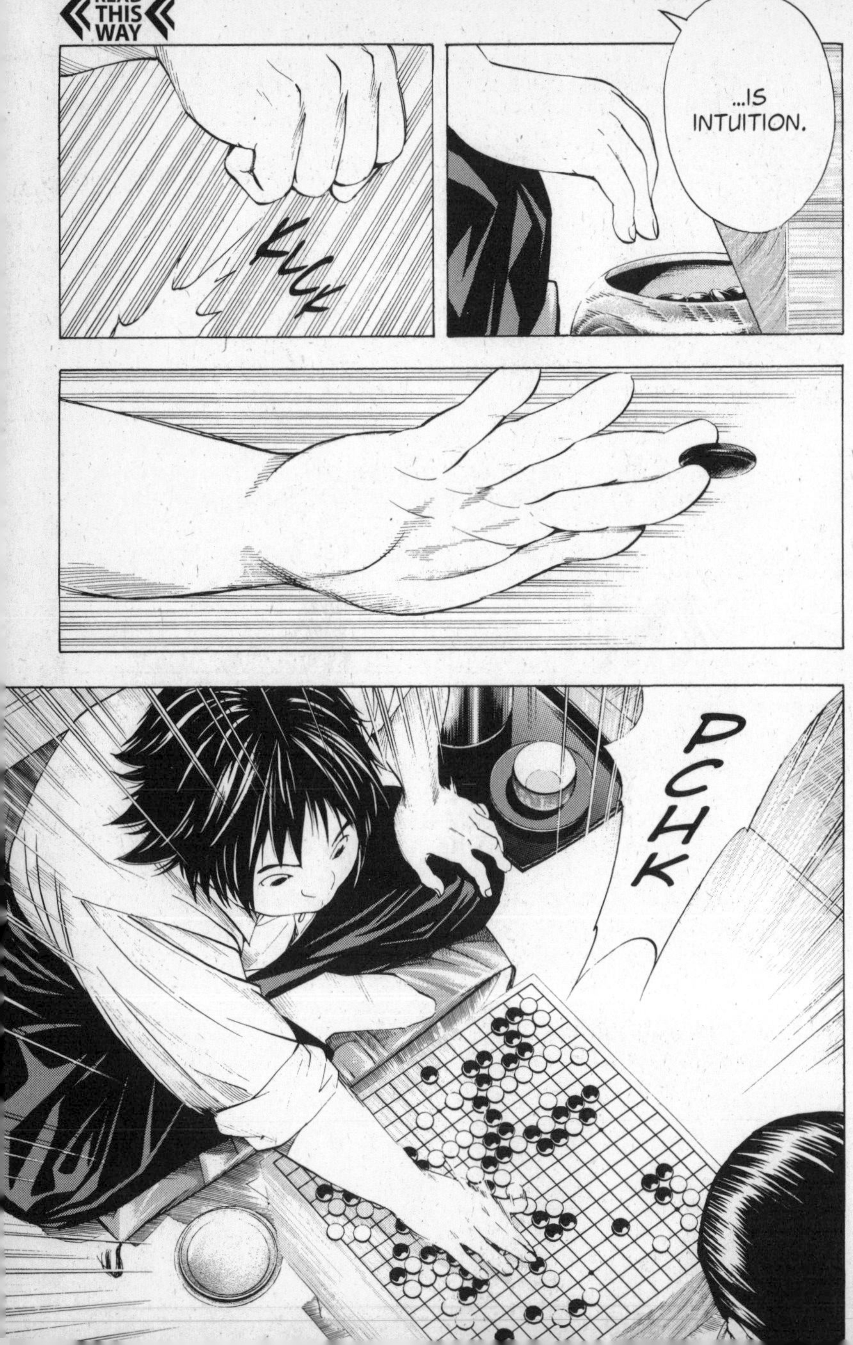
...IS INTUITION.
KLUCK
PCHK

YUMI HOTTA'S LONG INTERVIEW WITH TAKESHI OBATA SENSEI: 5

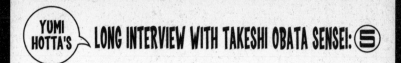

Ⓗ DO YOU LISTEN TO MUSIC WHILE YOU WORK?
Ⓞ NO, I LEAVE THE TV ON. I DON'T REALLY LOOK AT THE SCREEN. I JUST LISTEN TO THE NEWS BEHIND ME.

Ⓗ BY THE WAY, YOUR CELL PHONE IS COOL.
Ⓞ I BOUGHT IT BECAUSE IT LOOKED COOL. [LAUGHTER] IT'S PRETTY OLD.
Ⓗ DO YOU TEXT?
Ⓞ YES. I'LL TELL MY ASSISTANTS TO COME AT SUCH AND SUCH A TIME, FOR EXAMPLE. OR MY ASSISTANTS WILL TEXT ME TO SAY, "GIVE ME A RAISE!" [LAUGHTER]

Ⓗ I SEE YOU GOT A MOHAWK. DOES THAT REFLECT SOME INNER CHANGE?
Ⓞ IT'S TO CAMOUFLAGE MY THINNING HAIR. I SHOULD HAVE DONE IT SOONER. ONCE A WEEK I TEND TO IT MYSELF USING TWO MIRRORS, BUT I'VE GOTTEN BORED WITH IT. I'D LIKE A NEW HAIRSTYLE BUT I'VE BEEN STUCK BECAUSE THERE'S NO VARIATION.

Ⓗ LET'S FINISH WITH A QUICK BIO.
Ⓞ I WAS BORN FEBRUARY 11, 1969. I'M 174 CM TALL AND WEIGH 53 KG. BLOOD TYPE IS AB.
Ⓗ OH, I'M AB TOO. AND WE'RE THE SAME ZODIAC SIGN (THOUGH 12 YEARS APART). SO *HIKARU NO GO* IS CREATED BY A PAIR OF AB ROOSTERS! I LOOK FORWARD TO OUR CONTINUED COLLABORATION.

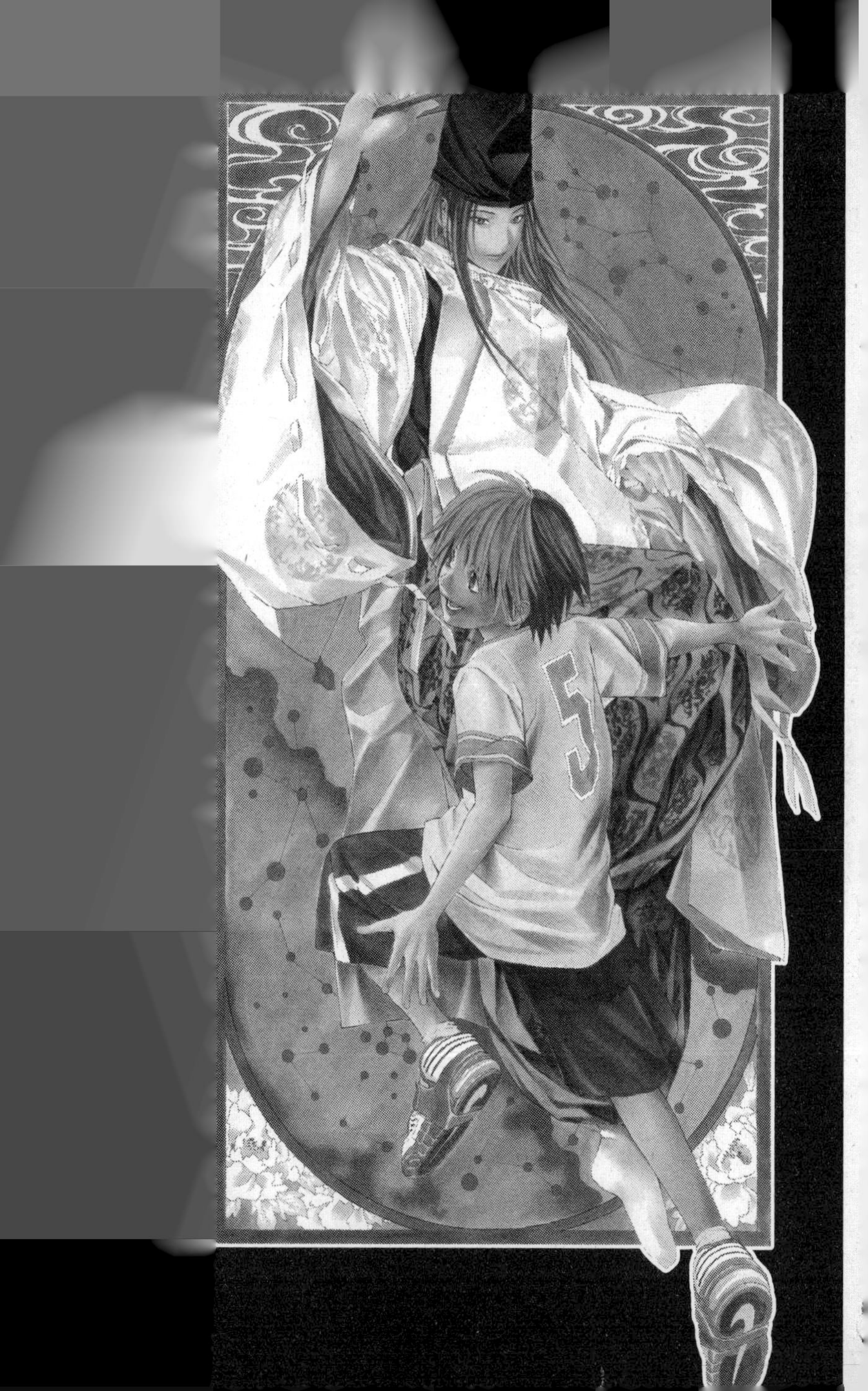

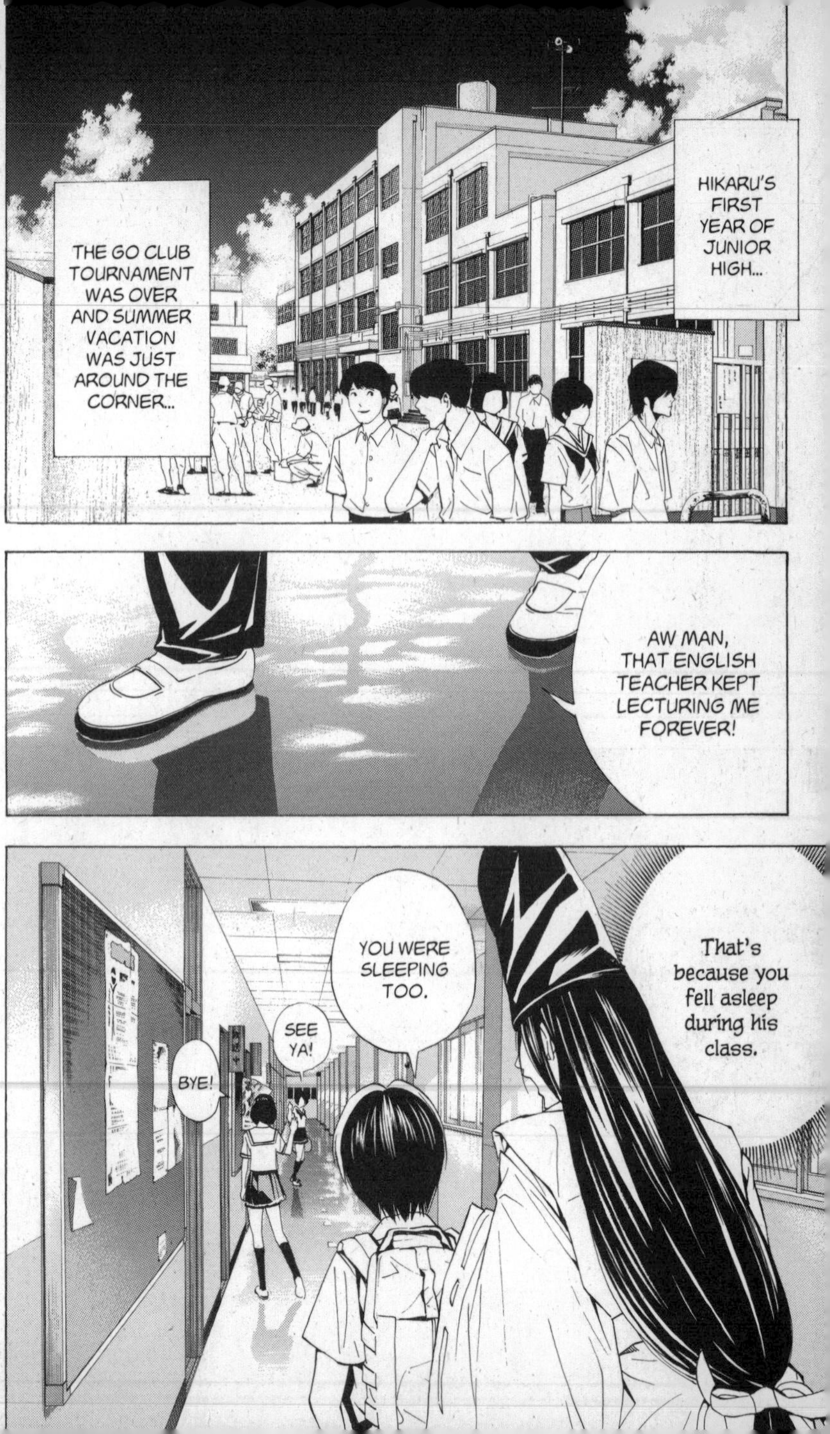
HIKARU'S FIRST YEAR OF JUNIOR HIGH...
THE GO CLUB TOURNAMENT WAS OVER AND SUMMER VACATION WAS JUST AROUND THE CORNER...
AW MAN, THAT ENGLISH TEACHER KEPT LECTURING ME FOREVER!
That's because you fell asleep during his class.
YOU WERE SLEEPING TOO.
SEE YA!
BYE!

READ THIS WAY

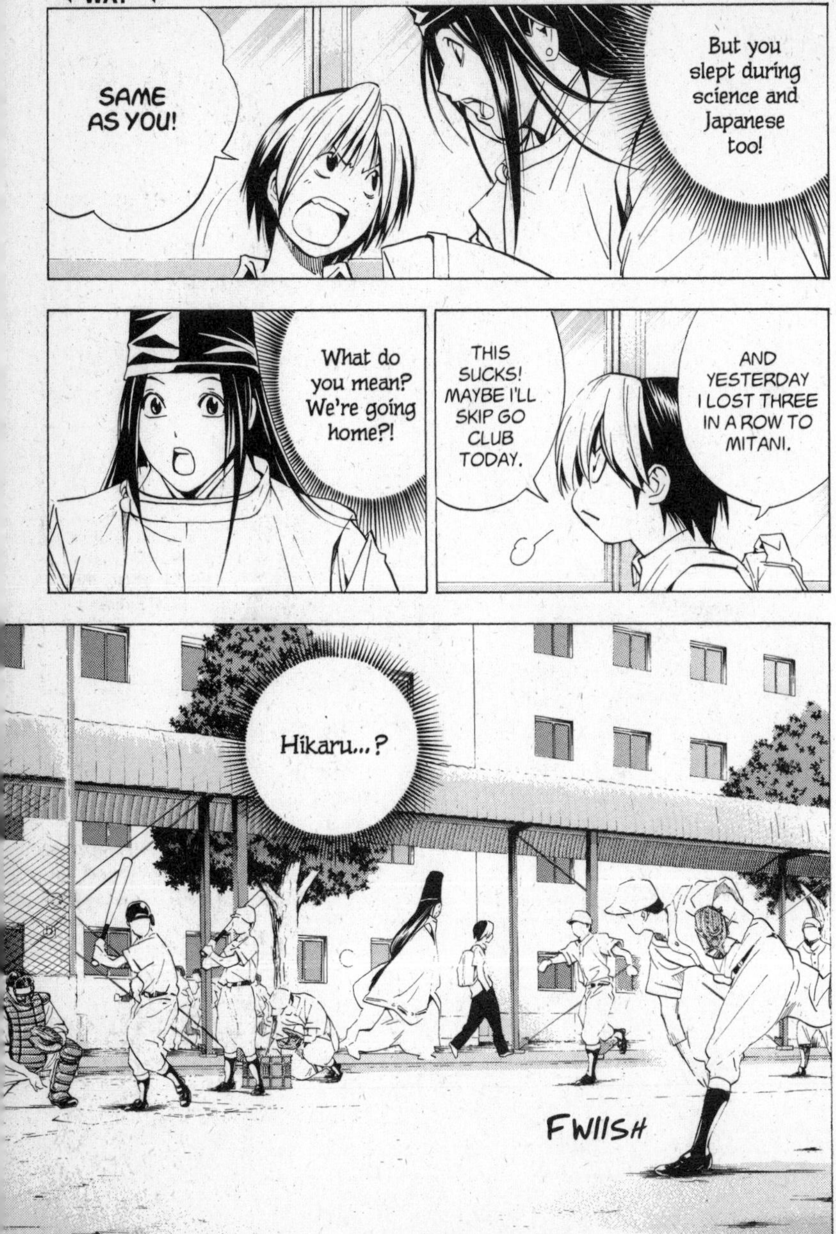
But you slept during science and Japanese too!
SAME AS YOU!
AND YESTERDAY I LOST THREE IN A ROW TO MITANI.
THIS SUCKS! MAYBE I'LL SKIP GO CLUB TODAY.
What do you mean? We're going home?!
Hikaru...?
FWIISH

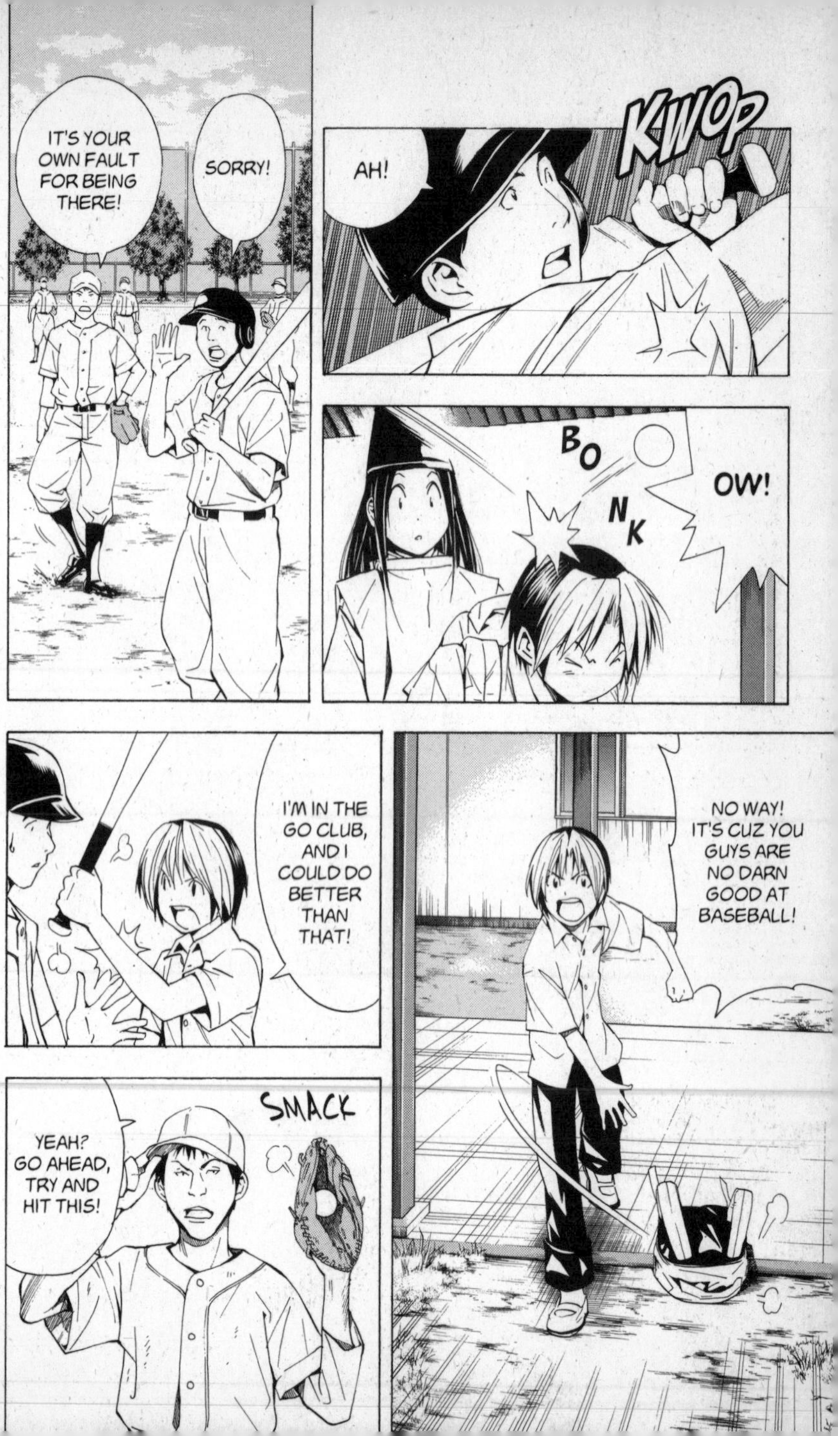
KWOP
AH!
BONK
OW!
SORRY!
IT'S YOUR OWN FAULT FOR BEING THERE!
NO WAY! IT'S CUZ YOU GUYS ARE NO DARN GOOD AT BASEBALL!
I'M IN THE GO CLUB, AND I COULD DO BETTER THAN THAT!
SMACK
YEAH? GO AHEAD, TRY AND HIT THIS!

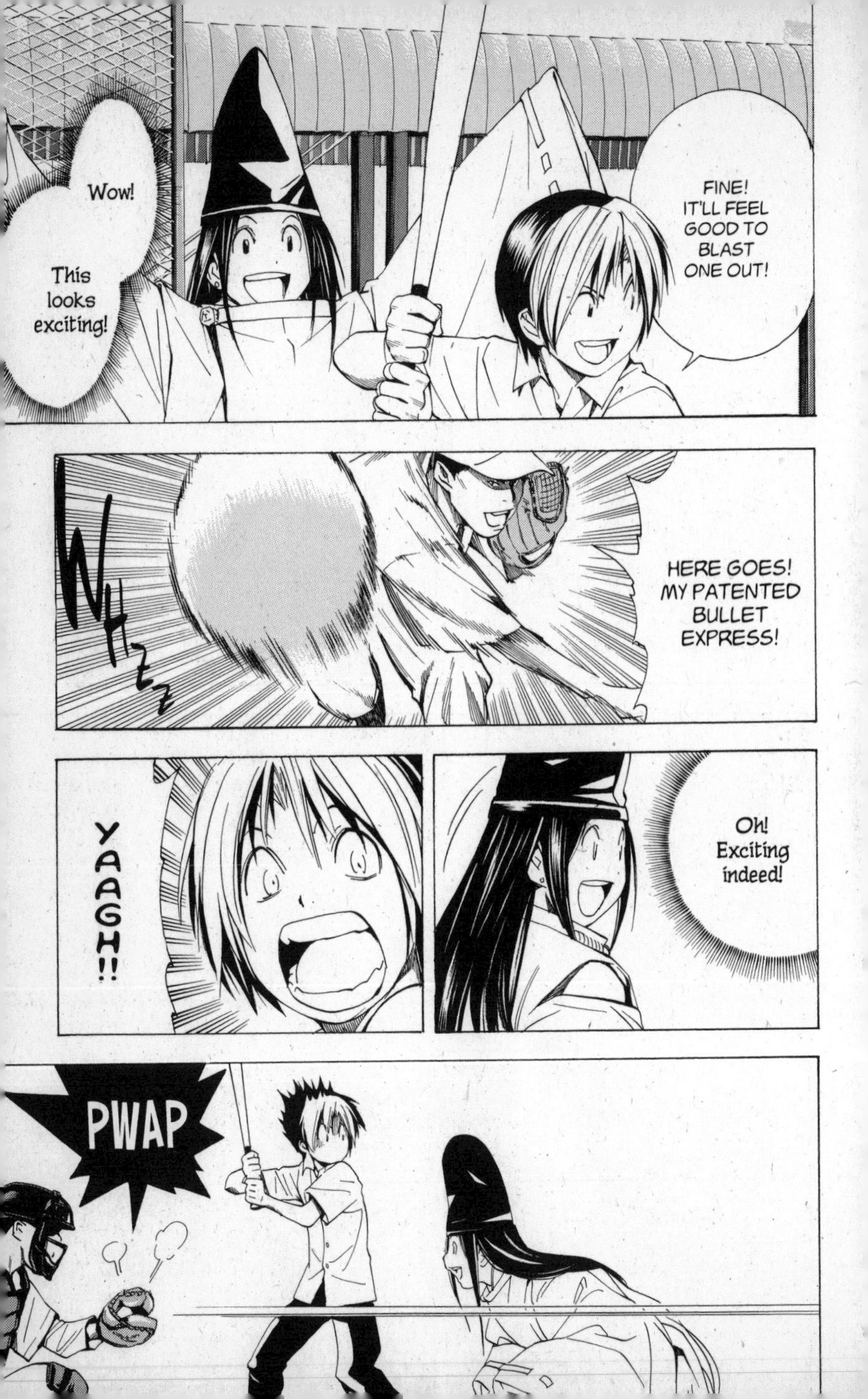
FINE! IT'LL FEEL GOOD TO BLAST ONE OUT!
Wow!
This looks exciting!
HERE GOES! MY PATENTED BULLET EXPRESS!
WHIZZZ
Oh! Exciting indeed!
YAAGH!!
PWAP

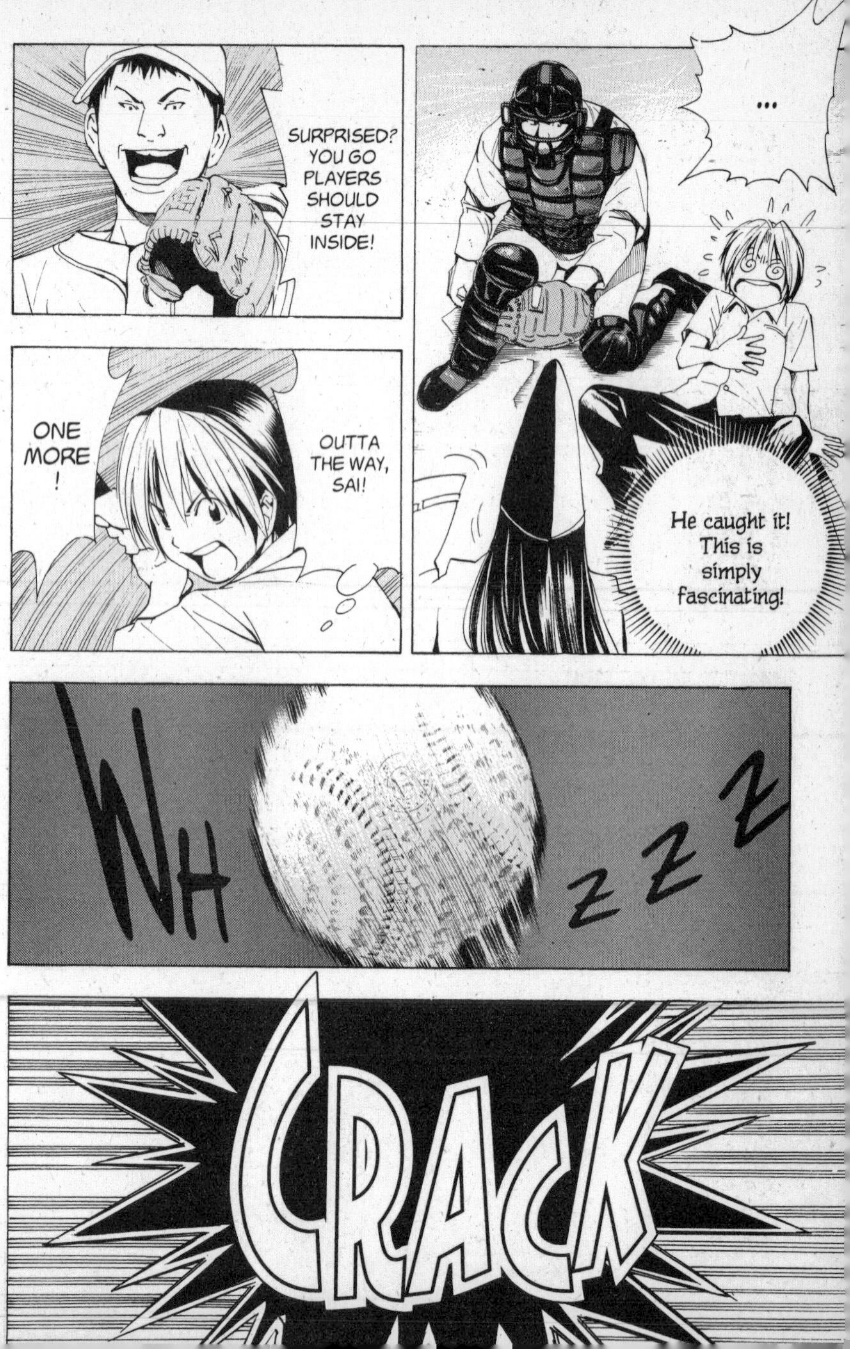
...
He caught it! This is simply fascinating!
SURPRISED? YOU GO PLAYERS SHOULD STAY INSIDE!
OUTTA THE WAY, SAI!
ONE MORE!
WHZZZ
CRACK

YESSS!

RIGHT INTO THE SHOGI CLUB'S ROOM...

BIG TIME...

FOUL BALL...

KRASH

KLANK

KLINK

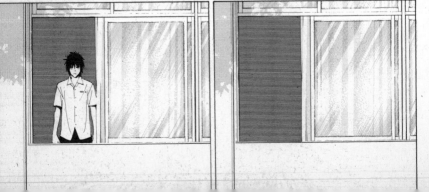

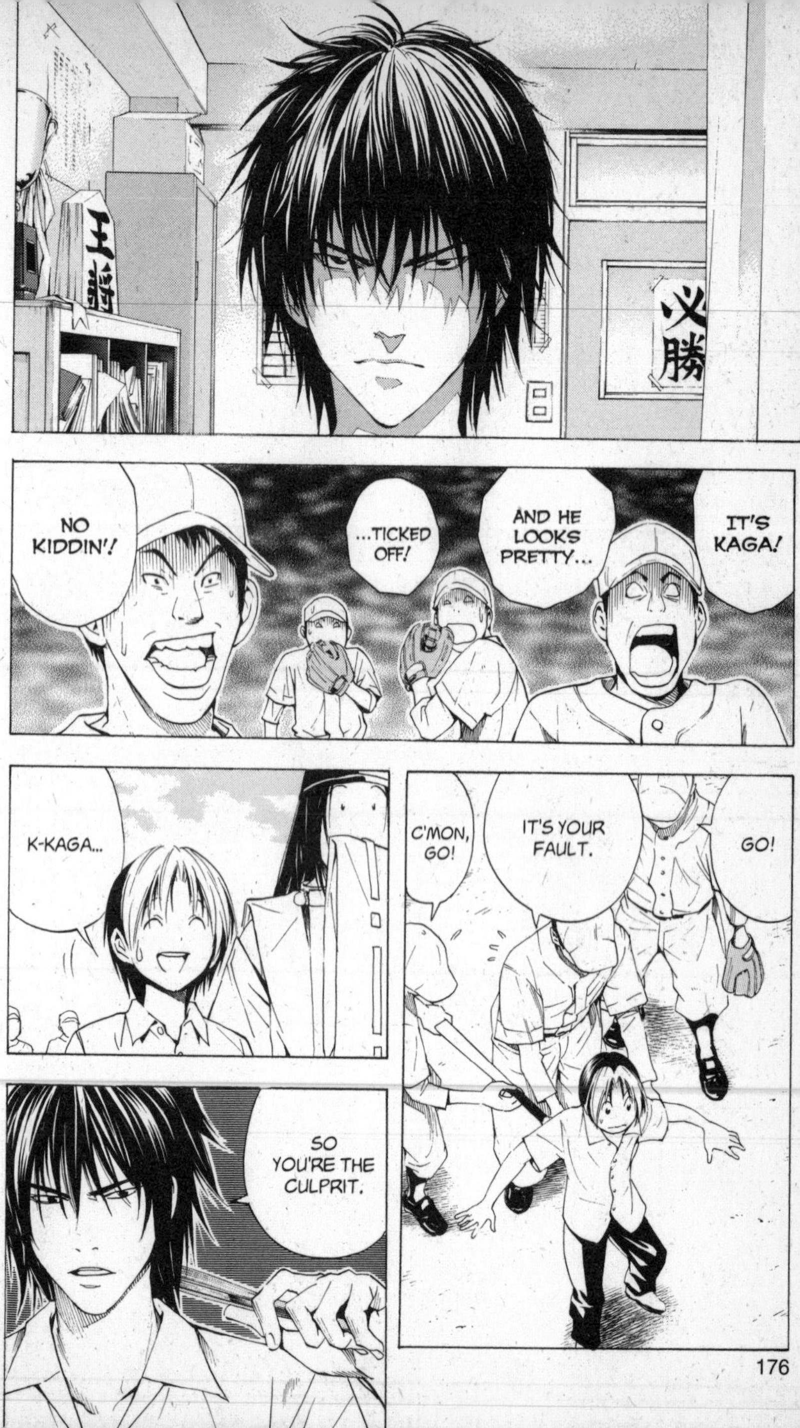
IT'S KAGA!
AND HE LOOKS PRETTY...
...TICKED OFF!
NO KIDDIN'!
GO!
IT'S YOUR FAULT.
C'MON, GO!
K-KAGA...
SO YOU'RE THE CULPRIT.

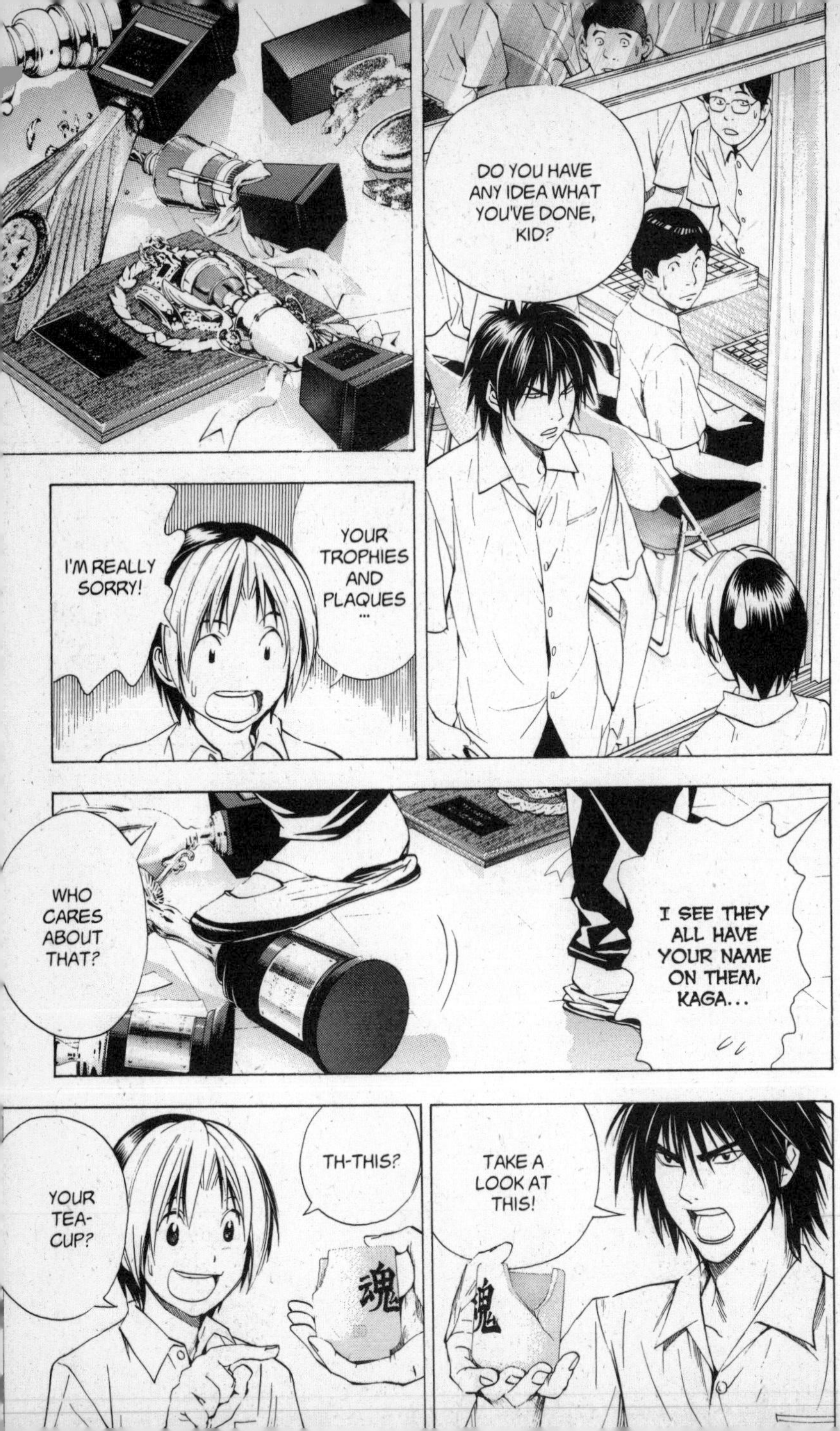
DO YOU HAVE ANY IDEA WHAT YOU'VE DONE, KID?
YOUR TROPHIES AND PLAQUES ...
I'M REALLY SORRY!
I SEE THEY ALL HAVE YOUR NAME ON THEM, KAGA...
WHO CARES ABOUT THAT?
TAKE A LOOK AT THIS!
魂
TH-THIS?
YOUR TEA-CUP?
魂

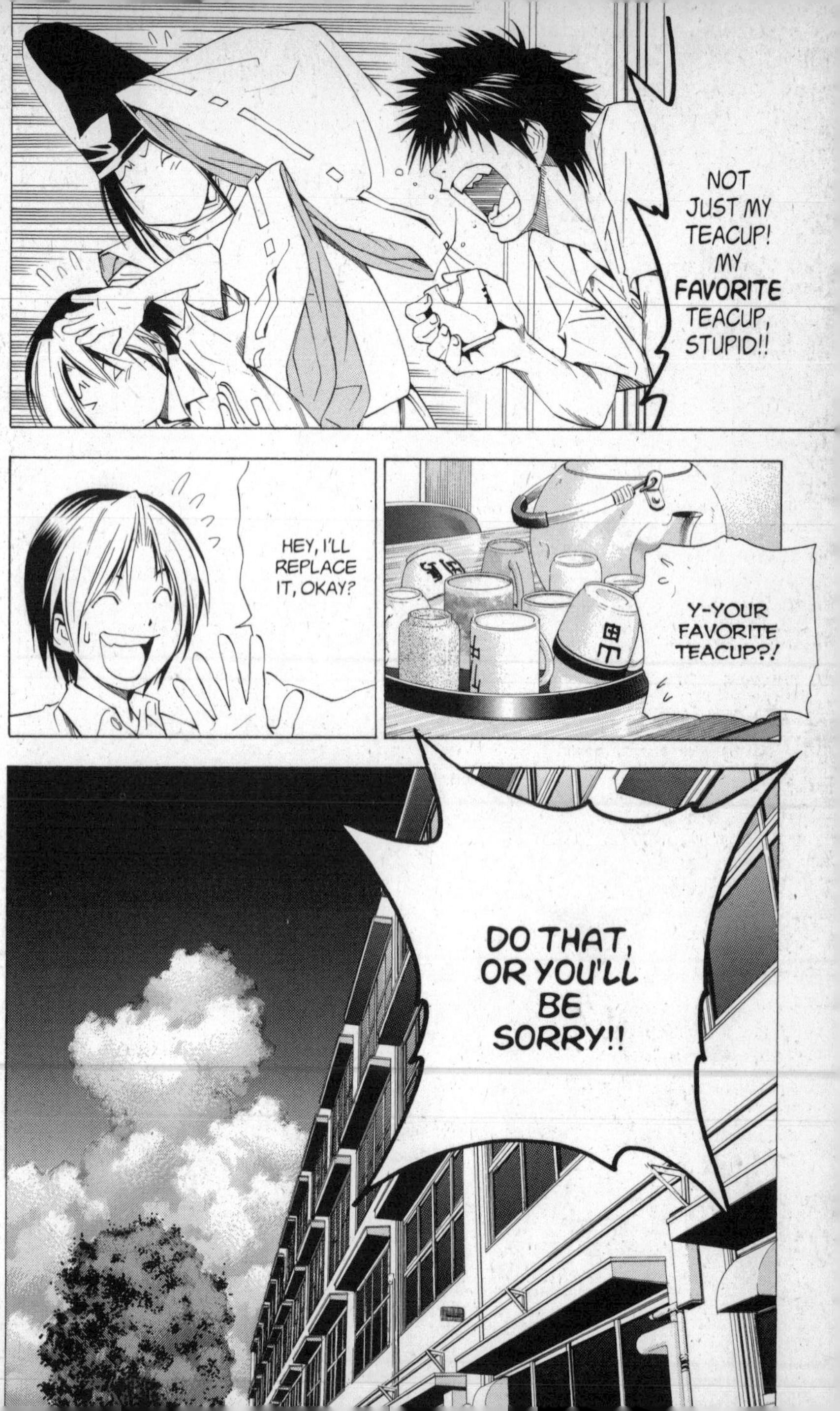
NOT JUST MY TEACUP! MY FAVORITE TEACUP, STUPID!!
Y-YOUR FAVORITE TEACUP?!
HEY, I'LL REPLACE IT, OKAY?
DO THAT, OR YOU'LL BE SORRY!!

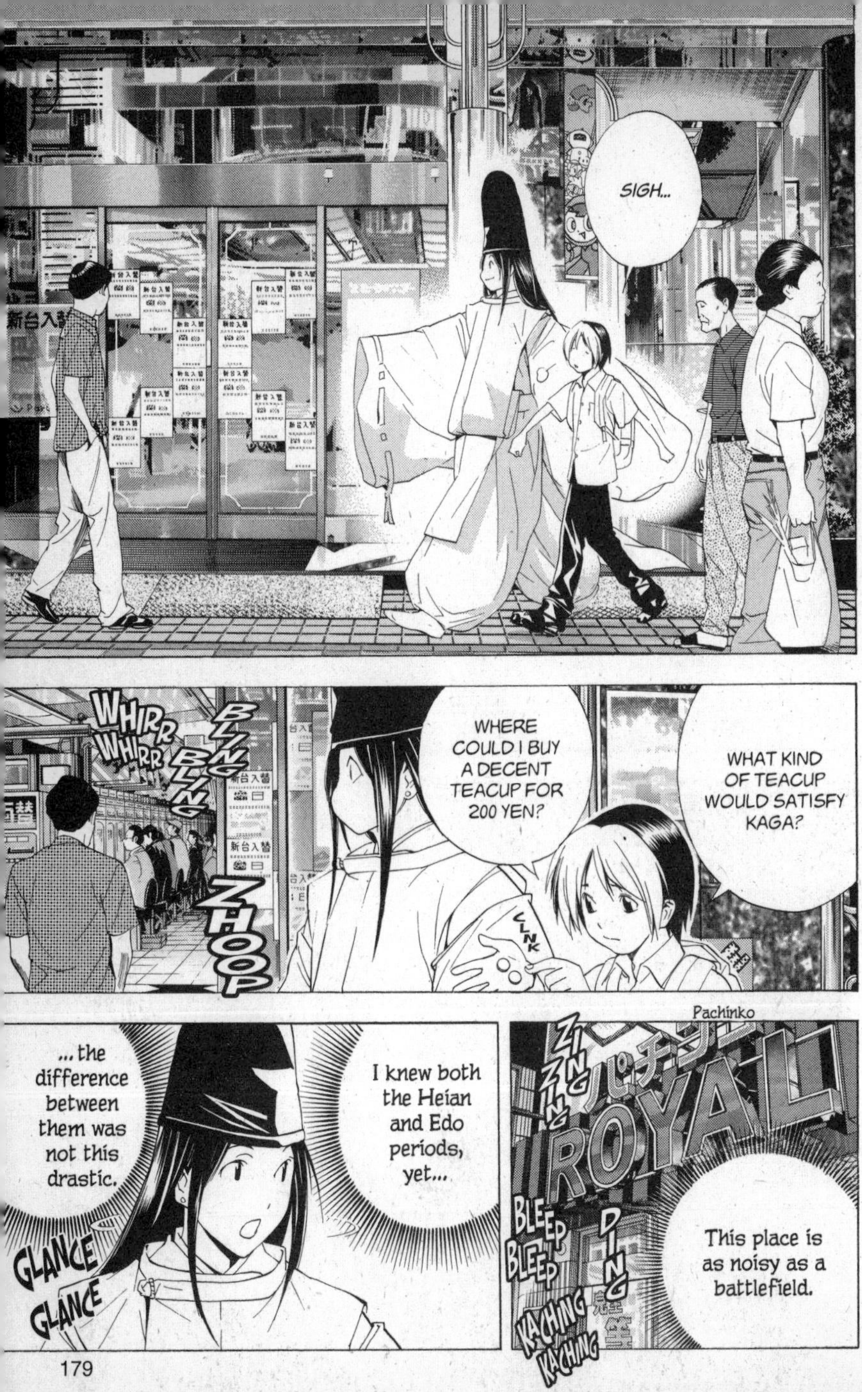
SIGH...
WHAT KIND OF TEACUP WOULD SATISFY KAGA?
WHERE COULD I BUY A DECENT TEACUP FOR 200 YEN?
CLNK
WHIRR WHIRR
BLING BLING
ZHOOP
Pachinko
ZING ZING
ROYAL
BLEEP BLEEP
DING
KACHING KACHING
This place is as noisy as a battlefield.
I knew both the Heian and Edo periods, yet...
...the difference between them was not this drastic.
GLANCE GLANCE

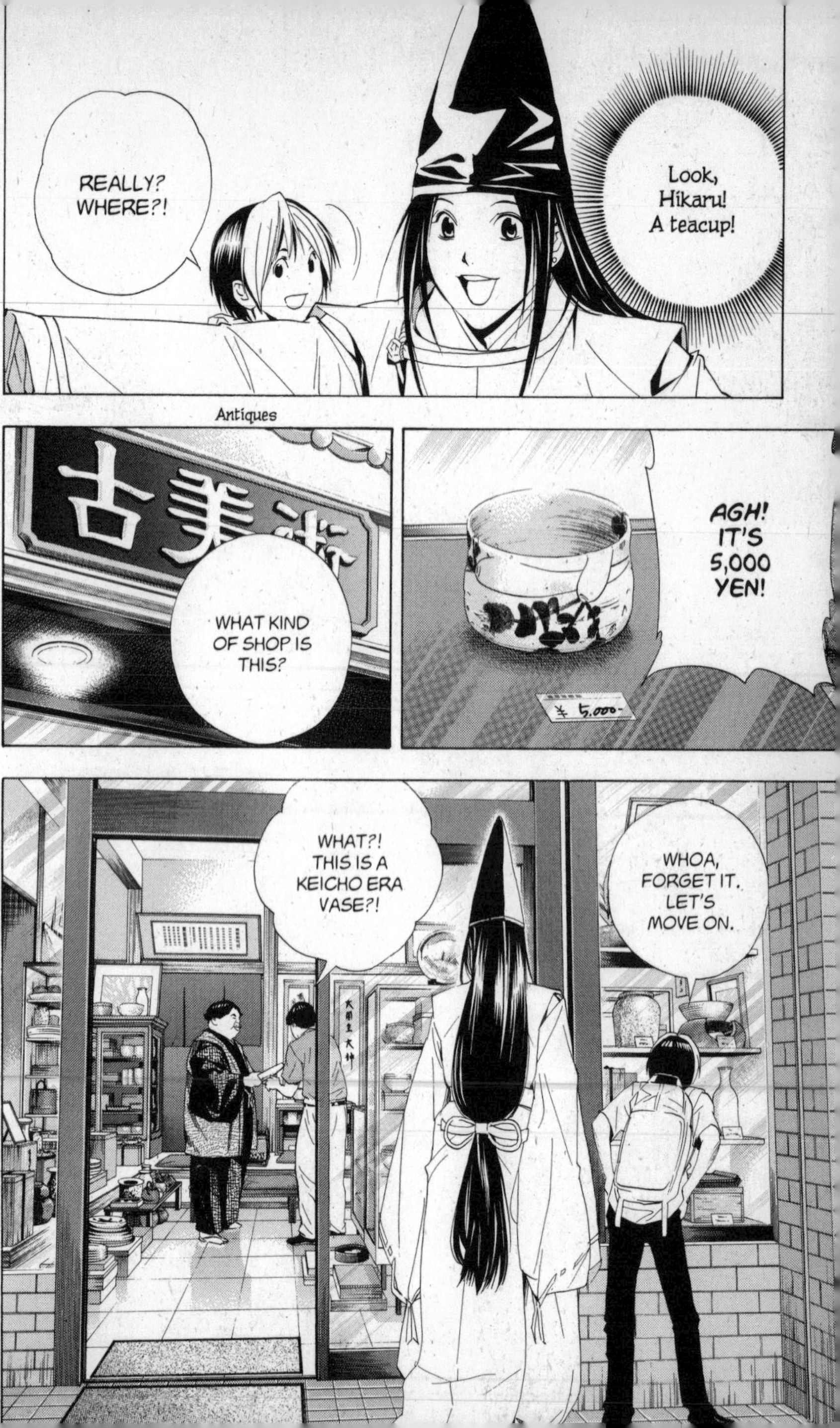
Look, Hikaru! A teacup!
REALLY? WHERE?!
AGH! IT'S 5,000 YEN!
¥ 5,000-
Antiques
古美術
WHAT KIND OF SHOP IS THIS?
WHAT?! THIS IS A KEICHO ERA VASE?!
WHOA, FORGET IT. LET'S MOVE ON.

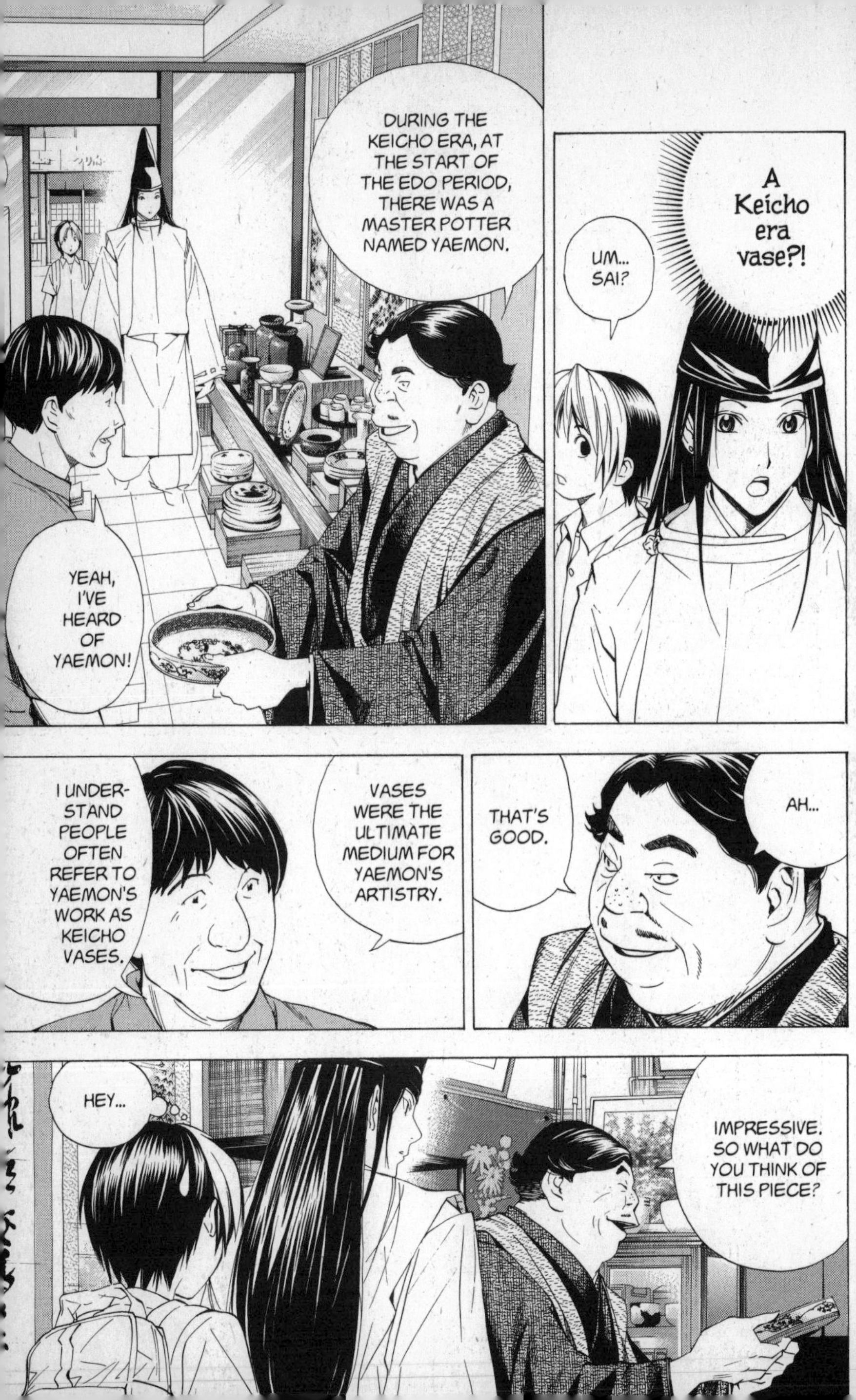
A Keicho era vase?!
UM... SAI?
DURING THE KEICHO ERA, AT THE START OF THE EDO PERIOD, THERE WAS A MASTER POTTER NAMED YAEMON.
YEAH, I'VE HEARD OF YAEMON!
AH...
THAT'S GOOD.
VASES WERE THE ULTIMATE MEDIUM FOR YAEMON'S ARTISTRY.
I UNDER-STAND PEOPLE OFTEN REFER TO YAEMON'S WORK AS KEICHO VASES.
IMPRESSIVE. SO WHAT DO YOU THINK OF THIS PIECE?
HEY...

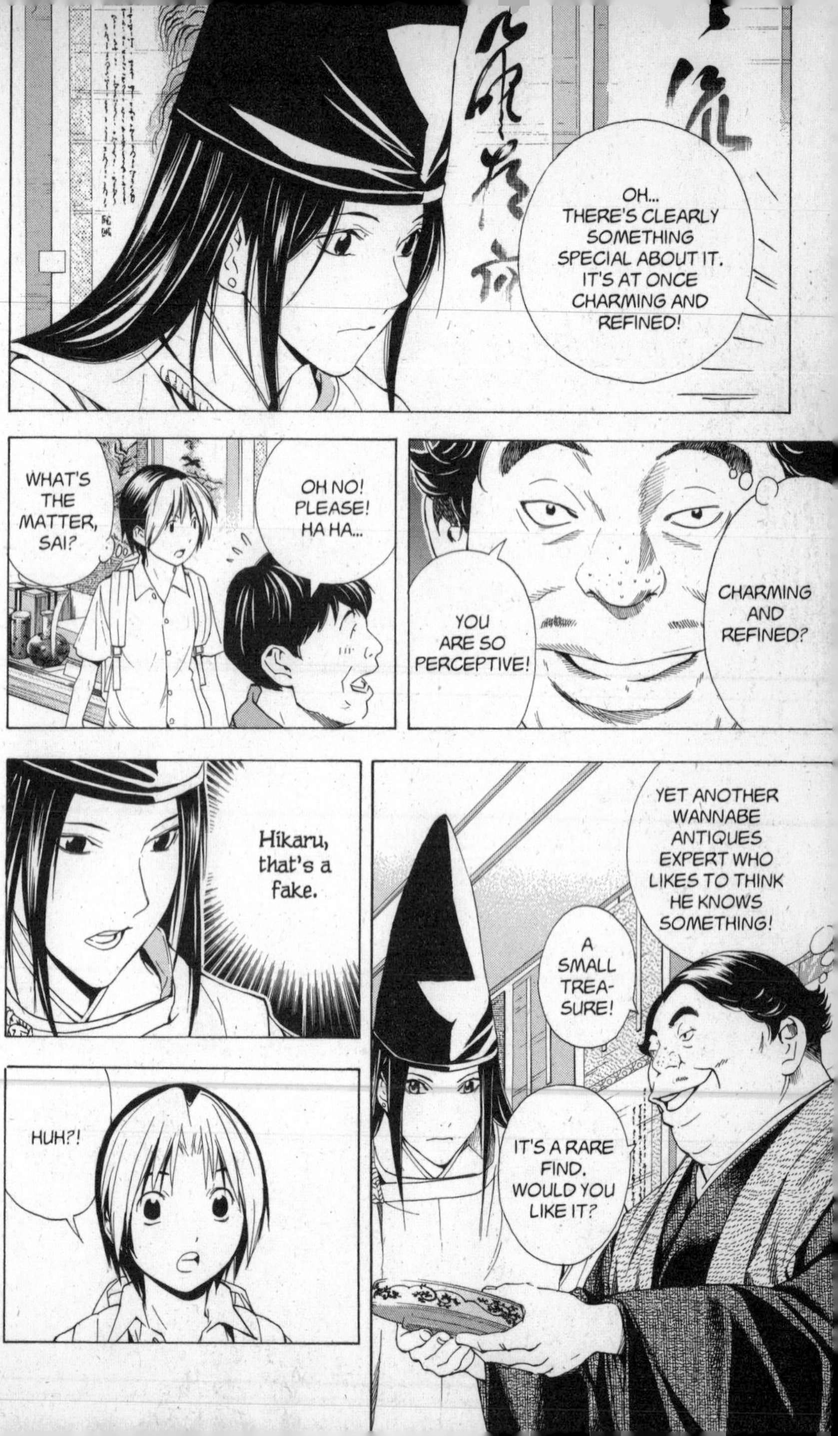
OH... THERE'S CLEARLY SOMETHING SPECIAL ABOUT IT. IT'S AT ONCE CHARMING AND REFINED!
CHARMING AND REFINED?
YOU ARE SO PERCEPTIVE!
OH NO! PLEASE! HA HA...
WHAT'S THE MATTER, SAI?
YET ANOTHER WANNABE ANTIQUES EXPERT WHO LIKES TO THINK HE KNOWS SOMETHING!
A SMALL TREASURE!
IT'S A RARE FIND. WOULD YOU LIKE IT?
Hikaru, that's a fake.
HUH?!

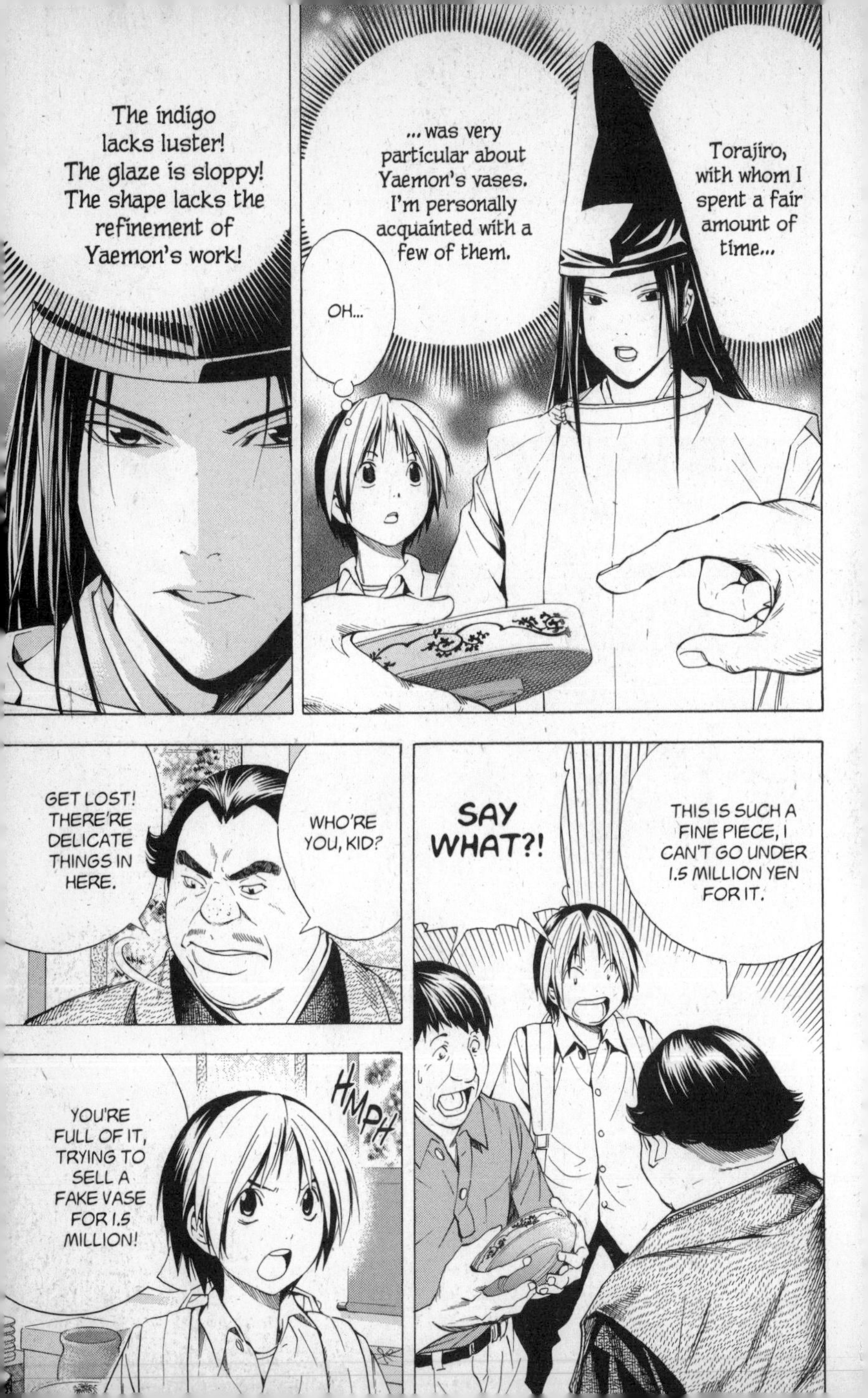
Torajiro, with whom I spent a fair amount of time...
... was very particular about Yaemon's vases. I'm personally acquainted with a few of them.
OH...
The indigo lacks luster! The glaze is sloppy! The shape lacks the refinement of Yaemon's work!
THIS IS SUCH A FINE PIECE, I CAN'T GO UNDER 1.5 MILLION YEN FOR IT.
SAY WHAT?!
WHO'RE YOU, KID?
GET LOST! THERE'RE DELICATE THINGS IN HERE.
HMPH
YOU'RE FULL OF IT, TRYING TO SELL A FAKE VASE FOR 1.5 MILLION!

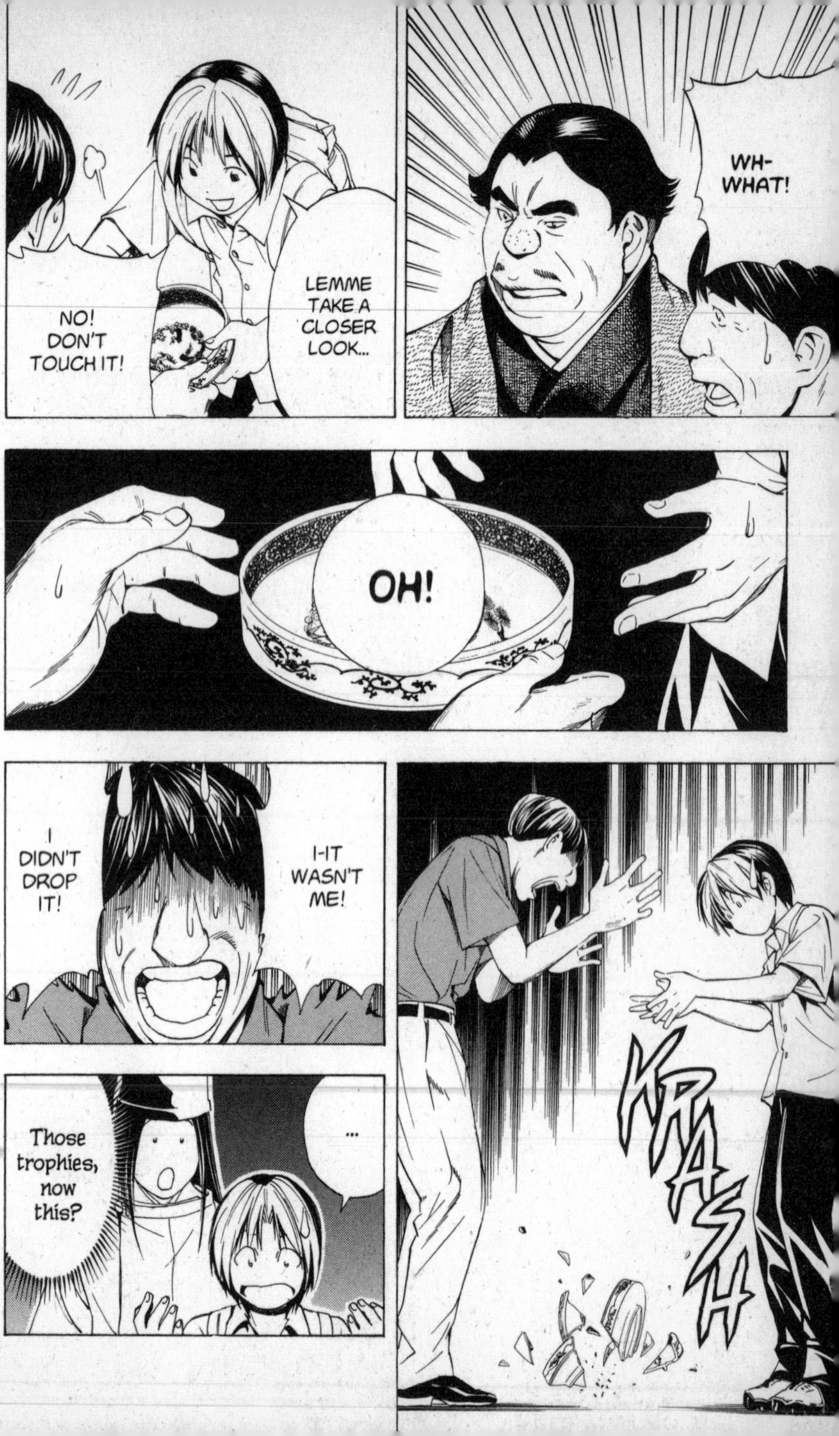
WH-
WHAT!
LEMME TAKE A CLOSER LOOK...
NO! DON'T TOUCH IT!
OH!
KRASH
I-IT WASN'T ME!
I DIDN'T DROP IT!
...
Those trophies, now this?

READ THIS WAY

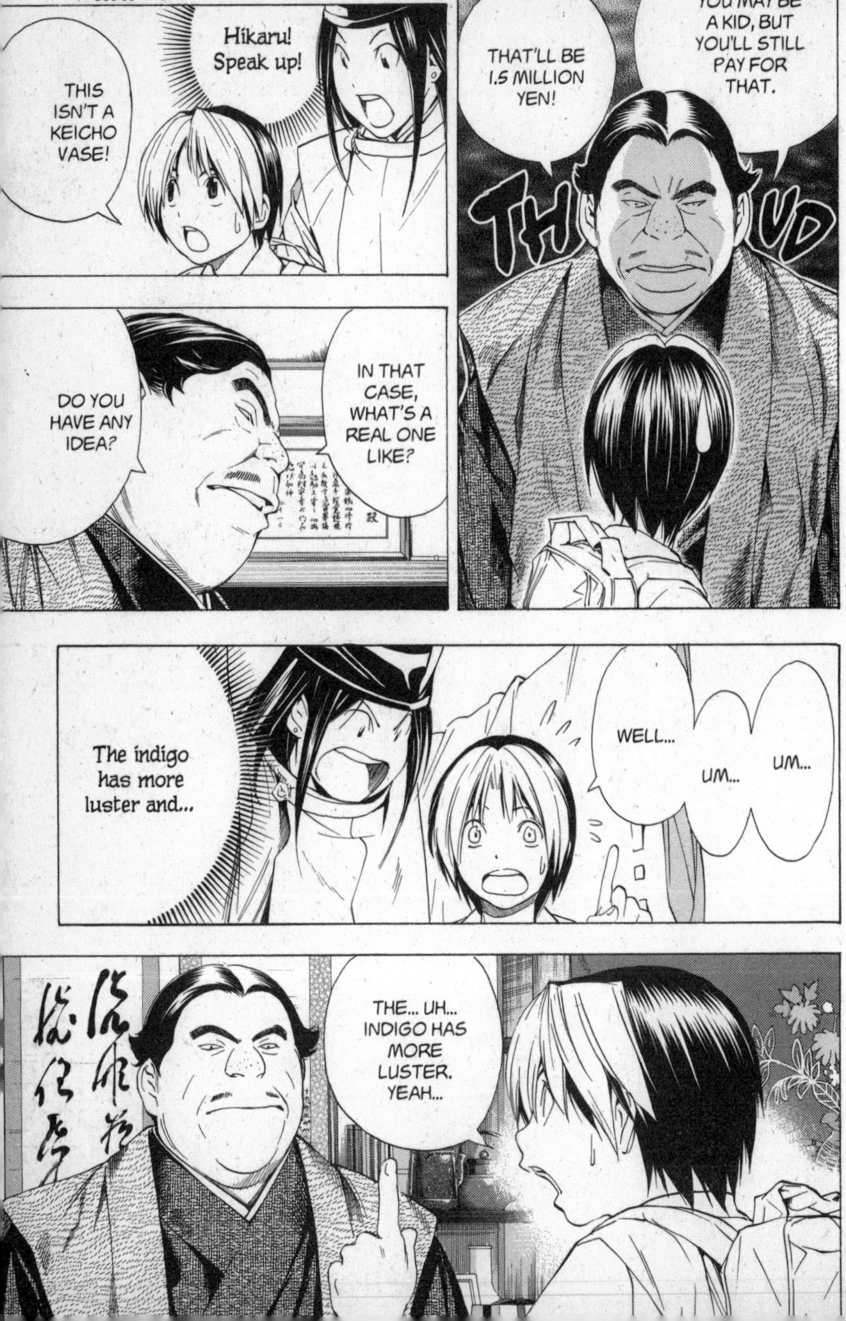
YOU MAY BE A KID, BUT YOU'LL STILL PAY FOR THAT.
THAT'LL BE 1.5 MILLION YEN!
THUD
Hikaru! Speak up!
THIS ISN'T A KEICHO VASE!
IN THAT CASE, WHAT'S A REAL ONE LIKE?
DO YOU HAVE ANY IDEA?
WELL...
UM...
UM...
The indigo has more luster and...
THE... UH... INDIGO HAS MORE LUSTER. YEAH...

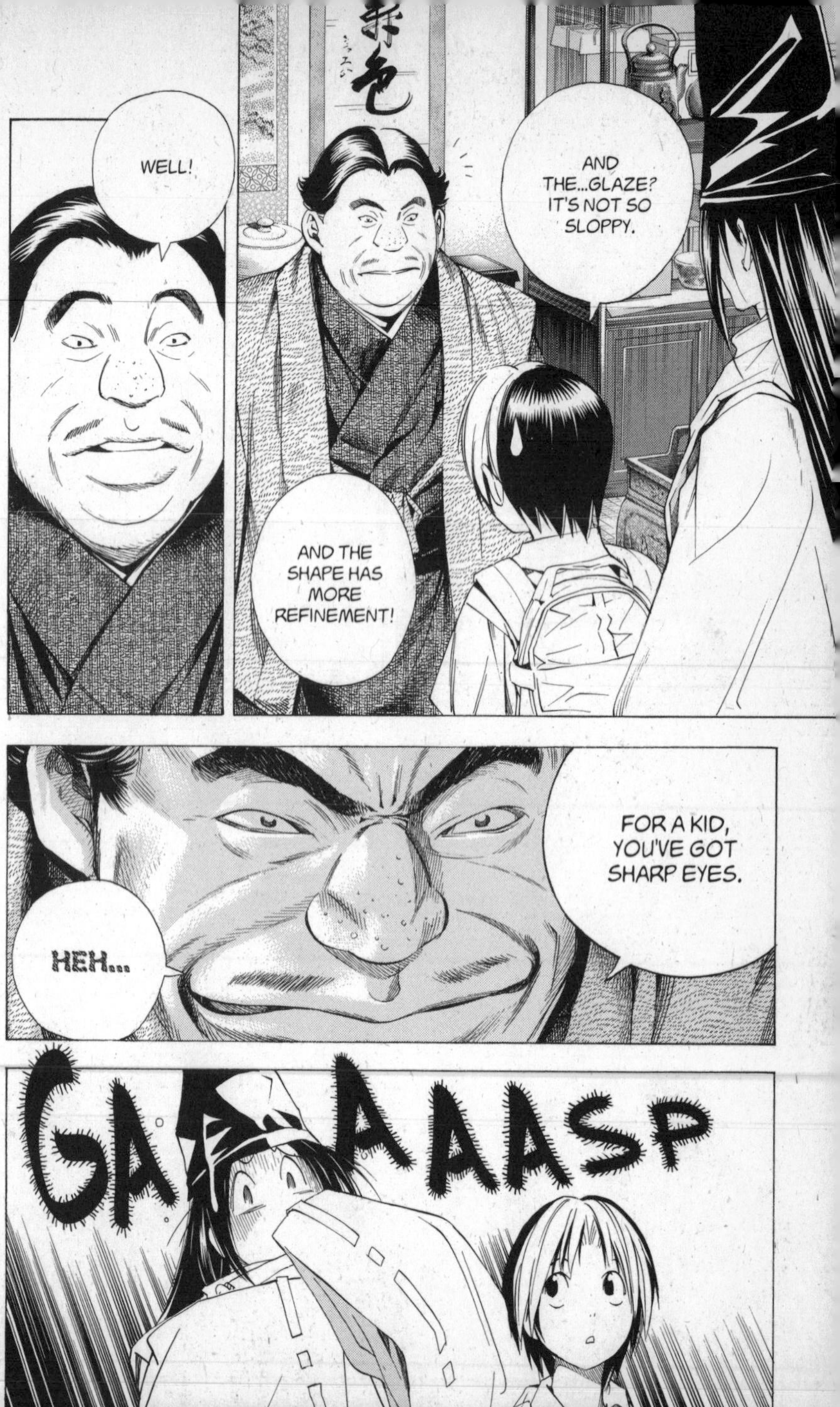
AND THE...GLAZE? IT'S NOT SO SLOPPY.
AND THE SHAPE HAS MORE REFINEMENT!
WELL!
FOR A KID, YOU'VE GOT SHARP EYES.
HEH...
GAAAASP

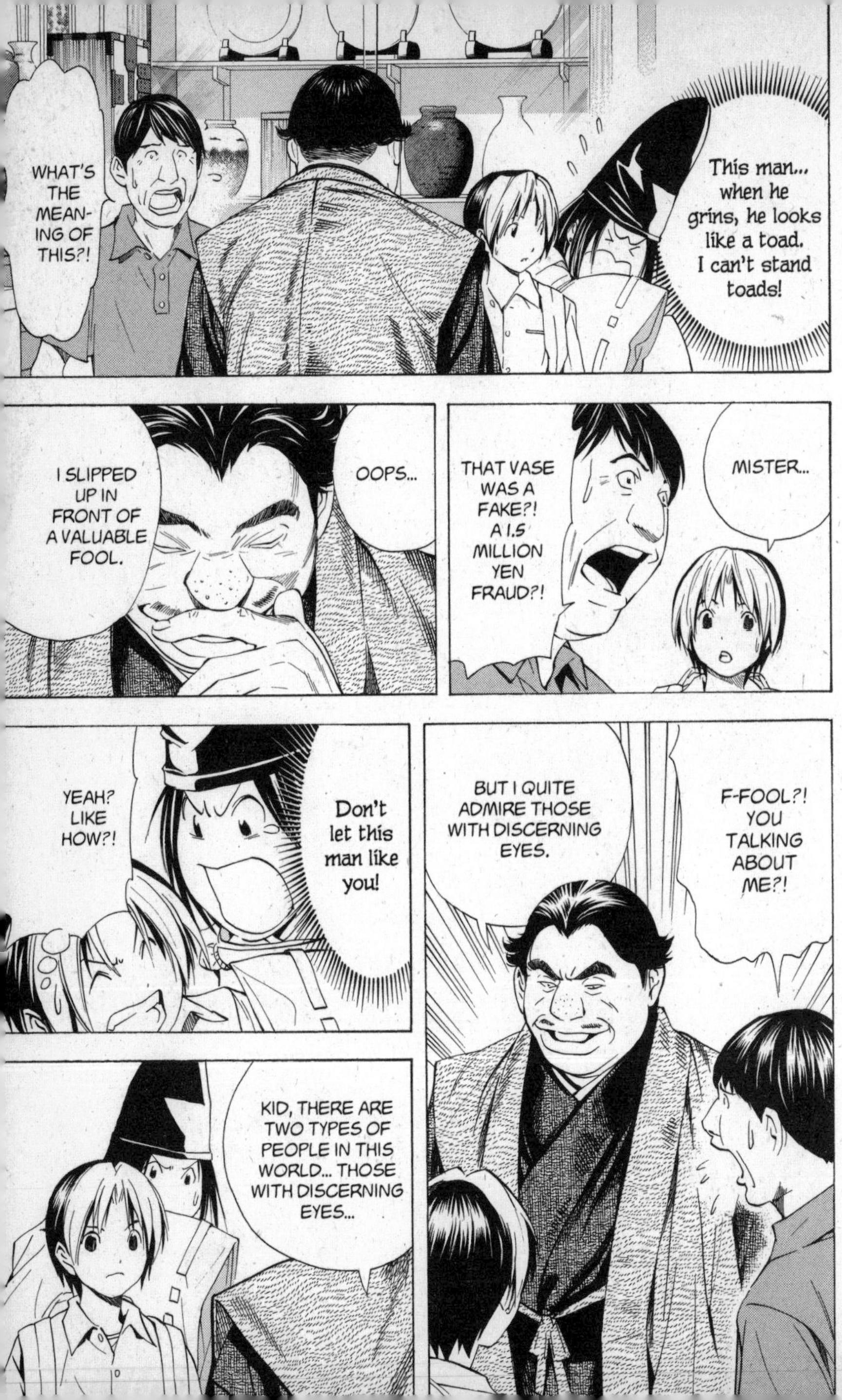
This man... when he grins, he looks like a toad. I can't stand toads!
WHAT'S THE MEAN-ING OF THIS?!
MISTER...
THAT VASE WAS A FAKE?! A 1.5 MILLION YEN FRAUD?!
OOPS...
I SLIPPED UP IN FRONT OF A VALUABLE FOOL.
F-FOOL?! YOU TALKING ABOUT ME?!
BUT I QUITE ADMIRE THOSE WITH DISCERNING EYES.
Don't let this man like you!
YEAH? LIKE HOW?!
KID, THERE ARE TWO TYPES OF PEOPLE IN THIS WORLD... THOSE WITH DISCERNING EYES...

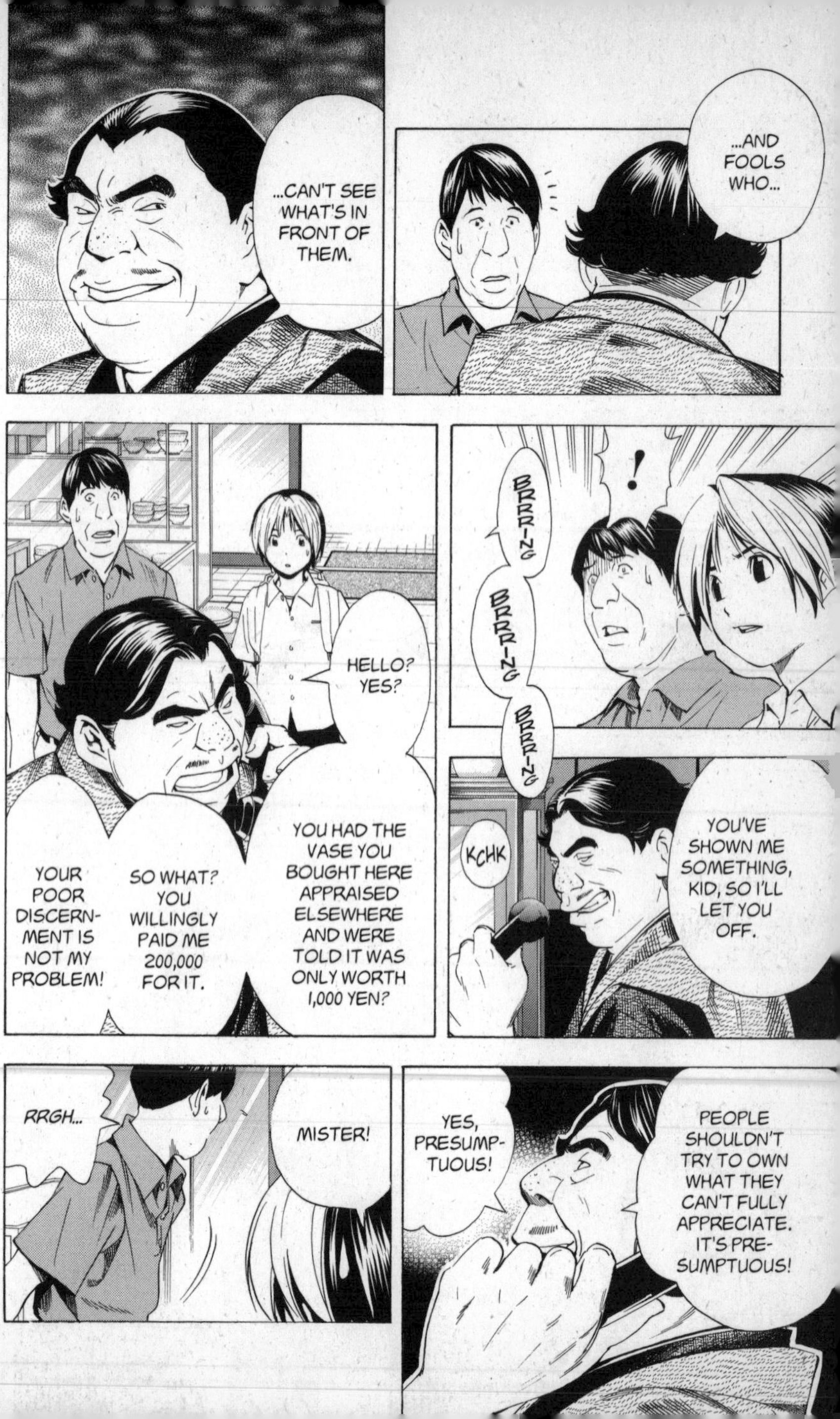
...AND FOOLS WHO...
...CAN'T SEE WHAT'S IN FRONT OF THEM.
!
BRRRING
BRRRING
BRRRING
KCHK
YOU'VE SHOWN ME SOMETHING, KID, SO I'LL LET YOU OFF.
HELLO? YES?
YOU HAD THE VASE YOU BOUGHT HERE APPRAISED ELSEWHERE AND WERE TOLD IT WAS ONLY WORTH 1,000 YEN?
SO WHAT? YOU WILLINGLY PAID ME 200,000 FOR IT.
YOUR POOR DISCERNMENT IS NOT MY PROBLEM!
PEOPLE SHOULDN'T TRY TO OWN WHAT THEY CAN'T FULLY APPRECIATE. IT'S PRESUMPTUOUS!
YES, PRESUMPTUOUS!
MISTER!
RRGH...

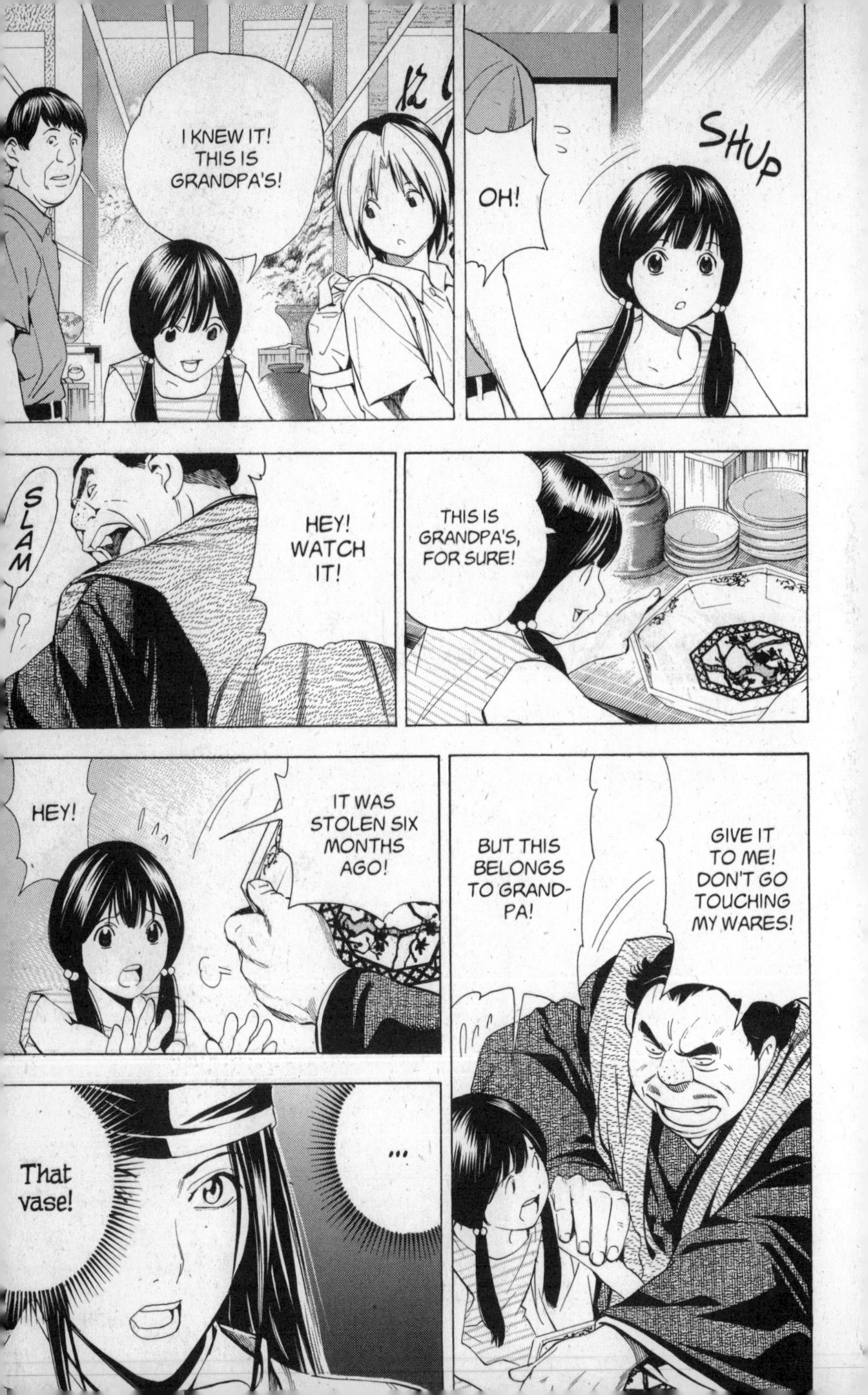
SHUP
OH!
I KNEW IT! THIS IS GRANDPA'S!
THIS IS GRANDPA'S, FOR SURE!
HEY! WATCH IT!
SLAM
GIVE IT TO ME! DON'T GO TOUCHING MY WARES!
BUT THIS BELONGS TO GRAND-PA!
IT WAS STOLEN SIX MONTHS AGO!
HEY!
...
That vase!

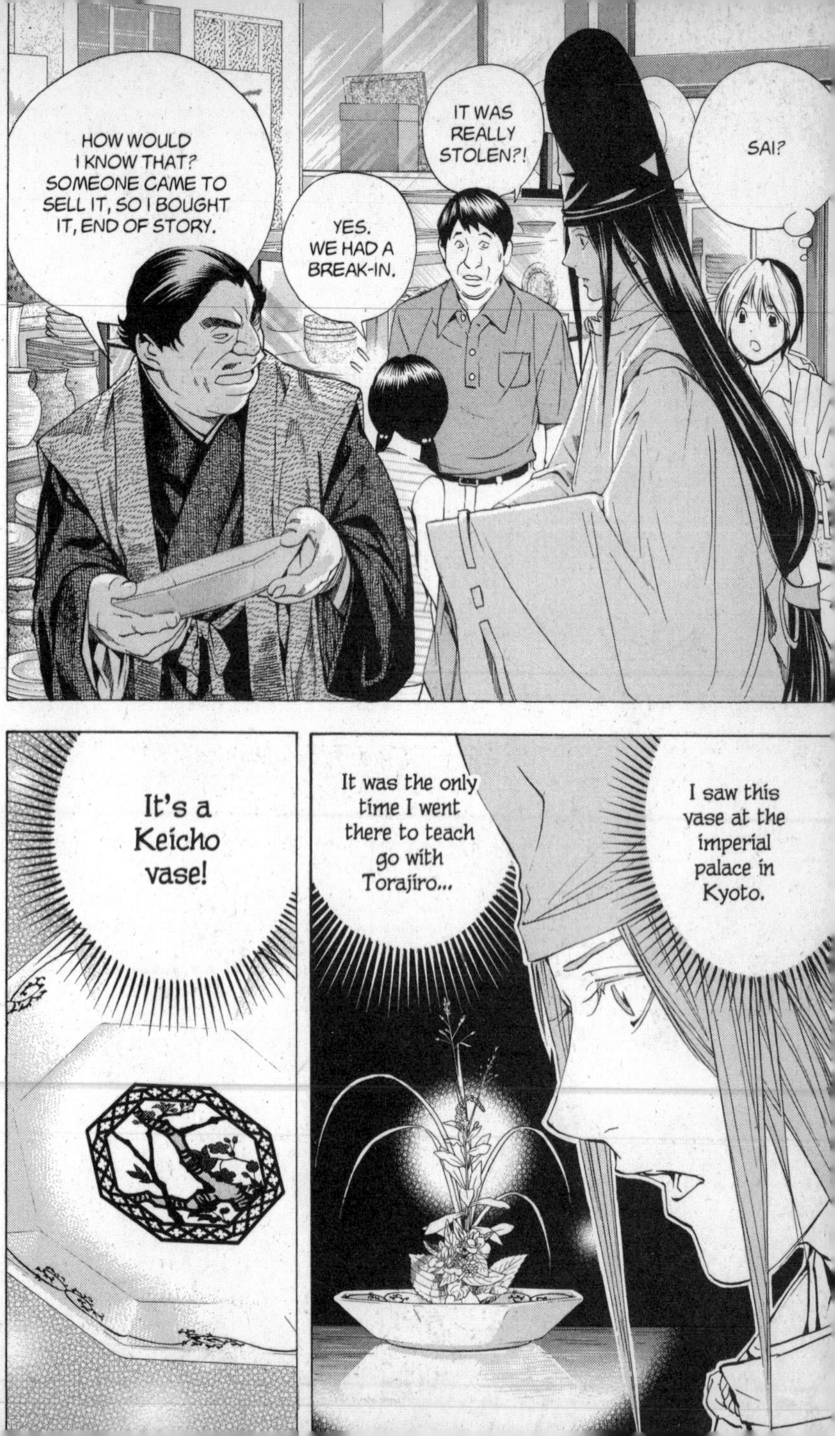
SAI?
IT WAS REALLY STOLEN?!
YES. WE HAD A BREAK-IN.
HOW WOULD I KNOW THAT? SOMEONE CAME TO SELL IT, SO I BOUGHT IT, END OF STORY.
I saw this vase at the imperial palace in Kyoto.
It was the only time I went there to teach go with Torajiro...
It's a Keicho vase!

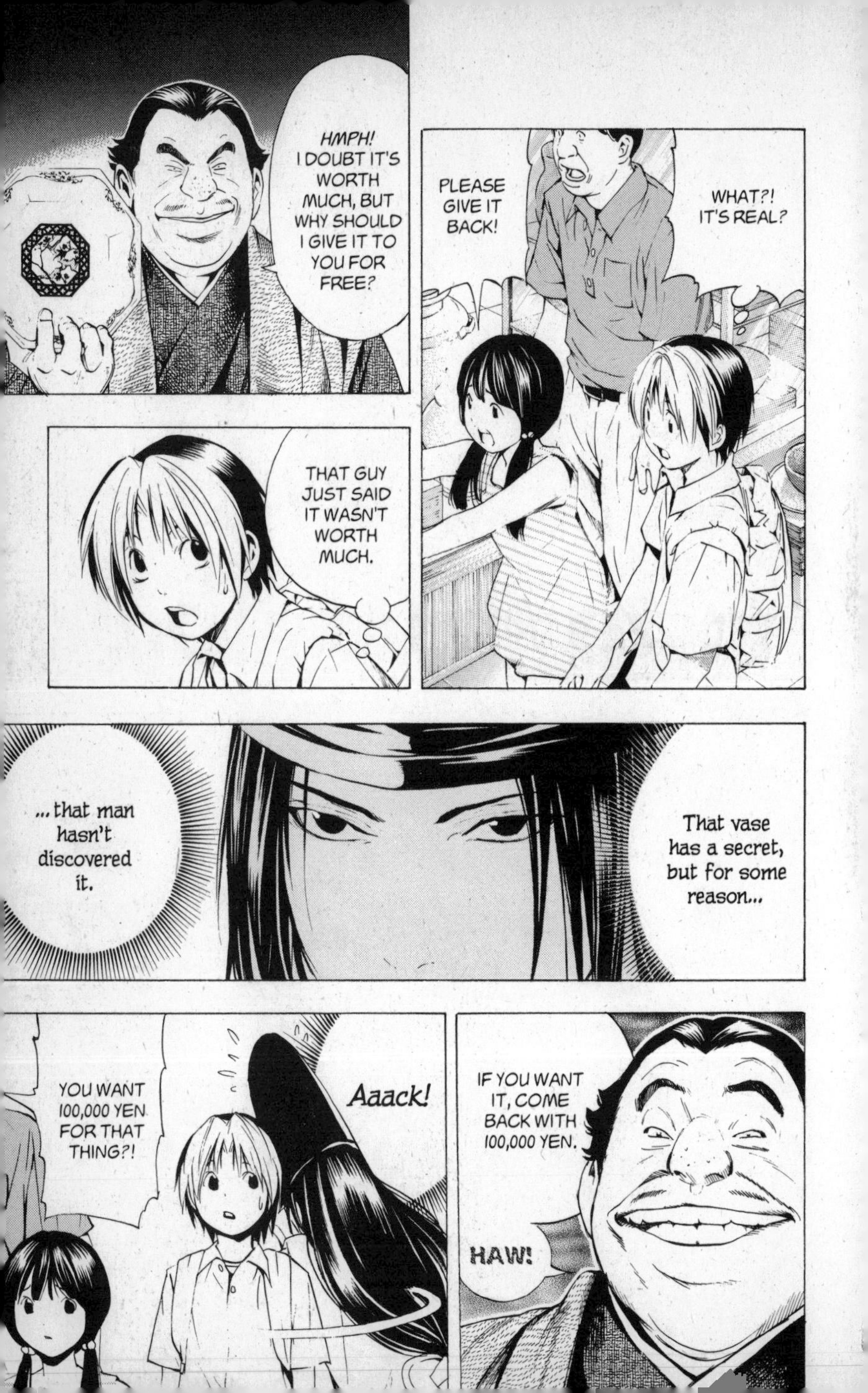
WHAT?! IT'S REAL?
PLEASE GIVE IT BACK!
HMPH! I DOUBT IT'S WORTH MUCH, BUT WHY SHOULD I GIVE IT TO YOU FOR FREE?
THAT GUY JUST SAID IT WASN'T WORTH MUCH.
That vase has a secret, but for some reason...
...that man hasn't discovered it.
IF YOU WANT IT, COME BACK WITH 100,000 YEN.
HAW!
Aaack!
YOU WANT 100,000 YEN FOR THAT THING?!

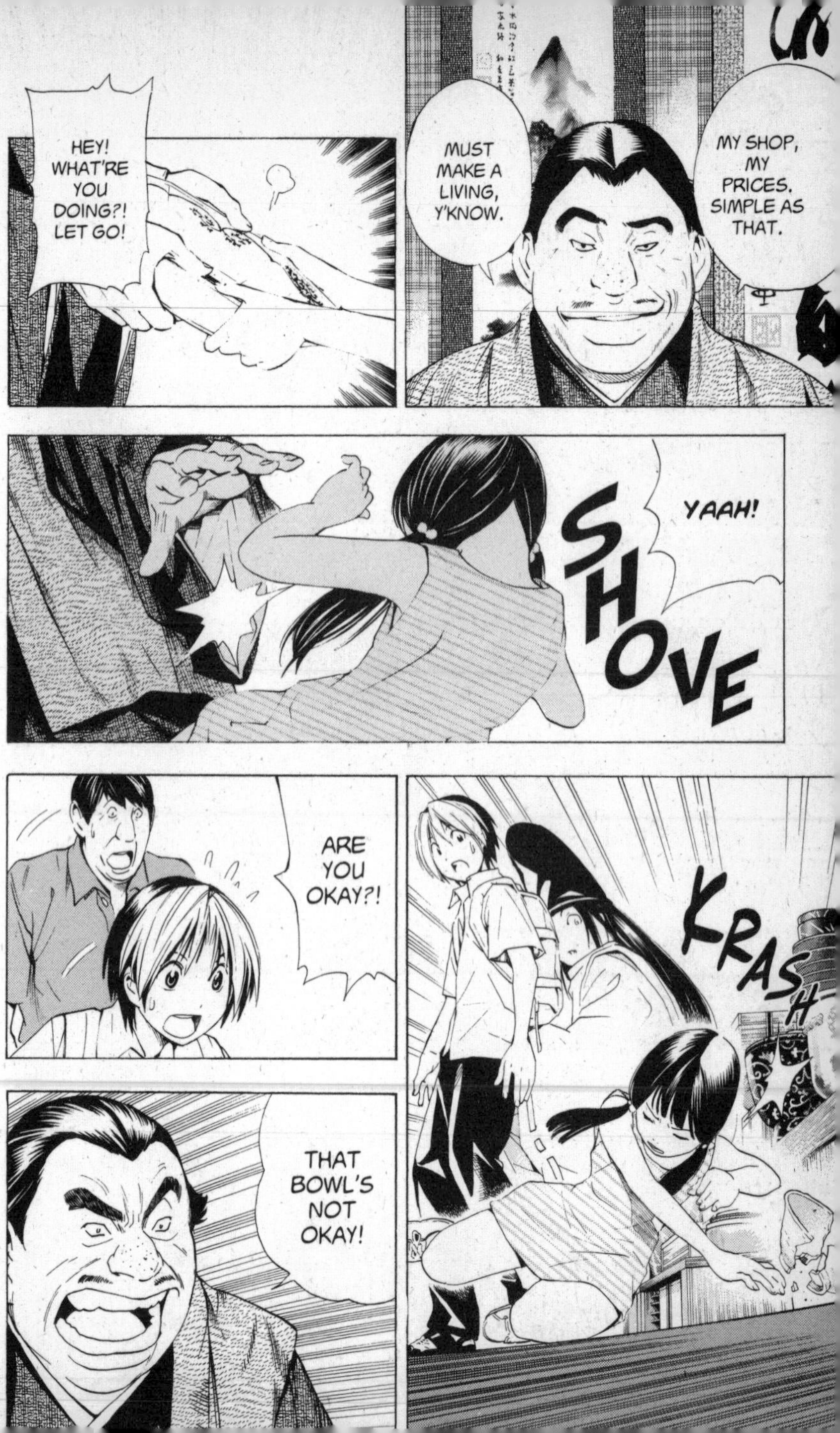
MY SHOP, MY PRICES. SIMPLE AS THAT.
MUST MAKE A LIVING, Y'KNOW.
HEY! WHAT'RE YOU DOING?! LET GO!
YAAH!
SHOVE
KRASH
ARE YOU OKAY?!
THAT BOWL'S NOT OKAY!

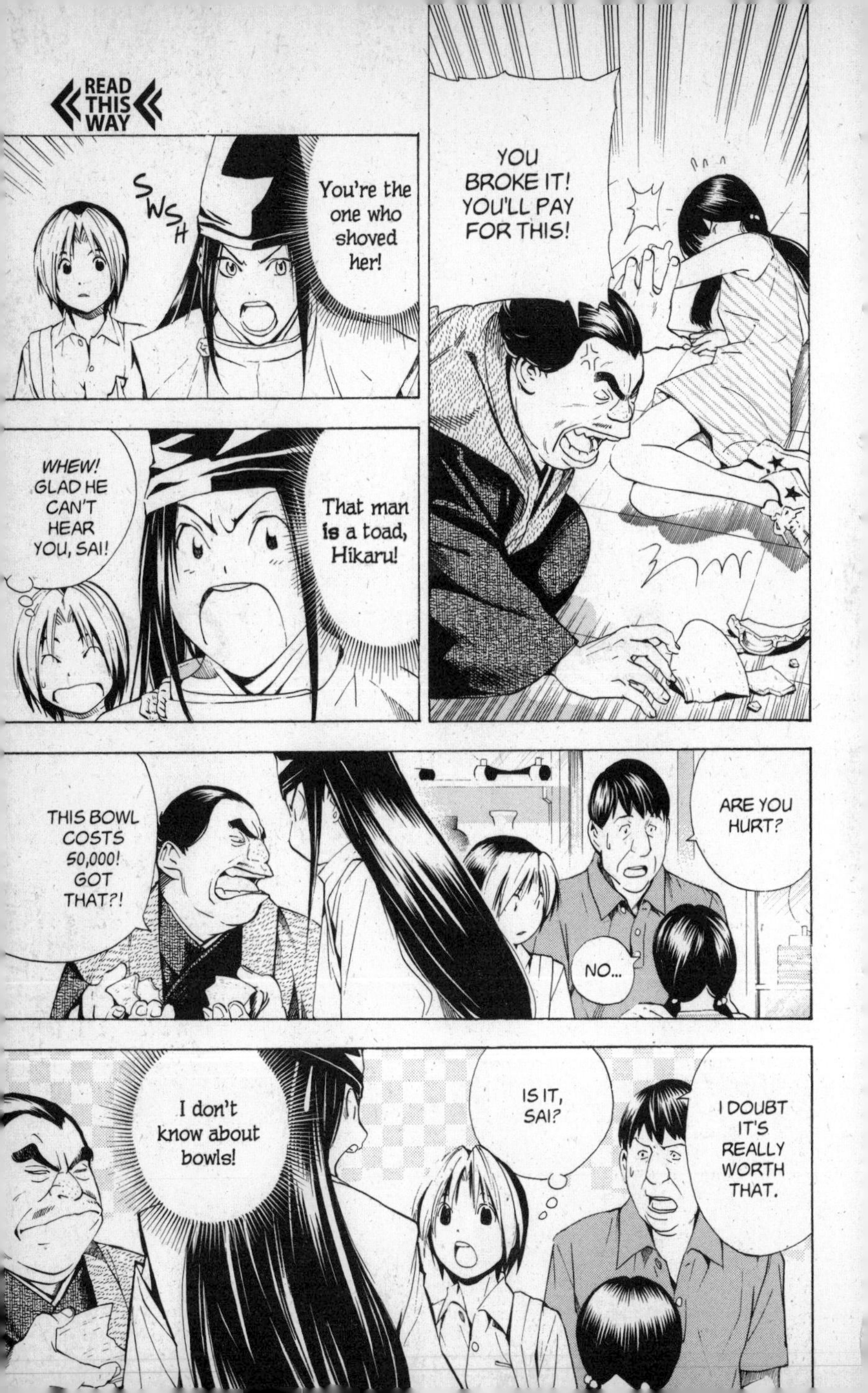
READ THIS WAY
YOU BROKE IT! YOU'LL PAY FOR THIS!
SWSH
You're the one who shoved her!
That man is a toad, Hikaru!
WHEW! GLAD HE CAN'T HEAR YOU, SAI!
ARE YOU HURT?
NO...
THIS BOWL COSTS 50,000! GOT THAT?!
I DOUBT IT'S REALLY WORTH THAT.
IS IT, SAI?
I don't know about bowls!

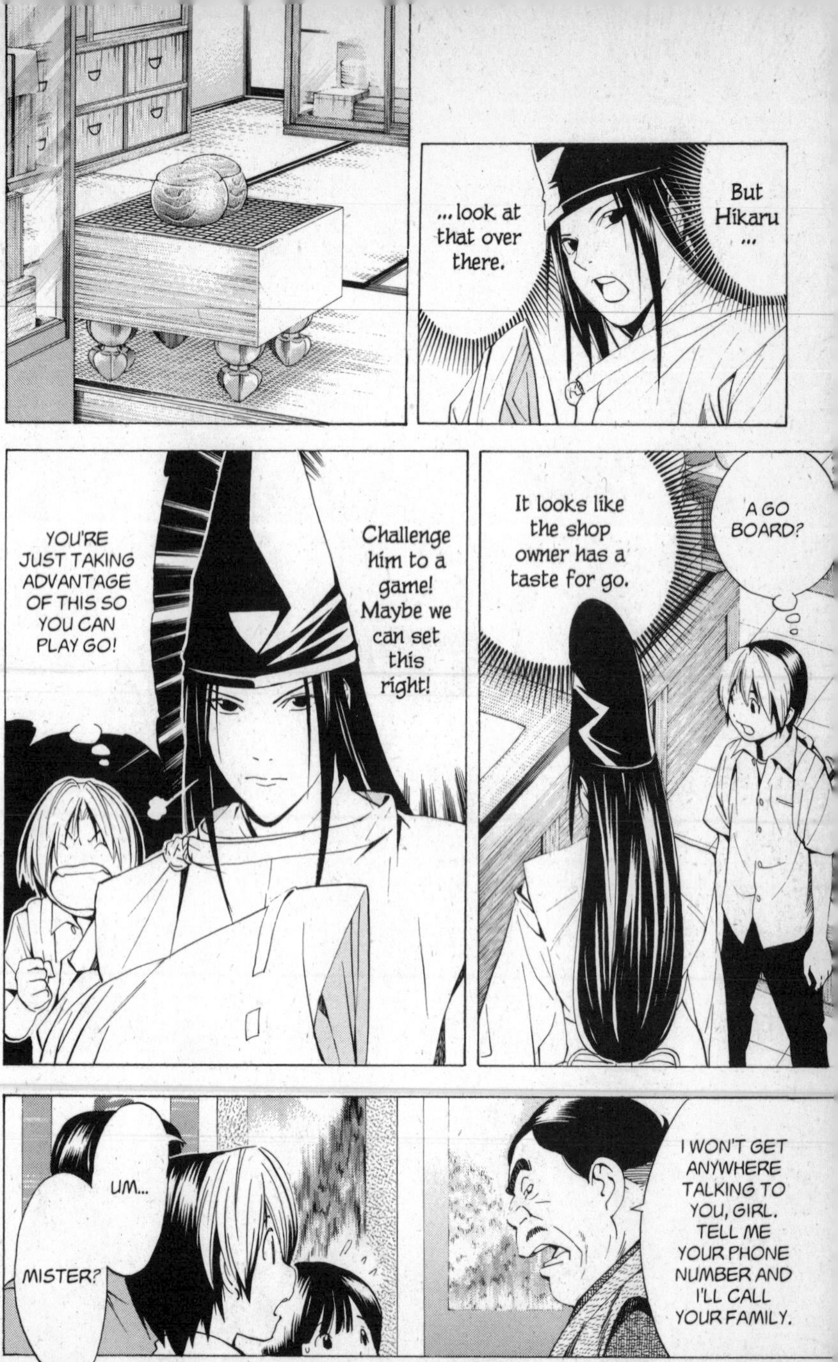
But Hikaru ...
...look at that over there.
A GO BOARD?
It looks like the shop owner has a taste for go.
Challenge him to a game! Maybe we can set this right!
YOU'RE JUST TAKING ADVANTAGE OF THIS SO YOU CAN PLAY GO!
I WON'T GET ANYWHERE TALKING TO YOU, GIRL. TELL ME YOUR PHONE NUMBER AND I'LL CALL YOUR FAMILY.
UM...
MISTER?

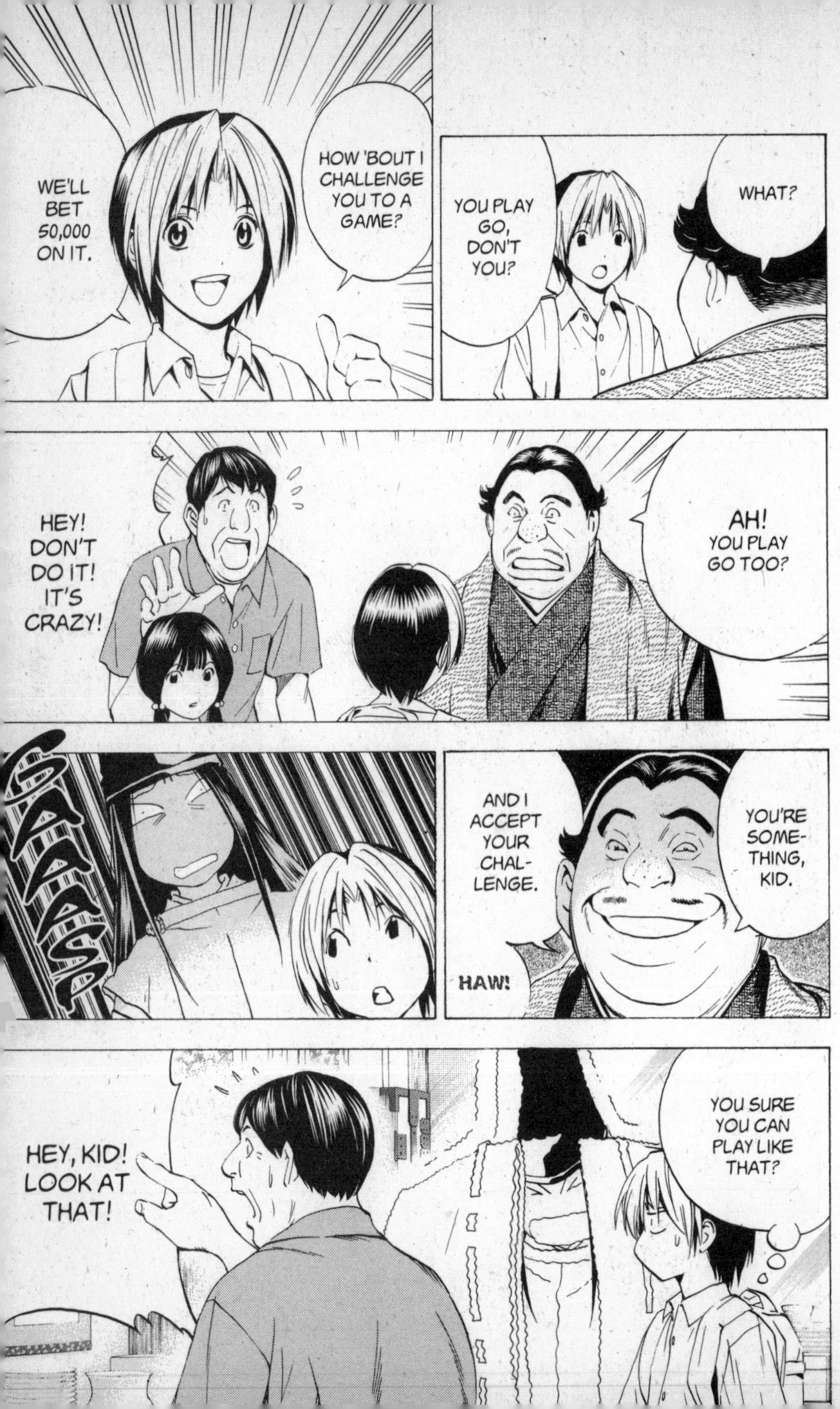
WHAT?
YOU PLAY GO, DON'T YOU?
HOW 'BOUT I CHALLENGE YOU TO A GAME?
WE'LL BET 50,000 ON IT.
AH! YOU PLAY GO TOO?
HEY! DON'T DO IT! IT'S CRAZY!
YOU'RE SOME-THING, KID.
AND I ACCEPT YOUR CHAL-LENGE.
HAW!
GAAASP
YOU SURE YOU CAN PLAY LIKE THAT?
HEY, KID! LOOK AT THAT!

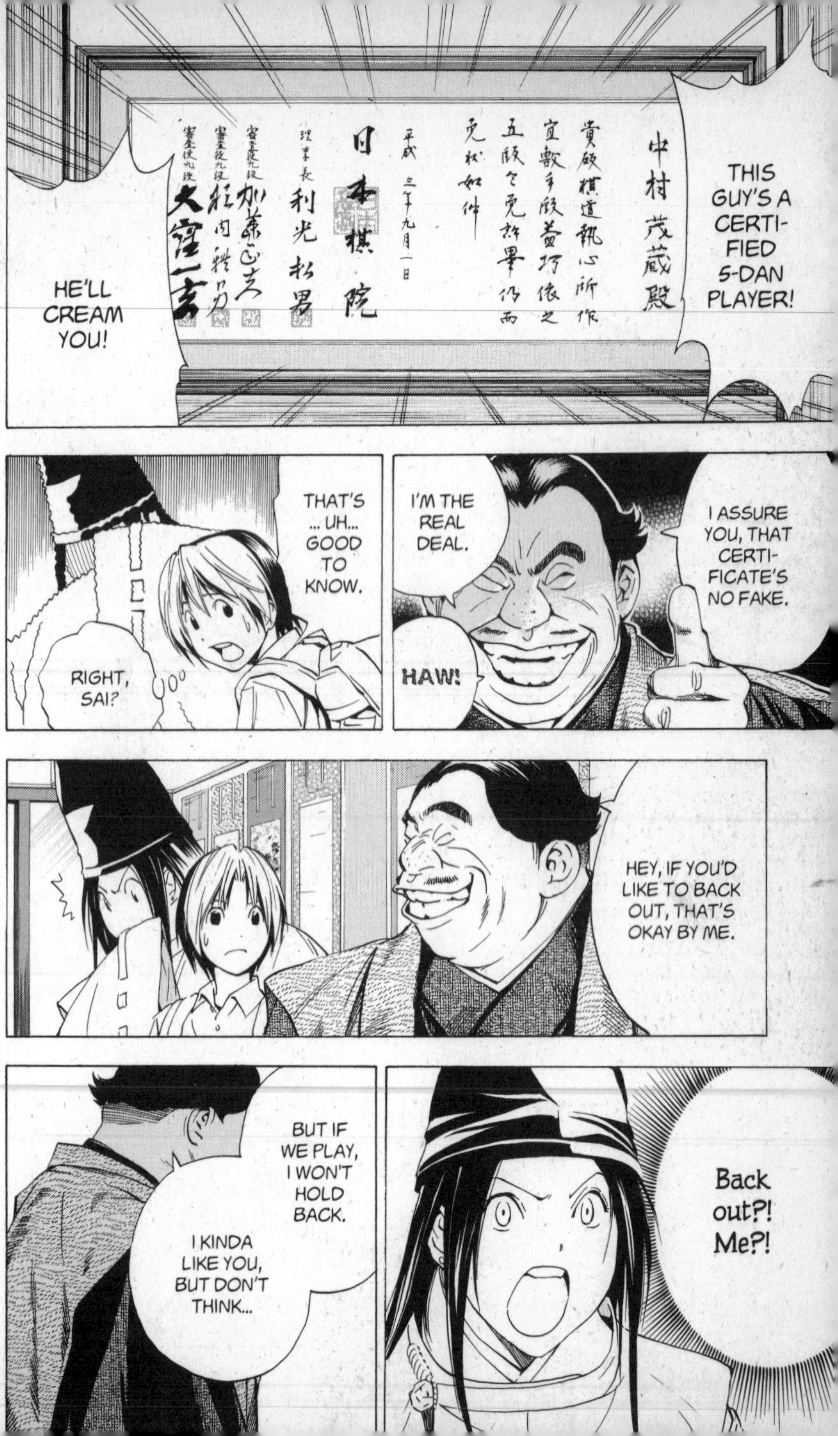
THIS GUY'S A CERTIFIED 5-DAN PLAYER!
中村茂蔵殿
貴殿棋道執心所作宜敷手段益巧依之五段之免許畢仍而免状如件
平成三年九月一日
日本棋院
理事長 利光松男
HE'LL CREAM YOU!
I ASSURE YOU, THAT CERTIFICATE'S NO FAKE.
I'M THE REAL DEAL.
HAW!
THAT'S ... UH... GOOD TO KNOW.
RIGHT, SAI?
HEY, IF YOU'D LIKE TO BACK OUT, THAT'S OKAY BY ME.
Back out?! Me?!
BUT IF WE PLAY, I WON'T HOLD BACK.
I KINDA LIKE YOU, BUT DON'T THINK...

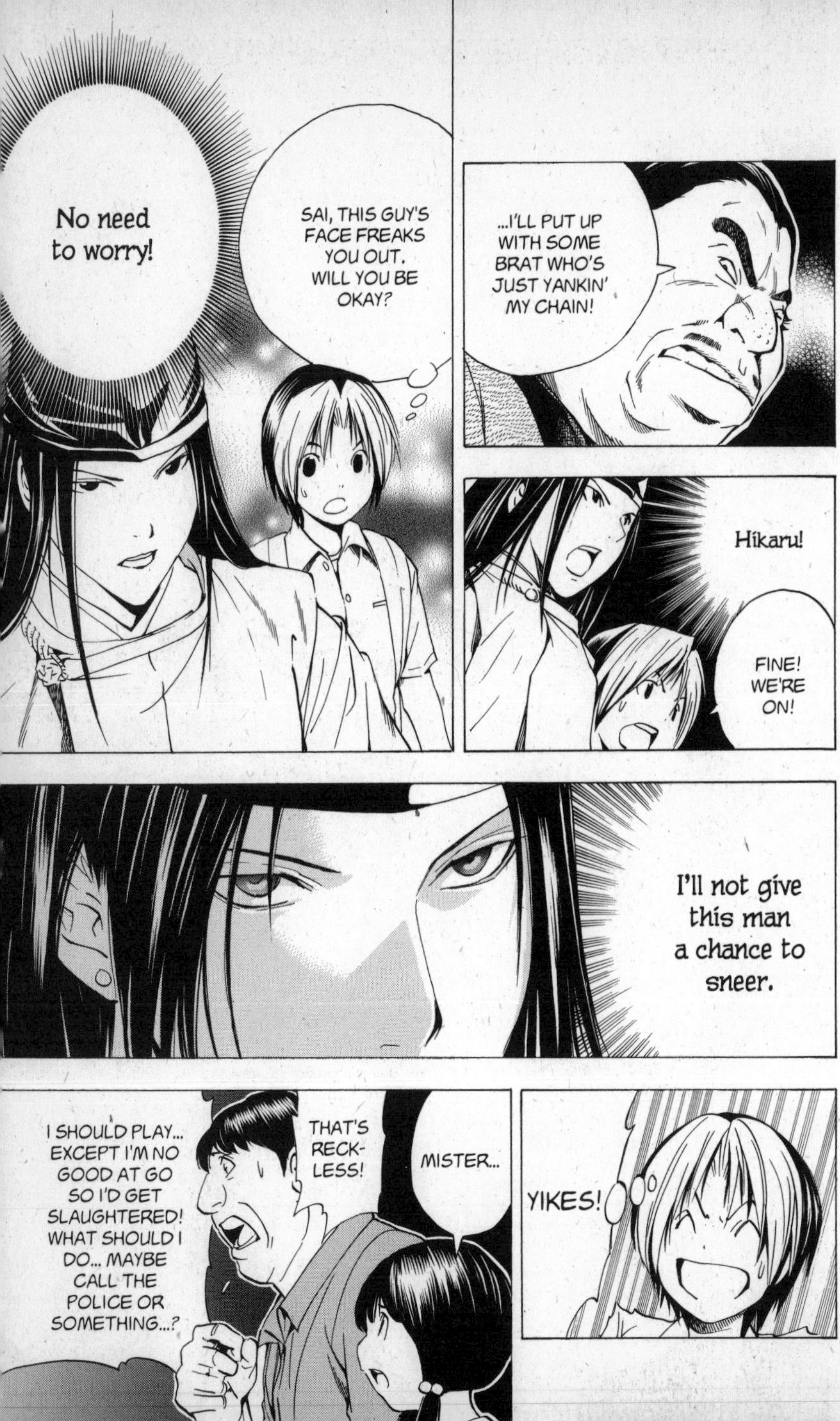
...I'LL PUT UP WITH SOME BRAT WHO'S JUST YANKIN' MY CHAIN!
Hikaru!
FINE! WE'RE ON!
SAI, THIS GUY'S FACE FREAKS YOU OUT. WILL YOU BE OKAY?
No need to worry!
I'll not give this man a chance to sneer.
YIKES!
MISTER...
THAT'S RECK-LESS!
I SHOULD PLAY... EXCEPT I'M NO GOOD AT GO SO I'D GET SLAUGHTERED! WHAT SHOULD I DO... MAYBE CALL THE POLICE OR SOMETHING...?

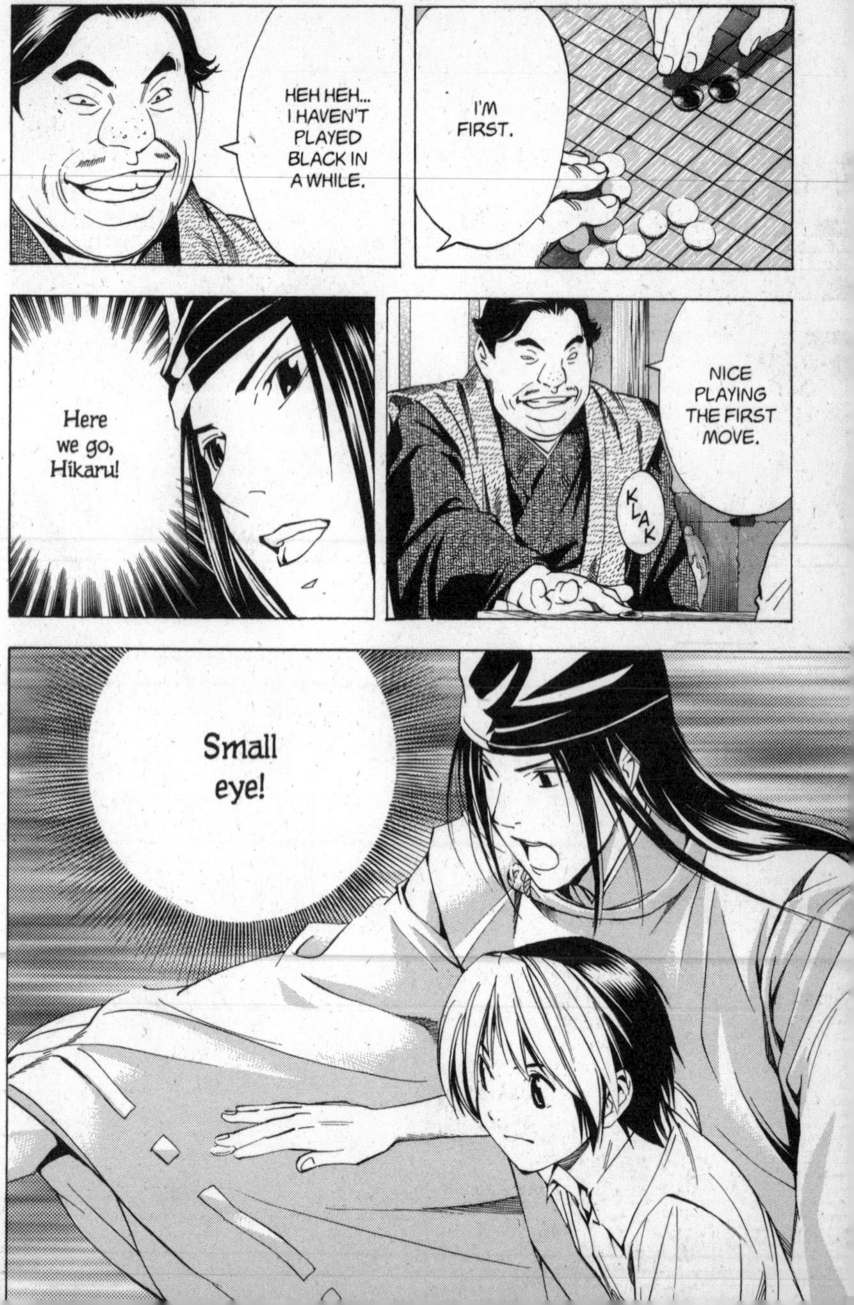
I'M FIRST.
HEH HEH... I HAVEN'T PLAYED BLACK IN A WHILE.
NICE PLAYING THE FIRST MOVE.
KLAK
Here we go, Hikaru!
Small eye!

Atari!

Tiger's mouth!

UNGH...

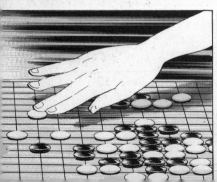

THIS KID'S UNBELIEV-ABLE!

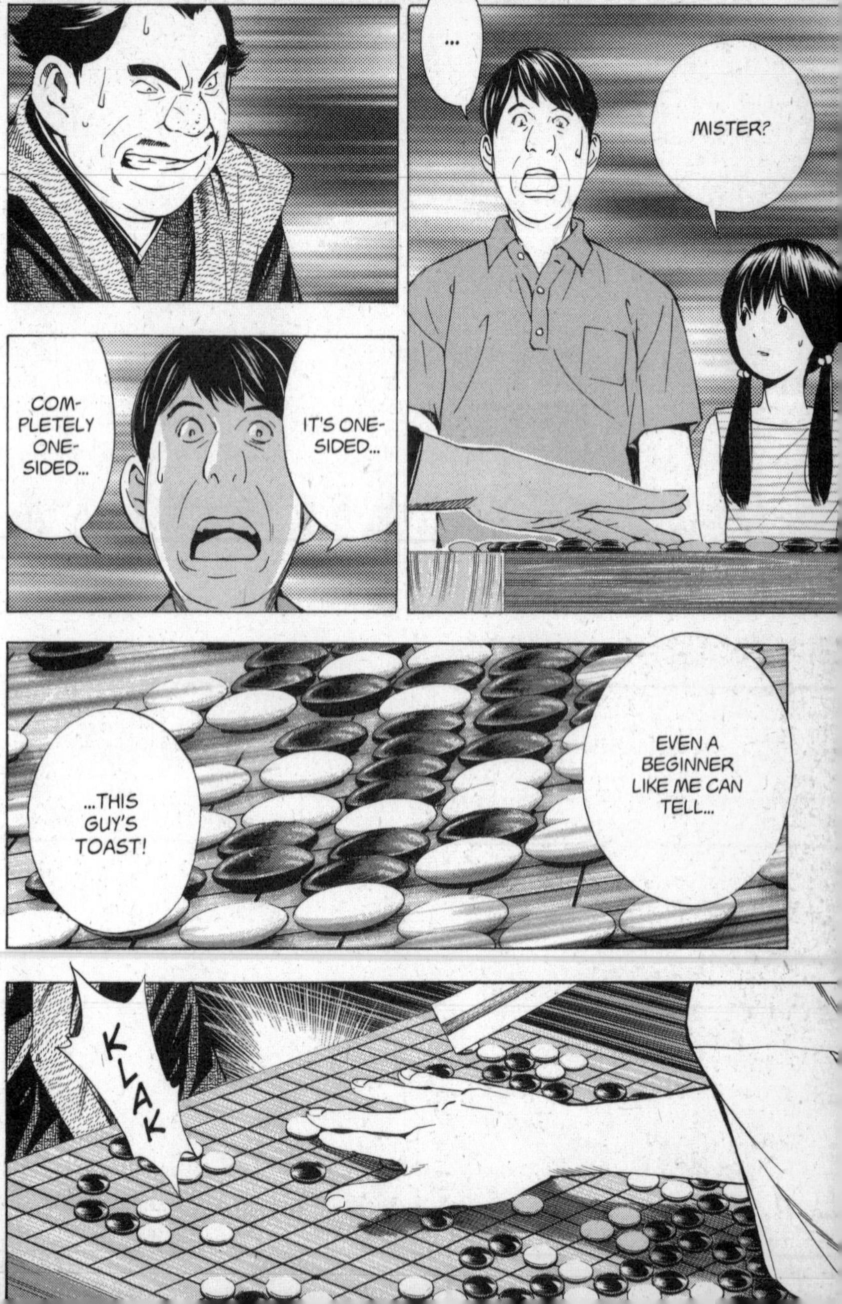
...
MISTER?
IT'S ONE-SIDED...
COMPLETELY ONE-SIDED...
EVEN A BEGINNER LIKE ME CAN TELL...
...THIS GUY'S TOAST!
KLAK

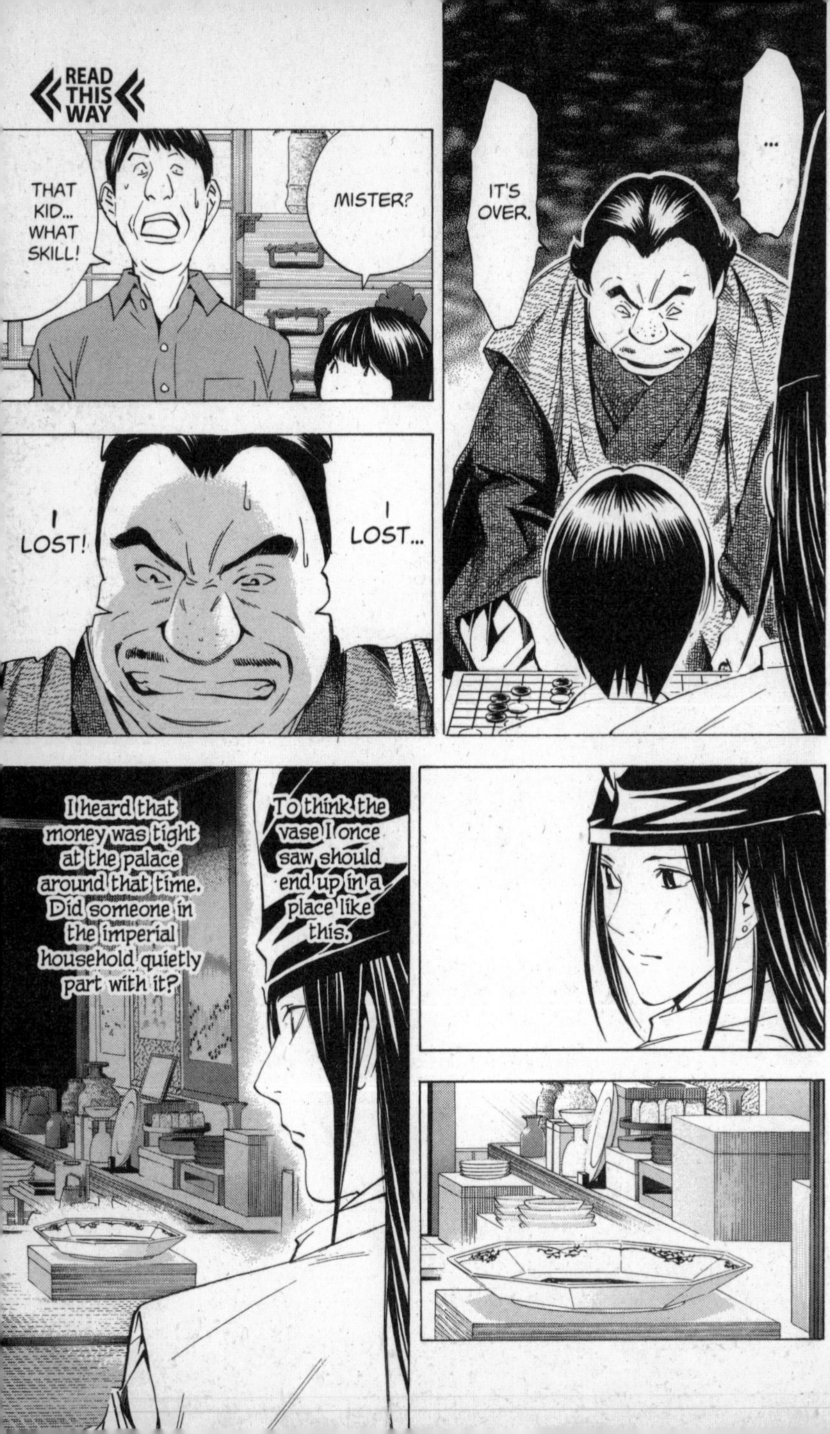
READ THIS WAY
...
IT'S OVER.
MISTER?
THAT KID... WHAT SKILL!
I LOST...
I LOST!
To think the vase I once saw should end up in a place like this.
I heard that money was tight at the palace around that time. Did someone in the imperial household quietly part with it?

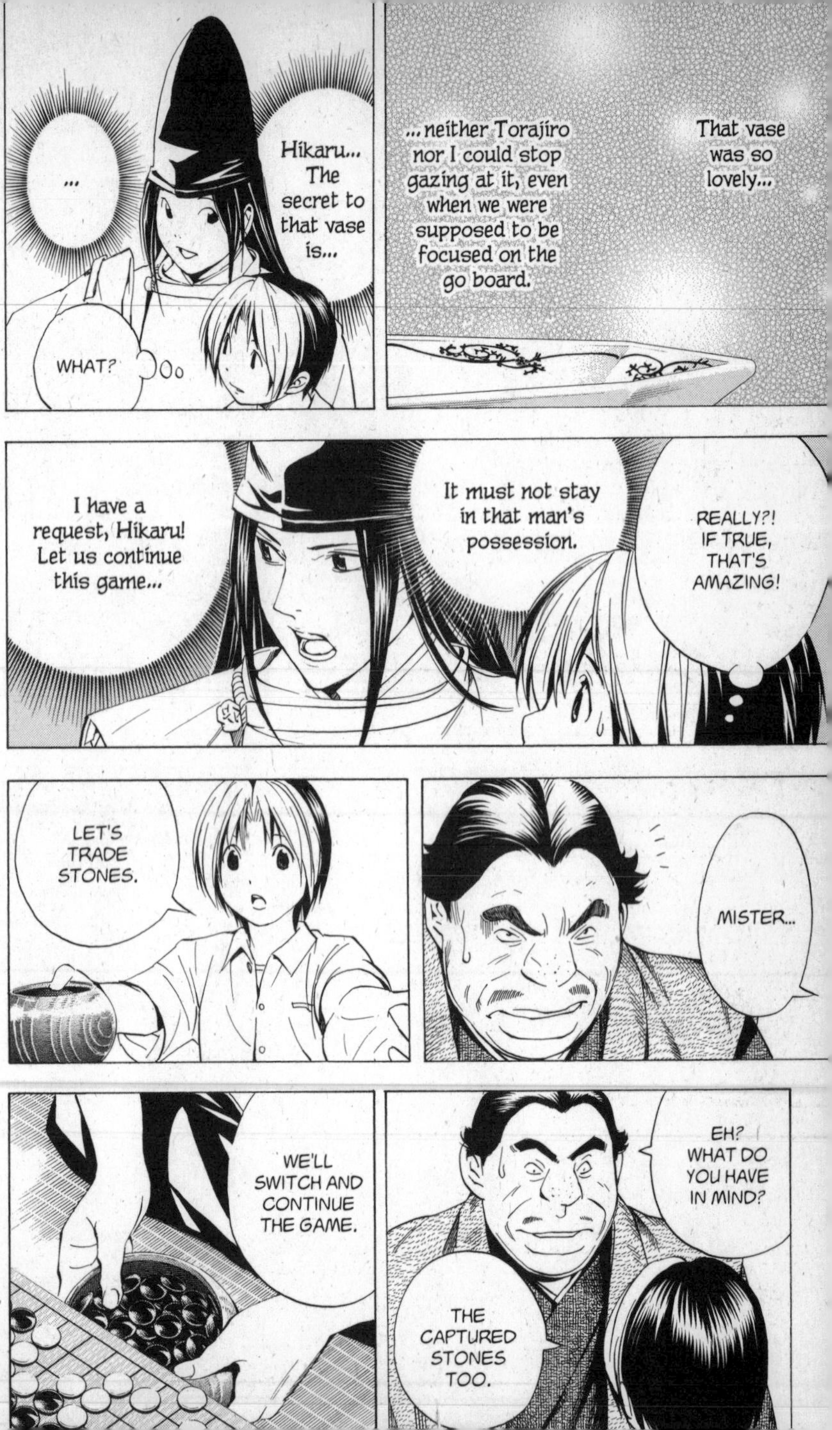
That vase was so lovely...
...neither Torajiro nor I could stop gazing at it, even when we were supposed to be focused on the go board.
Hikaru... The secret to that vase is...
...
WHAT?
REALLY?! IF TRUE, THAT'S AMAZING!
It must not stay in that man's possession.
I have a request, Hikaru! Let us continue this game...
MISTER...
LET'S TRADE STONES.
EH? WHAT DO YOU HAVE IN MIND?
THE CAPTURED STONES TOO.
WE'LL SWITCH AND CONTINUE THE GAME.

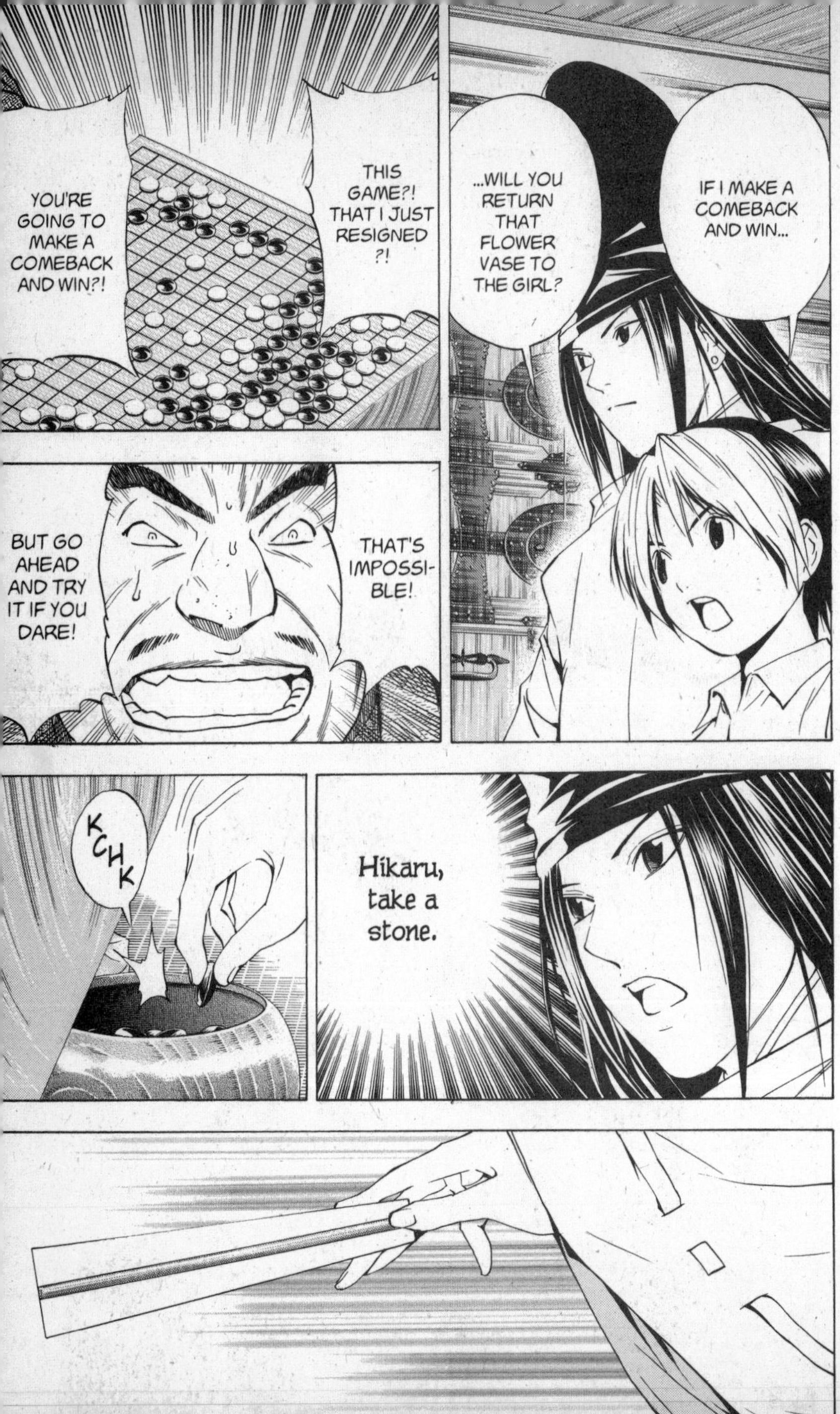
IF I MAKE A COMEBACK AND WIN...
...WILL YOU RETURN THAT FLOWER VASE TO THE GIRL?
THIS GAME?! THAT I JUST RESIGNED ?!
YOU'RE GOING TO MAKE A COMEBACK AND WIN?!
THAT'S IMPOSSI-BLE!
BUT GO AHEAD AND TRY IT IF YOU DARE!
Hikaru, take a stone.
KCHK

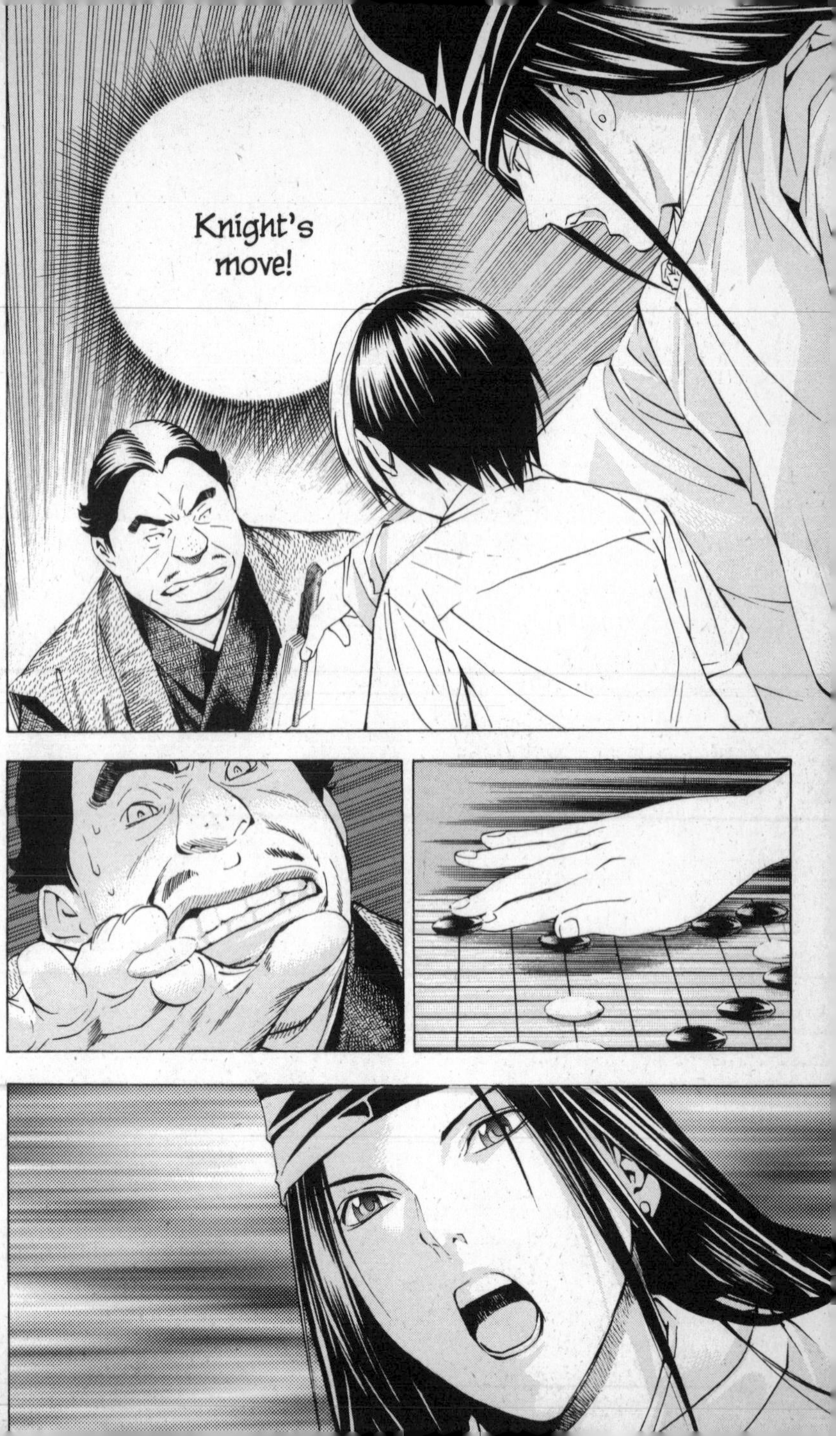
Knight's move!

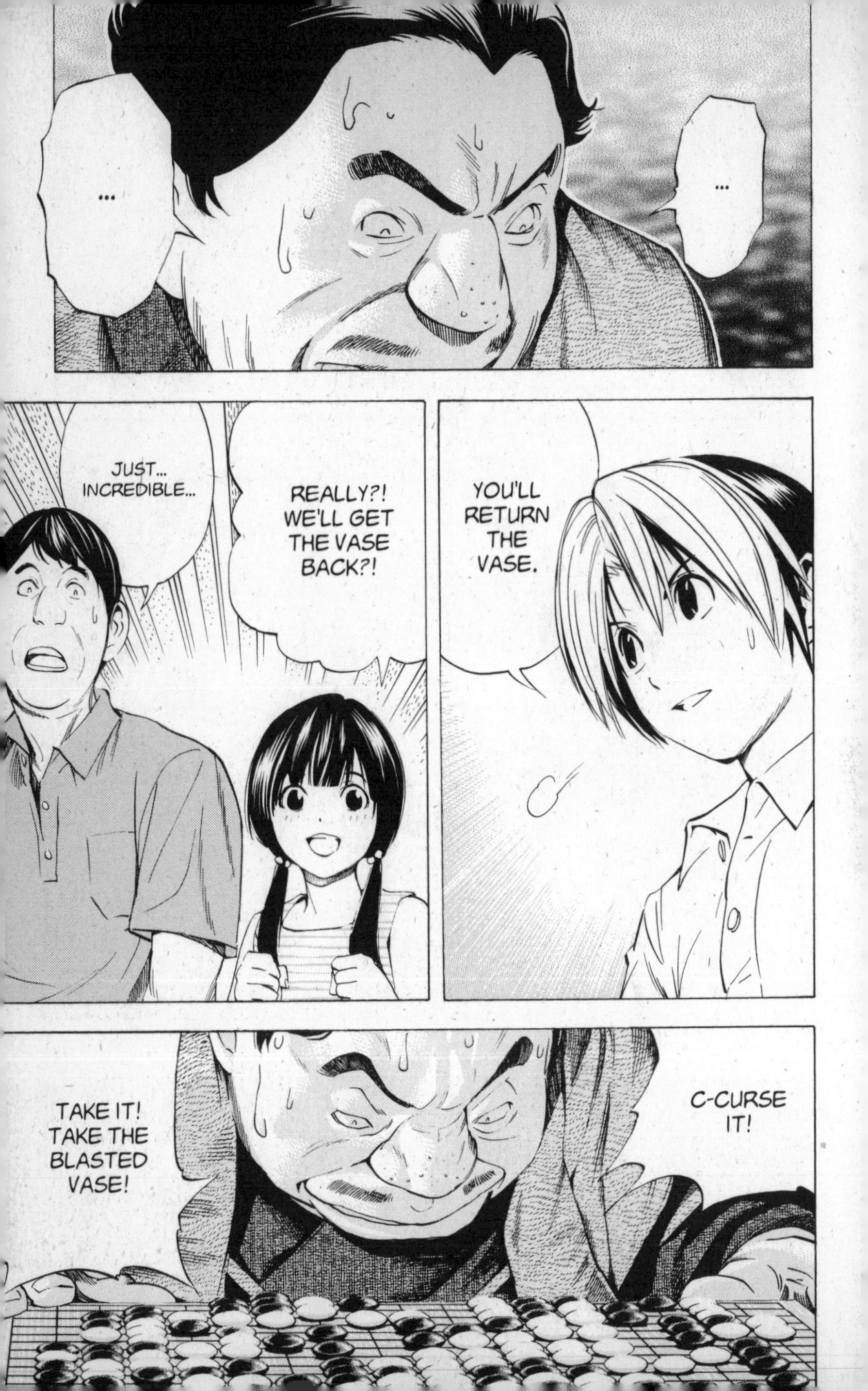
...
...
YOU'LL RETURN THE VASE.
REALLY?! WE'LL GET THE VASE BACK?!
JUST... INCREDIBLE...
C-CURSE IT!
TAKE IT! TAKE THE BLASTED VASE!

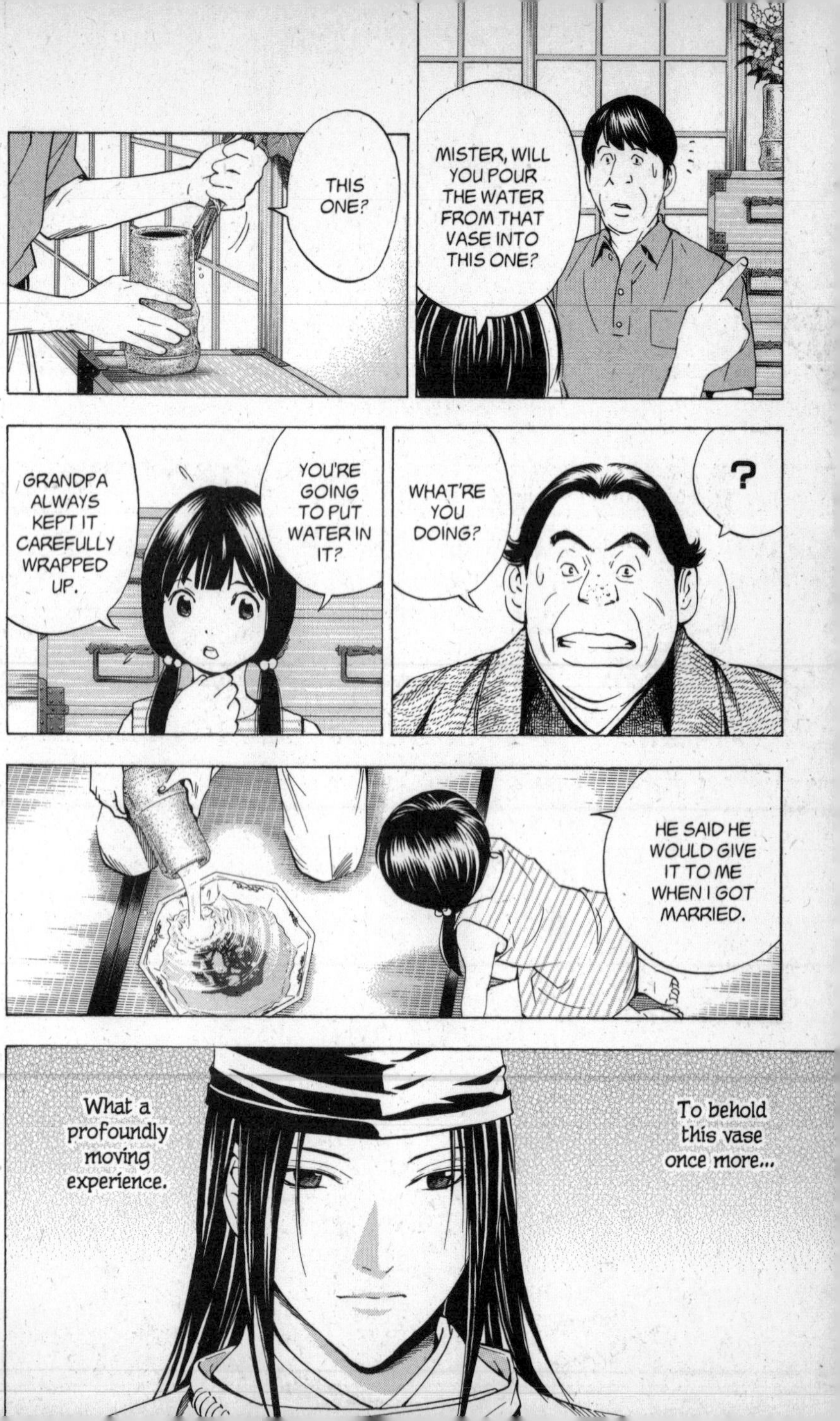
MISTER, WILL YOU POUR THE WATER FROM THAT VASE INTO THIS ONE?
THIS ONE?
?
WHAT'RE YOU DOING?
YOU'RE GOING TO PUT WATER IN IT?
GRANDPA ALWAYS KEPT IT CAREFULLY WRAPPED UP.
HE SAID HE WOULD GIVE IT TO ME WHEN I GOT MARRIED.
To behold this vase once more...
What a profoundly moving experience.

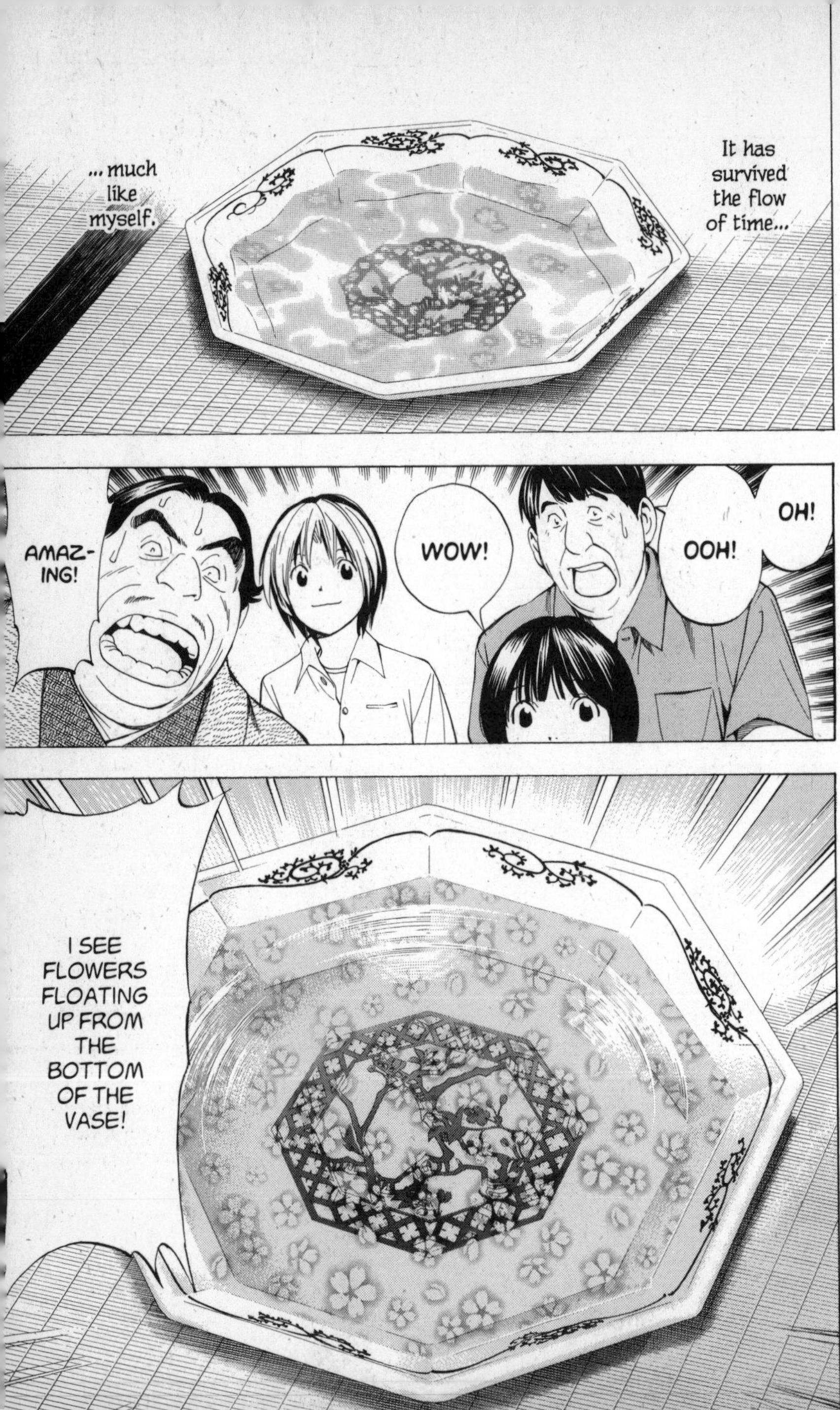
It has survived the flow of time...
...much like myself.
OH!
OOH!
WOW!
AMAZ-ING!
I SEE FLOWERS FLOATING UP FROM THE BOTTOM OF THE VASE!

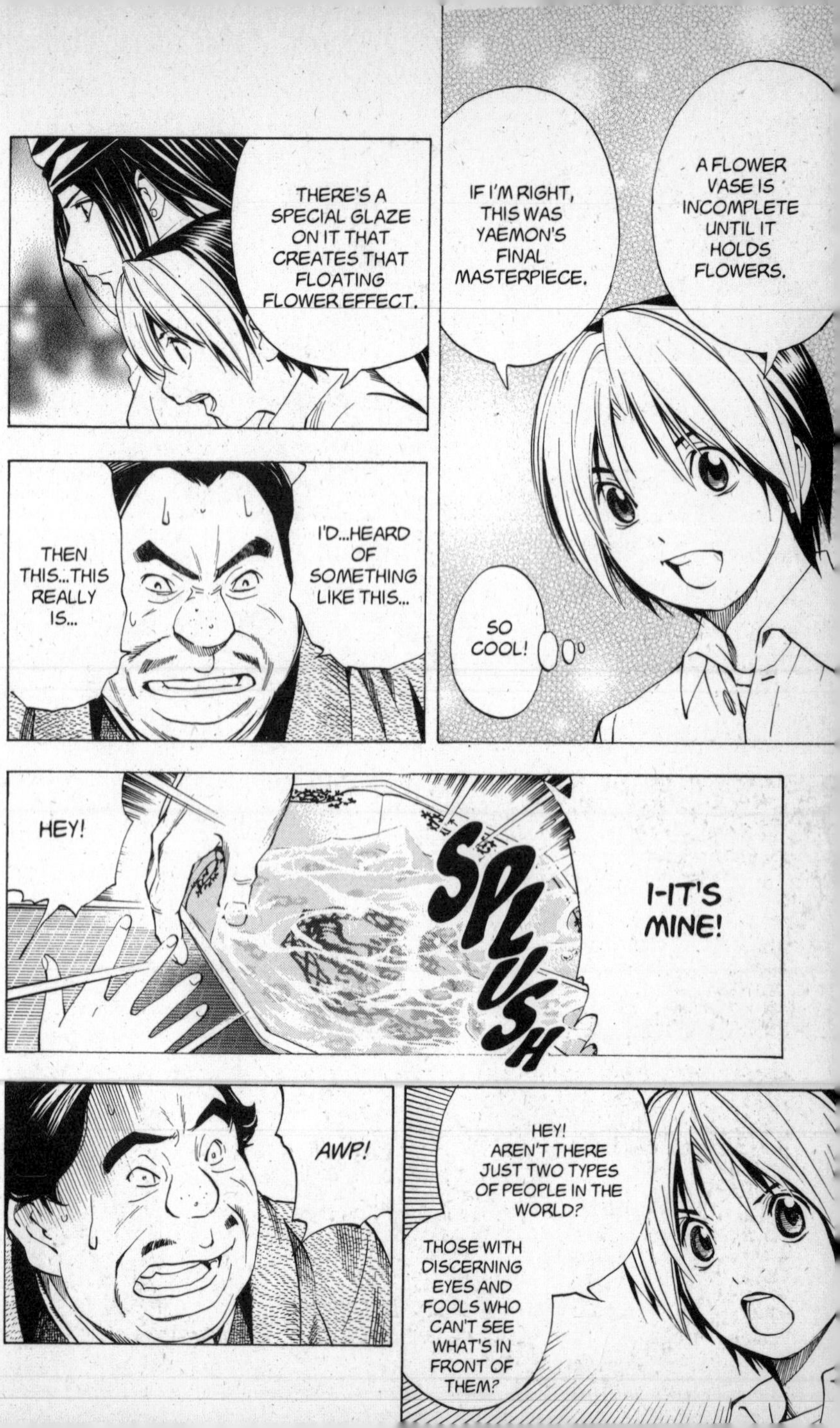
A FLOWER VASE IS INCOMPLETE UNTIL IT HOLDS FLOWERS.
IF I'M RIGHT, THIS WAS YAEMON'S FINAL MASTERPIECE.
SO COOL!
THERE'S A SPECIAL GLAZE ON IT THAT CREATES THAT FLOATING FLOWER EFFECT.
I'D...HEARD OF SOMETHING LIKE THIS...
THEN THIS...THIS REALLY IS...
I-IT'S MINE!
SPLUSH
HEY!
HEY! AREN'T THERE JUST TWO TYPES OF PEOPLE IN THE WORLD?
THOSE WITH DISCERNING EYES AND FOOLS WHO CAN'T SEE WHAT'S IN FRONT OF THEM?
AWP!

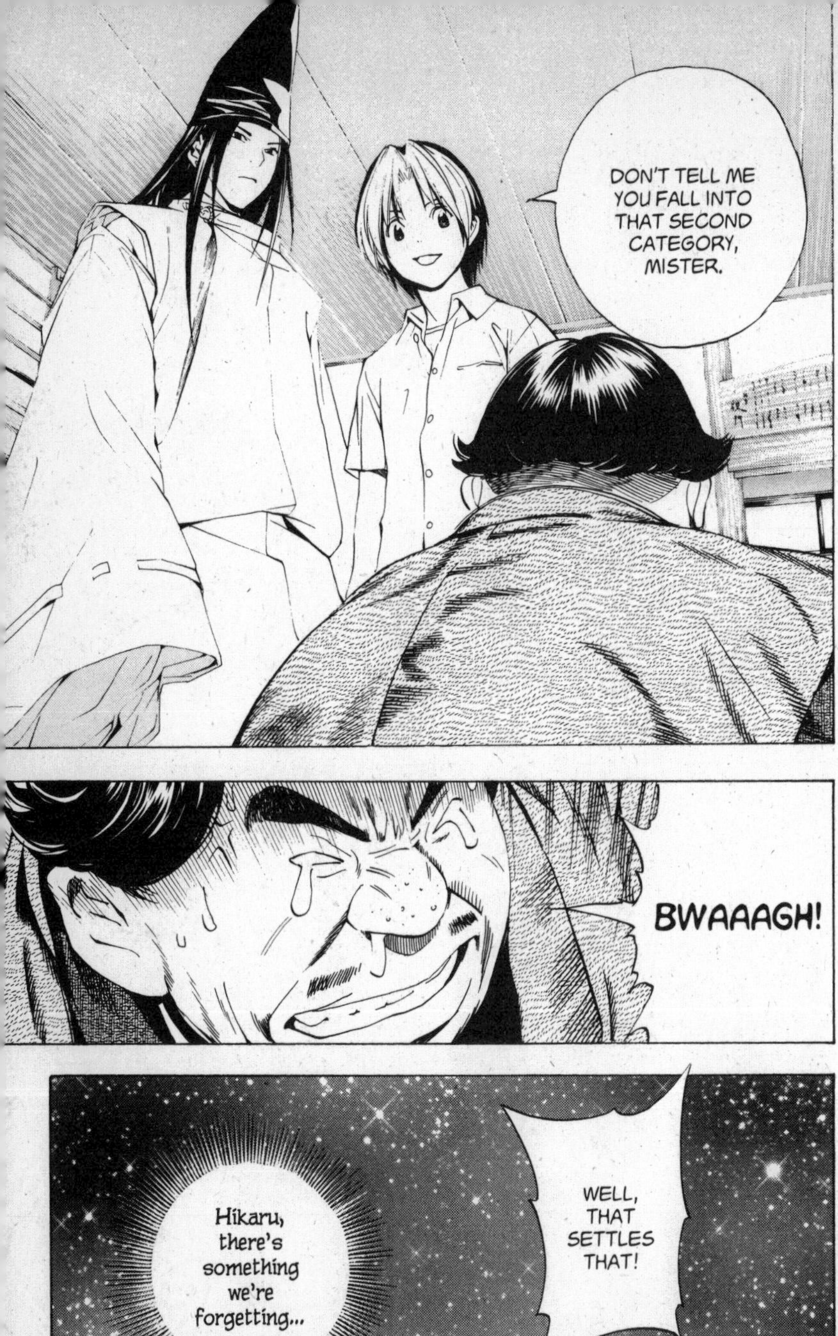
DON'T TELL ME YOU FALL INTO THAT SECOND CATEGORY, MISTER.
BWAAAGH!
WELL, THAT SETTLES THAT!
Hikaru, there's something we're forgetting...

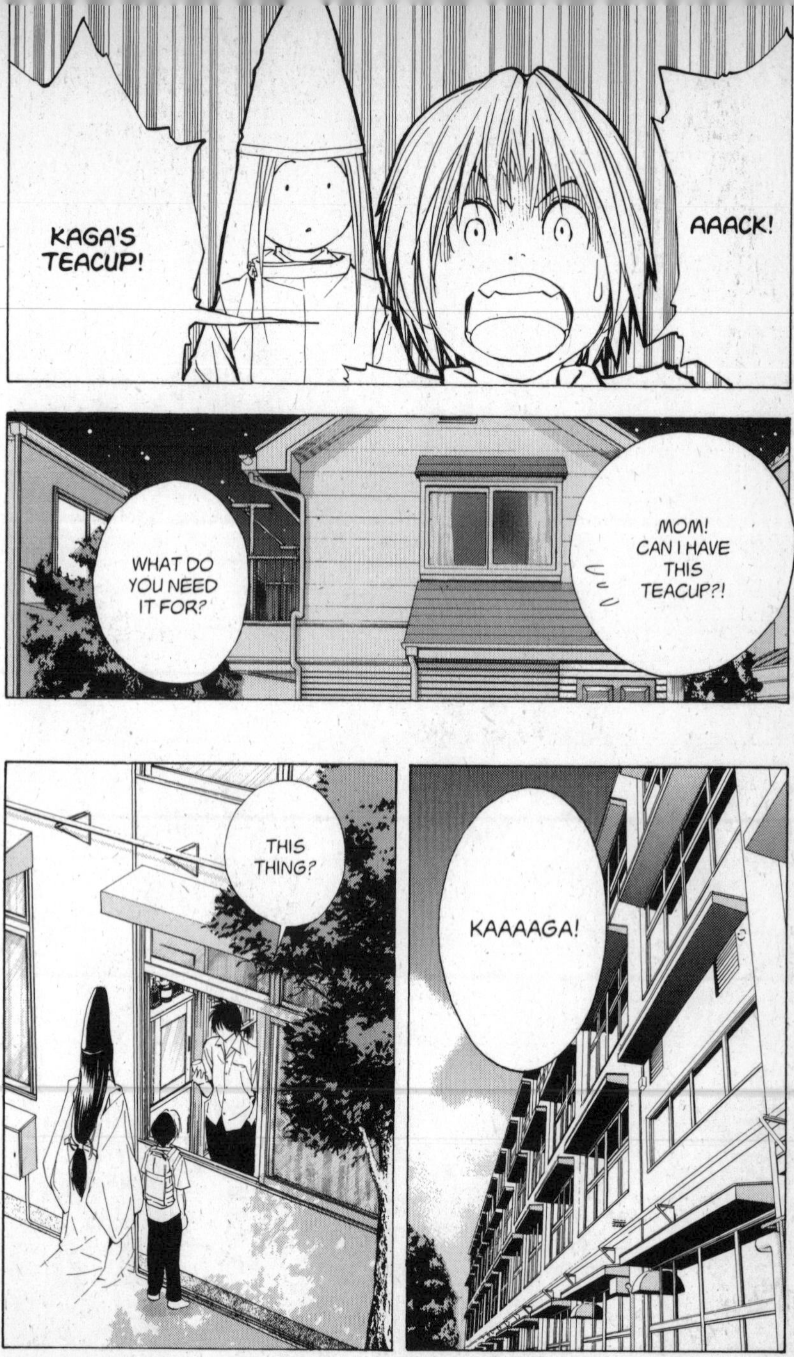
AAACK!
KAGA'S TEACUP!
MOM! CAN I HAVE THIS TEACUP?!
WHAT DO YOU NEED IT FOR?
KAAAAGA!
THIS THING?

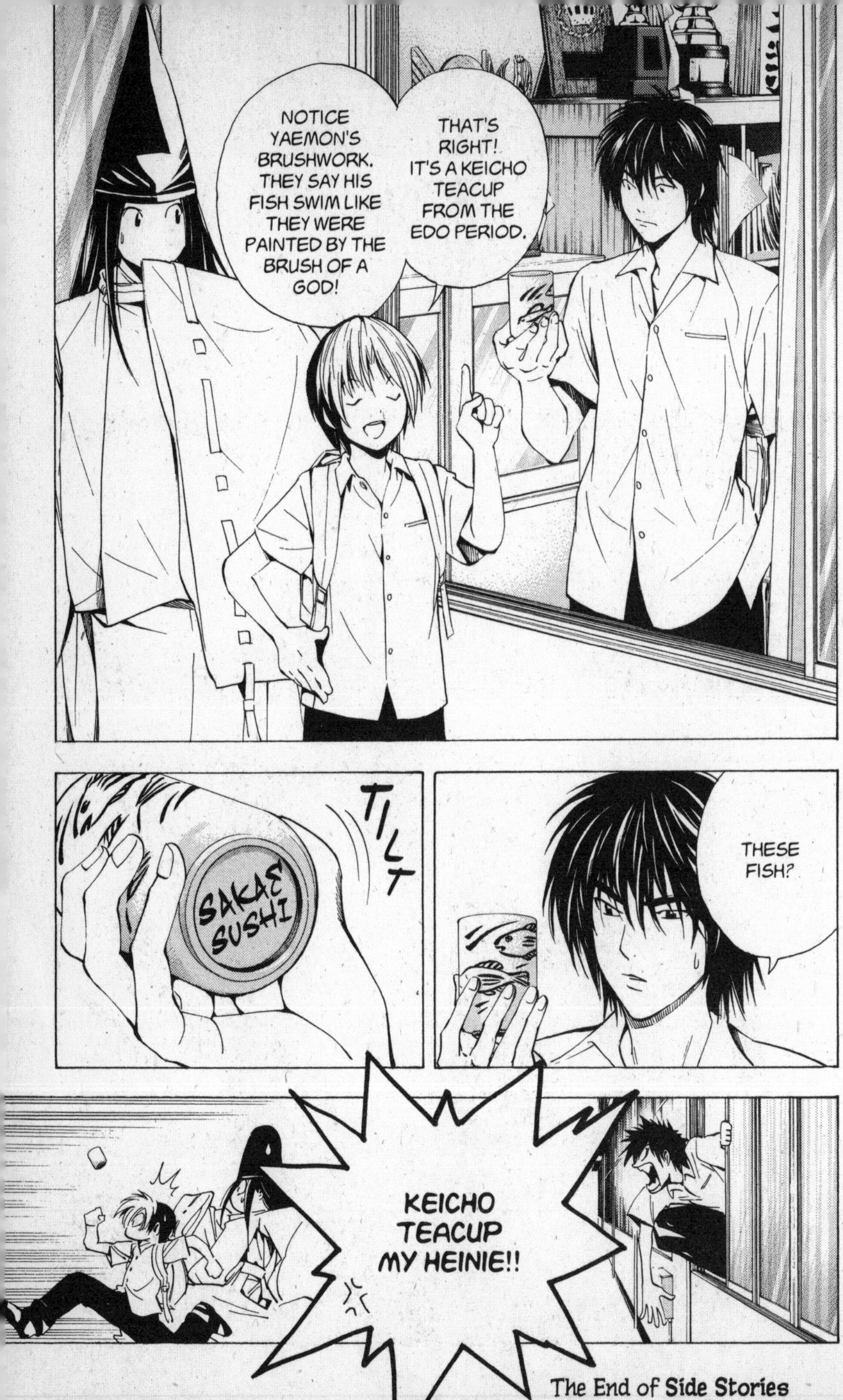
THAT'S RIGHT! IT'S A KEICHO TEACUP FROM THE EDO PERIOD.
NOTICE YAEMON'S BRUSHWORK. THEY SAY HIS FISH SWIM LIKE THEY WERE PAINTED BY THE BRUSH OF A GOD!
THESE FISH?
TILT
SAKAE SUSHI
KEICHO TEACUP MY HEINIE!!

The End of Side Stories

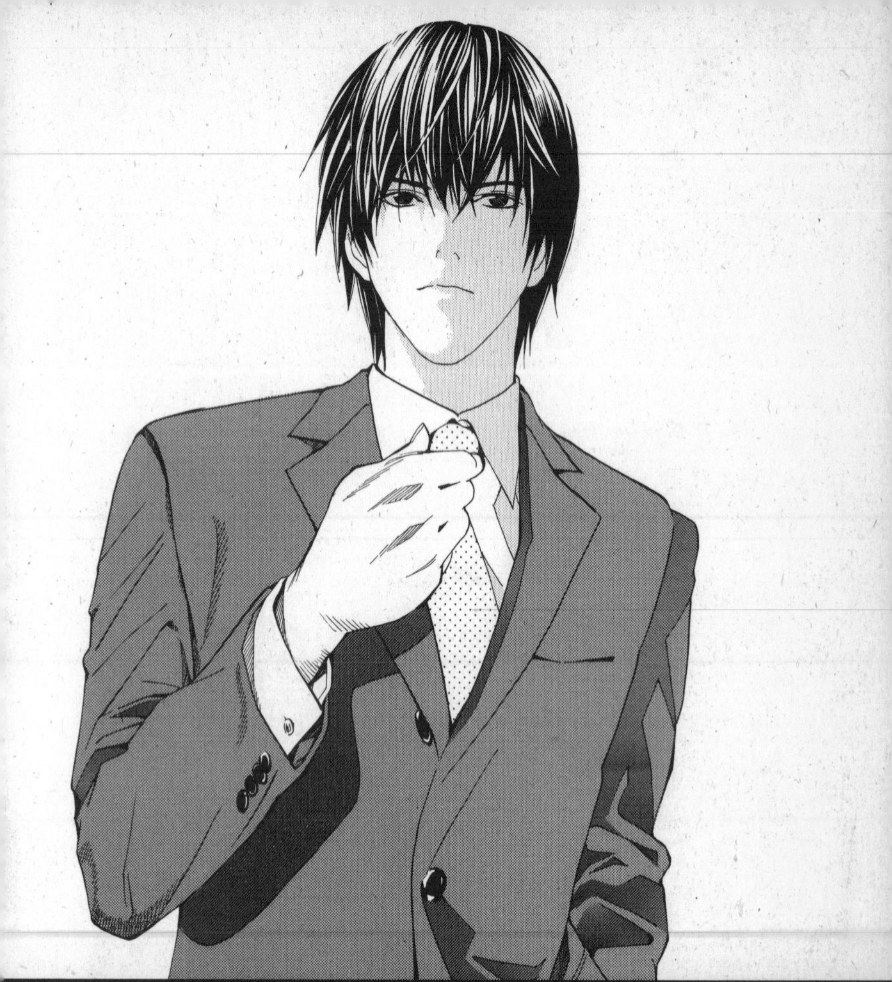

Hikaru's in a rut, facing what he feels are too many low-ranking players. Then he learns of a new Japan-China-Korea youth go tournament and sees this as a chance to shine. But he faces tough competition just to qualify for the Japanese team. He also gets a chance to play a 7-dan, but his opponent turns out to be a man he once denounced for passing off fake go merchandise!

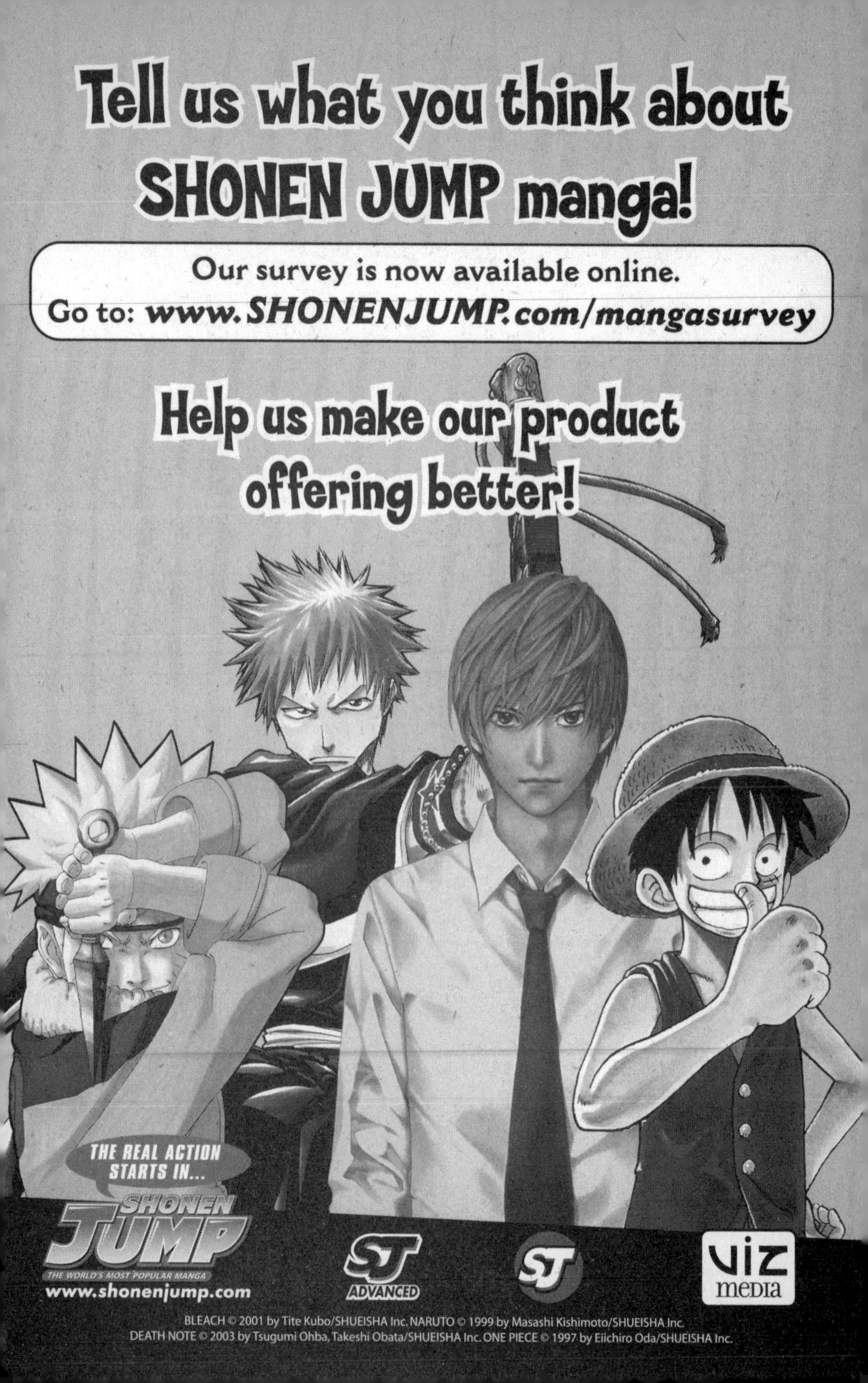

Tell us what you think about SHONEN JUMP manga!
Our survey is now available online.
Go to: www.SHONENJUMP.com/mangasurvey
Help us make our product offering better!
THE REAL ACTION STARTS IN...
SHONEN JUMP
THE WORLD'S MOST POPULAR MANGA
www.shonenjump.com
SJ ADVANCED
SJ
viz media
BLEACH © 2001 by Tite Kubo/SHUEISHA Inc. NARUTO © 1999 by Masashi Kishimoto/SHUEISHA Inc.
DEATH NOTE © 2003 by Tsugumi Ohba, Takeshi Obata/SHUEISHA Inc. ONE PIECE © 1997 by Eiichiro Oda/SHUEISHA Inc.

SHONEN JUMP

THE WORLD'S MOST POPULAR MANGA

350+ pages of the coolest manga available in the U.S., PLUS anime news, and info on video & card games, toys AND more!

SHONEN JUMP
PIRATE POWER!
SHONEN JUMP
ULTIMO
BLEACH
POWER UP!
PLUS: Cards! Video Games!! Anime!!!
SHONEN JUMP
CARD INSIDE!
ANIME UPDATE!
NARUTO
WHAT LURKS WITHIN
Movie Exclusive! Sneak Peek!

50% OFF the cover price!

That's like getting 6 issues

FREE!

12 HUGE issues for ONLY $29[95]*

3 EASY WAYS TO SUBCRIBE

1. Send in a subscription order form
2. Log on to: www.shonenjump.com
3. Call 1-800-541-7919

RATED T FOR TEEN ratings.viz.com

VIZ media www.viz.com

* Canada price: $41.95 USD, including GST, HST, and QST. US/CAN orders only. Allow 6-8 weeks for delivery.

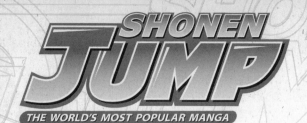

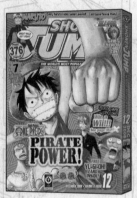

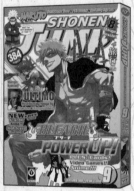

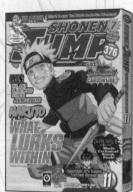